THE NEW FOLGER LIBRARY SHAKESPEARE

Designed to make Shakespeare's great plays available to all readers, the New Folger Library edition of Shakespeare's plays provides accurate texts in modern spelling and punctuation, as well as scene-by-scene action summaries, full explanatory notes, and notes recording the most significant departures from the early printed versions.

This collection of three of Shakespeare's greatest comedies is based on the acclaimed individual Folger editions of the plays. In those editions, each play is prefaced by a brief introduction and followed by a "Modern Perspective" written by an expert on that particular play, along with many pictures clarifying Shakespeare's language. Each is also prefaced by a guide to reading Shakespeare's language and by accounts of his life and theater, and is followed by an annotated list of further readings.

Barbara A. Mowat is Director of Academic Programs at the Folger Shakespeare Library, Executive Editor of *Shakespeare Quarterly*, Chair of the Folger Institute, and author of *The Dramaturgy of Shakespeare's Romances* and of essays on Shakespeare's plays and on the editing of the plays.

Paul Werstine is Professor of English at King's College and the Graduate School of the University of Western Ontario, Canada. He is general editor of the New Variorum Shakespeare and author of many papers and articles on the printing and editing of Shakespeare's plays.

The Folger Shakespeare Library

The Folger Shakespeare Library in Washington, D.C., a privately funded research library dedicated to Shakespeare and the civilization of early modern Europe, was founded in 1932 by Henry Clay and Emily Jordan Folger. In addition to its role as the world's preeminent Shakespeare collection and its emergence as a leading center for Renaissance studies, the Folger Library offers a wide array of cultural and educational programs and services for the general public.

·THE NEW·
FOLGER LIBRARY SHAKESPEARE

THREE COMEDIES

THE TAMING OF THE SHREW

A MIDSUMMER NIGHT'S DREAM

TWELFTH NIGHT

BY WILLIAM SHAKESPEARE

EDITED BY BARBARA A. MOWAT AND PAUL WERSTINE

WASHINGTON SQUARE PRESS

New York   London   Toronto   Sydney   Singapore

WSP

A WASHINGTON SQUARE PRESS Publication
1230 Avenue of the Americas, New York, NY 10020

The Taming of the Shrew copyright © 1992 by The Folger
Shakespeare Library
Twelfth Night copyright © 1993 by The Folger Shakespeare Library
A Midsummer Night's Dream copyright © 1993 by The Folger
Shakespeare Library

These titles were previously published individually by
Washington Square Press.

ISBN: 0-671-72260-3

This Washington Square Press New Folger Edition
November 2002

10 9 8 7 6 5 4 3 2 1

WASHINGTON SQUARE PRESS and colophon are
registered trademarks of Simon & Schuster, Inc.

For information regarding special discounts for bulk purchases,
please contact Simon & Schuster Special Sales at 1-800-456-6798
or business@simonandschuster.com

Cover design by Tom McKeveny
Cover art by Kinuko Y. Craft

Printed in the U.S.A.

From the Director of the Library

For over four decades, the Folger Library General Reader's Shakespeare provided accurate and accessible texts of the plays and poems to students, teachers, and millions of other interested readers. Today, in an age often impatient with the past, the passion for Shakespeare continues to grow. No author speaks more powerfully to the human condition, in all its variety, than this actor/playwright from a minor sixteenth-century English village.

Over the years vast changes have occurred in the way Shakespeare's works are edited, performed, studied, and taught. The New Folger Library Shakespeare replaces the earlier versions, bringing to bear the best and most current thinking concerning both the texts and their interpretation. Here is an edition which makes the plays and poems fully understandable for modern readers using uncompromising scholarship. Professors Barbara Mowat and Paul Werstine are uniquely qualified to produce this New Folger Shakespeare for a new generation of readers. The Library is grateful for the learning, clarity, and imagination they have brought to this ambitious project.

Werner Gundersheimer,
Director of the Folger Shakespeare
Library from 1984 to 2002

Acknowledgments

We are grateful to the Huntington and Newberry Libraries for fellowship support; to King's College for the grants it has provided to Paul Werstine; to the Social Sciences and Humanities Research Council of Canada, which provided him with a Research Time Stipend for 1990–91; to R. J. Shroyer of the University of Western Ontario for essential computer support; to the Folger Institute's Center for Shakespeare Studies for its fortuitous sponsorship of a workshop on "Shakespeare's Texts for Students and Teachers" (funded by the National Endowment for the Humanities and led by Richard Knowles of the University of Wisconsin), a workshop from which we learned an enormous amount about what is wanted by college and high-school teachers of Shakespeare today; to Alice Falk for her expert copyediting; and especially to Stephen Llano, our production editor at Washington Square Press, whose expertise and attention to detail are essential to this project.

Our biggest debt is to the Folger Shakespeare Library—to Werner Gundersheimer, Director of the Library from 1984 to 2002, who made possible our edition; to Deborah Curren-Aquino, who provides extensive editorial and production support; to Peggy O'Brien, former Director of Education at the Folger and now Director of Education Programs at the Corporation for Public Broadcasting, who gave us expert advice about the needs being expressed by Shakespeare teachers and students (and to Martha Christian and other "master teachers" who used our texts in manuscript in their classrooms); to Allan Shnerson and Mary Bloodworth for expert computer support;

to the staff of the Academic Programs Division, especially Rachel Kunkle (whose help is crucial), Mary Tonkinson, Kathleen Lynch, Carol Brobeck, Liz Pohland, Owen Williams, and Lisa Meyers; and, finally, to the generously supportive staff of the Library's Reading Room.

Barbara A. Mowat and Paul Werstine

Contents

An Introduction to the Texts of This Edition

In this collection of *Three Comedies* we reprint the single-volume editions of plays edited by Mowat and Werstine and published by Washington Square Press in 1992 (*The Taming of the Shrew*) and 1993 (*A Midsummer Night's Dream* and *Twelfth Night*). These single-volume editions are based directly upon the earliest printed texts of the plays. *A Midsummer Night's Dream* was first printed in a quarto dated 1600; *The Taming of the Shrew* and *Twelfth Night* were first printed in the 1623 collection of Shakespeare's plays now known as the First Folio. While the texts and explanatory notes are the same in this collection of *Three Comedies* (except for formatting) as in the 1992 and 1993 single-volume editions, the single-volume editions contain fuller discussions of the relation of our texts to the early printed versions, along with more extensive textual notes; an introduction to Shakespeare's language; information about Shakespeare, his theater, and the publication of his plays; a list of further readings; illustrations drawn from the Folger's holdings of rare books; and an essay about the play. Readers interested in such matters are encouraged to consult the 1992 and 1993 editions. In the present volume, we offer accurate texts in modern spelling, full explanatory notes, and scene-by-scene action summaries.

For the convenience of the reader, we have in our editions modernized the punctuation and the spelling of the early printed texts. Sometimes we go so far as to modernize certain old forms of words; for example, when *a* means *he,* we change it to *he;* we change *mo* to *more* and *ye* to *you.* But we have not modernized forms of words that sound distinctly different from modern forms. For example, when the early printed texts read *sith* or *apricocks* or *porpentine,* we have not modernized to *since, apricots, porcupine.* When the forms *an, and,* or *and if* appear instead of the modern form *if,* we have reduced *and* to *an* but have not changed any of these forms to their modern equivalent, *if.* We also modernize and, where necessary, correct passages in foreign languages, unless an error in the early printed text can be reasonably explained as a joke.

Whenever we change the wording of the early printed text or add anything to its stage directions, we mark the change by enclosing it in superior half-brackets (⌐ ⌐). We want our readers to be immediately aware when we have intervened. (Only when we correct an obvious typographical error in the early printed text does the change not get marked.) Whenever we change the wording of the early printed text, we list the change in the textual notes that follow each play. In this edition, when we have simply corrected an obvious error, we do not list the change in the textual notes, nor do we list punctuation changes. (For more complete textual notes, the reader is advised to consult the single-volume editions of the plays.)

Our editions differ from some earlier ones in trying to aid the reader in imagining the play as a performance rather than as a series of actual or novelistic events. Thus stage directions are written with reference to the stage. For example, when in 2.2 of *Twelfth Night* Viola refuses to take the ring offered to her by Malvolio, he throws it before her. If we were representing the play as pure fiction, our stage direction would read *"He throws the ring to the ground,"* but because we are representing the play as stage action, our stage direction reads, instead, *"He throws down the ring."* Whenever it is reasonably certain, in our view, that a speech is accompanied by a particular action, we provide a stage direction describing the action. (Occasional exceptions to this rule occur when the action is so obvious that to add a stage direction would insult the reader.) Stage directions for the entrance of characters in mid-scene are placed so that they immediately precede the characters' participation in the scene, even though these entrances may appear somewhat earlier in the early printed texts. We do not record these alterations in the position of stage directions in the textual notes. Latin stage directions (e.g., *Exeunt*) are translated into English (e.g., *They exit*).

In our editions, we regularize a number of the proper names, as is the usual practice in editions of Shakespeare's plays. For example, although *Twelfth Night*'s Viola enters once under the name "Violenta" in the First Folio, in our edition she is always designated "Viola."

We also expand the often severely abbreviated forms of names used as speech headings in early printed texts into the full names of the characters, and silently regularize the speakers' names in speech headings, using only a single designation for each character, even though the early printed texts sometimes use a variety of designations. For example, more often than not in the 1600 quarto of *A Midsummer Night's Dream*, the character Robin Goodfellow speaks (according to the speech prefixes) after his proper name "Robin," although more than a few times his speeches are prefixed with the generic form "Puck." (He is, as he himself tells us, a puck or hobgoblin.) Our editorial decision in this case is to regularize all the speech prefixes to the quarto's preferred form "Robin."

In our editions, as well, we mark with a dash any change of address within a speech, unless a stage direction intervenes. When the *-ed* ending of a word is to be pronounced, we mark it with an accent. Like editors for the last two centuries, we print metrically linked lines in the following way:

VIOLA
  I think not so, my lord.
ORSINO   Dear lad, believe it.

However, when there are a number of short verse-lines that can be linked in more than one way, we do not, with rare exceptions, indent any of them.

The Explanatory Notes

The notes that appear directly after each playtext are designed to provide readers with the help that they may need to enjoy the play. Whenever the meaning of a word in the text is not readily accessible in a good contemporary dictionary, we offer the meaning in a note. Sometimes we provide a note even when the relevant meaning is to be found in the dictionary but when the word has acquired since Shakespeare's time other potentially confusing meanings. In our notes, we try to offer modern synonyms for Shakespeare's words. We also try to indicate to the reader the connection between the word in the play and the modern synonym. For example, Shakespeare sometimes uses the word *head* to mean *source,* but, for modern readers, there may be no connection evident between these two words. We provide the connection by explaining Shakespeare's usage as follows: **"head:** fountainhead, source." On some occasions, a whole phrase or clause needs explanation. Then we rephrase in our own words the difficult passage, and add at the end synonyms for individual words in the passage. When scholars have been unable to determine the meaning of a word or phrase, we acknowledge the uncertainty.

THE
TAMING
OF THE
SHREW

Shakespeare's
The Taming of the Shrew

Love and marriage are the concerns of Shakespeare's *The Taming of the Shrew*. The play offers us some strikingly different models of the process of attracting and choosing a mate and then coming to terms with the mate one has chosen. Some of these models may still seem attractive to us, some not. Lucentio's courtship of and marriage to Bianca are prompted by his idealized love of an apparently ideal woman. When she first appears, Bianca is silent and perfectly obedient to her father. Lucentio then speaks of her as if she were a goddess come to earth. Because her father denies all men the opportunity openly to court Bianca, Lucentio spontaneously throws off his social status as a gentleman in order to disguise himself as a lowly tutor, the only kind of man that Bianca's father, Baptista, will let near her. All that matters to Lucentio is winning Bianca's heart. To marry her—even in secret and in shared defiance of her father—is surely, he believes, to be happy.

An alternative style of wooing adopted by Petruchio in quest of Katherine is notably free of idealism. Petruchio is concerned with money. He takes money from all Bianca's suitors for wooing her older sister, Katherine, who, Baptista has dictated, must be married before Bianca. When Petruchio comes to see Katherine, he first arranges with her father the dowry to be acquired by marrying her. Assured of the money, Petruchio is ready to marry Katherine even against her will. Katherine is the shrew named in the play's title; and, according to all

3

the men but Petruchio, her bad temper denies her the status of "ideal woman" accorded Bianca by Lucentio. Yet by the end of the play, Katherine, whether she has been tamed or not, certainly acts much changed. Petruchio then claims to have the more successful marriage. But is the marriage of Petruchio and Katherine a superior match—have they truly learned to love each other?—or is it based on terror and deception?

This question about Katherine and Petruchio is only one of the questions this play raises for us. How are we to respond to Kate's speech at the end of the play, with its celebration of the wife's subordinate position? What does it mean that Bianca, the "ideal" woman, at the end seems unpleasant and bad-tempered, now that she is married? How should we respond to the process by which Petruchio "tames" Kate? As with so many of Shakespeare's plays, how one answers these questions has a lot to do with one's own basic beliefs—here, one's beliefs about men and women, about love and marriage.

Characters in the Play

CHRISTOPHER SLY, a beggar
Hostess of an alehouse
A Lord
Huntsmen of the Lord
Page (disguised as a lady)
Players
Servingmen
Messenger

characters in the Induction

BAPTISTA MINOLA, father to Katherine and Bianca
KATHERINE, his elder daughter
BIANCA, his younger daughter

PETRUCHIO, suitor to Katherine

GREMIO
HORTENSIO (later disguised as the teacher Litio)
LUCENTIO (later disguised as the teacher Cambio)

suitors to Bianca

VINCENTIO, Lucentio's father

TRANIO (later impersonating Lucentio)
BIONDELLO

servants to Lucentio

A Merchant (later disguised as Vincentio)

GRUMIO
CURTIS
NATHANIEL
PHILLIP   *servants to Petruchio*
JOSEPH
NICHOLAS
PETER

Widow

Tailor
Haberdasher
Officer

Servants to Baptista and Petruchio

⌜INDUCTION⌝

Scene 1
Enter Beggar (Christopher Sly) and Hostess.

SLY   I'll feeze you, in faith.

HOSTESS   A pair of stocks, you rogue!

SLY   You're a baggage! The Slys are no rogues. Look
in the chronicles. We came in with Richard Conqueror. Therefore, *paucas pallabris*, let the world   5
slide. Sessa!

HOSTESS   You will not pay for the glasses you have
burst?

SLY   No, not a denier. Go, by ⌜Saint⌝ Jeronimy! Go to
thy cold bed and warm thee.   ⌜*He lies down.*⌝   10

HOSTESS   I know my remedy. I must go fetch the
headborough.   ⌜*She exits.*⌝

SLY   Third, or fourth, or fifth borough, I'll answer him
by law. I'll not budge an inch, boy. Let him come,
and kindly.   *Falls asleep.*   15

Wind horns ⌜*within.*⌝ *Enter a Lord from hunting, with
his train.*

LORD
Huntsman, I charge thee tender well my hounds.
⌜Breathe⌝ Merriman (the poor cur is embossed)
And couple Clowder with the deep-mouthed brach.
Saw'st thou not, boy, how Silver made it good
At the hedge corner, in the coldest fault?   20
I would not lose the dog for twenty pound!

7

FIRST HUNTSMAN
  Why, Bellman is as good as he, my lord.
  He cried upon it at the merest loss,
  And twice today picked out the dullest scent.
  Trust me, I take him for the better dog.   25
LORD
  Thou art a fool. If Echo were as fleet,
  I would esteem him worth a dozen such.
  But sup them well, and look unto them all.
  Tomorrow I intend to hunt again.
FIRST HUNTSMAN   I will, my lord.   30
                               ⌜*First Huntsman exits.*⌝
LORD, ⌜*noticing Sly*⌝
  What's here? One dead, or drunk? See doth he
    breathe.
SECOND HUNTSMAN
  He breathes, my lord. Were he not warmed with ale,
  This were a bed but cold to sleep so soundly.
LORD
  O monstrous beast, how like a swine he lies!   35
  Grim death, how foul and loathsome is thine image!
  Sirs, I will practice on this drunken man.
  What think you, if he were conveyed to bed,
  Wrapped in sweet clothes, rings put upon his
    fingers,   40
  A most delicious banquet by his bed,
  And brave attendants near him when he wakes,
  Would not the beggar then forget himself?
⌜THIRD⌝ HUNTSMAN
  Believe me, lord, I think he cannot choose.
SECOND HUNTSMAN
  It would seem strange unto him when he waked.   45
LORD
  Even as a flatt'ring dream or worthless fancy.
  Then take him up, and manage well the jest.

Carry him gently to my fairest chamber,
And hang it round with all my wanton pictures;
Balm his foul head in warm distillèd waters,   50
And burn sweet wood to make the lodging sweet;
Procure me music ready when he wakes
To make a dulcet and a heavenly sound.
And if he chance to speak, be ready straight
And, with a low, submissive reverence,   55
Say "What is it your Honor will command?"
Let one attend him with a silver basin
Full of rosewater and bestrewed with flowers,
Another bear the ewer, the third a diaper,
And say "Will 't please your Lordship cool your   60
   hands?"
Someone be ready with a costly suit,
And ask him what apparel he will wear.
Another tell him of his hounds and horse,
And that his lady mourns at his disease.   65
Persuade him that he hath been lunatic,
And when he says he is, say that he dreams,
For he is nothing but a mighty lord.
This do, and do it kindly, gentle sirs.
It will be pastime passing excellent   70
If it be husbanded with modesty.

⌜THIRD⌝ HUNTSMAN
My lord, I warrant you we will play our part
As he shall think by our true diligence
He is no less than what we say he is.

LORD
Take him up gently, and to bed with him,   75
And each one to his office when he wakes.
                              ⌜*Sly is carried out.*⌝
                              Sound trumpets ⌜*within.*⌝
Sirrah, go see what trumpet 'tis that sounds.
                              ⌜*Servingman exits.*⌝

Belike some noble gentleman that means
(Traveling some journey) to repose him here.

Enter Servingman.

How now? Who is it?   80
SERVINGMAN   An 't please your Honor, players
That offer service to your Lordship.
LORD
Bid them come near.

Enter Players.

                    Now, fellows, you are welcome.
PLAYERS   We thank your Honor.   85
LORD
Do you intend to stay with me tonight?
⌜FIRST PLAYER⌝
So please your Lordship to accept our duty.
LORD
With all my heart. This fellow I remember
Since once he played a farmer's eldest son.—
'Twas where you wooed the gentlewoman so well.   90
I have forgot your name, but sure that part
Was aptly fitted and naturally performed.
⌜SECOND PLAYER⌝
I think 'twas Soto that your Honor means.
LORD
'Tis very true. Thou didst it excellent.
Well, you are come to me in happy time,   95
The rather for I have some sport in hand
Wherein your cunning can assist me much.
There is a lord will hear you play tonight;
But I am doubtful of your modesties,
Lest, over-eying of his odd behavior   100
(For yet his Honor never heard a play),
You break into some merry passion,
And so offend him. For I tell you, sirs,
If you should smile, he grows impatient.

⌈FIRST PLAYER⌉
    Fear not, my lord, we can contain ourselves   105
    Were he the veriest antic in the world.
LORD, ⌈*to a Servingman*⌉
    Go, sirrah, take them to the buttery
    And give them friendly welcome every one.
    Let them want nothing that my house affords.
                    One exits with the Players.
    Sirrah, go you to Bartholomew, my page,   110
    And see him dressed in all suits like a lady.
    That done, conduct him to the drunkard's chamber,
    And call him "Madam," do him obeisance.
    Tell him from me, as he will win my love,
    He bear himself with honorable action,   115
    Such as he hath observed in noble ladies
    Unto their lords, by them accomplishèd.
    Such duty to the drunkard let him do
    With soft low tongue and lowly courtesy,
    And say "What is 't your Honor will command,   120
    Wherein your lady and your humble wife
    May show her duty and make known her love?"
    And then with kind embracements, tempting kisses,
    And with declining head into his bosom,
    Bid him shed tears, as being overjoyed   125
    To see her noble lord restored to health,
    Who, for this seven years, hath esteemed him
    No better than a poor and loathsome beggar.
    And if the boy have not a woman's gift
    To rain a shower of commanded tears,   130
    An onion will do well for such a shift,
    Which (in a napkin being close conveyed)
    Shall in despite enforce a watery eye.
    See this dispatched with all the haste thou canst.
    Anon I'll give thee more instructions.   135
                    A Servingman exits.
    I know the boy will well usurp the grace,

Voice, gait, and action of a gentlewoman.
I long to hear him call the drunkard "husband"!
And how my men will stay themselves from
    laughter   140
When they do homage to this simple peasant,
I'll in to counsel them. Haply my presence
May well abate the over-merry spleen
Which otherwise would grow into extremes.

⌜*They exit.*⌝

⌜Scene 2⌝

Enter aloft ⌜*Christopher Sly,*⌝ *the drunkard, with
Attendants, some with apparel, basin and ewer, and
other appurtenances, and Lord* ⌜*dressed as an Attendant.*⌝

SLY   For God's sake, a pot of small ale.

FIRST SERVINGMAN
  Will 't please your Lord drink a cup of sack?

SECOND SERVINGMAN
  Will 't please your Honor taste of these conserves?

THIRD SERVINGMAN
  What raiment will your Honor wear today?

SLY   I am Christophero Sly! Call not me "Honor" nor   5
  "Lordship." I ne'er drank sack in my life. An if you
  give me any conserves, give me conserves of beef.
  Ne'er ask me what raiment I'll wear, for I have no
  more doublets than backs, no more stockings than
  legs, nor no more shoes than feet, nay sometime   10
  more feet than shoes, or such shoes as my toes look
  through the over-leather.

LORD, ⌜*as* ATTENDANT⌝
  Heaven cease this idle humor in your Honor!
  O, that a mighty man of such descent,
  Of such possessions, and so high esteem   15
  Should be infusèd with so foul a spirit!

SLY   What, would you make me mad? Am not I Christopher Sly, old Sly's son of Burton Heath, by birth a
peddler, by education a cardmaker, by transmuta-
tion a bearherd, and now by present profession a   20
tinker? Ask Marian Hacket, the fat alewife of Wincot, if she know me not! If she say I am not fourteen
pence on the score for sheer ale, score me up for the
lying'st knave in Christendom. What, I am not
bestraught! Here's—   25

THIRD SERVINGMAN
    O, this it is that makes your lady mourn.
SECOND SERVINGMAN
    O, this is it that makes your servants droop.
LORD, ⌈*as* ATTENDANT⌉
    Hence comes it that your kindred shuns your house,
    As beaten hence by your strange lunacy.
    O noble lord, bethink thee of thy birth,   30
    Call home thy ancient thoughts from banishment,
    And banish hence these abject lowly dreams.
    Look how thy servants do attend on thee,
    Each in his office ready at thy beck.
    Wilt thou have music? Hark, Apollo plays,   *Music.* 35
    And twenty cagèd nightingales do sing.
    Or wilt thou sleep? We'll have thee to a couch
    Softer and sweeter than the lustful bed
    On purpose trimmed up for Semiramis.
    Say thou wilt walk, we will bestrew the ground.   40
    Or wilt thou ride? Thy horses shall be trapped,
    Their harness studded all with gold and pearl.
    Dost thou love hawking? Thou hast hawks will soar
    Above the morning lark. Or wilt thou hunt?
    Thy hounds shall make the welkin answer them   45
    And fetch shrill echoes from the hollow earth.
FIRST SERVINGMAN
    Say thou wilt course. Thy greyhounds are as swift
    As breathèd stags, ay, fleeter than the roe.

SECOND SERVINGMAN
  Dost thou love pictures? We will fetch thee straight
  Adonis painted by a running brook,   50
  And Cytherea all in sedges hid,
  Which seem to move and wanton with her breath,
  Even as the waving sedges play with wind.
LORD, ⌈*as* ATTENDANT⌉
  We'll show thee Io as she was a maid
  And how she was beguilèd and surprised,   55
  As lively painted as the deed was done.
THIRD SERVINGMAN
  Or Daphne roaming through a thorny wood,
  Scratching her legs that one shall swear she bleeds,
  And at that sight shall sad Apollo weep,
  So workmanly the blood and tears are drawn.   60
LORD, ⌈*as* ATTENDANT⌉
  Thou art a lord, and nothing but a lord;
  Thou hast a lady far more beautiful
  Than any woman in this waning age.
FIRST SERVINGMAN
  And till the tears that she hath shed for thee
  Like envious floods o'errun her lovely face,   65
  She was the fairest creature in the world—
  And yet she is inferior to none.
SLY
  Am I a lord, and have I such a lady?
  Or do I dream? Or have I dreamed till now?
  I do not sleep: I see, I hear, I speak,   70
  I smell sweet savors, and I feel soft things.
  Upon my life, I am a lord indeed
  And not a tinker, nor Christopher Sly.
  Well, bring our lady hither to our sight,
  And once again a pot o' the smallest ale.   75
SECOND SERVINGMAN
  Will 't please your Mightiness to wash your hands?
  O, how we joy to see your wit restored!

O, that once more you knew but what you are!
These fifteen years you have been in a dream,
Or, when you waked, so waked as if you slept.   80

SLY
These fifteen years! By my fay, a goodly nap.
But did I never speak of all that time?

FIRST SERVINGMAN
Oh, yes, my lord, but very idle words.
For though you lay here in this goodly chamber,
Yet would you say you were beaten out of door,   85
And rail upon the hostess of the house,
And say you would present her at the leet
Because she brought stone jugs and no sealed
  quarts.
Sometimes you would call out for Cicely Hacket.   90

SLY   Ay, the woman's maid of the house.

THIRD SERVINGMAN
Why, sir, you know no house, nor no such maid,
Nor no such men as you have reckoned up,
As Stephen Sly and old John Naps of ⌜Greete,⌝
And Peter Turph and Henry Pimpernell,   95
And twenty more such names and men as these,
Which never were, nor no man ever saw.

SLY   Now, Lord be thanked for my good amends!

ALL   Amen.

SLY   I thank thee. Thou shalt not lose by it.   100

Enter ⌜Page as⌝ Lady, with Attendants.

⌜PAGE, *as*⌝ LADY   How fares my noble lord?

SLY   Marry, I fare well, for here is cheer enough.
    Where is my wife?

⌜PAGE, *as*⌝ LADY
Here, noble lord. What is thy will with her?

SLY
Are you my wife, and will not call me "husband"?   105
My men should call me "lord." I am your goodman.

⌐PAGE, *as*⌐ LADY
  My husband and my lord, my lord and husband,
  I am your wife in all obedience.
SLY
  I know it well.—What must I call her?
LORD, ⌐*as* ATTENDANT⌐   "Madam."   110
SLY   "Alice Madam," or "Joan Madam"?
LORD
  "Madam," and nothing else. So lords call ladies.
SLY
  Madam wife, they say that I have dreamed
  And slept above some fifteen year or more.
⌐PAGE, *as*⌐ LADY
  Ay, and the time seems thirty unto me,   115
  Being all this time abandoned from your bed.
SLY
  'Tis much.—Servants, leave me and her alone.—
  Madam, undress you, and come now to bed.
⌐PAGE, *as*⌐ LADY
  Thrice noble lord, let me entreat of you
  To pardon me yet for a night or two;   120
  Or if not so, until the sun be set.
  For your physicians have expressly charged,
  In peril to incur your former malady,
  That I should yet absent me from your bed.
  I hope this reason stands for my excuse.   125
SLY   Ay, it stands so that I may hardly tarry so long; but
    I would be loath to fall into my dreams again. I will
    therefore tarry in despite of the flesh and the
    blood.

                    Enter a Messenger.

MESSENGER
  Your Honor's players, hearing your amendment,   130
  Are come to play a pleasant comedy,
  For so your doctors hold it very meet,

Seeing too much sadness hath congealed your
    blood,
And melancholy is the nurse of frenzy.   135
Therefore they thought it good you hear a play
And frame your mind to mirth and merriment,
Which bars a thousand harms and lengthens life.

SLY   Marry, I will. Let them play it.   ⌜*Messenger exits.*⌝
    Is not a comonty a Christmas gambold or a tum-   140
    bling trick?

⌜PAGE, *as*⌝ LADY
    No, my good lord, it is more pleasing stuff.

SLY   What, household stuff?

⌜PAGE, *as*⌝ LADY   It is a kind of history.

SLY   Well, we'll see 't. Come, madam wife, sit by my   145
    side, and let the world slip. We shall ne'er be
    younger.
                                        ⌜*They sit.*⌝

⌜ACT 1⌝

⌜Scene 1⌝

Flourish. Enter Lucentio, and his man Tranio.

LUCENTIO
Tranio, since for the great desire I had
To see fair Padua, nursery of arts,
I am arrived for fruitful Lombardy,
The pleasant garden of great Italy,
And by my father's love and leave am armed   5
With his goodwill and thy good company.
My trusty servant well approved in all,
Here let us breathe and haply institute
A course of learning and ingenious studies.
Pisa, renownèd for grave citizens,   10
Gave me my being, and my father first,
A merchant of great traffic through the world,
⌜Vincentio,⌝ come of the Bentivolii.
Vincentio's son, brought up in Florence,
It shall become to serve all hopes conceived   15
To deck his fortune with his virtuous deeds.
And therefore, Tranio, for the time I study
Virtue, and that part of philosophy
Will I apply that treats of happiness
By virtue specially to be achieved.   20
Tell me thy mind, for I have Pisa left
And am to Padua come, as he that leaves

19

A shallow plash to plunge him in the deep
And with satiety seeks to quench his thirst.

TRANIO
⌜*Mi perdonato,*⌝ gentle master mine.   25
I am in all affected as yourself,
Glad that you thus continue your resolve
To suck the sweets of sweet philosophy.
Only, good master, while we do admire
This virtue and this moral discipline,   30
Let's be no stoics nor no stocks, I pray,
Or so devote to Aristotle's checks
As Ovid be an outcast quite abjured.
Balk logic with acquaintance that you have,
And practice rhetoric in your common talk;   35
Music and poesy use to quicken you;
The mathematics and the metaphysics—
Fall to them as you find your stomach serves you.
No profit grows where is no pleasure ta'en.
In brief, sir, study what you most affect.   40

LUCENTIO
Gramercies, Tranio, well dost thou advise.
If, Biondello, thou wert come ashore,
We could at once put us in readiness
And take a lodging fit to entertain
Such friends as time in Padua shall beget.   45

*Enter Baptista with his two daughters, Katherine and
Bianca; Gremio, a pantaloon, ⌜and⌝ Hortensio, ⌜suitors⌝
to Bianca.*

But stay awhile! What company is this?

TRANIO
Master, some show to welcome us to town.
                    Lucentio ⌜and⌝ Tranio stand by.

BAPTISTA, ⌜*to Gremio and Hortensio*⌝
Gentlemen, importune me no farther,
For how I firmly am resolved you know:

That is, not to bestow my youngest daughter   50
Before I have a husband for the elder.
If either of you both love Katherine,
Because I know you well and love you well,
Leave shall you have to court her at your pleasure.

GREMIO
To cart her, rather. She's too rough for me.—   55
There, there, Hortensio, will you any wife?

KATHERINE, ⌈*to Baptista*⌉
I pray you, sir, is it your will
To make a stale of me amongst these mates?

HORTENSIO
"Mates," maid? How mean you that? No mates for
   you,   60
Unless you were of gentler, milder mold.

KATHERINE
I' faith, sir, you shall never need to fear.
Iwis it is not halfway to her heart.
But if it were, doubt not her care should be
To comb your noddle with a three-legged stool   65
And paint your face and use you like a fool.

HORTENSIO
From all such devils, good Lord, deliver us!

GREMIO   And me too, good Lord.

TRANIO, ⌈*aside to Lucentio*⌉
Husht, master, here's some good pastime toward;
That wench is stark mad or wonderful froward.   70

LUCENTIO, ⌈*aside to Tranio*⌉
But in the other's silence do I see
Maid's mild behavior and sobriety.
Peace, Tranio.

TRANIO, ⌈*aside to Lucentio*⌉
Well said, master. Mum, and gaze your fill.

BAPTISTA, ⌈*to Gremio and Hortensio*⌉
Gentlemen, that I may soon make good   75
What I have said—Bianca, get you in,

And let it not displease thee, good Bianca,
For I will love thee ne'er the less, my girl.

KATHERINE
A pretty peat! It is best
Put finger in the eye, an she knew why.   80

BIANCA
Sister, content you in my discontent.—
Sir, to your pleasure humbly I subscribe.
My books and instruments shall be my company,
On them to look and practice by myself.

LUCENTIO, ⌐*aside to Tranio*⌐
Hark, Tranio, thou mayst hear Minerva speak!   85

HORTENSIO
Signior Baptista, will you be so strange?
Sorry am I that our goodwill effects
Bianca's grief.

GREMIO   Why will you mew her up,
Signior Baptista, for this fiend of hell,   90
And make her bear the penance of her tongue?

BAPTISTA
Gentlemen, content you. I am resolved.—
Go in, Bianca.   ⌐*Bianca exits.*⌐
And for I know she taketh most delight
In music, instruments, and poetry,   95
Schoolmasters will I keep within my house
Fit to instruct her youth. If you, Hortensio,
Or, Signior Gremio, you know any such,
Prefer them hither. For to cunning men
I will be very kind, and liberal   100
To mine own children in good bringing up.
And so, farewell.—Katherine, you may stay,
For I have more to commune with Bianca.   *He exits.*

KATHERINE
Why, and I trust I may go too, may I not?
What, shall I be appointed hours as though, belike,   105
I knew not what to take and what to leave? Ha!
                                        She exits.

GREMIO   You may go to the devil's dam! Your gifts are
so good here's none will hold you.—Their love is
not so great, Hortensio, but we may blow our nails
together and fast it fairly out. Our cake's dough on   110
both sides. Farewell. Yet for the love I bear my
sweet Bianca, if I can by any means light on a fit
man to teach her that wherein she delights, I will
wish him to her father.

HORTENSIO   So will I, Signior Gremio. But a word, I   115
pray. Though the nature of our quarrel yet never
brooked parle, know now upon advice, it toucheth
us both (that we may yet again have access to our
fair mistress and be happy rivals in Bianca's love) to
labor and effect one thing specially.   120

GREMIO   What's that, I pray?

HORTENSIO   Marry, sir, to get a husband for her sister.

GREMIO   A husband? A devil!

HORTENSIO   I say "a husband."

GREMIO   I say "a devil." Think'st thou, Hortensio,   125
though her father be very rich, any man is so very a
fool to be married to hell?

HORTENSIO   Tush, Gremio. Though it pass your patience and mine to endure her loud alarums, why,
man, there be good fellows in the world, an a man   130
could light on them, would take her with all faults,
and money enough.

GREMIO   I cannot tell. But I had as lief take her dowry
with this condition: to be whipped at the high cross
every morning.   135

HORTENSIO   Faith, as you say, there's small choice in
rotten apples. But come, since this bar in law
makes us friends, it shall be so far forth friendly
maintained till by helping Baptista's eldest daughter to a husband we set his youngest free for a   140
husband, and then have to 't afresh. Sweet Bianca!
Happy man be his dole! He that runs fastest gets the
ring. How say you, Signior Gremio?

GREMIO I am agreed, and would I had given him the
best horse in Padua to begin his wooing that would 145
thoroughly woo her, wed her, and bed her, and rid
the house of her. Come on.
⌈*Gremio and Hortensio*⌉ *exit.*
Tranio and Lucentio remain onstage.

TRANIO
I pray, sir, tell me, is it possible
That love should of a sudden take such hold?

LUCENTIO
O Tranio, till I found it to be true, 150
I never thought it possible or likely.
But see, while idly I stood looking on,
I found the effect of love-in-idleness,
And now in plainness do confess to thee
That art to me as secret and as dear 155
As Anna to the Queen of Carthage was:
Tranio, I burn, I pine! I perish, Tranio,
If I achieve not this young modest girl.
Counsel me, Tranio, for I know thou canst.
Assist me, Tranio, for I know thou wilt. 160

TRANIO
Master, it is no time to chide you now.
Affection is not rated from the heart.
If love have touched you, naught remains but so:
Redime te ⌈*captum*⌉ *quam queas minimo.*

LUCENTIO
Gramercies, lad. Go forward. This contents; 165
The rest will comfort, for thy counsel's sound.

TRANIO
Master, you looked so longly on the maid,
Perhaps you marked not what's the pith of all.

LUCENTIO
O yes, I saw sweet beauty in her face,
Such as the daughter of Agenor had, 170
That made great Jove to humble him to her hand
When with his knees he kissed the Cretan strand.

TRANIO
Saw you no more? Marked you not how her sister
Began to scold and raise up such a storm
That mortal ears might hardly endure the din?   175
LUCENTIO
Tranio, I saw her coral lips to move,
And with her breath she did perfume the air.
Sacred and sweet was all I saw in her.
TRANIO, ⌈*aside*⌉
Nay, then 'tis time to stir him from his trance.—
I pray, awake, sir! If you love the maid,   :0
Bend thoughts and wits to achieve her. Thus it
    stands:
Her elder sister is so curst and shrewd
That till the father rid his hands of her,
Master, your love must live a maid at home,   185
And therefore has he closely mewed her up,
Because she will not be annoyed with suitors.
LUCENTIO
Ah, Tranio, what a cruel father's he!
But art thou not advised he took some care
To get her cunning schoolmasters to instruct her?   190
TRANIO
Ay, marry, am I, sir—and now 'tis plotted!
LUCENTIO
I have it, Tranio!
TRANIO   Master, for my hand,
Both our inventions meet and jump in one.
LUCENTIO
Tell me thine first.   195
TRANIO   You will be schoolmaster
And undertake the teaching of the maid:
That's your device.
LUCENTIO   It is. May it be done?
TRANIO
Not possible. For who shall bear your part   200

And be in Padua here Vincentio's son,
Keep house, and ply his book, welcome his friends,
Visit his countrymen and banquet them?

LUCENTIO
Basta, content thee, for I have it full.
We have not yet been seen in any house,   205
Nor can we be distinguished by our faces
For man or master. Then it follows thus:
Thou shalt be master, Tranio, in my stead,
Keep house, and port, and servants, as I should.
I will some other be, some Florentine,   210
Some Neapolitan, or meaner man of Pisa.
'Tis hatched, and shall be so. Tranio, at once
Uncase thee. Take my colored hat and cloak.
⌐*They exchange clothes.*⌐
When Biondello comes, he waits on thee,
But I will charm him first to keep his tongue.   215

TRANIO   So had you need.
In brief, sir, sith it your pleasure is,
And I am tied to be obedient
(For so your father charged me at our parting:
"Be serviceable to my son," quoth he,   220
Although I think 'twas in another sense),
I am content to be Lucentio,
Because so well I love Lucentio.

LUCENTIO
Tranio, be so, because Lucentio loves,
And let me be a slave, t' achieve that maid   225
Whose sudden sight hath thralled my wounded eye.

Enter Biondello.

Here comes the rogue.—Sirrah, where have you
    been?
BIONDELLO
Where have I been? Nay, how now, where are you?

Master, has my fellow Tranio stolen your clothes?   230
Or you stolen his? Or both? Pray, what's the news?

LUCENTIO
Sirrah, come hither. 'Tis no time to jest,
And therefore frame your manners to the time.
Your fellow, Tranio here, to save my life,
Puts my apparel and my count'nance on,   235
And I for my escape have put on his;
For in a quarrel since I came ashore
I killed a man and fear I was descried.
Wait you on him, I charge you, as becomes,
While I make way from hence to save my life.   240
You understand me?

BIONDELLO   Ay, sir. ⌜*Aside.*⌝ Ne'er a whit.

LUCENTIO
And not a jot of "Tranio" in your mouth.
Tranio is changed into Lucentio.

BIONDELLO
The better for him. Would I were so too.   245

TRANIO
So could I, faith, boy, to have the next wish after,
That Lucentio indeed had Baptista's youngest
    daughter.
But, sirrah, not for my sake, but your master's, I
    advise   250
You use your manners discreetly in all kind of
    companies.
When I am alone, why then I am Tranio;
But in all places else, ⌜your⌝ master Lucentio.

LUCENTIO   Tranio, let's go. One thing more rests, that   255
    thyself execute, to make one among these wooers. If
    thou ask me why, sufficeth my reasons are both
    good and weighty.   *They exit.*
                The Presenters above ⌜*speak.*⌝

FIRST SERVINGMAN
My lord, you nod. You do not mind the play.

SLY   Yes, by Saint Anne, do I. A good matter, surely.   260
     Comes there any more of it?

⌐PAGE, *as*⌐ LADY   My lord, 'tis but begun.

SLY   'Tis a very excellent piece of work, madam lady.
     Would 'twere done.

                                    They sit and mark.

                       ⌐Scene 2⌐
            Enter Petruchio and his man Grumio.

PETRUCHIO
   Verona, for a while I take my leave
   To see my friends in Padua, but of all
   My best belovèd and approvèd friend,
   Hortensio. And I trow this is his house.
   Here, sirrah Grumio, knock, I say.   5

GRUMIO   Knock, sir? Whom should I knock? Is there
     any man has rebused your Worship?

PETRUCHIO   Villain, I say, knock me here soundly.

GRUMIO   Knock you here, sir? Why, sir, what am I, sir,
     that I should knock you here, sir?   10

PETRUCHIO
   Villain, I say, knock me at this gate
   And rap me well, or I'll knock your knave's pate.

GRUMIO
   My master is grown quarrelsome. I should knock
      you first,
   And then I know after who comes by the worst.   15

PETRUCHIO   Will it not be?
   Faith, sirrah, an you'll not knock, I'll ring it.
   I'll try how you can *sol, fa,* and sing it.
            He wrings him by the ears. ⌐*Grumio falls.*⌐

GRUMIO   Help, mistress, help! My master is mad.

PETRUCHIO   Now knock when I bid you, sirrah   20
     villain.

Enter Hortensio.

HORTENSIO How now, what's the matter? My old
   friend Grumio and my good friend Petruchio? How
   do you all at Verona?

PETRUCHIO

   Signior Hortensio, come you to part the fray? 25
   ⌐*Con tutto il cuore ben trovato,*⌐ may I say.

HORTENSIO *Alla nostra casa* ⌐*ben*⌐ *venuto,* ⌐*molto
   honorato*⌐ *signor mio Petruchio.*—Rise, Grumio,
   rise. We will compound this quarrel. ⌐*Grumio rises.*⌐

GRUMIO Nay, 'tis no matter, sir, what he 'leges in 30
   Latin. If this be not a lawful cause for me to leave
   his service—look you, sir: he bid me knock him
   and rap him soundly, sir. Well, was it fit for a
   servant to use his master so, being perhaps, for
   aught I see, two-and-thirty, a pip out? 35
   Whom, would to God, I had well knocked at first,
   Then had not Grumio come by the worst.

PETRUCHIO

   A senseless villain, good Hortensio.
   I bade the rascal knock upon your gate
   And could not get him for my heart to do it. 40

GRUMIO Knock at the gate? O, heavens, spake you not
   these words plain: "Sirrah, knock me here, rap me
   here, knock me well, and knock me soundly"? And
   come you now with "knocking at the gate"?

PETRUCHIO

   Sirrah, begone, or talk not, I advise you. 45

HORTENSIO

   Petruchio, patience. I am Grumio's pledge.
   Why, this' a heavy chance 'twixt him and you,
   Your ancient, trusty, pleasant servant Grumio.
   And tell me now, sweet friend, what happy gale
   Blows you to Padua here from old Verona? 50

PETRUCHIO

   Such wind as scatters young men through the world

To seek their fortunes farther than at home,
Where small experience grows. But in a few,
Signior Hortensio, thus it stands with me:
Antonio, my father, is deceased,   55
And I have thrust myself into this maze,
Happily to wive and thrive, as best I may.
Crowns in my purse I have and goods at home,
And so am come abroad to see the world.

HORTENSIO
Petruchio, shall I then come roundly to thee   60
And wish thee to a shrewd ill-favored wife?
Thou'dst thank me but a little for my counsel—
And yet I'll promise thee she shall be rich,
And very rich. But thou'rt too much my friend,
And I'll not wish thee to her.   65

PETRUCHIO
Signior Hortensio, 'twixt such friends as we
Few words suffice. And therefore, if thou know
One rich enough to be Petruchio's wife
(As wealth is burden of my wooing dance),
Be she as foul as was Florentius' love,   70
As old as Sibyl, and as curst and shrewd
As Socrates' Xanthippe, or a worse,
She moves me not, or not removes at least
Affection's edge in me, were she as rough
As are the swelling Adriatic seas.   75
I come to wive it wealthily in Padua;
If wealthily, then happily in Padua.

GRUMIO, ⌈*to Hortensio*⌉ Nay, look you, sir, he tells you
flatly what his mind is. Why, give him gold enough
and marry him to a puppet or an aglet-baby, or an   80
old trot with ne'er a tooth in her head, though she
have as many diseases as two-and-fifty horses. Why,
nothing comes amiss, so money comes withal.

HORTENSIO
Petruchio, since we are stepped thus far in,

I will continue that I broached in jest.   85
I can, Petruchio, help thee to a wife
With wealth enough, and young and beauteous,
Brought up as best becomes a gentlewoman.
Her only fault, and that is faults enough,
Is that she is intolerable curst,   90
And shrewd, and froward, so beyond all measure
That, were my state far worser than it is,
I would not wed her for a mine of gold.

PETRUCHIO
Hortensio, peace. Thou know'st not gold's effect.
Tell me her father's name, and 'tis enough;   95
For I will board her, though she chide as loud
As thunder when the clouds in autumn crack.

HORTENSIO
Her father is Baptista Minola,
An affable and courteous gentleman.
Her name is Katherina Minola,   100
Renowned in Padua for her scolding tongue.

PETRUCHIO
I know her father, though I know not her,
And he knew my deceasèd father well.
I will not sleep, Hortensio, till I see her,
And therefore let me be thus bold with you   105
To give you over at this first encounter—
Unless you will accompany me thither.

GRUMIO, ⌈*to Hortensio*⌉ I pray you, sir, let him go while
   the humor lasts. O' my word, an she knew him as
   well as I do, she would think scolding would do little   110
   good upon him. She may perhaps call him half a
   score knaves or so. Why, that's nothing; an he begin
   once, he'll rail in his rope tricks. I'll tell you what,
   sir, an she stand him but a little, he will throw a
   figure in her face and so disfigure her with it that   115
   she shall have no more eyes to see withal than a cat.
   You know him not, sir.

HORTENSIO
  Tarry, Petruchio. I must go with thee,
  For in Baptista's keep my treasure is.
  He hath the jewel of my life in hold,   120
  His youngest daughter, beautiful Bianca,
  And her withholds from me ⌜and⌝ other more,
  Suitors to her and rivals in my love,
  Supposing it a thing impossible,
  For those defects I have before rehearsed,   125
  That ever Katherina will be wooed.
  Therefore this order hath Baptista ta'en,
  That none shall have access unto Bianca
  Till Katherine the curst have got a husband.
GRUMIO   "Katherine the curst,"   130
  A title for a maid, of all titles the worst.
HORTENSIO
  Now shall my friend Petruchio do me grace
  And offer me disguised in sober robes
  To old Baptista as a schoolmaster
  Well seen in music, to instruct Bianca,   135
  That so I may, by this device at least,
  Have leave and leisure to make love to her
  And unsuspected court her by herself.
GRUMIO   Here's no knavery! See, to beguile the old
  folks, how the young folks lay their heads together!   140

  *Enter Gremio and Lucentio, disguised ⌜as Cambio, a
            schoolmaster.⌝*

  Master, master, look about you. Who goes there, ha?
HORTENSIO
  Peace, Grumio, it is the rival of my love.
  Petruchio, stand by awhile.
      ⌜*Petruchio, Hortensio, and Grumio stand aside.*⌝
GRUMIO, ⌜*aside*⌝
  A proper stripling, and an amorous.

GREMIO, ⌜*to* LUCENTIO⌝
  O, very well, I have perused the note.   145
  Hark you, sir, I'll have them very fairly bound,
  All books of love. See that at any hand,
  And see you read no other lectures to her.
  You understand me. Over and beside
  Signior Baptista's liberality,   150
  I'll mend it with a largess. Take your paper too.
  And let me have them very well perfumed,
  For she is sweeter than perfume itself
  To whom they go to. What will you read to her?
LUCENTIO, ⌜*as* CAMBIO⌝
  Whate'er I read to her, I'll plead for you   155
  As for my patron, stand you so assured,
  As firmly as yourself were still in place,
  Yea, and perhaps with more successful words
  Than you—unless you were a scholar, sir.
GREMIO
  O this learning, what a thing it is!   160
GRUMIO, ⌜*aside*⌝
  O this woodcock, what an ass it is!
PETRUCHIO, ⌜*aside*⌝ Peace, sirrah.
HORTENSIO, ⌜*aside*⌝
  Grumio, mum.   ⌜*Coming forward.*⌝
          God save you, Signior Gremio.
GREMIO
  And you are well met, Signior Hortensio.   165
  Trow you whither I am going? To Baptista Minola.
  I promised to enquire carefully
  About a schoolmaster for the fair Bianca,
  And by good fortune I have lighted well
  On this young man, for learning and behavior   170
  Fit for her turn, well read in poetry
  And other books—good ones, I warrant you.
HORTENSIO
  'Tis well. And I have met a gentleman

Hath promised me to help ⌜me⌝ to another,
A fine musician to instruct our mistress.   175
So shall I no whit be behind in duty
To fair Bianca, so beloved of me.

GREMIO
Beloved of me, and that my deeds shall prove.

GRUMIO, ⌜*aside*⌝   And that his bags shall prove.

HORTENSIO
Gremio, 'tis now no time to vent our love.   180
Listen to me, and if you speak me fair
I'll tell you news indifferent good for either.
                              ⌜*Presenting Petruchio.*⌝
Here is a gentleman whom by chance I met,
Upon agreement from us to his liking,
Will undertake to woo curst Katherine,   185
Yea, and to marry her, if her dowry please.

GREMIO   So said, so done, is well.
Hortensio, have you told him all her faults?

PETRUCHIO
I know she is an irksome, brawling scold.
If that be all, masters, I hear no harm.   190

GREMIO
No? Sayst me so, friend? What countryman?

PETRUCHIO
Born in Verona, old Antonio's son.
My father dead, my fortune lives for me,
And I do hope good days and long to see.

GREMIO
Oh, sir, such a life with such a wife were strange.   195
But if you have a stomach, to 't, i' God's name!
You shall have me assisting you in all.
But will you woo this wildcat?

PETRUCHIO   Will I live?

GRUMIO
Will he woo her? Ay, or I'll hang her.   200

PETRUCHIO
   Why came I hither but to that intent?
   Think you a little din can daunt mine ears?
   Have I not in my time heard lions roar?
   Have I not heard the sea, puffed up with winds,
   Rage like an angry boar chafèd with sweat?   205
   Have I not heard great ordnance in the field
   And heaven's artillery thunder in the skies?
   Have I not in a pitchèd battle heard
   Loud 'larums, neighing steeds, and trumpets clang?
   And do you tell me of a woman's tongue,   210
   That gives not half so great a blow to hear
   As will a chestnut in a farmer's fire?
   Tush, tush, fear boys with bugs!
GRUMIO   For he fears none.
GREMIO   Hortensio, hark.   215
   This gentleman is happily arrived,
   My mind presumes, for his own good and yours.
HORTENSIO
   I promised we would be contributors
   And bear his charge of wooing whatsoe'er.
GREMIO
   And so we will, provided that he win her.   220
GRUMIO
   I would I were as sure of a good dinner.

   Enter Tranio, ⌜*disguised as Lucentio,*⌝ *and Biondello.*

TRANIO, ⌜*as* LUCENTIO⌝
   Gentlemen, God save you. If I may be bold,
   Tell me, I beseech you, which is the readiest way
   To the house of Signior Baptista Minola?
BIONDELLO   He that has the two fair daughters—is 't 225
      he you mean?
TRANIO, ⌜*as* LUCENTIO⌝   Even he, Biondello.
GREMIO
   Hark you, sir, you mean not her to—

TRANIO, ⌈*as* LUCENTIO⌉
  Perhaps him and her, sir. What have you to do?
PETRUCHIO
  Not her that chides, sir, at any hand, I pray.   230
TRANIO, ⌈*as* LUCENTIO⌉
  I love no chiders, sir. Biondello, let's away.
LUCENTIO, ⌈*aside*⌉
  Well begun, Tranio.
HORTENSIO   Sir, a word ere you go.
  Are you a suitor to the maid you talk of, yea or no?
TRANIO, ⌈*as* LUCENTIO⌉
  An if I be, sir, is it any offense?   235
GREMIO
  No, if without more words you will get you hence.
TRANIO, ⌈*as* LUCENTIO⌉
  Why sir, I pray, are not the streets as free
  For me, as for you?
GREMIO   But so is not she.
TRANIO, ⌈*as* LUCENTIO⌉
  For what reason, I beseech you?   240
GREMIO
  For this reason, if you'll know:
  That she's the choice love of Signior Gremio.
HORTENSIO
  That she's the chosen of Signior Hortensio.
TRANIO, ⌈*as* LUCENTIO⌉
  Softly, my masters. If you be gentlemen,
  Do me this right: hear me with patience.   245
  Baptista is a noble gentleman
  To whom my father is not all unknown,
  And were his daughter fairer than she is,
  She may more suitors have, and me for one.
  Fair Leda's daughter had a thousand wooers.   250
  Then well one more may fair Bianca have.
  And so she shall. Lucentio shall make one,
  Though Paris came in hope to speed alone.

GREMIO
  What, this gentleman will out-talk us all!
LUCENTIO, ⌈*as* CAMBIO⌉
  Sir, give him head; I know he'll prove a jade.   255
PETRUCHIO
  Hortensio, to what end are all these words?
HORTENSIO, ⌈*to Tranio*⌉
  Sir, let me be so bold as ask you,
  Did you yet ever see Baptista's daughter?
TRANIO, ⌈*as* LUCENTIO⌉
  No, sir, but hear I do that he hath two,
  The one as famous for a scolding tongue   260
  As is the other for beauteous modesty.
PETRUCHIO
  Sir, sir, the first's for me; let her go by.
GREMIO
  Yea, leave that labor to great Hercules,
  And let it be more than Alcides' twelve.
PETRUCHIO, ⌈*to Tranio*⌉
  Sir, understand you this of me, in sooth: 265
  The youngest daughter, whom you hearken for,
  Her father keeps from all access of suitors
  And will not promise her to any man
  Until the elder sister first be wed.
  The younger then is free, and not before.   270
TRANIO, ⌈*as* LUCENTIO⌉
  If it be so, sir, that you are the man
  Must stead us all, and me amongst the rest,
  And if you break the ice and do this ⌈feat,⌉
  Achieve the elder, set the younger free
  For our access, whose hap shall be to have her   275
  Will not so graceless be to be ingrate.
HORTENSIO
  Sir, you say well, and well you do conceive.
  And since you do profess to be a suitor,
  You must, as we do, gratify this gentleman,
  To whom we all rest generally beholding.   280

TRANIO, ⌐*as* LUCENTIO⌐

  Sir, I shall not be slack; in sign whereof,
  Please you we may contrive this afternoon
  And quaff carouses to our mistress' health,
  And do as adversaries do in law,
  Strive mightily, but eat and drink as friends.   285

GRUMIO ⌐*and*⌐ BIONDELLO

  O excellent motion! Fellows, let's be gone.

HORTENSIO

  The motion's good indeed, and be it so.—
  Petruchio, I shall be your ⌐*ben*⌐ *venuto*.

                          They exit.

⌜ACT 2⌝

⌜Scene 1⌝

Enter Katherine and Bianca ⌜with her hands tied.⌝

BIANCA
  Good sister, wrong me not, nor wrong yourself,
  To make a bondmaid and a slave of me.
  That I disdain. But for these other goods—
  Unbind my hands, I'll pull them off myself,
  Yea, all my raiment to my petticoat,   5
  Or what you will command me will I do,
  So well I know my duty to my elders.
KATHERINE
  Of all thy suitors here I charge ⌜thee⌝ tell
  Whom thou lov'st best. See thou dissemble not.
BIANCA
  Believe me, sister, of all the men alive   10
  I never yet beheld that special face
  Which I could fancy more than any other.
KATHERINE
  Minion, thou liest. Is 't not Hortensio?
BIANCA
  If you affect him, sister, here I swear
  I'll plead for you myself, but you shall have him.   15
KATHERINE
  O, then belike you fancy riches more.
  You will have Gremio to keep you fair.

39

BIANCA
　Is it for him you do envy me so?
　Nay, then, you jest, and now I well perceive
　You have but jested with me all this while.
　I prithee, sister Kate, untie my hands.   20
　　　　　　　　　　　　　　⌜*Katherine*⌝ *strikes her.*
KATHERINE
　If that be jest, then all the rest was so.

　　　　　　　　　Enter Baptista.

BAPTISTA
　Why, how now, dame, whence grows this
　　insolence?—
　Bianca, stand aside.—Poor girl, she weeps!   25
　　　　　　　　　　　　　　　　⌜*He unties her hands.*⌝
　⌜*To Bianca.*⌝ Go ply thy needle; meddle not with her.
　⌜*To Katherine.*⌝ For shame, thou hilding of a devilish
　　spirit!
　Why dost thou wrong her that did ne'er wrong
　　thee?   30
　When did she cross thee with a bitter word?
KATHERINE
　Her silence flouts me, and I'll be revenged!
　　　　　　　　　　　　　　⌜*She*⌝ *flies after Bianca.*
BAPTISTA
　What, in my sight?—Bianca, get thee in.
　　　　　　　　　　　　　　　　⌜*Bianca*⌝ *exits.*
KATHERINE
　What, will you not suffer me? Nay, now I see
　She is your treasure, she must have a husband,   35
　I must dance barefoot on her wedding day
　And, for your love to her, lead apes in hell.
　Talk not to me. I will go sit and weep
　Till I can find occasion of revenge.   ⌜*She exits.*⌝
BAPTISTA
　Was ever gentleman thus grieved as I?   40
　But who comes here?

Enter Gremio; Lucentio ⌜disguised as Cambio⌝
in the habit of a mean man; Petruchio with
⌜Hortensio disguised as Litio; and⌝ Tranio ⌜disguised
as Lucentio,⌝ with his boy, ⌜Biondello,⌝ bearing a lute
and books.

GREMIO Good morrow, neighbor Baptista.

BAPTISTA Good morrow, neighbor Gremio.—God
save you, gentlemen.

PETRUCHIO

And you, good sir. Pray, have you not a daughter   45
Called Katherina, fair and virtuous?

BAPTISTA

I have a daughter, sir, called Katherina.

GREMIO, ⌜to Petruchio⌝

You are too blunt. Go to it orderly.

PETRUCHIO

You wrong me, Signior Gremio. Give me leave.—
I am a gentleman of Verona, sir,   50
That hearing of her beauty and her wit,
Her affability and bashful modesty,
Her wondrous qualities and mild behavior,
Am bold to show myself a forward guest
Within your house, to make mine eye the witness   55
Of that report which I so oft have heard,
And, for an entrance to my entertainment,
I do present you with a man of mine,
⌜*Presenting Hortensio, disguised as Litio.*⌝
Cunning in music and the mathematics,
To instruct her fully in those sciences,   60
Whereof I know she is not ignorant.
Accept of him, or else you do me wrong.
His name is Litio, born in Mantua.

BAPTISTA

You're welcome, sir, and he for your good sake.

But for my daughter Katherine, this I know,   65
She is not for your turn, the more my grief.

PETRUCHIO
I see you do not mean to part with her,
Or else you like not of my company.

BAPTISTA
Mistake me not. I speak but as I find.
Whence are you, sir? What may I call your name?   70

PETRUCHIO
Petruchio is my name, Antonio's son,
A man well known throughout all Italy.

BAPTISTA
I know him well. You are welcome for his sake.

GREMIO
Saving your tale, Petruchio, I pray
Let us that are poor petitioners speak too!   75
Bacare, you are marvelous forward.

PETRUCHIO
O, pardon me, Signior Gremio, I would fain be
doing.

GREMIO
I doubt it not, sir. But you will curse your wooing.
⌈*To Baptista.* Neighbor,⌉ this is a gift very grateful,   80
I am sure of it. To express the like kindness, myself,
that have been more kindly beholding to you than
any, freely give unto ⌈you⌉ this young scholar ⌈*presenting Lucentio, disguised as Cambio*⌉ that hath
been long studying at Rheims, as cunning in Greek,   85
Latin, and other languages as the other in music and
mathematics. His name is Cambio. Pray accept his
service.

BAPTISTA A thousand thanks, Signior Gremio. Welcome, good Cambio. ⌈*To Tranio as Lucentio.*⌉ But,   90
gentle sir, methinks you walk like a stranger. May I
be so bold to know the cause of your coming?

TRANIO, ⌜*as* LUCENTIO⌝
  Pardon me, sir, the boldness is mine own,
  That being a stranger in this city here
  Do make myself a suitor to your daughter,   95
  Unto Bianca, fair and virtuous.
  Nor is your firm resolve unknown to me,
  In the preferment of the eldest sister.
  This liberty is all that I request,
  That, upon knowledge of my parentage,   100
  I may have welcome 'mongst the rest that woo
  And free access and favor as the rest.
  And toward the education of your daughters
  I here bestow a simple instrument
  And this small packet of Greek and Latin books.   105
      ⌜*Biondello comes forward with the gifts.*⌝
  If you accept them, then their worth is great.
BAPTISTA
  Lucentio is your name. Of whence, I pray?
TRANIO, ⌜*as* LUCENTIO⌝
  Of Pisa, sir, son to Vincentio.
BAPTISTA
  A mighty man of Pisa. By report
  I know him well. You are very welcome, sir.   110
  ⌜*To Hortensio as Litio.*⌝ Take you the lute, ⌜*To*
    Lucentio as Cambio.⌝ and you the set of books.
  You shall go see your pupils presently.
  Holla, within!

              Enter a Servant

              Sirrah, lead these gentlemen   115
  To my daughters, and tell them both
  These are their tutors. Bid them use them well.
      ⌜*Servant exits with Hortensio and Lucentio.*⌝
  We will go walk a little in the orchard,
  And then to dinner. You are passing welcome,
  And so I pray you all to think yourselves.   120

PETRUCHIO
  Signior Baptista, my business asketh haste,
  And every day I cannot come to woo.
  You knew my father well, and in him me,
  Left solely heir to all his lands and goods,
  Which I have bettered rather than decreased.   125
  Then tell me, if I get your daughter's love,
  What dowry shall I have with her to wife?
BAPTISTA
  After my death, the one half of my lands,
  And, in possession, twenty thousand crowns.
PETRUCHIO
  And, for that dowry, I'll assure her of   130
  Her widowhood, be it that she survive me,
  In all my lands and leases whatsoever.
  Let specialties be therefore drawn between us,
  That covenants may be kept on either hand.
BAPTISTA
  Ay, when the special thing is well obtained,   135
  That is, her love, for that is all in all.
PETRUCHIO
  Why, that is nothing. For I tell you, father,
  I am as peremptory as she proud-minded;
  And where two raging fires meet together,
  They do consume the thing that feeds their fury.   140
  Though little fire grows great with little wind,
  Yet extreme gusts will blow out fire and all.
  So I to her and so she yields to me,
  For I am rough and woo not like a babe.
BAPTISTA
  Well mayst thou woo, and happy be thy speed.   145
  But be thou armed for some unhappy words.
PETRUCHIO
  Ay, to the proof, as mountains are for winds,
  That shakes not, though they blow perpetually.

Enter Hortensio ⌈as Litio⌉ with his head broke.

BAPTISTA
  How now, my friend, why dost thou look so pale?
HORTENSIO, ⌈*as* LITIO⌉
  For fear, I promise you, if I look pale.   150
BAPTISTA
  What, will my daughter prove a good musician?
HORTENSIO, ⌈*as* LITIO⌉
  I think she'll sooner prove a soldier!
  Iron may hold with her, but never lutes.
BAPTISTA
  Why, then thou canst not break her to the lute?
HORTENSIO, ⌈*as* LITIO⌉
  Why, no, for she hath broke the lute to me.   155
  I did but tell her she mistook her frets,
  And bowed her hand to teach her fingering,
  When, with a most impatient devilish spirit,
  " 'Frets' call you these?" quoth she. "I'll fume with
    them!"   160
  And with that word she struck me on the head,
  And through the instrument my pate made way,
  And there I stood amazèd for a while,
  As on a pillory, looking through the lute,
  While she did call me "rascal fiddler,"   165
  And "twangling Jack," with twenty such vile terms,
  As had she studied to misuse me so.
PETRUCHIO
  Now, by the world, it is a lusty wench.
  I love her ten times more than e'er I did.
  O, how I long to have some chat with her!   170
BAPTISTA, ⌈*to Hortensio as Litio*⌉
  Well, go with me, and be not so discomfited.
  Proceed in practice with my younger daughter.
  She's apt to learn, and thankful for good turns.—
  Signior Petruchio, will you go with us,
  Or shall I send my daughter Kate to you?   175

PETRUCHIO
 I pray you do. I'll attend her here—
       All but Petruchio exit.
 And woo her with some spirit when she comes!
 Say that she rail, why then I'll tell her plain
 She sings as sweetly as a nightingale.
 Say that she frown, I'll say she looks as clear   180
 As morning roses newly washed with dew.
 Say she be mute and will not speak a word,
 Then I'll commend her volubility
 And say she uttereth piercing eloquence.
 If she do bid me pack, I'll give her thanks   185
 As though she bid me stay by her a week.
 If she deny to wed, I'll crave the day
 When I shall ask the banns, and when be marrièd.
 But here she comes—and now, Petruchio, speak.

     Enter Katherine

 Good morrow, Kate, for that's your name, I hear. 190
KATHERINE
 Well have you heard, but something hard of hearing.
 They call me Katherine that do talk of me.
PETRUCHIO
 You lie, in faith, for you are called plain Kate,
 And bonny Kate, and sometimes Kate the curst.
 But Kate, the prettiest Kate in Christendom,   195
 Kate of Kate Hall, my super-dainty Kate
 (For dainties are all Kates)—and therefore, Kate,
 Take this of me, Kate of my consolation:
 Hearing thy mildness praised in every town,
 Thy virtues spoke of, and thy beauty sounded 200
 (Yet not so deeply as to thee belongs),
 Myself am moved to woo thee for my wife.
KATHERINE
 "Moved," in good time! Let him that moved you
  hither

Remove you hence. I knew you at the first   205
You were a movable.

PETRUCHIO
Why, what's a movable?

KATHERINE   A joint stool.

PETRUCHIO
Thou hast hit it. Come, sit on me.

KATHERINE
Asses are made to bear, and so are you.   210

PETRUCHIO
Women are made to bear, and so are you.

KATHERINE
No such jade as you, if me you mean.

PETRUCHIO
Alas, good Kate, I will not burden thee,
For knowing thee to be but young and light—

KATHERINE
Too light for such a swain as you to catch,   215
And yet as heavy as my weight should be.

PETRUCHIO
"Should be"—should buzz!

KATHERINE   Well ta'en, and like a
    buzzard.

PETRUCHIO
O slow-winged turtle, shall a buzzard take thee?   220

KATHERINE
Ay, for a turtle, as he takes a buzzard.

PETRUCHIO
Come, come, you wasp! I' faith, you are too angry.

KATHERINE
If I be waspish, best beware my sting.

PETRUCHIO
My remedy is then to pluck it out.

KATHERINE
Ay, if the fool could find it where it lies.   225

PETRUCHIO
   Who knows not where a wasp does wear his sting?
   In his tail.
KATHERINE   In his tongue.
PETRUCHIO   Whose tongue?
KATHERINE
   Yours, if you talk of tales, and so farewell.   230
PETRUCHIO   What, with my tongue in your tail?
   Nay, come again, good Kate. I am a gentleman—
KATHERINE   That I'll try.   *She strikes him.*
PETRUCHIO
   I swear I'll cuff you if you strike again.
KATHERINE   So may you lose your arms.   235
   If you strike me, you are no gentleman,
   And if no gentleman, why then no arms.
PETRUCHIO
   A herald, Kate? O, put me in thy books.
KATHERINE   What is your crest? A coxcomb?
PETRUCHIO
   A combless cock, so Kate will be my hen.   240
KATHERINE
   No cock of mine. You crow too like a craven.
PETRUCHIO
   Nay, come, Kate, come. You must not look so sour.
KATHERINE
   It is my fashion when I see a crab.
PETRUCHIO
   Why, here's no crab, and therefore look not sour.
KATHERINE   There is, there is.   245
PETRUCHIO
   Then show it me.
KATHERINE   Had I a glass, I would.
PETRUCHIO   What, you mean my face?
KATHERINE   Well aimed of such a young one.
PETRUCHIO
   Now, by Saint George, I am too young for you.   250

KATHERINE
  Yet you are withered.

PETRUCHIO   'Tis with cares.

KATHERINE   I care not.

PETRUCHIO
  Nay, hear you, Kate—in sooth, you 'scape not so.

KATHERINE
  I chafe you if I tarry. Let me go.   255

PETRUCHIO
  No, not a whit. I find you passing gentle.
  'Twas told me you were rough, and coy, and sullen,
  And now I find report a very liar.
  For thou art pleasant, gamesome, passing
    courteous,   260
  But slow in speech, yet sweet as springtime flowers.
  Thou canst not frown, thou canst not look askance,
  Nor bite the lip as angry wenches will,
  Nor hast thou pleasure to be cross in talk.
  But thou with mildness entertain'st thy wooers,   265
  With gentle conference, soft, and affable.
  Why does the world report that Kate doth limp?
  O sland'rous world! Kate like the hazel twig
  Is straight, and slender, and as brown in hue
  As hazel nuts, and sweeter than the kernels.   270
  O, let me see thee walk! Thou dost not halt.

KATHERINE
  Go, fool, and whom thou keep'st command.

PETRUCHIO
  Did ever Dian so become a grove
  As Kate this chamber with her princely gait?
  O, be thou Dian and let her be Kate,   275
  And then let Kate be chaste and Dian sportful.

KATHERINE
  Where did you study all this goodly speech?

PETRUCHIO
  It is extempore, from my mother wit.

KATHERINE
  A witty mother, witless else her son.

PETRUCHIO   Am I not wise?   280

KATHERINE   Yes, keep you warm.

PETRUCHIO
  Marry, so I mean, sweet Katherine, in thy bed.
  And therefore, setting all this chat aside,
  Thus in plain terms: your father hath consented
  That you shall be my wife, your dowry 'greed on,   285
  And, will you, nill you, I will marry you.
  Now, Kate, I am a husband for your turn,
  For by this light, whereby I see thy beauty,
  Thy beauty that doth make me like thee well,
  Thou must be married to no man but me.   290
  For I am he am born to tame you, Kate,
  And bring you from a wild Kate to a Kate
  Conformable as other household Kates.

  Enter Baptista, Gremio, ⌜and⌝ Tranio ⌜as Lucentio.⌝

  Here comes your father. Never make denial.
  I must and will have Katherine to my wife.   295

BAPTISTA
  Now, Signior Petruchio, how speed you with my
    daughter?

PETRUCHIO   How but well, sir? How but well?
  It were impossible I should speed amiss.

BAPTISTA
  Why, how now, daughter Katherine? In your   300
    dumps?

KATHERINE
  Call you me daughter? Now I promise you
  You have showed a tender fatherly regard,
  To wish me wed to one half lunatic,
  A madcap ruffian and a swearing Jack,   305
  That thinks with oaths to face the matter out.

PETRUCHIO
   Father, 'tis thus: yourself and all the world
   That talked of her have talked amiss of her.
   If she be curst, it is for policy,
   For she's not froward, but modest as the dove;   310
   She is not hot, but temperate as the morn.
   For patience she will prove a second Grissel,
   And Roman Lucrece for her chastity.
   And to conclude, we have 'greed so well together
   That upon Sunday is the wedding day.   315

KATHERINE
   I'll see thee hanged on Sunday first.

GREMIO Hark, Petruchio, she says she'll see thee
   hanged first.

TRANIO, ⌐*as* LUCENTIO⌐ Is this your speeding? Nay,
   then, goodnight our part.   320

PETRUCHIO
   Be patient, gentlemen. I choose her for myself.
   If she and I be pleased, what's that to you?
   'Tis bargained 'twixt us twain, being alone,
   That she shall still be curst in company.
   I tell you, 'tis incredible to believe   325
   How much she loves me. O, the kindest Kate!
   She hung about my neck, and kiss on kiss
   She vied so fast, protesting oath on oath,
   That in a twink she won me to her love.
   O, you are novices! 'Tis a world to see   330
   How tame, when men and women are alone,
   A meacock wretch can make the curstest shrew.—
   Give me thy hand, Kate. I will unto Venice
   To buy apparel 'gainst the wedding day.—
   Provide the feast, father, and bid the guests.   335
   I will be sure my Katherine shall be fine.

BAPTISTA
   I know not what to say, but give me your hands.
   God send you joy, Petruchio. 'Tis a match.

GREMIO and TRANIO, ⌈*as* LUCENTIO⌉
Amen, say we. We will be witnesses.

PETRUCHIO
Father, and wife, and gentlemen, adieu.   340
I will to Venice. Sunday comes apace.
We will have rings, and things, and fine array,
And kiss me, Kate. We will be married o' Sunday.

                         Petruchio and Katherine exit
                              ⌈*through different doors.*⌉

GREMIO
Was ever match clapped up so suddenly?

BAPTISTA
Faith, gentlemen, now I play a merchant's part   345
And venture madly on a desperate mart.

TRANIO, ⌈*as* LUCENTIO⌉
'Twas a commodity lay fretting by you.
'Twill bring you gain, or perish on the seas.

BAPTISTA
The gain I seek, is quiet ⌈in⌉ the match.

GREMIO
No doubt but he hath got a quiet catch.   350
But now, Baptista, to your younger daughter.
Now is the day we long have lookèd for.
I am your neighbor and was suitor first.

TRANIO, ⌈*as* LUCENTIO⌉
And I am one that love Bianca more
Than words can witness or your thoughts can guess.   355

GREMIO
Youngling, thou canst not love so dear as I.

TRANIO, ⌈*as* LUCENTIO⌉
Graybeard, thy love doth freeze.

GREMIO   But thine doth fry!
Skipper, stand back. 'Tis age that nourisheth.

TRANIO, ⌈*as* LUCENTIO⌉
But youth in ladies' eyes that flourisheth.   360

BAPTISTA
    Content you, gentlemen. I will compound this strife.
    'Tis deeds must win the prize, and he of both
    That can assure my daughter greatest dower
    Shall have my Bianca's love.
    Say, Signior Gremio, what can you assure her?   365

GREMIO
    First, as you know, my house within the city
    Is richly furnishèd with plate and gold,
    Basins and ewers to lave her dainty hands;
    My hangings all of Tyrian tapestry;
    In ivory coffers I have stuffed my crowns,   370
    In cypress chests my arras counterpoints,
    Costly apparel, tents, and canopies,
    Fine linen, Turkey cushions bossed with pearl,
    Valance of Venice gold in needlework,
    Pewter and brass, and all things that belongs   375
    To house or housekeeping. Then, at my farm
    I have a hundred milch-kine to the pail,
    Six score fat oxen standing in my stalls,
    And all things answerable to this portion.
    Myself am struck in years, I must confess,   380
    And if I die tomorrow this is hers,
    If whilst I live she will be only mine.

TRANIO, ⌜*as* LUCENTIO⌝
    That "only" came well in. ⌜*To Baptista.*⌝ Sir, list to
      me:
    I am my father's heir and only son.   385
    If I may have your daughter to my wife,
    I'll leave her houses three or four as good,
    Within rich Pisa walls, as any one
    Old Signior Gremio has in Padua,
    Besides two thousand ducats by the year   390
    Of fruitful land, all which shall be her jointure.—
    What, have I pinched you, Signior Gremio?

GREMIO
  Two thousand ducats by the year of land?
  ⌐*Aside.*⌐ My land amounts not to so much in all.—
  That she shall have, besides an argosy   395
  That now is lying in Marcellus' road.
  ⌐*To Tranio.*⌐ What, have I choked you with an argosy?
TRANIO, ⌐*as* LUCENTIO⌐
  Gremio, 'tis known my father hath no less
  Than three great argosies, besides two galliasses
  And twelve tight galleys. These I will assure her,   400
  And twice as much whate'er thou off'rest next.
GREMIO
  Nay, I have offered all. I have no more,
  And she can have no more than all I have.
  ⌐*To Baptista.*⌐ If you like me, she shall have me and
      mine.   405
TRANIO, ⌐*as* LUCENTIO⌐
  Why, then, the maid is mine from all the world,
  By your firm promise. Gremio is outvied.
BAPTISTA
  I must confess your offer is the best,
  And, let your father make her the assurance,
  She is your own; else, you must pardon me.   410
  If you should die before him, where's her dower?
TRANIO, ⌐*as* LUCENTIO⌐
  That's but a cavil. He is old, I young.
GREMIO
  And may not young men die as well as old?
BAPTISTA
  Well, gentlemen, I am thus resolved:
  On Sunday next, you know   415
  My daughter Katherine is to be married.
  ⌐*To Tranio as Lucentio.*⌐ Now, on the Sunday
      following, shall Bianca
  Be bride to you, if you make this assurance.
  If not, to Signior Gremio.   420
  And so I take my leave, and thank you both.

GREMIO
    Adieu, good neighbor.   ⌜*Baptista*⌝ *exits.*
                    Now I fear thee not.
    Sirrah young gamester, your father were a fool
    To give thee all and in his waning age   425
    Set foot under thy table. Tut, a toy!
    An old Italian fox is not so kind, my boy.
                                    ⌜*Gremio*⌝ *exits.*

TRANIO
    A vengeance on your crafty withered hide!—
    Yet I have faced it with a card of ten.
    'Tis in my head to do my master good.   430
    I see no reason but supposed Lucentio
    Must get a father, called "supposed Vincentio"—
    And that's a wonder. Fathers commonly
    Do get their children. But in this case of wooing,
    A child shall get a sire, if I fail not of my cunning.   435
                                    He exits.

ACT 3

Enter Lucentio ⌜*as Cambio,*⌝ *Hortensio* ⌜*as Litio,*⌝ *and Bianca.*

LUCENTIO, ⌜*as* CAMBIO⌝
  Fiddler, forbear. You grow too forward, sir.
  Have you so soon forgot the entertainment
  Her sister Katherine welcomed you withal?
HORTENSIO, ⌜*as* LITIO⌝ But, wrangling pedant, this is
  The patroness of heavenly harmony.   5
  Then give me leave to have prerogative,
  And when in music we have spent an hour,
  Your lecture shall have leisure for as much.
LUCENTIO, ⌜*as* CAMBIO⌝
  Preposterous ass, that never read so far
  To know the cause why music was ordained.   10
  Was it not to refresh the mind of man
  After his studies or his usual pain?
  Then give me leave to read philosophy,
  And, while I pause, serve in your harmony.
HORTENSIO, ⌜*as* LITIO⌝
  Sirrah, I will not bear these braves of thine.   15
BIANCA
  Why, gentlemen, you do me double wrong
  To strive for that which resteth in my choice.
  I am no breeching scholar in the schools.
  I'll not be tied to hours, nor 'pointed times,

56

But learn my lessons as I please myself.   20
And, to cut off all strife, here sit we down.
⌐*To Hortensio.*⌐ Take you your instrument, play you
   the whiles;
His lecture will be done ere you have tuned.
HORTENSIO, ⌐*as* LITIO⌐
You'll leave his lecture when I am in tune?   25
LUCENTIO, ⌐*aside*⌐
That will be never. ⌐*To Hortensio.*⌐ Tune your
   instrument.   ⌐*Hortensio steps aside to tune his lute.*⌐
BIANCA   Where left we last?
LUCENTIO, ⌐*as* CAMBIO⌐ Here, madam:
                           ⌐*Showing her a book.*⌐
Hic ibat Simois, hic est ⌐*Sigeia*⌐ *tellus,*   30
Hic steterat Priami regia celsa senis.
BIANCA   Conster them.
LUCENTIO   *Hic ibat,* as I told you before, *Simois,* I am
   Lucentio, *hic est,* son unto Vincentio of Pisa,
   ⌐*Sigeia*⌐ *tellus,* disguised thus to get your love, *Hic*   35
   steterat, and that "Lucentio" that comes a-wooing,
   Priami, is my man Tranio, *regia,* bearing my port,
   celsa senis, that we might beguile the old pantaloon.
HORTENSIO, ⌐*as* LITIO⌐ Madam, my instrument's in
   tune.   40
BIANCA   Let's hear. ⌐*He plays.*⌐ Oh fie, the treble jars!
LUCENTIO, ⌐*as* CAMBIO⌐   Spit in the hole, man, and tune
   again.   ⌐*Hortensio tunes his lute again.*⌐
BIANCA   Now let me see if I can conster it. *Hic ibat*
   Simois, I know you not; *hic est* ⌐*Sigeia*⌐ *tellus,* I trust   45
   you not; *Hic* ⌐*steterat*⌐ *Priami,* take heed he hear us
   not; *regia,* presume not; *celsa senis,* despair not.
HORTENSIO, ⌐*as* LITIO⌐
   Madam, 'tis now in tune.   ⌐*He plays again.*⌐
LUCENTIO, ⌐*as* CAMBIO⌐   All but the bass.
HORTENSIO, ⌐*as* LITIO⌐
The bass is right. 'Tis the base knave that jars.   50

⌜*Aside.*⌝ How fiery and forward our pedant is.
Now for my life the knave doth court my love!
Pedascule, I'll watch you better yet.
⌜BIANCA, *to Lucentio*⌝
In time I may believe, yet I mistrust.
⌜LUCENTIO⌝
Mistrust it not, for sure Aeacides   55
Was Ajax, called so from his grandfather.
⌜BIANCA⌝
I must believe my master; else, I promise you,
I should be arguing still upon that doubt.
But let it rest.—Now, Litio, to you.
Good master, take it not unkindly, pray,   60
That I have been thus pleasant with you both.
HORTENSIO, ⌜*as* LITIO, *to Lucentio*⌝
You may go walk, and give me leave awhile.
My lessons make no music in three parts.
LUCENTIO, ⌜*as* CAMBIO⌝
Are you so formal, sir? Well, I must wait
⌜*Aside.*⌝ And watch withal, for, but I be deceived,   65
Our fine musician groweth amorous.
                                        ⌜*He steps aside.*⌝
HORTENSIO, ⌜*as* LITIO⌝
Madam, before you touch the instrument,
To learn the order of my fingering
I must begin with rudiments of art,
To teach you gamut in a briefer sort,   70
More pleasant, pithy, and effectual
Than hath been taught by any of my trade.
And there it is in writing fairly drawn.
BIANCA
Why, I am past my gamut long ago.
HORTENSIO
Yet read the gamut of Hortensio.   75
                                ⌜*Giving her a paper.*⌝

BIANCA ⌜*reads*⌝
"*Gamut* I am, the ground of all accord:
⌜*A re,*⌝ to plead Hortensio's passion;
⌜*B mi,*⌝ Bianca, take him for thy lord,
⌜*C fa ut,*⌝ that loves with all affection;
D sol re, one clef, two notes have I;   80
E la mi, show pity or I die."
Call you this "gamut"? Tut, I like it not.
Old fashions please me best. I am not so nice
To ⌜change⌝ true rules for ⌜odd⌝ inventions.

                    Enter a ⌜*Servant.*⌝

⌜SERVANT⌝
Mistress, your father prays you leave your books   85
And help to dress your sister's chamber up.
You know tomorrow is the wedding day.

BIANCA
Farewell, sweet masters both. I must be gone.

LUCENTIO
Faith, mistress, then I have no cause to stay.
          ⌜*Bianca, the Servant, and Lucentio exit.*⌝

HORTENSIO
But I have cause to pry into this pedant.   90
Methinks he looks as though he were in love.
Yet if thy thoughts, Bianca, be so humble
To cast thy wand'ring eyes on every stale,
Seize thee that list! If once I find thee ranging,
Hortensio will be quit with thee by changing.   95
                                        He exits.

                    ⌜Scene 2⌝
Enter Baptista, Gremio, Tranio ⌜*as Lucentio,*⌝ *Katherine,
Bianca,* ⌜*Lucentio as Cambio,*⌝ *and others, Attendants.*

BAPTISTA, ⌜*to Tranio*⌝
Signior Lucentio, this is the 'pointed day

That Katherine and Petruchio should be married,
And yet we hear not of our son-in-law.
What will be said? What mockery will it be,
To want the bridegroom when the priest attends   5
To speak the ceremonial rites of marriage?
What says Lucentio to this shame of ours?

KATHERINE
No shame but mine. I must, forsooth, be forced
To give my hand, opposed against my heart,
Unto a mad-brain rudesby, full of spleen,   10
Who wooed in haste and means to wed at leisure.
I told you, I, he was a frantic fool,
Hiding his bitter jests in blunt behavior,
And, to be noted for a merry man,
He'll woo a thousand, 'point the day of marriage,   15
Make friends, invite, and proclaim the banns,
Yet never means to wed where he hath wooed.
Now must the world point at poor Katherine
And say "Lo, there is mad Petruchio's wife,
If it would please him come and marry her."   20

TRANIO, ⌈*as* LUCENTIO⌉
Patience, good Katherine, and Baptista too.
Upon my life, Petruchio means but well,
Whatever fortune stays him from his word.
Though he be blunt, I know him passing wise;
Though he be merry, yet withal he's honest.   25

KATHERINE
Would Katherine had never seen him, though!
                                        She exits weeping.

BAPTISTA
Go, girl. I cannot blame thee now to weep,
For such an injury would vex a very saint,
Much more a shrew of ⌈thy⌉ impatient humor.

                    Enter Biondello.

BIONDELLO   Master, master, news! And such ⌈old⌉   30
    news as you never heard of!

BAPTISTA

  Is it new and old too? How may that be?

BIONDELLO Why, is it not news to ⌜hear⌝ of Petruchio's
  coming?

BAPTISTA Is he come? 35

BIONDELLO Why, no, sir.

BAPTISTA

  What then?

BIONDELLO   He is coming.

BAPTISTA   When will he be here?

BIONDELLO

  When he stands where I am, and sees you there. 40

TRANIO, ⌜*as* LUCENTIO⌝ But say, what to thine old news?

BIONDELLO Why, Petruchio is coming in a new hat and
  an old jerkin, a pair of old breeches thrice turned,
  a pair of boots that have been candle-cases, one
  buckled, another laced; an old rusty sword ta'en 45
  out of the town armory, with a broken hilt, and
  chapeless; with two broken points; his horse
  hipped, with an old mothy saddle and stirrups of no
  kindred, besides possessed with the glanders and
  like to mose in the chine, troubled with the lam- 50
  pass, infected with the fashions, full of windgalls,
  sped with spavins, rayed with the yellows, past cure
  of the fives, stark spoiled with the staggers, begnawn
  with the bots, ⌜swayed⌝ in the back and shoulder-
  shotten, near-legged before, and with a half- 55
  checked bit and a headstall of sheep's leather,
  which, being restrained to keep him from stum-
  bling, hath been often burst, and now repaired with
  knots; one girth six times pieced, and a woman's
  crupper of velour, which hath two letters for her 60
  name fairly set down in studs, and here and there
  pieced with packthread.

BAPTISTA Who comes with him?

BIONDELLO　Oh, sir, his lackey, for all the world capari-
　　soned like the horse: with a linen stock on one leg　65
　　and a kersey boot-hose on the other, gartered with
　　a red and blue list; an old hat, and the humor of
　　forty fancies pricked in 't for a feather. A monster,
　　a very monster in apparel, and not like a Christian
　　footboy or a gentleman's lackey.　70

TRANIO, ⌈*as* LUCENTIO⌉
　'Tis some odd humor pricks him to this fashion,
　Yet oftentimes he goes but mean-appareled.

BAPTISTA
　I am glad he's come, howsoe'er he comes.

BIONDELLO　Why, sir, he comes not.

BAPTISTA　Didst thou not say he comes?　75

BIONDELLO　Who? That Petruchio came?

BAPTISTA　Ay, that Petruchio came!

BIONDELLO　No, sir, I say his horse comes with him on
　his back.

BAPTISTA　Why, that's all one.　80

BIONDELLO

　　　　Nay, by Saint Jamy.
　　　　I hold you a penny,
　　　　A horse and a man
　　　　Is more than one,
　　　　And yet not many.　85

　　　　Enter Petruchio and Grumio.

PETRUCHIO
　Come, where be these gallants? Who's at home?

BAPTISTA　You are welcome, sir.

PETRUCHIO　And yet I come not well.

BAPTISTA　And yet you halt not.

TRANIO, ⌈*as* LUCENTIO⌉　Not so well appareled as I wish　90
　you were.

PETRUCHIO
　Were it better I should rush in thus—

But where is Kate? Where is my lovely bride?
How does my father? Gentles, methinks you frown.
And wherefore gaze this goodly company   95
As if they saw some wondrous monument,
Some comet or unusual prodigy?

BAPTISTA
Why, sir, you know this is your wedding day.
First were we sad, fearing you would not come,
Now sadder that you come so unprovided.   100
Fie, doff this habit, shame to your estate,
An eyesore to our solemn festival.

TRANIO, ⌜*as* LUCENTIO⌝
And tell us what occasion of import
Hath all so long detained you from your wife
And sent you hither so unlike yourself.   105

PETRUCHIO
Tedious it were to tell, and harsh to hear.
Sufficeth I am come to keep my word,
Though in some part enforcèd to digress,
Which at more leisure I will so excuse
As you shall well be satisfied with all.   110
But where is Kate? I stay too long from her.
The morning wears. 'Tis time we were at church.

TRANIO, ⌜*as* LUCENTIO⌝
See not your bride in these unreverent robes.
Go to my chamber, put on clothes of mine.

PETRUCHIO
Not I, believe me. Thus I'll visit her.   115

BAPTISTA
But thus, I trust, you will not marry her.

PETRUCHIO
Good sooth, even thus. Therefore, ha' done with
    words.
To me she's married, not unto my clothes.
Could I repair what she will wear in me,   120
As I can change these poor accoutrements,

'Twere well for Kate and better for myself.
But what a fool am I to chat with you
When I should bid good morrow to my bride
And seal the title with a lovely kiss!   125
                    Petruchio exits, ⌐with Grumio.¬

TRANIO, ⌐*as* LUCENTIO¬
  He hath some meaning in his mad attire.
  We will persuade him, be it possible,
  To put on better ere he go to church.

BAPTISTA
  I'll after him, and see the event of this.
                    ⌐*All except Tranio and Lucentio*¬ *exit.*

TRANIO
  But, sir, ⌐to¬ love concerneth us to add   130
  Her father's liking, which to bring to pass,
  As ⌐I¬ before imparted to your Worship,
  I am to get a man (whate'er he be
  It skills not much, we'll fit him to our turn),
  And he shall be "Vincentio of Pisa,"   135
  And make assurance here in Padua
  Of greater sums than I have promisèd.
  So shall you quietly enjoy your hope
  And marry sweet Bianca with consent.

LUCENTIO
  Were it not that my fellow schoolmaster   140
  Doth watch Bianca's steps so narrowly,
  'Twere good, methinks, to steal our marriage,
  Which, once performed, let all the world say no,
  I'll keep mine own despite of all the world.

TRANIO
  That by degrees we mean to look into,   145
  And watch our vantage in this business.
  We'll overreach the graybeard, Gremio,
  The narrow prying father, Minola,
  The quaint musician, amorous Litio,
  All for my master's sake, Lucentio.   150

Enter Gremio.

TRANIO, ⌜*as* LUCENTIO⌝
  Signior Gremio, came you from the church?
GREMIO
  As willingly as e'er I came from school.
TRANIO, ⌜*as* LUCENTIO⌝
  And is the bride and bridegroom coming home?
GREMIO
  A bridegroom, say you? 'Tis a groom indeed,
  A grumbling groom, and that the girl shall find.   155
TRANIO, ⌜*as* LUCENTIO⌝
  Curster than she? Why, 'tis impossible.
GREMIO
  Why, he's a devil, a devil, a very fiend.
TRANIO, ⌜*as* LUCENTIO⌝
  Why, she's a devil, a devil, the devil's dam.
GREMIO
  Tut, she's a lamb, a dove, a fool to him.
  I'll tell you, Sir Lucentio: when the priest   160
  Should ask if Katherine should be his wife,
  "Ay, by gog's wouns!" quoth he, and swore so loud
  That, all amazed, the priest let fall the book,
  And as he stooped again to take it up,
  This mad-brained bridegroom took him such a cuff   165
  That down fell priest and book, and book and priest.
  "Now, take them up," quoth he, "if any list."
TRANIO, ⌜*as* LUCENTIO⌝
  What said the wench when he rose again?
GREMIO
  Trembled and shook, for why he stamped and swore
  As if the vicar meant to cozen him.   170
  But after many ceremonies done,
  He calls for wine. "A health!" quoth he, as if
  He had been aboard, carousing to his mates
  After a storm; quaffed off the muscatel

And threw the sops all in the sexton's face,   175
Having no other reason
But that his beard grew thin and hungerly,
And seemed to ask him sops as he was drinking.
This done, he took the bride about the neck
And kissed her lips with such a clamorous smack   180
That at the parting all the church did echo.
And I, seeing this, came thence for very shame,
And after me I know the rout is coming.
Such a mad marriage never was before!   *Music plays.*
Hark, hark, I hear the minstrels play.   185

Enter Petruchio, Katherine, Bianca, Hortensio, Baptista,
                ⌜*Grumio, and Attendants.*⌝

PETRUCHIO
  Gentlemen and friends, I thank you for your pains.
  I know you think to dine with me today
  And have prepared great store of wedding cheer,
  But so it is, my haste doth call me hence,
  And therefore here I mean to take my leave.   190
BAPTISTA
  Is 't possible you will away tonight?
PETRUCHIO
  I must away today, before night come.
  Make it no wonder. If you knew my business,
  You would entreat me rather go than stay.
  And, honest company, I thank you all,   195
  That have beheld me give away myself
  To this most patient, sweet, and virtuous wife.
  Dine with my father, drink a health to me,
  For I must hence, and farewell to you all.
TRANIO, ⌜*as* LUCENTIO⌝
  Let us entreat you stay till after dinner.   200
PETRUCHIO   It may not be.
GREMIO   Let me entreat you.
PETRUCHIO   It cannot be.

KATHERINE   Let me entreat you.

PETRUCHIO
 I am content.   205

KATHERINE   Are you content to stay?

PETRUCHIO
 I am content you shall entreat me stay,
 But yet not stay, entreat me how you can.

KATHERINE
 Now, if you love me, stay.

PETRUCHIO   Grumio, my horse.   210

GRUMIO Ay, sir, they be ready; the oats have eaten the
 horses.

KATHERINE   Nay, then,
 Do what thou canst, I will not go today,
 No, nor tomorrow, not till I please myself.   215
 The door is open, sir. There lies your way.
 You may be jogging whiles your boots are green.
 For me, I'll not be gone till I please myself.
 'Tis like you'll prove a jolly surly groom,
 That take it on you at the first so roundly.   220

PETRUCHIO
 O Kate, content thee. Prithee, be not angry.

KATHERINE
 I will be angry. What hast thou to do?—
 Father, be quiet. He shall stay my leisure.

GREMIO
 Ay, marry, sir, now it begins to work.

KATHERINE
 Gentlemen, forward to the bridal dinner.   225
 I see a woman may be made a fool
 If she had not a spirit to resist.

PETRUCHIO
 They shall go forward, Kate, at thy command.—
 Obey the bride, you that attend on her.
 Go to the feast, revel and domineer,   230
 Carouse full measure to her maidenhead,

Be mad and merry, or go hang yourselves.
But for my bonny Kate, she must with me.
Nay, look not big, nor stamp, nor stare, nor fret;
I will be master of what is mine own.   235
She is my goods, my chattels; she is my house,
My household stuff, my field, my barn,
My horse, my ox, my ass, my anything.
And here she stands, touch her whoever dare.
I'll bring mine action on the proudest he   240
That stops my way in Padua.—Grumio,
Draw forth thy weapon. We are beset with thieves.
Rescue thy mistress if thou be a man!—
Fear not, sweet wench, they shall not touch thee,
    Kate.   245
I'll buckler thee against a million.
          Petruchio and Katherine exit, ⌜with Grumio.⌝

BAPTISTA
Nay, let them go. A couple of quiet ones!

GREMIO
Went they not quickly, I should die with laughing.

TRANIO, ⌜*as* LUCENTIO⌝
Of all mad matches never was the like.

LUCENTIO, ⌜*as* CAMBIO⌝
Mistress, what's your opinion of your sister?   250

BIANCA
That being mad herself, she's madly mated.

GREMIO
I warrant him, Petruchio is Kated.

BAPTISTA
Neighbors and friends, though bride and
    bridegroom wants
For to supply the places at the table,   255
You know there wants no junkets at the feast.
⌜*To Tranio.*⌝ Lucentio, you shall supply the
    bridegroom's place,
And let Bianca take her sister's room.

TRANIO, ⌜*as* LUCENTIO⌝
  Shall sweet Bianca practice how to bride it?   260
BAPTISTA, ⌜*to Tranio*⌝
  She shall, Lucentio. Come, gentlemen, let's go.
                                        They exit.

⌜ACT 4⌝

⌜Scene 1⌝
Enter Grumio.

GRUMIO Fie, fie on all tired jades, on all mad masters,
and all foul ways! Was ever man so beaten? Was
ever man so 'rayed? Was ever man so weary? I am
sent before to make a fire, and they are coming
after to warm them. Now were not I a little pot and   5
soon hot, my very lips might freeze to my teeth, my
tongue to the roof of my mouth, my heart in my
belly, ere I should come by a fire to thaw me. But I
with blowing the fire shall warm myself. For, considering the weather, a taller man than I will take   10
cold.—Holla, ho, Curtis!

Enter Curtis.

CURTIS Who is that calls so coldly?
GRUMIO A piece of ice. If thou doubt it, thou mayst
slide from my shoulder to my heel with no greater
a run but my head and my neck. A fire, good Curtis!   15
CURTIS Is my master and his wife coming, Grumio?
GRUMIO Oh, ay, Curtis, ay, and therefore fire, fire! Cast
on no water.
CURTIS Is she so hot a shrew as she's reported?
GRUMIO She was, good Curtis, before this frost. But   20
thou know'st winter tames man, woman, and

70

beast, for it hath tamed my old master and my new
mistress and myself, fellow Curtis.

⌈CURTIS⌉ Away, you three-inch fool, I am no beast!

GRUMIO Am I but three inches? Why, thy horn is a   25
foot, and so long am I, at the least. But wilt thou
make a fire? Or shall I complain on thee to our
mistress, whose hand (she being now at hand) thou
shalt soon feel, to thy cold comfort, for being slow in
thy hot office?   30

CURTIS I prithee, good Grumio, tell me, how goes the
world?

GRUMIO A cold world, Curtis, in every office but thine,
and therefore fire! Do thy duty, and have thy duty,
for my master and mistress are almost frozen to   35
death.

CURTIS There's fire ready. And therefore, good Grumio, the news!

GRUMIO Why, "Jack boy, ho boy!" and as much news
as wilt thou.   40

CURTIS Come, you are so full of cony-catching.

GRUMIO Why, therefore fire, for I have caught extreme
cold. Where's the cook? Is supper ready, the house
trimmed, rushes strewed, cobwebs swept, the servingmen in their new fustian, ⌈their⌉ white stock-   45
ings, and every officer his wedding garment on? Be
the Jacks fair within, the Jills fair without, the
carpets laid, and everything in order?

CURTIS All ready. And therefore, I pray thee, news.

GRUMIO First, know my horse is tired, my master and   50
mistress fallen out.

CURTIS How?

GRUMIO Out of their saddles into the dirt, and thereby
hangs a tale.

CURTIS Let's ha' t, good Grumio.   55

GRUMIO Lend thine ear.

CURTIS Here.

GRUMIO   There!   ⌐*He slaps Curtis on the ear.*⌐
CURTIS   This 'tis to feel a tale, not to hear a tale.
GRUMIO   And therefore 'tis called a sensible tale. And   60
         this cuff was but to knock at your ear and beseech
         list'ning. Now I begin: *Imprimis*, we came down a
         foul hill, my master riding behind my mistress—
CURTIS   Both of one horse?
GRUMIO   What's that to thee?   65
CURTIS   Why, a horse.
GRUMIO   Tell thou the tale! But hadst thou not crossed
         me, thou shouldst have heard how her horse fell,
         and she under her horse; thou shouldst have heard
         in how miry a place, how she was bemoiled, how he   70
         left her with the horse upon her, how he beat me
         because her horse stumbled, how she waded
         through the dirt to pluck him off me, how he swore,
         how she prayed that never prayed before, how I
         cried, how the horses ran away, how her bridle was   75
         burst, how I lost my crupper, with many things of
         worthy memory which now shall die in oblivion,
         and thou return unexperienced to thy grave.
CURTIS   By this reck'ning, he is more shrew than she.
GRUMIO   Ay, and that thou and the proudest of you all   80
         shall find when he comes home. But what talk I of
         this? Call forth Nathaniel, Joseph, Nicholas, Phil-
         lip, Walter, Sugarsop, and the rest. Let their heads
         be slickly combed, their blue coats brushed, and
         their garters of an indifferent knit. Let them curtsy   85
         with their left legs, and not presume to touch a hair
         of my master's horse-tail till they kiss their hands.
         Are they all ready?
CURTIS   They are.
GRUMIO   Call them forth.   90
CURTIS, ⌐*calling out*⌐ Do you hear, ho? You must meet
         my master to countenance my mistress.
GRUMIO   Why, she hath a face of her own.

CURTIS   Who knows not that?

GRUMIO   Thou, it seems, that calls for company to   95
   countenance her.

CURTIS   I call them forth to credit her.

GRUMIO   Why, she comes to borrow nothing of them.

Enter four or five Servingmen.

NATHANIEL   Welcome home, Grumio.

PHILLIP   How now, Grumio?   100

JOSEPH   What, Grumio!

NICHOLAS   Fellow Grumio!

NATHANIEL   How now, old lad?

GRUMIO   Welcome, you!—How now, you?—What,
   you!—Fellow, you!—And thus much for greeting.   105
   Now, my spruce companions, is all ready and all
   things neat?

NATHANIEL   All things is ready. How near is our master?

⌈GRUMIO⌉   E'en at hand, alighted by this. And therefore   110
   be not—Cock's passion, silence! I hear my master.

Enter Petruchio and Katherine.

PETRUCHIO
   Where be these knaves? What, no man at door
   To hold my stirrup nor to take my horse?
   Where is Nathaniel, Gregory, Phillip?

ALL THE SERVANTS   Here! Here, sir, here, sir!   115

PETRUCHIO
   "Here, sir! Here, sir! Here, sir! Here, sir!"
   You loggerheaded and unpolished grooms.
   What? No attendance? No regard? No duty?
   Where is the foolish knave I sent before?

GRUMIO
   Here, sir, as foolish as I was before.   120

PETRUCHIO
   You peasant swain, you whoreson malt-horse
   drudge!

Did I not bid thee meet me in the park
And bring along these rascal knaves with thee?

GRUMIO
Nathaniel's coat, sir, was not fully made,   125
And Gabriel's pumps were all unpinked i' th' heel.
There was no link to color Peter's hat,
And Walter's dagger was not come from sheathing.
There were none fine but Adam, Rafe, and Gregory.
The rest were ragged, old, and beggarly.   130
Yet, as they are, here are they come to meet you.

PETRUCHIO
Go, rascals, go, and fetch my supper in!
                                    The Servants exit.
⌜*Sings.*⌝   *Where is the life that late I led?*
                Where are those—
Sit down, Kate, and welcome.—   135
                        ⌜*They sit at a table.*⌝
Soud, soud, soud, soud!

                Enter Servants with supper.

Why, when, I say?—Nay, good sweet Kate, be
    merry.—
Off with my boots, you rogues, you villains! When?
⌜*Sings.*⌝   *It was the friar of orders gray,*   140
                As he forth walkèd on his way—

        ⌜*Servant begins to remove Petruchio's boots.*⌝

Out, you rogue! You pluck my foot awry.
Take that!   ⌜*He hits the Servant.*⌝
            And mend the plucking of the other.—
Be merry, Kate.—Some water here! What ho!   145

                Enter one with water.

Where's my spaniel Troilus? Sirrah, get you hence
And bid my cousin Ferdinand come hither.
                            ⌜*A Servant exits.*⌝

One, Kate, that you must kiss and be acquainted
  with.—
Where are my slippers? Shall I have some water?— 150
Come, Kate, and wash, and welcome heartily.—
You whoreson villain, will you let it fall?
                   ⌜*He hits the Servant.*⌝

KATHERINE
Patience, I pray you, 'twas a fault unwilling.

PETRUCHIO
A whoreson beetle-headed flap-eared knave!—
Come, Kate, sit down. I know you have a stomach. 155
Will you give thanks, sweet Kate, or else shall I?—
What's this? Mutton?

FIRST SERVANT   Ay.

PETRUCHIO   Who brought it?

PETER   I. 160

PETRUCHIO 'Tis burnt, and so is all the meat.
What dogs are these? Where is the rascal cook?
How durst you, villains, bring it from the dresser
And serve it thus to me that love it not?
There, take it to you, trenchers, cups, and all! 165
      ⌜*He throws the food and dishes at them.*⌝
You heedless joltheads and unmannered slaves!
What, do you grumble? I'll be with you straight.
                        ⌜*The Servants exit.*⌝

KATHERINE
I pray you, husband, be not so disquiet.
The meat was well, if you were so contented.

PETRUCHIO
I tell thee, Kate, 'twas burnt and dried away, 170
And I expressly am forbid to touch it,
For it engenders choler, planteth anger,
And better 'twere that both of us did fast
(Since of ourselves, ourselves are choleric)
Than feed it with such over-roasted flesh. 175
Be patient. Tomorrow 't shall be mended,

And for this night we'll fast for company.
Come, I will bring thee to thy bridal chamber.

They exit.

Enter Servants severally.

NATHANIEL   Peter, didst ever see the like?
PETER   He kills her in her own humor.   180

Enter Curtis.

GRUMIO   Where is he?
CURTIS   In her chamber,
    Making a sermon of continency to her,
    And rails and swears and rates, that she (poor soul)
    Knows not which way to stand, to look, to speak,   185
    And sits as one new-risen from a dream.
    Away, away, for he is coming hither!

⌜*The Servants exit.*⌝

Enter Petruchio.

PETRUCHIO
    Thus have I politicly begun my reign,
    And 'tis my hope to end successfully.
    My falcon now is sharp and passing empty,   190
    And, till she stoop, she must not be full-gorged,
    For then she never looks upon her lure.
    Another way I have to man my haggard,
    To make her come and know her keeper's call.
    That is, to watch her, as we watch these kites   195
    That bate and beat and will not be obedient.
    She ate no meat today, nor none shall eat.
    Last night she slept not, nor tonight she shall not.
    As with the meat, some undeservèd fault
    I'll find about the making of the bed,   200
    And here I'll fling the pillow, there the bolster,
    This way the coverlet, another way the sheets.
    Ay, and amid this hurly I intend

That all is done in reverend care of her.
And, in conclusion, she shall watch all night,   205
And, if she chance to nod, I'll rail and brawl,
And with the clamor keep her still awake.
This is a way to kill a wife with kindness.
And thus I'll curb her mad and headstrong humor.
He that knows better how to tame a shrew,   210
Now let him speak; 'tis charity to shew.

                                        He exits.

                        ⌐Scene 2¬
    Enter Tranio ⌐*as Lucentio*¬ *and Hortensio* ⌐*as Litio.*¬

TRANIO, ⌐*as* LUCENTIO¬
  Is 't possible, friend Litio, that mistress Bianca
  Doth fancy any other but Lucentio?
  I tell you, sir, she bears me fair in hand.
⌐HORTENSIO, *as* LITIO¬
  Sir, to satisfy you in what I have said,
  Stand by, and mark the manner of his teaching.   5
                            ⌐*They stand aside.*¬

    Enter Bianca ⌐*and Lucentio as Cambio.*¬

⌐LUCENTIO, *as* CAMBIO¬
  Now mistress, profit you in what you read?
BIANCA
  What, master, read you? First resolve me that.
⌐LUCENTIO, *as* CAMBIO¬
  I read that I profess, *The Art to Love.*
BIANCA
  And may you prove, sir, master of your art.
LUCENTIO, ⌐*as* CAMBIO¬
  While you, sweet dear, prove mistress of my heart.   10
                  ⌐*They move aside and kiss and talk.*¬
HORTENSIO, ⌐*as* LITIO¬
  Quick proceeders, marry! Now tell me, I pray,

You that durst swear that your mistress Bianca
Loved ⌜none⌝ in the world so well as Lucentio.

TRANIO, ⌜*as* LUCENTIO⌝
  O despiteful love, unconstant womankind!
  I tell thee, Litio, this is wonderful!   15

HORTENSIO
  Mistake no more. I am not Litio,
  Nor a musician as I seem to be,
  But one that scorn to live in this disguise
  For such a one as leaves a gentleman
  And makes a god of such a cullion.   20
  Know, sir, that I am called Hortensio.

TRANIO, ⌜*as* LUCENTIO⌝
  Signior Hortensio, I have often heard
  Of your entire affection to Bianca,
  And since mine eyes are witness of her lightness,
  I will with you, if you be so contented,   25
  Forswear Bianca and her love forever.

HORTENSIO
  See how they kiss and court! Signior Lucentio,
  Here is my hand, and here I firmly vow
  Never to woo her more, but do forswear her
  As one unworthy all the former favors   30
  That I have fondly flattered ⌜her⌝ withal.

TRANIO, ⌜*as* LUCENTIO⌝
  And here I take the like unfeignèd oath,
  Never to marry with her, though she would entreat.
  Fie on her, see how beastly she doth court him!

HORTENSIO
  Would all the world but he had quite forsworn!   35
  For me, that I may surely keep mine oath,
  I will be married to a wealthy widow
  Ere three days pass, which hath as long loved me
  As I have loved this proud disdainful haggard.
  And so farewell, Signior Lucentio.   40
  Kindness in women, not their beauteous looks,

Shall win my love, and so I take my leave,
In resolution as I swore before.

⌐*Hortensio exits;*
Bianca and Lucentio come forward.⌐

TRANIO
Mistress Bianca, bless you with such grace
As 'longeth to a lover's blessèd case!   45
Nay, I have ta'en you napping, gentle love,
And have forsworn you with Hortensio.

BIANCA
Tranio, you jest. But have you both forsworn me?

TRANIO
Mistress, we have.

LUCENTIO   Then we are rid of Litio.   50

TRANIO
I' faith, he'll have a lusty widow now
That shall be wooed and wedded in a day.

BIANCA   God give him joy.

TRANIO
Ay, and he'll tame her.

BIANCA   He says so, Tranio?   55

TRANIO
Faith, he is gone unto the taming school.

BIANCA
The taming school? What, is there such a place?

TRANIO
Ay, mistress, and Petruchio is the master,
That teacheth tricks eleven and twenty long
To tame a shrew and charm her chattering tongue.   60

Enter Biondello

BIONDELLO
O master, master, I have watched so long
That I am dog-weary, but at last I spied
An ancient angel coming down the hill
Will serve the turn.

TRANIO   What is he, Biondello?   65
BIONDELLO
  Master, a marcantant, or a pedant,
  I know not what, but formal in apparel,
  In gait and countenance surely like a father.
LUCENTIO   And what of him, Tranio?
TRANIO
  If he be credulous, and trust my tale,   70
  I'll make him glad to seem Vincentio
  And give assurance to Baptista Minola
  As if he were the right Vincentio.
  Take ⌈in⌉ your love, and then let me alone.
                        ⌈*Lucentio and Bianca exit.*⌉

               Enter a ⌈*Merchant.*⌉

⌈MERCHANT⌉
  God save you, sir.
TRANIO, ⌈*as* LUCENTIO⌉ And you, sir. You are welcome.   75
  Travel you far on, or are you at the farthest?
⌈MERCHANT⌉
  Sir, at the farthest for a week or two,
  But then up farther, and as far as Rome,
  And so to Tripoli, if God lend me life.   80
TRANIO, ⌈*as* LUCENTIO⌉
  What countryman, I pray?
⌈MERCHANT⌉   Of Mantua.
TRANIO, ⌈*as* LUCENTIO⌉
  Of Mantua, sir? Marry, God forbid!
  And come to Padua, careless of your life?
⌈MERCHANT⌉
  My life, sir? How, I pray? For that goes hard.   85
TRANIO, ⌈*as* LUCENTIO⌉
  'Tis death for anyone in Mantua
  To come to Padua. Know you not the cause?
  Your ships are stayed at Venice, and the Duke,
  For private quarrel 'twixt your duke and him,

Hath published and proclaimed it openly.   90
'Tis marvel, but that you are but newly come,
You might have heard it else proclaimed about.
⌜MERCHANT⌝
    Alas, sir, it is worse for me than so,
    For I have bills for money by exchange
    From Florence, and must here deliver them.   95
TRANIO, ⌜*as* LUCENTIO⌝
    Well, sir, to do you courtesy,
    This will I do, and this I will advise you.
    First tell me, have you ever been at Pisa?
⌜MERCHANT⌝
    Ay, sir, in Pisa have I often been,
    Pisa renownèd for grave citizens.   100
TRANIO, ⌜*as* LUCENTIO⌝
    Among them know you one Vincentio?
⌜MERCHANT⌝
    I know him not, but I have heard of him:
    A merchant of incomparable wealth.
TRANIO, ⌜*as* LUCENTIO⌝
    He is my father, sir, and sooth to say,
    In count'nance somewhat doth resemble you.   105
BIONDELLO, ⌜*aside*⌝ As much as an apple doth an
    oyster, and all one.
TRANIO, ⌜*as* LUCENTIO⌝
    To save your life in this extremity,
    This favor will I do you for his sake
    (And think it not the worst of all your fortunes   110
    That you are like to Sir Vincentio):
    His name and credit shall you undertake,
    And in my house you shall be friendly lodged.
    Look that you take upon you as you should.
    You understand me, sir. So shall you stay   115
    Till you have done your business in the city.
    If this be court'sy, sir, accept of it.

⌐MERCHANT⌐

   O sir, I do, and will repute you ever
   The patron of my life and liberty.

TRANIO, ⌐*as* LUCENTIO⌐

   Then go with me, to make the matter good. 120
   This, by the way, I let you understand:
   My father is here looked for every day
   To pass assurance of a dower in marriage
   'Twixt me and one Baptista's daughter here.
   In all these circumstances I'll instruct you. 125
   Go with me to clothe you as becomes you.

                            They exit.

⌐Scene 3⌐
Enter Katherine and Grumio.

GRUMIO

   No, no, forsooth, I dare not for my life.

KATHERINE

   The more my wrong, the more his spite appears.
   What, did he marry me to famish me?
   Beggars that come unto my father's door
   Upon entreaty have a present alms. 5
   If not, elsewhere they meet with charity.
   But I, who never knew how to entreat,
   Nor never needed that I should entreat,
   Am starved for meat, giddy for lack of sleep,
   With oaths kept waking and with brawling fed. 10
   And that which spites me more than all these wants,
   He does it under name of perfect love,
   As who should say, if I should sleep or eat
   'Twere deadly sickness or else present death.
   I prithee, go, and get me some repast, 15
   I care not what, so it be wholesome food.

GRUMIO   What say you to a neat's foot?

KATHERINE
  'Tis passing good. I prithee let me have it.
GRUMIO
  I fear it is too choleric a meat.
  How say you to a fat tripe finely broiled?   20
KATHERINE
  I like it well. Good Grumio, fetch it me.
GRUMIO
  I cannot tell. I fear 'tis choleric.
  What say you to a piece of beef and mustard?
KATHERINE
  A dish that I do love to feed upon.
GRUMIO
  Ay, but the mustard is too hot a little.   25
KATHERINE
  Why then, the beef, and let the mustard rest.
GRUMIO
  Nay then, I will not. You shall have the mustard
  Or else you get no beef of Grumio.
KATHERINE
  Then both, or one, or any thing thou wilt.
GRUMIO
  Why then, the mustard without the beef.   30
KATHERINE
  Go, get thee gone, thou false deluding slave,
                                    ⌜*She*⌝ *beats him.*
  That feed'st me with the very name of meat.
  Sorrow on thee, and all the pack of you
  That triumph thus upon my misery.
  Go, get thee gone, I say.   35

          Enter Petruchio and Hortensio with meat.

PETRUCHIO
  How fares my Kate? What, sweeting, all amort?
HORTENSIO
  Mistress, what cheer?
KATHERINE   Faith, as cold as can be.

PETRUCHIO
　Pluck up thy spirits. Look cheerfully upon me.
　Here, love, thou seest how diligent I am,　　　　　　40
　To dress thy meat myself and bring it thee.
　I am sure, sweet Kate, this kindness merits thanks.
　What, not a word? Nay then, thou lov'st it not,
　And all my pains is sorted to no proof.
　Here, take away this dish.　　　　　　　　　　　45
KATHERINE　I pray you, let it stand.
PETRUCHIO
　The poorest service is repaid with thanks,
　And so shall mine before you touch the meat.
KATHERINE　I thank you, sir.
HORTENSIO
　Signior Petruchio, fie, you are to blame.　　　　50
　Come, Mistress Kate, I'll bear you company.
PETRUCHIO, ⌜*aside to Hortensio*⌝
　Eat it up all, Hortensio, if thou lovest me.—
　Much good do it unto thy gentle heart.
　Kate, eat apace.
　　　　　⌜*Katherine and Hortensio prepare to eat.*⌝
　　　　　　　And now, my honey love,　　　　　55
　Will we return unto thy father's house
　And revel it as bravely as the best,
　With silken coats and caps and golden rings,
　With ruffs and cuffs and farthingales and things,
　With scarves and fans and double change of brav'ry,　60
　With amber bracelets, beads, and all this knav'ry.
　What, hast thou dined? The tailor stays thy leisure
　To deck thy body with his ruffling treasure.

　　　　　　　　Enter Tailor.

　Come, tailor, let us see these ornaments.
　Lay forth the gown.　　　　　　　　　　　　65

　　　　　　　　Enter Haberdasher.

　　　　　　　What news with you, sir?

⌜HABERDASHER⌝
  Here is the cap your Worship did bespeak.
PETRUCHIO
  Why, this was molded on a porringer!
  A velvet dish! Fie, fie, 'tis lewd and filthy.
  Why, 'tis a cockle or a walnut shell,   70
  A knack, a toy, a trick, a baby's cap.
  Away with it! Come, let me have a bigger.
KATHERINE
  I'll have no bigger. This doth fit the time,
  And gentlewomen wear such caps as these.
PETRUCHIO
  When you are gentle, you shall have one too,   75
  And not till then.
HORTENSIO, ⌜*aside*⌝ That will not be in haste.
KATHERINE
  Why, sir, I trust I may have leave to speak,
  And speak I will. I am no child, no babe.
  Your betters have endured me say my mind,   80
  And if you cannot, best you stop your ears.
  My tongue will tell the anger of my heart,
  Or else my heart, concealing it, will break,
  And, rather than it shall, I will be free
  Even to the uttermost, as I please, in words.   85
PETRUCHIO
  Why, thou sayst true. It is ⌜a⌝ paltry cap,
  A custard-coffin, a bauble, a silken pie.
  I love thee well in that thou lik'st it not.
KATHERINE
  Love me, or love me not, I like the cap,
  And it I will have, or I will have none.   90
                              ⌜*Exit Haberdasher.*⌝
PETRUCHIO
  Thy gown? Why, ay. Come, tailor, let us see 't.
  O mercy God, what masking-stuff is here?

What's this? A sleeve? 'Tis like ⌜a⌝ demi-cannon.
What, up and down carved like an apple tart?
Here's snip and nip and cut and slish and slash, 95
Like to a censer in a barber's shop.
Why, what a devil's name, tailor, call'st thou this?

HORTENSIO, ⌜*aside*⌝
I see she's like to have neither cap nor gown.

TAILOR
You bid me make it orderly and well,
According to the fashion and the time. 100

PETRUCHIO
Marry, and did. But if you be remembered,
I did not bid you mar it to the time.
Go, hop me over every kennel home,
For you shall hop without my custom, sir.
I'll none of it. Hence, make your best of it. 105

KATHERINE
I never saw a better-fashioned gown,
More quaint, more pleasing, nor more
  commendable.
Belike you mean to make a puppet of me.

PETRUCHIO
Why, true, he means to make a puppet of thee. 110

TAILOR
She says your Worship means to make a puppet of
  her.

PETRUCHIO
O monstrous arrogance! Thou liest, thou thread,
  thou thimble,
Thou yard, three-quarters, half-yard, quarter, nail! 115
Thou flea, thou nit, thou winter cricket, thou!
Braved in mine own house with a skein of thread?
Away, thou rag, thou quantity, thou remnant,
Or I shall so be-mete thee with thy yard
As thou shalt think on prating whilst thou liv'st. 120
I tell thee, I, that thou hast marred her gown.

TAILOR
  Your Worship is deceived. The gown is made
  Just as my master had direction.
  Grumio gave order how it should be done.
GRUMIO   I gave him no order. I gave him the stuff.   125
TAILOR
  But how did you desire it should be made?
GRUMIO   Marry, sir, with needle and thread.
TAILOR
  But did you not request to have it cut?
GRUMIO   Thou hast faced many things.
TAILOR   I have.   130
GRUMIO   Face not me. Thou hast braved many men;
  brave not me. I will neither be faced nor braved. I
  say unto thee, I bid thy master cut out the gown,
  but I did not bid him cut it to pieces. *Ergo*, thou
  liest.   135
TAILOR   Why, here is the note of the fashion to testify.
                              ⌜*He shows a paper.*⌝
PETRUCHIO   Read it.
GRUMIO   The note lies in 's throat, if he say I said so.
TAILOR ⌜*reads*⌝ "*Imprimis*, a loose-bodied gown—"
GRUMIO   Master, if ever I said "loose-bodied gown,"   140
  sew me in the skirts of it and beat me to death with
  a bottom of brown thread. I said "a gown."
PETRUCHIO   Proceed.
TAILOR ⌜*reads*⌝ "With a small-compassed cape—"
GRUMIO   I confess the cape.   145
TAILOR ⌜*reads*⌝ "With a trunk sleeve—"
GRUMIO   I confess two sleeves.
TAILOR ⌜*reads*⌝ "The sleeves curiously cut."
PETRUCHIO   Ay, there's the villainy.
GRUMIO   Error i' th' bill, sir, error i' th' bill! I com-   150
  manded the sleeves should be cut out and sewed
  up again, and that I'll prove upon thee, though thy
  little finger be armed in a thimble.

TAILOR This is true that I say. An I had thee in place
where, thou shouldst know it.   155

GRUMIO I am for thee straight. Take thou the bill, give
me thy mete-yard, and spare not me.

HORTENSIO God-a-mercy, Grumio, then he shall have
no odds.

PETRUCHIO
Well, sir, in brief, the gown is not for me.   160

GRUMIO You are i' th' right, sir, 'tis for my mistress.

PETRUCHIO
Go, take it up unto thy master's use.

GRUMIO Villain, not for thy life! Take up my mistress'
gown for thy master's use!

PETRUCHIO Why, sir, what's your conceit in that?   165

GRUMIO O, sir, the conceit is deeper than you think
for. Take up my mistress' gown to his master's use!
O, fie, fie, fie!

PETRUCHIO, ⌜*aside to Hortensio*⌝
Hortensio, say thou wilt see the tailor paid.
⌜*To Tailor.*⌝ Go, take it hence. Begone, and say no   170
more.

HORTENSIO, ⌜*aside to Tailor*⌝
Tailor, I'll pay thee for thy gown tomorrow.
Take no unkindness of his hasty words.
Away, I say. Commend me to thy master.
                                            Tailor exits.

PETRUCHIO
Well, come, my Kate, we will unto your father's,   175
Even in these honest mean habiliments.
Our purses shall be proud, our garments poor,
For 'tis the mind that makes the body rich,
And as the sun breaks through the darkest clouds,
So honor peereth in the meanest habit.   180
What, is the jay more precious than the lark
Because his feathers are more beautiful?
Or is the adder better than the eel

Because his painted skin contents the eye?
O no, good Kate. Neither art thou the worse   185
For this poor furniture and mean array.
If thou ⌜account'st⌝ it shame, lay it on me,
And therefore frolic! We will hence forthwith
To feast and sport us at thy father's house.
⌜*To Grumio.*⌝ Go, call my men, and let us straight to   190
    him,
And bring our horses unto Long-lane end.
There will we mount, and thither walk on foot.
Let's see, I think 'tis now some seven o'clock,
And well we may come there by dinner time.   195

KATHERINE
I dare assure you, sir, 'tis almost two,
And 'twill be supper time ere you come there.

PETRUCHIO
It shall be seven ere I go to horse.
Look what I speak, or do, or think to do,
You are still crossing it. Sirs, let 't alone.   200
I will not go today, and, ere I do,
It shall be what o'clock I say it is.

HORTENSIO, ⌜*aside*⌝
Why, so, this gallant will command the sun!
                                        ⌜*They exit.*⌝

                    ⌜Scene 4⌝
Enter Tranio ⌜*as Lucentio,*⌝ *and the* ⌜*Merchant,*⌝ *booted,*
              and dressed like Vincentio.

TRANIO, ⌜*as* LUCENTIO⌝
⌜Sir,⌝ this is the house. Please it you that I call?

⌜MERCHANT⌝
Ay, what else? And but I be deceived,
Signior Baptista may remember me,
Near twenty years ago, in Genoa,
Where we were lodgers at the Pegasus.   5

TRANIO, ⌜*as* LUCENTIO⌝
    'Tis well. And hold your own in any case
    With such austerity as 'longeth to a father.
⌜MERCHANT⌝
    I warrant you.

            Enter Biondello.

                        But, sir, here comes your boy.
    'Twere good he were schooled.   10
TRANIO, ⌜*as* LUCENTIO⌝
    Fear you not him.—Sirrah Biondello,
    Now do your duty throughly, I advise you.
    Imagine 'twere the right Vincentio.
BIONDELLO   Tut, fear not me.
TRANIO, ⌜*as* LUCENTIO⌝
    But hast thou done thy errand to Baptista?   15
BIONDELLO
    I told him that your father was at Venice,
    And that you looked for him this day in Padua.
TRANIO, ⌜*as* LUCENTIO⌝
    Thou'rt a tall fellow. Hold thee that to drink.
                            ⌜*He gives him money.*⌝

    Enter Baptista and Lucentio ⌜*as Cambio.*⌝

    Here comes Baptista. Set your countenance, sir.
                    ⌜*Merchant stands*⌝ *bareheaded.*
TRANIO, ⌜*as* LUCENTIO⌝
    Signior Baptista, you are happily met.—   20
    Sir, this is the gentleman I told you of.
    I pray you stand good father to me now.
    Give me Bianca for my patrimony.
⌜MERCHANT, *as* VINCENTIO⌝   Soft, son.—
    Sir, by your leave, having come to Padua   25
    To gather in some debts, my son Lucentio
    Made me acquainted with a weighty cause
    Of love between your daughter and himself.

And, for the good report I hear of you,
And for the love he beareth to your daughter   30
And she to him, to stay him not too long,
I am content, in a good father's care,
To have him matched. And if you please to like
No worse than I, upon some agreement
Me shall you find ready and willing   35
With one consent to have her so bestowed,
For curious I cannot be with you,
Signior Baptista, of whom I hear so well.

BAPTISTA
Sir, pardon me in what I have to say.
Your plainness and your shortness please me well.   40
Right true it is your son Lucentio here
Doth love my daughter, and she loveth him,
Or both dissemble deeply their affections.
And therefore, if you say no more than this,
That like a father you will deal with him   45
And pass my daughter a sufficient dower,
The match is made, and all is done.
Your son shall have my daughter with consent.

TRANIO, ⌐*as* LUCENTIO⌐
I thank you, sir. Where then do you know best
We be affied and such assurance ta'en   50
As shall with either part's agreement stand?

BAPTISTA
Not in my house, Lucentio, for you know
Pitchers have ears, and I have many servants.
Besides, old Gremio is heark'ning still,
And happily we might be interrupted.   55

TRANIO, ⌐*as* LUCENTIO⌐
Then at my lodging, an it like you.
There doth my father lie, and there this night
We'll pass the business privately and well.
Send for your daughter by your servant here.
          ⌐*He indicates Lucentio, and winks at him.*⌐

My boy shall fetch the scrivener presently.   60
The worst is this: that at so slender warning
You are like to have a thin and slender pittance.

BAPTISTA
It likes me well.—Cambio, hie you home,
And bid Bianca make her ready straight.
And, if you will, tell what hath happenèd: 65
Lucentio's father is arrived in Padua,
And how she's like to be Lucentio's wife.

⌜*Lucentio exits.*⌝

BIONDELLO
I pray the gods she may, with all my heart.

TRANIO, ⌜*as* LUCENTIO⌝
Dally not with the gods, but get thee gone.—
Signior Baptista, shall I lead the way?   70
Welcome! One mess is like to be your cheer.
Come, sir, we will better it in Pisa.

BAPTISTA   I follow you.

⌜*All but Biondello*⌝ *exit.*

Enter Lucentio.

BIONDELLO   Cambio.
LUCENTIO   What sayst thou, Biondello?   75
BIONDELLO   You saw my master wink and laugh upon
you?
LUCENTIO   Biondello, what of that?
BIONDELLO   Faith, nothing; but 'has left me here be-
hind to expound the meaning or moral of his signs   80
and tokens.
LUCENTIO   I pray thee, moralize them.
BIONDELLO   Then thus: Baptista is safe, talking with
the deceiving father of a deceitful son.
LUCENTIO   And what of him?   85
BIONDELLO   His daughter is to be brought by you to the
supper.

LUCENTIO And then?

BIONDELLO The old priest at Saint Luke's Church is at
your command at all hours.   90

LUCENTIO And what of all this?

BIONDELLO I cannot tell, ⌈except⌉ they are busied
about a counterfeit assurance. Take you assurance
of her *cum privilegio ad imprimendum solum.* To th'
church take the priest, clerk, and some sufficient   95
honest witnesses.

If this be not that you look for, I have no more to
say,

But bid Bianca farewell forever and a day.

LUCENTIO Hear'st thou, Biondello?   100

BIONDELLO I cannot tarry. I knew a wench married in
an afternoon as she went to the garden for parsley
to stuff a rabbit, and so may you, sir. And so adieu,
sir. My master hath appointed me to go to Saint
Luke's to bid the priest be ready to come against   105
you come with your appendix.   *He exits.*

LUCENTIO

I may, and will, if she be so contented.

She will be pleased. Then wherefore should I
doubt?

Hap what hap may, I'll roundly go about her.   110

It shall go hard if "Cambio" go without her.

                                            He exits.

⌈Scene 5⌉

Enter Petruchio, Katherine, Hortensio, ⌈and Servants.⌉

PETRUCHIO

Come on, i' God's name, once more toward our
father's.

Good Lord, how bright and goodly shines the moon!

KATHERINE

The moon? The sun! It is not moonlight now.

PETRUCHIO
    I say it is the moon that shines so bright. 5
KATHERINE
    I know it is the sun that shines so bright.
PETRUCHIO
    Now, by my mother's son, and that's myself,
    It shall be moon, or star, or what I list,
    Or e'er I journey to your father's house.
    ⌐*To Servants.*¬ Go on, and fetch our horses back 10
      again.—
    Evermore crossed and crossed, nothing but crossed!
HORTENSIO, ⌐*to Katherine*¬
    Say as he says, or we shall never go.
KATHERINE
    Forward, I pray, since we have come so far,
    And be it moon, or sun, or what you please.
    And if you please to call it a rush candle, 15
    Henceforth I vow it shall be so for me.
PETRUCHIO   I say it is the moon.
KATHERINE   I know it is the moon.
PETRUCHIO
    Nay, then you lie. It is the blessèd sun. 20
KATHERINE
    Then God be blest, it ⌐is¬ the blessèd sun.
    But sun it is not, when you say it is not,
    And the moon changes even as your mind.
    What you will have it named, even that it is,
    And so it shall be so for Katherine. 25
HORTENSIO
    Petruchio, go thy ways, the field is won.
PETRUCHIO
    Well, forward, forward. Thus the bowl should run,
    And not unluckily against the bias.
    But soft! Company is coming here.

Enter Vincentio.

⌈*To Vincentio.*⌉ Good morrow, gentle mistress, where   30
    away?—
Tell me, sweet Kate, and tell me truly, too,
Hast thou beheld a fresher gentlewoman?
Such war of white and red within her cheeks!
What stars do spangle heaven with such beauty   35
As those two eyes become that heavenly face?—
Fair lovely maid, once more good day to thee.—
Sweet Kate, embrace her for her beauty's sake.

HORTENSIO, ⌈*aside*⌉
He will make the man mad, to make the woman of
    him.   40

KATHERINE
Young budding virgin, fair and fresh and sweet,
Whither away, or ⌈where⌉ is thy abode?
Happy the parents of so fair a child!
Happier the man whom favorable stars
⌈Allots⌉ thee for his lovely bedfellow.   45

PETRUCHIO
Why, how now, Kate? I hope thou art not mad!
This is a man—old, wrinkled, faded, withered—
And not a maiden, as thou sayst he is.

KATHERINE
Pardon, old father, my mistaking eyes
That have been so bedazzled with the sun   50
That everything I look on seemeth green.
Now I perceive thou art a reverend father.
Pardon, I pray thee, for my mad mistaking.

PETRUCHIO
Do, good old grandsire, and withal make known
Which way thou travelest. If along with us,   55
We shall be joyful of thy company.

VINCENTIO
Fair sir, and you, my merry mistress,
That with your strange encounter much amazed me,
My name is called Vincentio, my dwelling Pisa,

And bound I am to Padua, there to visit   60
A son of mine which long I have not seen.

PETRUCHIO
What is his name?

VINCENTIO   Lucentio, gentle sir.

PETRUCHIO
Happily met, the happier for thy son.
And now by law as well as reverend age,   65
I may entitle thee my loving father.
The sister to my wife, this gentlewoman,
Thy son by this hath married. Wonder not,
Nor be not grieved. She is of good esteem,
Her dowry wealthy, and of worthy birth;   70
Beside, so qualified as may beseem
The spouse of any noble gentleman.
Let me embrace with old Vincentio,
And wander we to see thy honest son,
Who will of thy arrival be full joyous.   75

VINCENTIO
But is this true, or is it else your pleasure,
Like pleasant travelers, to break a jest
Upon the company you overtake?

HORTENSIO
I do assure thee, father, so it is.

PETRUCHIO
Come, go along and see the truth hereof,   80
For our first merriment hath made thee jealous.
                    ⌐*All but Hortensio*⌐ *exit.*

HORTENSIO
Well, Petruchio, this has put me in heart!
Have to my widow, and if she ⌐be⌐ froward,
Then hast thou taught Hortensio to be untoward.
                                        He exits.

⌜ACT 5⌝

⌜Scene 1⌝
Enter Biondello, Lucentio ⌜as himself,⌝ and Bianca.
Gremio is out before ⌜and stands to the side.⌝

BIONDELLO Softly and swiftly, sir, for the priest is
  ready.
LUCENTIO I fly, Biondello. But they may chance to
  need thee at home. Therefore leave us.
                    ⌜*Lucentio exits with Bianca.*⌝
BIONDELLO Nay, faith, I'll see the church a' your back,   5
  and then come back to my ⌜master's⌝ as soon as I
  can.   ⌜*He exits.*⌝
GREMIO I marvel Cambio comes not all this while.

Enter Petruchio, Katherine, Vincentio, Grumio, with
Attendants.

PETRUCHIO
  Sir, here's the door. This is Lucentio's house.
  My father's bears more toward the marketplace.   10
  Thither must I, and here I leave you, sir.
VINCENTIO
  You shall not choose but drink before you go.
  I think I shall command your welcome here,
  And by all likelihood some cheer is toward.
                              ⌜*He⌝ knocks.*

97

GREMIO, ⌜*coming forward*⌝
They're busy within. You were best knock louder.   15
                    ⌜*Merchant*⌝ *looks out of the window.*
⌜MERCHANT, *as* VINCENTIO⌝ What's he that knocks as
he would beat down the gate?

VINCENTIO   Is Signior Lucentio within, sir?

⌜MERCHANT, *as* VINCENTIO⌝ He's within, sir, but not to
be spoken withal.   20

VINCENTIO   What if a man bring him a hundred pound
or two to make merry withal?

⌜MERCHANT, *as* VINCENTIO⌝ Keep your hundred
pounds to yourself. He shall need none so long as I
live.   25

PETRUCHIO, ⌜*to Vincentio*⌝ Nay, I told you your son was
well beloved in Padua.—Do you hear, sir? To leave
frivolous circumstances, I pray you tell Signior
Lucentio that his father is come from Pisa and is
here at the door to speak with him.   30

⌜MERCHANT, *as* VINCENTIO⌝ Thou liest. His father is
come from Padua and here looking out at the
window.

VINCENTIO   Art thou his father?

⌜MERCHANT, *as* VINCENTIO⌝ Ay, sir, so his mother says,   35
if I may believe her.

PETRUCHIO, ⌜*to Vincentio*⌝ Why, how now, gentleman!
Why, this is flat knavery, to take upon you another
man's name.

⌜MERCHANT, *as* VINCENTIO⌝ Lay hands on the villain. I   40
believe he means to cosen somebody in this city
under my countenance.

Enter Biondello.

BIONDELLO, ⌜*aside*⌝ I have seen them in the church
together. God send 'em good shipping! But who is
here? Mine old master Vincentio! Now we are   45
undone and brought to nothing.

VINCENTIO, ⌜*to Biondello*⌝ Come hither, crack-hemp.

BIONDELLO I hope I may choose, sir.

VINCENTIO Come hither, you rogue! What, have you
forgot me?   50

BIONDELLO Forgot you? No, sir. I could not forget you,
for I never saw you before in all my life.

VINCENTIO What, you notorious villain, didst thou
never see thy ⌜master's⌝ father, Vincentio?

BIONDELLO What, my old worshipful old master? Yes,   55
marry, sir. See where he looks out of the window.

VINCENTIO Is't so indeed?   *He beats Biondello.*

BIONDELLO Help, help, help! Here's a madman will
murder me.   ⌜*Biondello exits.*⌝

⌜MERCHANT, *as* VINCENTIO⌝ Help, son! Help, Signior   60
Baptista!   ⌜*He exits from window.*⌝

PETRUCHIO Prithee, Kate, let's stand aside and see the
end of this controversy.   ⌜*They move aside.*⌝

Enter ⌜*Merchant*⌝ *with Servants,* ⌜*and*⌝ *Baptista* ⌜*and*⌝
Tranio ⌜*disguised as Lucentio.*⌝

TRANIO, ⌜*as* LUCENTIO⌝ Sir, what are you that offer to
beat my servant?   65

VINCENTIO What am I, sir? Nay, what are you, sir! O
immortal gods! O fine villain! A silken doublet, a
velvet hose, a scarlet cloak, and a copatain hat! O, I
am undone, I am undone! While I play the good
husband at home, my son and my servant spend all   70
at the university.

TRANIO, ⌜*as* LUCENTIO⌝ How now, what's the matter?

BAPTISTA What, is the man lunatic?

TRANIO, ⌜*as* LUCENTIO⌝ Sir, you seem a sober ancient
gentleman by your habit, but your words show you   75
a madman. Why, sir, what 'cerns it you if I wear
pearl and gold? I thank my good father, I am able
to maintain it.

VINCENTIO   Thy father! O villain, he is a sailmaker in
    Bergamo.   80
BAPTISTA   You mistake, sir, you mistake, sir! Pray, what
    do you think is his name?
VINCENTIO   His name? As if I knew not his name! I have
    brought him up ever since he was three years old,
    and his name is Tranio.   85
⌜MERCHANT, *as* VINCENTIO⌝   Away, away, mad ass! His
    name is Lucentio and he is mine only son, and heir
    to the lands of me, Signior Vincentio.
VINCENTIO   Lucentio? O, he hath murdered his master!
    Lay hold on him, I charge you in the Duke's name.   90
    O, my son, my son! Tell me, thou villain, where is
    my son Lucentio?
TRANIO, ⌜*as* LUCENTIO⌝   Call forth an officer.

                    ⌜*Enter an Officer.*⌝

    Carry this mad knave to the jail.—Father Baptista, I
    charge you see that he be forthcoming.   95
VINCENTIO   Carry me to the jail?
GREMIO   Stay, officer. He shall not go to prison.
BAPTISTA   Talk not, Signior Gremio. I say he shall go to
    prison.
GREMIO   Take heed, Signior Baptista, lest you be cony-   100
    catched in this business. I dare swear this is the
    right Vincentio.
⌜MERCHANT, *as* VINCENTIO⌝   Swear, if thou dar'st.
GREMIO   Nay, I dare not swear it.
TRANIO, ⌜*as* LUCENTIO⌝   Then thou wert best say that I   105
    am not Lucentio.
GREMIO   Yes, I know thee to be Signior Lucentio.
BAPTISTA   Away with the dotard, to the jail with him.
VINCENTIO   Thus strangers may be haled and abused.—
    O monstrous villain!   110

            Enter Biondello, Lucentio and Bianca.

BIONDELLO   O, we are spoiled, and yonder he is! Deny
   him, forswear him, or else we are all undone.
                 Biondello, Tranio, and ⌐*Merchant*¬
                 exit as fast as may be.

LUCENTIO
   Pardon, sweet father.   ⌐*Lucentio and Bianca*¬ *kneel.*
VINCENTIO   Lives my sweet son?
BIANCA
   Pardon, dear father.   115
BAPTISTA   How hast thou offended?
   Where is Lucentio?
LUCENTIO   Here's Lucentio,
   Right son to the right Vincentio,
   That have by marriage made thy daughter mine   120
   While counterfeit supposes bleared thine eyne.
GREMIO
   Here's packing, with a witness, to deceive us all!
VINCENTIO
   Where is that damnèd villain, Tranio,
   That faced and braved me in this matter so?
BAPTISTA
   Why, tell me, is not this my Cambio?   125
BIANCA
   Cambio is changed into Lucentio.
LUCENTIO
   Love wrought these miracles. Bianca's love
   Made me exchange my state with Tranio,
   While he did bear my countenance in the town,
   And happily I have arrivèd at the last   130
   Unto the wishèd haven of my bliss.
   What Tranio did, myself enforced him to.
   Then pardon him, sweet father, for my sake.
VINCENTIO   I'll slit the villain's nose that would have
   sent me to the jail!   135
BAPTISTA   But do you hear, sir, have you married my
   daughter without asking my goodwill?

VINCENTIO   Fear not, Baptista, we will content you. Go
to! But I will in to be revenged for this villainy.
He exits.

BAPTISTA   And I to sound the depth of this knavery.   140
He exits.

LUCENTIO   Look not pale, Bianca. Thy father will not
frown.   *They exit.*

GREMIO
My cake is dough, but I'll in among the rest,
Out of hope of all but my share of the feast.
⌜*He exits.*⌝

KATHERINE   Husband, let's follow to see the end of   145
this ado.

PETRUCHIO   First kiss me, Kate, and we will.

KATHERINE   What, in the midst of the street?

PETRUCHIO   What, art thou ashamed of me?

KATHERINE   ⌜No,⌝ sir, God forbid, but ashamed to kiss.   150

PETRUCHIO
Why, then, let's home again. ⌜*To Grumio.*⌝ Come,
sirrah, let's away.

KATHERINE
Nay, I will give thee a kiss.   ⌜*She kisses him.*⌝
Now pray thee, love, stay.

PETRUCHIO
Is not this well? Come, my sweet Kate.   155
Better once than never, for never too late.
They exit.

⌜Scene 2⌝

Enter Baptista, Vincentio, Gremio, the ⌜*Merchant,*⌝
Lucentio, and Bianca; ⌜*Hortensio*⌝ *and* ⌜*the*⌝ *Widow,*
⌜*Petruchio and Katherine;*⌝ *Tranio, Biondello,* ⌜*and*⌝
Grumio, ⌜*with*⌝ *Servingmen bringing in a banquet.*

LUCENTIO
At last, though long, our jarring notes agree,

And time it is when raging war is ⌜done⌝
To smile at 'scapes and perils overblown.
My fair Bianca, bid my father welcome,
While I with selfsame kindness welcome thine.   5
Brother Petruchio, sister Katherina,
And thou, Hortensio, with thy loving widow,
Feast with the best, and welcome to my house.
My banquet is to close our stomachs up
After our great good cheer. Pray you, sit down,   10
For now we sit to chat as well as eat.   ⌜*They sit.*⌝

PETRUCHIO
Nothing but sit and sit, and eat and eat!

BAPTISTA
Padua affords this kindness, son Petruchio.

PETRUCHIO
Padua affords nothing but what is kind.

HORTENSIO
For both our sakes I would that word were true.   15

PETRUCHIO
Now, for my life, Hortensio fears his widow!

WIDOW
Then never trust me if I be afeard.

PETRUCHIO
You are very sensible, and yet you miss my sense:
I mean Hortensio is afeard of you.

WIDOW
He that is giddy thinks the world turns round.   20

PETRUCHIO
Roundly replied.

KATHERINE   Mistress, how mean you that?

WIDOW   Thus I conceive by him.

PETRUCHIO
Conceives by me? How likes Hortensio that?

HORTENSIO
My widow says, thus she conceives her tale.   25

PETRUCHIO
  Very well mended. Kiss him for that, good widow.
KATHERINE
  "He that is giddy thinks the world turns round"—
  I pray you tell me what you meant by that.
WIDOW
  Your husband being troubled with a shrew
  Measures my husband's sorrow by his woe.   30
  And now you know my meaning.
KATHERINE
  A very mean meaning.
WIDOW   Right, I mean you.
KATHERINE
  And I am mean indeed, respecting you.
PETRUCHIO   To her, Kate!   35
HORTENSIO   To her, widow!
PETRUCHIO
  A hundred marks, my Kate does put her down.
HORTENSIO   That's my office.
PETRUCHIO
  Spoke like an officer! Ha' to thee, lad.
                    ⌜*He*⌝ *drinks to Hortensio.*
BAPTISTA
  How likes Gremio these quick-witted folks?   40
GREMIO
  Believe me, sir, they butt together well.
BIANCA
  Head and butt! An hasty-witted body
  Would say your head and butt were head and horn.
VINCENTIO
  Ay, mistress bride, hath that awakened you?
BIANCA
  Ay, but not frighted me. Therefore I'll sleep again.   45
PETRUCHIO
  Nay, that you shall not. Since you have begun,
  Have at you for a ⌜bitter⌝ jest or two.

BIANCA
　Am I your bird? I mean to shift my bush,
　And then pursue me as you draw your bow.—
　You are welcome all.   50
　　　　　Bianca, ⌜Katherine, and the Widow⌝ exit.

PETRUCHIO
　She hath prevented me. Here, Signior Tranio,
　This bird you aimed at, though you hit her not.—
　Therefore a health to all that shot and missed.

TRANIO
　O, sir, Lucentio slipped me like his greyhound,
　Which runs himself and catches for his master.   55

PETRUCHIO
　A good swift simile, but something currish.

TRANIO
　'Tis well, sir, that you hunted for yourself.
　'Tis thought your deer does hold you at a bay.

BAPTISTA
　O, O, Petruchio! Tranio hits you now.

LUCENTIO
　I thank thee for that gird, good Tranio.   60

HORTENSIO
　Confess, confess! Hath he not hit you here?

PETRUCHIO
　He has a little galled me, I confess.
　And as the jest did glance away from me,
　'Tis ten to one it maimed you two outright.

BAPTISTA
　Now, in good sadness, son Petruchio,   65
　I think thou hast the veriest shrew of all.

PETRUCHIO
　Well, I say no. And therefore, ⌜for⌝ assurance,
　Let's each one send unto his wife,
　And he whose wife is most obedient
　To come at first when he doth send for her   70
　Shall win the wager which we will propose.

HORTENSIO
  Content, what's the wager?
LUCENTIO   Twenty crowns.
PETRUCHIO   Twenty crowns?
  I'll venture so much of my hawk or hound,   75
  But twenty times so much upon my wife.
LUCENTIO
  A hundred, then.
HORTENSIO   Content.
PETRUCHIO   A match! 'Tis done.
HORTENSIO   Who shall begin?   80
LUCENTIO   That will I.
  Go, Biondello, bid your mistress come to me.
BIONDELLO   I go.   *He exits.*
BAPTISTA
  Son, I'll be your half Bianca comes.
LUCENTIO
  I'll have no halves. I'll bear it all myself.   85

                   Enter Biondello

  How now, what news?
BIONDELLO   Sir, my mistress sends you
    word
  That she is busy, and she cannot come.
PETRUCHIO
  How? "She's busy, and she cannot come"?   90
  Is that an answer?
GREMIO   Ay, and a kind one, too.
  Pray God, sir, your wife send you not a worse.
PETRUCHIO   I hope better.
HORTENSIO
  Sirrah Biondello, go and entreat my wife   95
  To come to me forthwith.   *Biondello exits.*
PETRUCHIO   O ho, entreat her!
  Nay, then, she must needs come.

HORTENSIO   I am afraid, sir,
  Do what you can, yours will not be entreated.   100

                    Enter Biondello

  Now, where's my wife?
BIONDELLO
  She says you have some goodly jest in hand.
  She will not come. She bids you come to her.
PETRUCHIO   Worse and worse. She will not come!
  O vile, intolerable, not to be endured!—   105
  Sirrah Grumio, go to your mistress,
  Say I command her come to me.   ⌜*Grumio*⌝ *exits.*
HORTENSIO
  I know her answer.
PETRUCHIO   What?
HORTENSIO   She will not.   110
PETRUCHIO
  The fouler fortune mine, and there an end.

                    Enter Katherine.

BAPTISTA
  Now by my holidam, here comes Katherina!
KATHERINE
  What is your will, sir, that you send for me?
PETRUCHIO
  Where is your sister, and Hortensio's wife?
KATHERINE
  They sit conferring by the parlor fire.   115
PETRUCHIO
  Go fetch them hither. If they deny to come,
  Swinge me them soundly forth unto their husbands.
  Away, I say, and bring them hither straight.
                              ⌜*Katherine exits.*⌝
LUCENTIO
  Here is a wonder, if you talk of a wonder.
HORTENSIO
  And so it is. I wonder what it bodes.   120

PETRUCHIO
  Marry, peace it bodes, and love, and quiet life,
  An awful rule, and right supremacy,
  And, to be short, what not that's sweet and happy.
BAPTISTA
  Now fair befall thee, good Petruchio!
  The wager thou hast won, and I will add   125
  Unto their losses twenty thousand crowns,
  Another dowry to another daughter,
  For she is changed as she had never been.
PETRUCHIO
  Nay, I will win my wager better yet,
  And show more sign of her obedience,   130
  Her new-built virtue and obedience.

      Enter Katherine, Bianca, and Widow.

  See where she comes, and brings your froward
    wives
  As prisoners to her womanly persuasion.—
  Katherine, that cap of yours becomes you not.   135
  Off with that bauble, throw it underfoot.
                        ⌜*She obeys.*⌝
WIDOW
  Lord, let me never have a cause to sigh
  Till I be brought to such a silly pass.
BIANCA
  Fie, what a foolish duty call you this?
LUCENTIO
  I would your duty were as foolish too.   140
  The wisdom of your duty, fair Bianca,
  Hath cost me ⌜a⌝ hundred crowns since suppertime.
BIANCA
  The more fool you for laying on my duty.
PETRUCHIO
  Katherine, I charge thee tell these headstrong
    women   145
  What duty they do owe their lords and husbands.

WIDOW
  Come, come, ⌜you're⌝ mocking. We will have no
    telling.
PETRUCHIO
  Come on, I say, and first begin with her.
WIDOW   She shall not.   150
PETRUCHIO
  I say she shall.—And first begin with her.
KATHERINE
  Fie, fie! Unknit that threat'ning unkind brow,
  And dart not scornful glances from those eyes
  To wound thy lord, thy king, thy governor.
  It blots thy beauty as frosts do bite the meads,   155
  Confounds thy fame as whirlwinds shake fair buds,
  And in no sense is meet or amiable.
  A woman moved is like a fountain troubled,
  Muddy, ill-seeming, thick, bereft of beauty,
  And while it is so, none so dry or thirsty   160
  Will deign to sip or touch one drop of it.
  Thy husband is thy lord, thy life, thy keeper,
  Thy head, thy sovereign, one that cares for thee,
  And for thy maintenance commits his body
  To painful labor both by sea and land,   165
  To watch the night in storms, the day in cold,
  Whilst thou liest warm at home, secure and safe,
  And craves no other tribute at thy hands
  But love, fair looks, and true obedience—
  Too little payment for so great a debt.   170
  Such duty as the subject owes the prince,
  Even such a woman oweth to her husband;
  And when she is froward, peevish, sullen, sour,
  And not obedient to his honest will,
  What is she but a foul contending rebel   175
  And graceless traitor to her loving lord?
  I am ashamed that women are so simple
  To offer war where they should kneel for peace,

Or seek for rule, supremacy, and sway
When they are bound to serve, love, and obey.   180
Why are our bodies soft and weak and smooth,
Unapt to toil and trouble in the world,
But that our soft conditions and our hearts
Should well agree with our external parts?
Come, come, you froward and unable worms!   185
My mind hath been as big as one of yours,
My heart as great, my reason haply more,
To bandy word for word and frown for frown;
But now I see our lances are but straws,
Our strength as weak, our weakness past compare,   190
That seeming to be most which we indeed least are.
Then vail your stomachs, for it is no boot,
And place your hands below your husband's foot;
In token of which duty, if he please,
My hand is ready, may it do him ease.   195

PETRUCHIO
Why, there's a wench! Come on, and kiss me, Kate.
                                        ⌐*They kiss.*¬

LUCENTIO
Well, go thy ways, old lad, for thou shalt ha 't.
VINCENTIO
'Tis a good hearing when children are toward.
LUCENTIO
But a harsh hearing when women are froward.
PETRUCHIO   Come, Kate, we'll to bed.   200
We three are married, but you two are sped.
⌐*To Lucentio.*¬ 'Twas I won the wager, though you
    hit the white,
And being a winner, God give you good night.
                            Petruchio ⌐*and Katherine*¬ *exit.*

HORTENSIO
Now, go thy ways, thou hast tamed a curst shrow.   205
LUCENTIO
'Tis a wonder, by your leave, she will be tamed so.
                                        ⌐*They exit.*¬

Explanatory Notes

Ind.1 Christopher Sly, a drunken beggar, is driven out of an alehouse by its hostess. A great lord, returning from the hunt, finds Sly in a drunken sleep and decides to play an elaborate trick on him. The lord orders his servants to place Sly in a luxurious bedroom and, when the beggar awakes, to tell him he is a great lord who has long been out of his mind. A troupe of traveling actors present themselves to the lord, who, by way of further elaborating his trick, instructs them to stage a play for Sly.

1. **feeze you:** fix you, do for you
2. **stocks:** a heavy timber frame with holes for the ankles used to punish disturbers of the peace
4. **chronicles:** histories, such as Holinshed's *Chronicles* (1577 and 1587), often used by Shakespeare
4–5. **Richard Conqueror:** i.e., William the Conqueror
5. **paucas pallabris:** i.e., *pocas palabras*, Spanish for "few words," i.e., enough
6. **Sessa:** perhaps French *cessez* or Spanish *cesa*, both meaning "stop" or "be silent"
9. **denier:** small copper coin of little value; **Saint Jeronimy:** St. Jerome (Some scholars think **Jeronimy** a reference to Hieronimo, the hero of Kyd's play *The Spanish Tragedy*.)
12. **headborough:** constable
13. **Third . . . borough:** "Thirdborough" was another term for constable.
15. **kindly:** i.e., welcome
15 SD. **Wind:** blow
16. **tender well:** take good care of
17. **Breathe Merriman:** let Merriman get his breath back; **embossed:** exhausted

111

19. **made it good:** i.e., picked up the scent
20. **in . . . fault:** i.e., when the scent was lost
23. **it:** i.e., the scent; **at the merest loss:** i.e., when the scent was absolutely lost
36. **thine image:** i.e., sleep, which looks like death
37. **practice:** play a trick
42. **brave:** splendidly dressed
44. **cannot choose:** i.e., will have no other choice
54. **straight:** immediately
55. **reverence:** bow
59. **diaper:** small towel
67. **when . . . is:** i.e., when he says he is now mad
69. **kindly:** (1) naturally—with no sign that you are feigning; (2) in a friendly way
70. **passing:** surpassingly
71. **husbanded with modesty:** conducted with restraint
73. **As:** i.e., so that
76. **office:** assigned part; **he:** i.e., Sly
77. **Sirrah:** a term of address to a social inferior
78. **Belike:** probably; **means:** intends
81. **An 't:** if it; **players:** actors
87. **So please:** if it please; **duty:** respect
91. **sure:** certainly
92. **aptly fitted:** well cast
93. **Soto:** The earliest surviving play with a character named Soto is John Fletcher's *Women Pleased* (1619). Since only a fraction of the drama of Shakespeare's time survives, it is likely that the reference here is to a lost play.
95. **in happy time:** i.e., at just the right moment
96. **The rather for:** i.e., especially because
97. **cunning:** skill
99. **doubtful of your modesties:** i.e., suspicious about how well you can control yourselves
100. **over-eying of:** observing
102. **merry passion:** i.e., laughter
106. **veriest antic:** most peculiar person

107. **buttery:** storeroom for food and drink
109. **want:** lack; **affords:** can provide
110. **Bartholomew:** pronounced "Bartelmy"
111. **in all suits:** in every way
113–14. **him . . . him . . . him:** i.e., the page
114. **as he will:** i.e., if he wishes to
115. **He bear:** i.e., he should conduct
117. **accomplishèd:** performed
119. **tongue:** voice
124. **with . . . bosom:** with his (the page's) head lowered onto Sly's breast
125. **him:** i.e., the page; **as being:** i.e., as if he were
127. **esteemed him:** i.e., thought himself to be
131. **shift:** trick
132. **napkin:** handkerchief; **close conveyed:** secretly carried
133. **Shall . . . eye:** despite his inability to cry, will force his eyes to water
135. **Anon:** soon
136. **usurp:** take on
139. **stay:** stop, keep
141. **do homage:** show respect
142. **Haply:** perhaps
143. **over-merry spleen:** excess of laughter (The spleen was thought to be the seat of laughter, as well as of other strong emotions.)

Ind.2 The newly awakened Sly is offered delicacies and fine clothes. When he demands his usual ale and beef, the lord and servants tell him that he is suffering from delusions. After they inform him that he has a beautiful wife, he asks to see her. The lord's page, who impersonates the wife, persuades Sly to watch the play that is about to begin.

1. **small:** thin, weak, and therefore cheap
2. **sack:** costly dry Spanish wine, such as sherry

3. **conserves:** candied fruit

6. **An if:** i.e., if

7. **conserves of beef:** salted beef

9. **doublets:** i.e., jackets

13. **idle humor:** groundless fantasy

18. **Burton Heath:** perhaps Barton-on-the-Heath, a village about a dozen miles from Shakespeare's native Stratford

19. **cardmaker:** maker of cards used to comb wool

20. **bearherd:** keeper of a tame, performing bear

21. **alewife:** woman alehousekeeper

21–22. **Wincot:** another village near Stratford

23. **on the score:** on account (Charges for drink were cut or scored on a stick or tally.); **sheer ale:** ale alone; or, perhaps, "small ale"; **score me up:** chalk me up

25. **bestraught:** distracted

30. **bethink thee:** think

31. **ancient:** former

34. **office:** assignment

35. **Apollo:** here, patron god of music

39. **Semiramis:** queen of Assyria, noted for her sexual escapades

40. **bestrew:** cover with flowers or rushes

41. **trapped:** dressed in trappings

43. **hawking:** hunting for birds with trained hawks

45–46. **Thy hounds ... earth:** i.e., the sound of the hounds' barking will strike the sky and then return to echo from the earth **welkin:** the sky

47. **course:** hunt hares with greyhounds

48. **breathèd stags:** stags with good wind or endurance; **roe:** small deer

49. **pictures:** These are presumably the "wanton pictures" mentioned by the lord in Induction 1. Now, in lines 49–60, are described pictures of seductions and rapes based on stories told in Ovid's *Metamorphoses:* the story of Venus and Adonis, of Jove and Io, of Apollo and Daphne.

50. **Adonis:** a mortal loved by Cytherea (i.e., Venus)

51. **sedges:** marsh grass

52. **wanton:** move playfully and lovingly

54. **Io:** a maiden raped by Jove and transformed into a heifer

55. **beguilèd and surprised:** tricked and captured

56. **As lively . . . done:** i.e., painted as vividly as if it were the actual deed

57. **Daphne:** a maiden desired and pursued by Apollo (She escaped when she was transformed into a laurel tree.)

60. **workmanly:** expertly

65. **envious:** malicious; **o'errun:** overran

67. **yet:** even now

71. **savors:** odors

74. **our:** Sly now uses the royal "we."

75. **smallest:** thinnest, weakest, cheapest

77. **wit:** mind

78. **knew but:** only knew

79. **These:** i.e., these last

81. **fay:** faith

82. **of:** in

83. **idle:** silly

86. **house:** alehouse

87. **present . . . leet:** accuse her before the court of the lord of the manor

88–89. **stone jugs . . . quarts:** Customers preferred sealed quarts, which bore official stamps (seals) guaranteeing the quantity they contained, rather than stone jars that could hold indeterminate quantities.

91. **Ay:** yes

93. **reckoned up:** listed

94. **Greete:** a hamlet in Gloucestershire, near Stratford (The Folio reading, "Greece," seems to be a misreading.)

98. **amends:** recovery

102. **Marry:** i.e., indeed (originally an oath on the name of the Virgin Mary); **cheer:** food and drink

106. **goodman:** the form in which a lower-class wife addressed her husband

114. **above:** more than

116. **abandoned:** banished

123. **In peril . . . malady:** because of the danger that you will again fall ill

125. **stands:** will serve (There is a bawdy pun on **stands** when it is repeated in the next line.)

126. **tarry:** wait

130. **players:** actors; **amendment:** recovery

132. **hold . . . meet:** regard it to be most suitable

138. **bars:** prevents

140. **comonty:** i.e., comedy; **gambold:** i.e., frolic, merrymaking

143. **household stuff:** goods, utensils, dishes, etc., belonging to a household

144. **history:** i.e., story

1.1 Lucentio has come with his servant Tranio to Padua to study philosophy. They witness an encounter between Baptista and his daughters, in which Baptista announces that Bianca cannot marry until the elder and bad-tempered Katherine does. Bianca's suitors decide to search for a husband for Katherine. Meanwhile Lucentio has fallen in love with Bianca and decides to have Tranio impersonate him so that Lucentio, in the disguise of a schoolmaster, can secretly woo Bianca. The two men exchange clothes.

0 SD. **Flourish:** a fanfare of trumpets

1. **for:** because of

2. **nursery of arts:** Padua was famous for its university. **arts:** i.e., the liberal arts

3. **am arrived for:** i.e., have arrived in

5. **leave:** permission

7. **well approved:** found perfectly reliable

8. **breathe:** pause, rest, remain; **haply:** perhaps; **institute:** i.e., begin

9. **ingenious:** highly intellectual

10. **grave:** worthy and serious

11. **my father first:** i.e., my father before me

12. **of great traffic:** i.e., trading extensively

13. **come of:** descended from

14–16. **Vincentio's son . . . deeds:** i.e., it will be fitting for me, Vincentio's son, to fulfill all expectations by adorning his good fortune with good deeds

17. **the:** i.e., this

19–20. **Will I apply . . . achieved:** i.e., I will devote myself to that part of philosophy that deals with the happiness achieved through virtue

23. **plash:** pool, puddle

25. **Mi perdonato:** excuse me, pardon me

26. **affected:** i.e., of the same feeling

30. **discipline:** i.e., philosophy

31. **stoics:** persons who put aside all pleasures, refusing to give in to emotion and desire (There is a play here on the word **stocks,** i.e., unfeeling people.)

32. **devote:** devoted; **Aristotle's checks:** the self-restraint which the Greek philosopher Aristotle (384–322 B.C.E.) advocated

33. **As:** i.e., so that; **Ovid:** Roman love poet (In his *Art of Love*, Ovid names himself the Professor of Love.); **abjured:** renounced

34. **Balk logic:** avoid the study of logic; or, chop logic, bandy words

35. **practice . . . talk:** i.e., instead of studying rhetoric in the university, practice rhetoric by talking with friends

36. **Music . . . quicken you:** i.e., use music and poetry to enliven you

38. **your stomach serves you:** you have an appetite for them

40. **affect:** like

41. **Gramercies:** thanks
42. **Biondello:** an (absent) servant of Lucentio's
43. **put us in readiness:** prepare ourselves
45 SD. **pantaloon:** ridiculous old man, a stock character in Italian comedy of the period
47. **show:** entertainment, spectacle
50. **bestow:** give in marriage
54. **Leave:** permission
55. **cart:** Women who transgressed community standards were shamed by being paraded through the streets in open carts.
58. **stale:** laughingstock; also prostitute (Prostitutes were among those "carted."); **mates:** fellows
59. **mates:** spouses
63. **Iwis:** certainly; **it:** i.e., marriage; **her:** i.e., Katherine's
65. **noddle:** head (slang)
66. **paint your face:** i.e., scratch **your face** until it bleeds
69. **pastime toward:** entertainment about to take place
70. **wonderful froward:** amazingly ungovernable
79. **peat:** pet, favorite
79–80. **It is . . . why:** she should make herself cry, if she had some excuse
82. **subscribe:** give in, submit
83. **instruments:** musical instruments
85. **Minerva:** goddess of wisdom, also credited with inventing musical instruments
86. **strange:** uncooperative, unfriendly
89. **mew her up:** cage her
90. **for:** because of
91. **her . . . her:** i.e., Bianca . . . Katherine's
99. **Prefer:** recommend; **cunning:** learned
103. **commune:** talk over together
105. **belike:** as is probable
107. **devil's dam:** devil's mother (in proverbs, said to be worse than the devil)

108. **hold:** restrain; **Their love:** perhaps, the love of women (Some editors print this as "There! Love . . .")

109. **blow our nails:** i.e., wait patiently

110–11. **Our cake's . . . sides:** proverbial for "we've both lost"

114. **wish:** recommend

117. **brooked parle:** i.e., allowed for discussion; **advice:** careful consideration; **toucheth:** concerns

126–27. **so very a fool:** so entirely a fool as

129. **alarums:** brawlings

131. **light on:** i.e., find

132. **and:** if (there were)

133. **had as lief:** would just as soon

134. **high cross:** the cross at the town center

137. **bar in law:** legal barrier (i.e., Baptista's insistence that Katherine must be married before Bianca)

141. **have to 't afresh:** i.e., compete anew, go to it again

142. **Happy . . . dole:** i.e., may the winner find happiness; or, may the best man win

144–45. **would I . . . wooing:** i.e., I wish I had already given Katherine's wooer the best horse in Padua as encouragement to begin his wooing

153. **I found . . . love-in-idleness:** i.e., I fell in love (Lucentio plays with the idea that idleness begets love, "love-in-idleness" being the name of a flower whose juice in one's eyes, according to Shakespeare's *A Midsummer Night's Dream,* causes one to love the next thing that one sees.)

155. **to me as secret:** as much in my confidence

156. **Anna to the Queen of Carthage:** In Virgil's *Aeneid,* Dido, queen of Carthage, has a sister, Anna, to whom the queen reveals her love for Aeneas.

162. **rated:** chided, scolded

164. **Redime . . . minimo:** i.e., ransom yourself from capture for as little money as possible

165. **Gramercies:** thanks; **contents:** i.e., makes me content

167. **longly:** long; perhaps also longingly

168. **marked not:** did not notice; **pith:** essence

170. **daughter of Agenor:** Europa, whom Jove, in the form of a bull, took to Crete (The story is told in Ovid's *Metamorphoses*.)

176. **her:** i.e., Bianca's

183. **curst and shrewd:** bad-tempered and loud

186. **mewed:** caged

187. **Because:** i.e., so that

191. **'tis plotted:** i.e., I've a scheme

193. **for my hand:** i.e., I'll bet my hand

194. **meet . . . one:** i.e., coincide perfectly

202. **Keep house:** establish a household

204. **Basta:** Italian for "enough"; **have it full:** i.e., have worked out a whole plan

209. **port:** style of life fitting my station

211. **meaner:** less socially important

213. **Uncase thee:** i.e., undress

214. **waits on:** serves

215. **charm . . . tongue:** first conjure him to stay quiet

218. **tied:** bound, obligated

220. **quoth:** said

226. **Whose sudden sight:** i.e., the sudden sight of whom; **thralled:** enthralled, enslaved

233. **frame:** adjust

235. **count'nance:** appearance, manner

236. **for:** i.e., to make good

238. **descried:** identified, recognized

239. **becomes:** is becoming or appropriate

242. **Ne'er a whit:** i.e., not a bit

255. **rests:** remains

256. **make:** become

258 SD. **Presenters:** characters in the Induction (who "presented" the play)

259. **mind:** pay attention to

264. **Would:** i.e., I wish

264 SD. **mark:** i.e., watch

1.2 Petruchio, with his servant Grumio, has just arrived in Padua. His friend Hortensio suggests that Petruchio woo Katherine. Petruchio enthusiastically agrees. He agrees also to present Hortensio, in disguise, to Baptista as a music teacher named Litio. Gremio appears with Lucentio, who is disguised as a teacher named Cambio. Last of all comes Tranio, now impersonating Lucentio and declaring his intention to woo Bianca. Gremio, Hortensio, and Tranio (as Lucentio) agree to help Petruchio win Katherine.

0 SD. **man:** i.e., servant

2. **of all:** especially

3. **approvèd:** tried, tested

4. **trow:** think

7. **rebused:** Grumio's error for "abused"

8. **knock me:** i.e., knock (rap on the gate) for me (Grumio takes **me** to be the object of **knock,** and continues to define **knock me** as "hit me.")

12. **pate:** head

13–15. **I . . . worst:** i.e., if I were to hit you first, I know who would afterward get the worst of it

17. **ring it:** perhaps, use the ring fastened to the door as a knocker (with a pun on "wring")

18. **sol, fa:** notes on the scale; **sing it:** i.e., wail

25. **part the fray:** i.e., stop the fight

26. **Con tutto il cuore ben trovato:** Italian for "Well found (i.e., welcome) with all [my] heart"

27–28. **Alla . . . Petruchio:** Italian for "Welcome to our house, my much honored Master Petruchio"

29. **compound:** settle

30. **'leges:** i.e., alleges

31. **Latin:** Grumio seems to be presented as an Englishman who cannot tell the difference between Italian and Latin.

35. **two-and-thirty . . . out:** i.e., not quite right in the head (The allusion is to a card game called "one-in-thirty."

According to Grumio, Petruchio is one "pip"—i.e., one mark on the card—over the goal of the game.)

46. **pledge:** guarantor
47. **this':** i.e., this is; **heavy chance:** grave misfortune
48. **ancient:** longtime
53. **in a few:** i.e., in a few words
56. **maze:** intricate puzzle
57. **Happily:** perhaps; or, with pleasure
58. **Crowns:** i.e., coins
60. **come roundly to thee:** speak to you bluntly
61. **ill-favored:** unattractive (because bad-tempered)
69. **burden:** refrain; or, bass accompaniment
70. **foul:** ugly; **Florentius' love:** Florentius, in John Gower's fourteenth-century *Confessio Amantis*, agrees to marry an old hag, who is later transformed into a young beauty.
71. **Sibyl:** the Sibyl of Cumae, granted as many years of life as there are grains in a handful of sand; **curst and shrewd:** bad-tempered
72. **Socrates' Xanthippe:** The wife of Socrates is usually represented as a shrew.
73. **moves:** disturbs, dislodges
80. **aglet-baby:** i.e., doll decked with spangles
81. **trot:** hag
83. **withal:** with it
85. **that:** i.e., that which
91. **shrewd, and froward:** shrewish and perverse
92. **state:** financial status
96. **board her:** i.e., woo her
106. **give you over:** leave you right now
109. **humor:** whim, mood
111–12. **half a score:** ten
113. **rail ... tricks:** perhaps, scold in his "rhetorics"; or, use abusive language for which he should be hanged (The passage is very obscure.)
114. **stand him:** i.e., stand up to him (with a sexual meaning as well)

114–16. These lines suggest that Petruchio will throw "figures of speech" at Katherine until she is overcome. But they also suggest physical violence, and, perhaps, rape.

118. Tarry: wait

119. keep: i.e., keeping; or, castle keep, the heavily fortified inner tower of a castle

120. hold: i.e., his stronghold; safekeeping

122. other more: i.e., others too

124. Supposing: i.e., Baptista supposes

125. For: i.e., because of; **rehearsed:** itemized

127. this . . . ta'en: i.e., Baptista has arranged

132. do me grace: do me a favor

133. sober: dark

135. Well seen: well trained

136. device: scheme

137. leave: opportunity; **make love to:** pay amorous attention to, woo

144. proper stripling: handsome youngster (sarcastic reference to Gremio)

145. the note: i.e., perhaps, a list of the books mentioned at line 147

146. bound: books were sold unbound

147. See . . . hand: i.e., see to that in any case

148. lectures: lessons

150. liberality: generosity; probably, here, "what Baptista pays you"

151. mend: improve; **a largess:** a gift of money; **paper:** probably the note mentioned above

152. them: i.e., the books

156. stand: i.e., rest

157. as yourself . . . place: as if you were present the whole time

161. woodcock: i.e., dupe (A woodcock is a bird easily snared and therefore thought to be foolish.)

166. Trow: know

172. warrant: guarantee

179. **bags:** i.e., moneybags

180. **vent:** express

181. **fair:** courteously

182. **indifferent:** equally

184. **Upon agreement . . . liking:** i.e., if we agree to terms that he likes (Hortensio and Gremio are to pay the expenses that Petruchio incurs in his courtship of Katherine; see lines 218–19.)

187. **So said, so done, is well:** i.e., if the deeds match the words, this is good

191. **What countryman?:** i.e., from what country are you?

196. **stomach:** desire, spirit, courage; **to 't:** go to it; **i':** i.e., in

206. **ordnance:** heavy guns

209. **'larums:** i.e., alarums, or calls to battle

213. **fear boys with bugs:** frighten little boys with bugbears or bogeymen

216. **happily:** opportunely, at just the right time

219. **bear . . . of:** pay his expenses for

223. **readiest:** i.e., shortest

225. **fair:** beautiful

228. **her to—:** Gremio seems to be interrupted here before he finishes the question "you mean not her to woo?" (Some editors print the line as "mean not her too?")

229. **What . . . do?:** i.e., what business is it of yours?

230. **her that chides:** i.e., Katherine; **at any hand:** in any case

233. **ere:** before

236. **get you hence:** i.e., go away

242. **choice:** i.e., chosen

244. **Softly:** gently

248. **And were his daughter fairer:** We would probably say: "Even if she were less fair than she is."

250. **Leda's daughter:** the legendarily beautiful Helen of Troy, daughter of the god Jove and the woman Leda

251. **well . . . have:** i.e., Bianca may well have one more

252. **make one:** i.e., be one

253. **Paris:** lover of Helen of Troy; **speed:** prevail, succeed

254. **What:** an interjection introducing a question or an exclamation

255. **give him head:** i.e., let him run (as if he were a horse); **jade:** a worthless horse

257. **as:** i.e., as to

262. **let her go by:** leave her alone

263. **Hercules:** Also called Alcides, he was required to undertake twelve seemingly impossible labors.

266. **hearken:** ask

272. **stead:** help

275. **hap:** fortune

276. **so graceless . . . ingrate:** i.e., be so ungracious as to be ungrateful

277. **conceive:** understand

279. **gratify:** i.e., pay

282. **Please . . . contrive:** i.e., if it please you, let us spend

283. **quaff carouses:** drink copiously

286. **motion:** proposal

288. **I . . . venuto:** i.e., I will introduce you; I will ensure your welcome

2.1 Baptista stops Katherine from abusing Bianca and receives a visit from Petruchio, who presents Hortensio (disguised as Litio, a music teacher); Gremio introduces Lucentio (disguised as Cambio, a teacher of languages). Tranio, impersonating Lucentio, announces his wish to marry Bianca, and Petruchio his desire to marry Katherine. Baptista insists that Petruchio must get Katherine's love. Petruchio and Katherine, left alone, enter into a furious bout of wordplay. Petruchio then lies to Baptista, insisting

that Katherine loves him but that the couple have agreed
that she will pretend to dislike him in public. Katherine's
wedding is arranged, and Baptista hears the offers that
Gremio and Tranio (as Lucentio) make for Bianca. Tranio-
Lucentio outbids Gremio and is awarded Bianca, provided
that Vincentio, Lucentio's father, will guarantee the dowry.
Tranio-Lucentio sets out to find someone to impersonate
Vincentio and provide the guarantee.

2. **bondmaid:** same as slave
3. **goods:** things; articles of clothing
4. **Unbind:** i.e., if you will unbind
8. **charge:** command
13. **Minion:** hussy
14. **affect:** like
15. **but . . . him:** i.e., but in any case you shall have him
16. **belike:** perhaps
17. **fair:** i.e., in beautiful clothes
18. **envy:** hate (pronounced "en-vigh' ")
27. **hilding:** beast
32. **flouts:** mocks, insults
34. **suffer me:** allow me to be, tolerate me
36. **dance . . . day:** the proverbial misfortune of the
unmarried elder daughter on her sister's wedding day
37. **for:** because of; **lead . . . hell:** the proverbial fate of
unmarried women
41 SD. **mean man:** man of low status
49. **Give me leave:** permit me to continue
57. **entrance:** price of admission; **entertainment:**
reception as a guest
62. **Accept of:** i.e., accept
66. **is not for your turn:** i.e., is not right for you
68. **like not of:** i.e., do not like
74. **Saving:** with all respect to
76. **Bacare:** corrupt Latin for "get back"
77. **fain:** rather

80. **gift:** i.e., Litio, given to Baptista by Petruchio; **very grateful:** i.e., for which you are very grateful

86. **the other:** i.e., Litio

98. **In the preferment of:** granting precedence to

116. **them both:** i.e., Katherine and Bianca

118. **orchard:** garden

119. **passing:** very

129. **in possession:** for immediate possession

131. **widowhood:** her rights as a widow; **be it:** i.e., if it be

133. **specialties:** special contracts

134. **on either hand:** i.e., on both sides

145. **happy:** fortunate; **speed:** progress

147. **to the proof:** (1) in strong armor; (2) to the test

147–48. **as mountains . . . perpetually:** i.e., as mountains, which do not shake, even though winds blow against them perpetually

153. **hold with her:** withstand her use

154. **break:** tame, train

155. **broke the lute:** Usually in productions Hortensio enters with the lute broken over his head.

156. **did but tell:** only told; **mistook her frets:** placed her fingers the wrong way on the ridges or bars (**frets**) on the neck of the lute

159. **fume:** rage (as in "frets and fumes")

162. **pate:** head

163. **amazèd:** astounded

166. **Jack:** rascal

167. **As had she:** i.e., as if she had

168. **lusty:** lively

173. **apt:** inclined

176. **attend:** await

178. **rail:** scold; **plain:** directly, simply

185. **pack:** i.e., pack up and leave

187. **deny:** refuse; **crave the day:** beg her to name the day

191. **but:** i.e., but you are

194. **curst:** ill-tempered, quarrelsome

196. **super-dainty:** especially choice, precious

197. **dainties:** delicacies to eat, also called "cates"

200. **sounded:** (1) spoken of; (2) measured for depth—hence **deeply** in the next line

202. **moved:** inspired

203. **in good time:** indeed

206. **movable:** (1) piece of furniture; (2) whimsical person

208. **joint stool:** stool made of parts joined or fitted together

211. **bear:** (1) bear children; (2) bear the weight of a man in sexual intercourse

212. **jade:** worthless horse that lacks endurance

214. **light:** Since Petruchio is interrupted, it is impossible to say which of the many meanings of **light** might apply here.

215. **light:** quick; **swain:** rustic lover; bumpkin

217. **buzz:** i.e., the sound of a bee, the **be** of **should be**

218. **ta'en:** taken or understood (sarcastic)

219. **buzzard:** (1) a buzzing insect; (2) a stupid person

220. **turtle:** turtle dove, symbolic of love; **buzzard:** a bird of prey; **take:** (1) capture; (2) mistake

233. **try:** test

237. **arms:** i.e., coat of arms, the mark of a gentleman

238. **herald:** the officer who determined who had the right to bear arms; **in thy books:** in your herald's books; in your good books, i.e., in your favor

239. **crest:** (1) a figure worn atop a knight's helmet; (2) the comb on a rooster or cock; **coxcomb:** fool's cap

241. **craven:** coward; a defeated cock

243. **crab:** (1) crab apple; (2) sour-faced person

247. **glass:** mirror

249. **aimed:** guessed; **of:** i.e., by

254. **sooth:** truth

255. **chafe:** irritate; **tarry:** stay
256. **whit:** bit; **passing:** very
257. **coy:** distant, aloof
258. **a very:** an utter
259. **gamesome:** playful
262. **askance:** aside (in scorn or contempt)
264. **cross:** inclined to oppose or contradict
266. **conference:** conversation
271. **halt:** limp
272. **whom thou keep'st:** i.e., your servants
273. **Dian:** i.e., Diana, the huntress-goddess of chastity
276. **sportful:** lustful
277. **study:** i.e., prepare
278. **mother wit:** natural intelligence
279. **else:** otherwise
281. **keep you warm:** Proverbial: "He is wise enough that can keep himself warm."
286. **will you, nill you:** i.e., whether you like it or not
287. **for your turn:** just right for you
292. **wild Kate:** pun on "wildcat"
296. **speed:** succeed
300–301. **In your dumps:** depressed, out of sorts
302. **promise:** assure
306. **face:** brazen
309. **curst:** quarrelsome, ill-tempered
310. **froward:** strong-willed
311. **hot:** angry
312. **Grissel:** Griselda, the legendary wife who, with superhuman patience, remained obedient and faithful to a cruel husband (Her story is told by Chaucer in *The Clerk's Tale.*)
313. **Lucrece:** After being raped by Tarquin, she committed suicide. (Shakespeare tells her story in *The Rape of Lucrece.*)
319. **speeding:** success
320. **goodnight our part:** i.e., we'll say good-bye to our suits to Bianca

323. **bargained:** agreed; **'twixt:** between
324. **still:** always
328. **vied:** repeated, piled up
329. **twink:** i.e., twinkling of an eye
332. **meacock:** meek
334. **'gainst:** in preparation for
335. **bid:** invite
336. **fine:** splendidly dressed
341. **apace:** quickly
344. **clapped up:** hurriedly arranged
345–48. **Faith, gentlemen . . . the seas:** In these lines Baptista compares himself—and is compared—to a merchant who takes a great gamble to dispose of goods (Katherine) which are wearing out from being long kept in storage. **desperate mart:** risky market **commodity:** goods **fretting:** (1) wearing out (of goods); (2) irritable (of Katherine)
350. **he:** i.e., Petruchio
359. **Skipper:** i.e., one young enough that he can skip (term of contempt)
361. **compound:** settle, reconcile
362. **he of both:** i.e., the one of you two
368. **lave:** wash
369. **hangings:** i.e., wall hangings; **Tyrian:** purple
370. **crowns:** gold coins
371. **arras counterpoints:** counterpanes of Arras tapestry
372. **tents:** perhaps, bed-curtains
373. **Turkey:** Turkish; **bossed:** i.e., embossed
374. **Valance:** drapery; **gold:** i.e., gold thread
377. **milch-kine to the pail:** cows providing milk
378. **Six score:** one hundred twenty
379. **answerable to:** i.e., consistent with; **portion:** estate
380. **struck in years:** stricken with age
383. **list:** listen

390. **ducats:** gold coins; **by the:** per
391. **Of:** from; **fruitful:** fertile; **jointure:** estate, which she will inherit at his death
392. **pinched you:** put you in a tight spot
395. **argosy:** largest of trading ships
396. **Marcellus' road:** sheltered anchorage outside the harbor at Marseilles
399. **galliasses:** large galleys
400. **tight:** watertight, sound; **assure:** promise
407. **outvied:** outbid
409. **let . . . assurance:** i.e., if your father provides her the guarantee
412. **cavil:** meaningless objection
424. **gamester:** gambler, betting on his father's generosity; **were:** i.e., would be
426. **Set foot under thy table:** i.e., be reduced to a guest in your house; **toy:** joke
428. **A vengeance on:** i.e., may I be avenged on
429. **faced . . . ten:** i.e., bluffed it without even a face card
434. **get:** i.e., beget
435. **sire:** father; **of:** i.e., in

3.1 Under cover of their disguises as schoolmasters, first Lucentio (as Cambio) and then Hortensio (as Litio) try for Bianca's love. Hortensio notices Lucentio-Cambio's affection for Bianca and determines to abandon her if she shows any interest in such a social inferior as Hortensio believes Cambio to be.

1. **forbear:** stop
3. **withal:** i.e., with
4. **this:** i.e., Bianca
6. **leave:** permission; **to have prerogative:** i.e., to go first
8. **Your lecture . . . much:** i.e., your lesson will be given equal time

9. **Preposterous:** literally, putting first what belongs last (Music is to follow work, not precede it.)

10. **ordained:** instituted, created

12. **usual pain:** i.e., daily labor

14. **serve in:** i.e., perform, present

15. **bear these braves:** endure these taunts

18. **breeching scholar:** young student liable to be breeched (i.e., whipped)

19. **'pointed:** i.e., appointed

30–31. **Hic . . . senis:** "Here flowed the Simois; here is the Sigeian land; / Here had stood old Priam's high palace" (Ovid).

32. **Conster:** construe, interpret

35. **thus:** i.e., as the tutor Cambio

37. **bearing my port:** assuming my social position

38. **pantaloon:** i.e., Gremio (see note to 1.1.45 SD)

41. **jars:** is out of tune

42–43. **Spit . . . again:** an ironic twist on the proverbial "Spit on your hands and try again"

50. **base knave:** i.e., "Cambio"

53. **Pedascule:** corrupt Latin for "little pedant" (pronounced with four syllables)

55. **Aeacides:** Lucentio is pretending to interpret Ovid to Bianca. The reference to **Aeacides** ("descendant of Aeacus") follows in Ovid the passage quoted at lines 30–31.

61. **pleasant:** merry

62. **give me leave:** let me alone

65. **withal:** as well; **but:** unless

68. **learn:** i.e., teach; **order:** system

70. **gamut:** the musical scale devised in the 11th century (The notes—known as A, B, C, etc.—were sung to the syllables *re, mi, fa, sol, la,* and *ut* [see lines 76–81]. The "gamut" was also the ground note of the scale.)

73. **drawn:** set out

83. **nice:** hard to please

84. **To:** i.e., so as to

91. **Methinks:** I think
92. **humble:** common, low, base
93. **stale:** decoy, lure (term from falconry)
94–95. **Seize . . . changing:** i.e., Let anyone who wants you capture you. If I once find you untrue, I will get even with you by turning to someone else.

3.2 Petruchio is late arriving for his wedding, to Katherine's great embarrassment. When he finally presents himself, he is dressed in ridiculous clothes. At the wedding, according to Gremio's report, Petruchio behaves rudely and abusively. He refuses to attend the supper that traditionally follows a wedding, and he insists on taking Katherine away as well. Over her protests, he forces her to go with him, making a show of defending her against the interference of her family and friends.

1. **'pointed:** i.e., appointed
5. **want:** lack; **attends:** awaits; is present
8. **forsooth:** indeed
10. **rudesby:** rude, disorderly fellow; **spleen:** impulsiveness, changeableness
12. **frantic:** lunatic, insane
13. **blunt:** rude
14. **noted for:** known as
16. **proclaim the banns:** announce the intended marriage
22. **means but:** only means
23. **Whatever . . . word:** whatever accident prevents him from keeping his promise to be married
24. **passing:** very
27. **to weep:** i.e., for weeping
29. **humor:** temperament
41. **to:** i.e., about
43. **jerkin:** short jacket; **turned:** i.e., turned inside out in order to get more wear out of them

44. **candle-cases:** i.e., used as places to throw candle ends

47. **chapeless:** without the metal plate (**chape**) on its sheath; **points:** laces to hold up stockings

48. **hipped:** lame in the hip

48–49. **of no kindred:** i.e., that do not match

49. **glanders:** swelling glands and nasal discharge

50. **like ... chine:** possibly, likely to decay in the backbone; or possibly, susceptible to glanders

50–51. **lampass:** swelling in the mouth

51. **fashions:** i.e., farcins, a disease in horses causing painful ulcerations, especially on the legs; **windgalls:** tumors on its legs

52. **sped with spavins:** ruined by inflamed cartilage; **rayed with the yellows:** berayed or disfigured by jaundice

53. **fives:** avives, a disease causing swelling below the ears; **stark:** entirely; **the staggers:** staggering, giddiness; **begnawn:** gnawed; eaten away

54. **bots:** intestinal worms

54–55. **shoulder-shotten:** lame in the shoulder

55. **near-legged before:** with knock-kneed forelegs

55–56. **half-checked bit:** i.e., a faulty bit

56. **headstall:** part of the bridle; **sheep's leather:** i.e., inferior leather, not the preferable pigskin

59. **pieced:** repaired

60. **crupper:** the strap under the horse's tail that keeps the saddle steady; **velour:** velvet (thus less sturdy than a leather crupper)

62. **pieced ... packthread:** held together with string

64–65. **caparisoned:** outfitted

65. **stock:** stocking

66. **kersey boot-hose:** coarse wool stocking

67. **list:** cloth border

67–68. **humor ... in 't:** perhaps, decorated in a wildly extravagant way

69. **monster:** beast that combines several forms

71. **humor:** whim, mood; **pricks:** urges
72. **mean-appareled:** dressed poorly
80. **all one:** i.e., the same thing
82. **hold:** bet
86. **gallants:** fine gentlemen
89. **halt:** limp
94. **Gentles:** i.e., gentlemen
95. **wherefore:** why
97. **prodigy:** wonder
100. **unprovided:** unprepared
101. **this habit:** these clothes; **estate:** status
102. **solemn:** ceremonial
103. **import:** importance
108. **in some part:** to some extent; **enforcèd to digress:** forced to deviate (from his promise)
113. **unreverent:** unrespectable
117. **Good sooth:** in truth
121. **accoutrements:** clothes
125. **seal:** i.e., ratify; **lovely:** i.e., loving
127. **be it:** i.e., if it be
129. **event:** outcome
130. **love:** i.e., Bianca's love (The abruptness of the change of subject may reflect some lost lines of text. It has been suggested that Tranio and Lucentio should enter at this point, and that the lines earlier in the scene given to Tranio should, in fact, be given to Hortensio, for whom they are much more appropriate.)
134. **skills:** i.e., matters; **turn:** purpose
136. **make assurance:** provide guarantees
141. **narrowly:** closely
142. **steal our marriage:** i.e., elope (**marriage** pronounced as a three-syllable word)
145. **That:** i.e., the marriage; **by degrees:** gradually
146. **watch our vantage:** look out for opportunities that favor us
148. **narrow prying:** i.e., overly watchful

149. **quaint:** cunning, crafty
156. **Curster:** more perverse
158. **dam:** mother
159. **fool:** pitiable creature
161. **Should ask:** i.e., asked; **should:** would
162. **gog's wouns:** i.e., God's wounds (a strong oath)
163. **amazed:** astounded
165. **took:** hit
167. **he:** i.e., Petruchio; **list:** wishes to
169. **for why:** because
170. **vicar:** priest; **cozen:** cheat
172. **health:** toast
173. **aboard:** i.e., on shipboard
174. **quaffed:** drank
175. **sops:** cake that had been broken up and soaked in the wine; **sexton:** church officer
177. **his:** i.e., the sexton's; **hungerly:** sparsely
178. **to ask him sops:** i.e., to require sops
183. **rout:** crowd
185 SD. **Hortensio:** It is unclear whether Hortensio enters here as "Litio" or as himself.
188. **store:** quantities; **cheer:** food and drink
193. **Make it no wonder:** do not wonder at it
198. **my father:** i.e., my father-in-law, Baptista
217. **jogging . . . green:** going while your boots are new (an invitation to leave)
219. **like:** i.e., likely; **jolly:** i.e., overbearing
220. **That take . . . roundly:** i.e., in that you immediately presume to take command so completely
222. **What . . . do?:** i.e., what business is it of yours?
223. **stay my leisure:** i.e., wait until I am ready
224. **marry:** i.e., indeed
230. **domineer:** feast riotously (Dutch *domineren*, to feast luxuriously)
234. **big:** challenging, defiant
236. **chattels:** property, goods

237. **stuff:** goods
240. **bring mine action:** (1) bring legal action; (2) attack physically; **he:** i.e., one
246. **buckler:** i.e., defend
248. **Went they not:** i.e., if they had not gone
251. **mated:** matched, married
254–55. **wants . . . supply:** i.e., are not present to occupy
256. **wants:** are lacking; **junkets:** confections
259. **room:** place

4.1 At Petruchio's house in the country, Grumio tells his fellow servant Curtis about the wild journey home to Petruchio's after the wedding. When Petruchio and Katherine arrive, Petruchio attacks his servants verbally and physically. He refuses to let Katherine eat, saying the dinner is burnt and throwing it to the floor. At the end of the scene he confides to the audience that he intends to tame Katherine in the same way that a hunter tames a falcon—by starving it and keeping it sleepless.

1. **jades:** worthless horses
2. **foul ways:** dirty roads
3. **'rayed:** i.e., berayed, dirty
6. **hot:** Proverbial: "A small pot is soon hot."
24. **three-inch fool:** another reference to Grumio's short stature (compare **little pot,** line 5)
25. **horn:** the symbol of the cuckold (the husband whose wife is unfaithful)
27. **on:** i.e., about
28. **at hand:** nearby
30. **office:** duty (of lighting a fire)
34. **have thy duty:** i.e., get what is due to you
39. **"Jack boy, ho boy!":** a line from a song
41. **cony-catching:** deception (Literally, a cony is a rabbit. In **cony-catching,** the cony is the victim of trickery and deception.)

44. **rushes strewed:** i.e., as floor covering.
45. **fustian:** coarse-cloth work-clothes
46. **officer:** household servant
47. **Jacks:** (1) menservants; (2) large leather drinking cups; **Jills:** (1) women servants; (2) small metal drinking cups
48. **carpets:** probably, woolen table covers
60. **sensible:** (1) making sense; (2) felt by the senses
62. **Imprimis:** Latin for "first"
63. **foul:** dirty
64. **of:** i.e., on
70. **miry:** swampy; **bemoiled:** muddied
74. **that:** i.e., who
78. **unexperienced:** uninformed
79. **reck'ning:** account
81. **what:** i.e., why
84. **blue coats:** servants' uniforms
85. **indifferent:** equal, i.e., matched
92. **to countenance:** to show respect (pun on the meaning "to face" in the next line)
97. **credit her:** pay respect to her (but "lend her money" in the next line)
106. **spruce:** (1) lively; (2) smart in appearance
111. **Cock's:** i.e., God or Christ's
117. **loggerheaded:** blockheaded
121. **swain:** country bumpkin; **whoreson:** literally, son of a whore; a good-for-nothing
121–22. **malt-horse drudge:** stupid slave (literally, a horse on a treadmill that grinds malt in a brewery)
123. **park:** grounds
126. **unpinked:** undecorated (literally, without ornamental holes punched in them)
127. **link:** blacking from a torch
136. **Soud:** No meaning for this word is recorded; it is often changed to "Food" in texts of this play.
139. **When:** i.e., how long do I have to wait

144. **mend . . . other:** do better in removing the other boot
152. **it:** i.e., the basin of water
153. **unwilling:** involuntary
154. **beetle-headed:** thickheaded (A *beetle* was a mallet with a heavy head.)
155. **stomach:** appetite
163. **dresser:** sideboard; or, person who prepared it
165. **trenchers:** wooden platters
166. **joltheads:** blockheads
167. **be . . . straight:** deal with you immediately
172. **choler:** one of the four bodily humors (Excess choler made one angry.)
175. **it:** i.e., our predisposition to anger
180. **humor:** disposition
183. **continency:** self-restraint
184. **rails . . . rates:** i.e., scolds and berates; **that:** i.e., so that
188. **politicly:** shrewdly
190. **sharp:** hungry; **passing:** completely
191. **stoop:** fly directly to the keeper or to the prey
192. **lure:** the bait held by the keeper
193. **man my haggard:** train my falcon
195. **watch her:** force her to stay awake; **kites:** falcons
196. **bate:** beat their wings
203. **hurly:** commotion; **intend:** (1) pretend; (2) propose
204. **reverend:** respectful
205. **watch:** be kept awake
206. **rail and brawl:** scold and make noise
211. **shew:** reveal (a better way)

4.2 In Padua, Hortensio (as Litio) leads Tranio (as Lucentio) to spy on Bianca and Lucentio-Cambio as the couple kiss and talk of love. Hortensio, doffing his disguise as Litio, then rejects Bianca forever, resolves to marry a wealthy widow who loves him, and sets off to observe

Petruchio's taming of Katherine. In the meantime, Biondello has found a traveling merchant whom Tranio persuades to impersonate Lucentio's father, Vincentio.

   3. **bears . . . hand:** deceives me beautifully
   4. **satisfy you in:** convince you of
   7. **resolve:** answer
   8. **that I profess:** that which I teach; **The Art to Love:** the *Ars Amatoria*, by the Roman poet Ovid
   11. **proceeders:** workers (with wordplay on "proceeding" to an academic degree like master of arts, alluded to in line 9); **marry:** i.e., indeed
   15. **wonderful:** astounding
   18. **scorn:** i.e., scorns
   20. **cullion:** low fellow (term of contempt)
   24. **lightness:** inconstancy
   31. **fondly:** foolishly; **withal:** i.e., with
   34. **beastly:** shamelessly
   35. **but he:** i.e., except "Cambio"
   38. **Ere:** before; **which:** i.e., who (i.e., the widow)
   39. **haggard:** a wild female hawk
   45. **'longeth:** i.e., belongeth
   59. **eleven and twenty long:** i.e., exactly right (The allusion is to the card game "Thirty-one.")
   60. **charm:** magically silence
   63. **ancient angel:** i.e., reliable old man (literally, a coin [**angel**] whose value is above suspicion, unlike that of newer coins)
   64. **serve the turn:** suit the purpose
   66. **marcantant:** Biondello's version of *mercatante*, Italian for "merchant"
   72. **give assurance:** i.e., provide guarantees of the dowry that Tranio (as Lucentio) has promised
   74 SD. Although the Folio has this character enter and speak under the designation "Pedant," his words (lines 94–95) suggest that he is no pedant (schoolmaster), but is

rather Biondello's **marcantant,** or merchant. We have therefore followed editor Ann Thompson in emending "Pedant" to "Merchant" throughout.

77. **far on:** i.e., farther on; **the farthest:** i.e., the end of your journey

81. **What countryman:** i.e., from what country are you?

84. **careless:** without regard for

85. **goes hard:** is serious

88. **stayed:** detained

90. **it:** i.e., the death sentence upon citizens of Mantua

91. **but . . . but:** except . . . only

92. **else:** otherwise

94. **bills . . . exchange:** papers to be exchanged for money

100. **grave:** worthy and serious

104. **sooth:** truth

107. **all one:** no matter

111. **are like to:** i.e., look like

112. **credit:** reputation; **undertake:** take on, assume

114. **take . . . should:** i.e., be careful to assume the proper manner

117. **accept of:** i.e., accept

118. **repute:** consider

120. **make . . . good:** carry out the plan

123. **pass assurance of:** formally guarantee

4.3 At Petruchio's home, Grumio torments Katherine by promising her food that he fails to bring. Petruchio then serves Katherine himself, demanding her thanks. The Haberdasher and Tailor bring in the cap and gown that Katherine plans to wear for Bianca's wedding feast, but Petruchio refuses them. Petruchio threatens that she may not return to her father's for Bianca's wedding feast unless Katherine agrees with everything he says, no matter how self-evidently false it is.

2. **my wrong:** the wrong that I suffer

5. **present:** immediate

8. **needed . . . should:** i.e., needed to

9. **meat:** food

11. **spites:** angers; **wants:** deprivations

13. **As who should say:** i.e., as if to say

16. **so it be:** i.e., so long as it is

17. **neat's:** calf's

18. **passing:** very

19. **choleric:** liable to promote choler (see note to 4.1.172)

26. **let . . . rest:** i.e., do without **the mustard**

32. **the very name:** only the name

33. **Sorrow on thee:** i.e., may sorrow come upon thee

36. **all amort:** (French: *à la mort*) dejected

41. **dress thy meat:** prepare your food

44. **is sorted to no proof:** i.e., turn out to have no effect

46. **stand:** i.e., stay

54. **apace:** right now, immediately

57. **bravely:** splendidly (in our dress)

59. **ruffs:** starched wheel-like collars; **farthingales:** hooped petticoats

60. **brav'ry:** splendid dress

61. **knav'ry:** i.e., nonsense

62. **stays thy leisure:** i.e., awaits your pleasure

63. **ruffling:** i.e., ruffled

67. **bespeak:** order

68. **porringer:** porridge bowl

69. **lewd:** low, vulgar; **filthy:** mean, disgusting

70. **cockle:** cockleshell

71. **knack:** knickknack; **toy, trick:** both mean "trifle," something worthless

73. **doth fit the time:** is fashionable now

78. **leave:** permission

87. **custard-coffin:** crust for a custard

92. **masking-stuff:** costumes for maskers (i.e., people who came to parties wearing disguises)

93. **demi-cannon:** large cannon

94. **carved ... tart:** i.e., with slits like the upper crust of a pie

96. **censer:** perhaps, incense burner

98. **like:** i.e., likely

101. **Marry, and did:** i.e., indeed I did; **be remembered:** i.e., remember

103. **hop ... kennel:** i.e., hop over every gutter

104. **custom:** trade, patronage

107. **quaint:** elegant

108. **commendable:** accent on first syllable

109. **Belike:** perhaps; **puppet:** plaything

115. **yard:** yardstick; **quarter:** quarter-yard; **nail:** one-sixteenth yard

116. **nit:** louse egg

117. **Braved:** defied; **with:** i.e., by

119. **be-mete:** intensive form of **mete,** meaning "measure"; i.e., measure thoroughly; beat you

120. **As ... liv'st:** i.e., remembering this thrashing, you will think before chattering as long as you live

123. **had direction:** i.e., was directed

125. **stuff:** material (for the gown)

129. **faced:** (1) sewed on trim; (2) defied

131. **braved:** made to look splendid

132. **brave:** defy

134. **Ergo:** Latin for "therefore"

136. **note ... fashion:** written instruction for the style of the gown

138. **in 's:** in his

139. **Imprimis:** Latin for "first"

142. **bottom:** ball or skein

144. **small-compassed:** i.e., in the form of a small semicircle

146. **trunk sleeve:** wide sleeve

148. **curiously:** exquisitely
152. **prove upon thee:** i.e., make good in a fight
154. **An:** i.e., if
154–55. **place where:** a suitable place
156. **straight:** straightway, immediately; **bill:** (1) note; (2) long-handled weapon
157. **mete-yard:** measuring stick
159. **odds:** i.e., advantage
162. **unto . . . use:** i.e., for your master to use
165. **what's . . . that:** i.e., what do you mean by that
173. **of:** i.e., at
176. **mean habiliments:** common clothes
180. **peereth in:** i.e., shows through; **habit:** clothes
181. **What:** interjection at the beginning of a question or exclamation
186. **furniture:** accessories; **mean array:** ordinary clothes
189. **sport:** i.e., disport, entertain ourselves
194. **some:** i.e., about
195. **dinner time:** i.e., noon
199. **Look what:** i.e., whatever
200. **still:** always; **crossing:** opposing; **let 't alone:** i.e., abandon preparations for departure

4.4 In Padua, the Merchant impersonating Vincentio visits Baptista with Tranio, who is still disguised as Lucentio. Baptista accepts the Merchant's guarantee of Bianca's dowry and sends "Cambio" to Bianca to tell her the marriage plans. Meanwhile, Baptista arranges to visit "Lucentio" and "Vincentio" at their lodging to finalize the marriage contract. Biondello tells Lucentio that all the arrangements have been made for Lucentio to elope with Bianca.

0 SD. **booted:** in riding boots
2. **And but:** unless (The Merchant may be practicing his role as Vincentio.)

4. **Near:** i.e., nearly

5. **Pegasus:** i.e., an inn named after the mythical winged horse

7. **'longeth:** i.e., belongeth

10. **schooled:** instructed

12. **throughly:** thoroughly

13. **right:** true

18. **tall:** fine, bold

20. **happily:** opportunely

24. **Soft:** i.e., enough, hush

25. **by your leave:** a polite phrase

27. **weighty cause:** serious matter

29, 30. **for:** because of

31. **stay:** delay

32. **in . . . care:** i.e., with the care that a good father ought to have

37. **curious:** overparticular, too demanding

46. **pass:** transfer to

50. **affied:** formally betrothed; **such assurance ta'en:** such guarantees provided

51. **either part's agreement:** what each party has agreed to

53. **Pitchers have ears:** i.e., we might be overheard (proverbial)

54. **heark'ning still:** listening constantly

55. **happily:** perhaps

56. **an it like you:** i.e., if it please you

57. **lie:** stay

58. **pass:** i.e., transact

60. **scrivener:** notary public

61. **slender warning:** short notice

62. **pittance:** i.e., refreshment

63. **likes:** pleases; **hie you:** hurry

64. **straight:** straightway, immediately

67. **like:** i.e., likely

71. **mess:** dish; **cheer:** food and drink

79. **'has:** i.e., he has

82. **moralize:** i.e., explain

93. **assurance:** marriage contract

93–94. **Take ... of her:** i.e., make sure of her

94. **cum ... solum:** "with the exclusive right to print," a formula often appearing on the title pages of books in this period (Biondello plays with the formula as a description of legal marriage.)

97. **that:** i.e., what

101. **tarry:** wait

105–106. **against you come:** in preparation for your coming

106. **appendix:** appendage (spouse)

108. **wherefore:** why

110. **Hap what hap may:** i.e., whatever may happen; **roundly ... her:** perhaps, approach her boldly

111. **shall go hard:** i.e., will not be for lack of effort

4.5 Katherine now gives assent to every word Petruchio says. On their way to her father's, they meet the true Vincentio, who is going to Padua to visit his son. They travel together to Padua.

1–2. **our father's:** i.e., Baptista's

8. **list:** choose; or, please

9. **Or e'er I:** before I ever will

12. **crossed:** opposed, contradicted

16. **rush candle:** cheap candle made by dipping a rush in grease or fat

26. **field:** i.e., battlefield

27–28. **Thus ... bias:** Petruchio claims that Katherine is now acting naturally, no longer being perverse. (In the game of bowls, the ball is weighted so that it follows a curved path [its **bias**]; **against the bias,** thus, means "off its natural course.")

29. **soft:** i.e., wait a minute

30–31. **where away:** i.e., where are you going?

33. **fresher:** more radiant

34. **war . . . red:** language typical of love poetry of the period as it described womanly beauty

36. **become:** fit

42. **Whither away:** i.e., where are you going?

44–45. **whom . . . thee:** i.e., to whom you have been given by fortune **Allots:** i.e., allot

51. **green:** i.e., young, fresh

52. **reverend:** worthy of respect

54. **withal:** in addition

58. **encounter:** i.e., greeting; **amazed:** astounded

68. **by this:** by now

69. **esteem:** repute

71. **so qualified:** with such qualities; **beseem:** suit, become

75. **of:** i.e., at, with

76. **else:** instead

77. **pleasant:** merry; **break a jest:** play a joke

80. **hereof:** of it

81. **merriment:** joke; **jealous:** suspicious

82. **in heart:** in good spirits

83. **Have to:** i.e., now for; **froward:** perverse

84. **untoward:** stubborn, intractable

5.1 After Bianca has secretly married Lucentio, Petruchio, Katherine, and Lucentio's father arrive at Lucentio's lodging. They are rebuffed by the Merchant impersonating Vincentio. Vincentio denounces as frauds the Merchant and then Tranio, who turns up still disguised as Lucentio. As Vincentio is about to be carried off to jail by an officer, the true Lucentio arrives with his bride, successfully begs his father's pardon for the secret marriage, and explains the disguises.

10. **bears more toward:** is closer to

14. **cheer is toward:** refreshment can be expected

20, 22. **withal:** i.e., with

28. **frivolous circumstances:** i.e., silly details

38. **flat:** downright

41. **cosen:** cheat

42. **under my countenance:** i.e., by exploiting my good name

44. **good shipping:** i.e., good luck

47. **crack-hemp:** i.e., rogue (literally, someone who will stretch the hangman's rope)

48. **I may choose:** i.e., go my own way

67. **fine villain:** splendidly dressed rogue; **doublet:** jacket

68. **hose:** breeches; **copatain:** high-crowned

69. **undone:** ruined, destroyed

69–70. **play the good husband:** i.e., conserve, save money

75. **habit:** clothes

76. **'cerns:** i.e., concerns

78. **maintain:** afford

82. **his name:** i.e., Tranio's name

95. **forthcoming:** produced (at the time of his trial)

100–101. **cony-catched:** deceived and victimized

102. **right:** true

108. **dotard:** foolish old man

109. **haled:** molested

111. **spoiled:** ruined

119. **Right:** true

121. **counterfeit supposes:** false impersonations; **eyne:** i.e., eyes

122. **packing:** plotting, conspiracy; **with a witness:** i.e., with a vengeance

124. **faced and braved:** i.e., defied

128. **state:** status

129. **countenance:** i.e., position and reputation

131. **Unto:** i.e., at

138–39. **Go to!:** expression of angry impatience

139. **will in:** i.e., will go in
143. **My cake is dough:** proverbial for "I've failed"
144. **Out ... but:** without hope of anything except
146. **ado:** fuss
156. **Better ... late:** Petruchio combines two proverbs—"Better once than never" (i.e., "Better late than never") and "It is never too late to mend."

5.2 Three couples attend the wedding banquet—Lucentio and Bianca, Petruchio and Katherine, and Hortensio and the Widow. Petruchio is repeatedly teased about being married to a shrew. In retaliation Petruchio wagers with Lucentio and Hortensio that if they all summon their wives to them, his Katherine will be the most obedient in responding. When Bianca and the Widow refuse to come at all and Katherine promptly appears, Petruchio wins, and then he sends Katherine to bring the other wives to their husbands. When they return, Petruchio tells Katherine to instruct the other wives in their wifely duty. Katherine delivers a long speech in praise of women's submission to their husbands. Petruchio kisses Katherine, and they go off to bed.

 0 SD. **banquet:** dessert and wine
 1. **At last, though long:** i.e., at long last
 3. **'scapes:** i.e., escapes; **overblown:** i.e., past
 10. **great good cheer:** i.e., the wedding feast
 15. **would:** wish
 16. **fears:** is afraid of (The Widow [line 17] takes **fears** to mean "frightens.")
 17. **afeard:** afraid
 21. **Roundly:** bluntly
 23. **Thus I conceive by him:** i.e., I come to this understanding through observing him
 30. **his:** i.e., his own (Petruchio's)

34. **mean . . . you:** (1) temperate compared to you; (2) nasty, where you are concerned

37. **marks:** i.e., coins (A "mark" was worth 13 shillings.); **put her down:** defeat her

38. **office:** duty, privilege (Hortensio takes "put her down" in the sexual sense.)

39. **Ha' to:** i.e., here's to

41. **butt together:** knock heads

42. **body:** i.e., person

43. **horn:** symbol of a cuckold

47. **Have at you for:** i.e., I challenge you to

48. **bird:** i.e., target

51. **prevented me:** stopped me in advance

53. **health:** toast

54. **slipped:** loosed

56. **something:** i.e., somewhat

58. **deer . . . bay:** The image is perhaps of the cornered animal defending itself against the attacking hounds; or, perhaps, Tranio is picturing Kate as a deer cornering the hunter.

60. **gird:** biting remark

62. **galled:** scratched, irritated

65. **in good sadness:** i.e., seriously

66. **veriest shrew:** i.e., shrew in the truest sense, the most complete shrew

67. **for assurance:** i.e., to put it to the test

75. **of:** i.e., on

84. **be your half:** assume half your bet

96. **forthwith:** immediately

112. **holidam:** a confusion of "holidom," meaning a relic or the state of holiness, with "holidame," or the Virgin Mary

116. **deny:** i.e., refuse

117. **Swinge me them:** beat them

118. **straight:** immediately

119. **wonder:** miracle

120. **bodes:** foretells, presages

122. **awful rule:** rule by commanding respect or awe; **right:** proper

123. **what not:** i.e., anything and everything

124. **fair befall thee:** i.e., good fortune come to you

128. **as:** i.e., as though

132. **froward:** perverse

136. **bauble:** showy trifle

137. **cause:** reason

138. **pass:** state of affairs

139. **duty:** obedience

143. **laying:** betting

155. **meads:** meadows

156. **Confounds thy fame:** i.e., spoils your reputation

157. **meet:** appropriate

158. **moved:** angry

159. **ill-seeming:** unbecoming

162–70. **Thy husband . . . debt:** See Paul's Letter to the Ephesians 3.22–28 ("Wives, submit yourselves unto your husbands, . . . for the husband is the head of the wife, even as Christ is the head of the Church . . ."). In the Geneva Bible, the marginal gloss adds "So the husband ought to nourish, govern, and defend his wife from perils."

166. **To watch:** i.e., to keep watch throughout

168. **at:** i.e., from

171–76. **Such duty . . . lord:** See 1 Peter 2.13–3.7: "Submit yourselves to every ordinance of man for the Lord's sake: whether it be to the king . . . or unto governors. . . . Likewise, ye wives, be in subjection to your own husbands. . . ."

177. **simple:** foolish

179. **sway:** power

182. **Unapt:** unsuited

183. **conditions:** qualities

185. **unable:** helpless

186. **big:** self-important

187. **heart:** courage

188. **bandy:** exchange; literally, hit back and forth

190. **as weak:** i.e., as weak as **straws; past compare:** beyond comparison

192. **vail your stomachs:** i.e., subdue your pride; **no boot:** i.e., bootless, futile

195. **may it:** i.e., if it may

197. **ha 't:** have it (i.e., you win)

198. **a good hearing:** i.e., good to hear; **toward:** compliant, cooperative

201. **We three:** i.e., Petruchio, Hortensio, Lucentio; **sped:** done for

203. **the white:** the bull's eye (i.e., won the woman prized by all, Bianca, whose name in Italian means "white")

204. **God:** i.e., I pray God to

Textual Notes

The reading of the present text appears to the left of the square bracket. The earliest sources of readings not in F, the First Folio text, are indicated as follows: **Q** is *The Taming of a Shrew* 1594; **F2** is the Second Folio of 1632; **F3** is the Third Folio of 1663–64; **F4** is the Fourth Folio of 1685. **Ed.** is an earlier editor of Shakespeare, beginning with Rowe in 1709. **SD** means stage direction; **SP** means speech prefix.

	Ind.1]	Ed.; *Actus primus. Scœna Prima.* F
Ind.1	0.	SD *Enter Begger and Hostes, Christophero Sly.* F
	9.	Saint] Ed.; *S.* F
	17.	Breathe] Ed.; *Brach* F
	44.	SP THIRD HUNTSMAN] This ed.; *1. Hun.* F
	72.	SP THIRD HUNTSMAN] This ed.; *1. Hunts.* F
	87.	SP FIRST PLAYER] Ed.; *2. Player* F
	93.	SP SECOND PLAYER] Ed.; *Sincklo* (*the name of an actor in Shakespeare's company*) F
	105.	SP FIRST PLAYER] Ed.; *Plai.* F
Ind.2	18.	Sly's] Ed.; *Sies* F
	94.	Greete] Ed.; *Greece* F
	144.	a] *a a* F
1.1	13.	Vincentio] Ed.; *Vincentio's* F
	25.	*Mi perdonato*] Ed.; *Me Pardonato* F
	45.	SD *suitors*] This ed.; *sister* F; *suitor* F2

153

147. SD *Gremio . . . onstage.*] *Exeunt ambo.*
     Manet Tranio and Lucentio F
164. *captum*] F2; *captam* F
242. Ay, sir] Ed.; I sir F
254. your] F2; you F
258. SD *speak*] Ed.; *speakes* F

1.2   26. *Con tutto il cuore ben trovato*] Ed.; *Contut-*
           ti le core bene trobatto F
       27. *ben*] Ed.; *bene* F
       27. *molto*] Ed.; *multo* F
       28. *honorato*] Ed.; *honorata* F
       28. *signor*] Ed.; *signior* F
       74. she as] Ed.; she is as F
      122. me and other] Ed.; me. Other F
      174. me] Ed.; one F
      221. SD *disguised as Lucentio*] Ed.; *braue* F
      273. feat] Ed.; seeke F
      288. *ben*] F2; *Been* F

2.1   8. thee] F2; *omit* F
    79–80. wooing. Neighbor, this] Ed.; wooing neigh-
           bors: this F
       83. you] Ed.; *omit* F
      262. askance] Ed.; a sconce F
      349. in] Ed.; me F

3.1 30, 35, 45. *Sigeia*] F2; *sigeria* F
       46. *steterat*] F2; *staterat* F
       51. SP How] Ed.; *Luc.* How F
       54. SP BIANCA In] Ed.; In F
       55. SP LUCENTIO] Ed.; *Bian.* F
       57. SP BIANCA] Ed.; *Hort.* F
       77. *A re*] Q; *Are* F
       78. *B mi*] Ed.; *Beeme* F
       79. *C fa ut*] Q; *C favt* F
       84. change] F2; charge F
       84. odd] Ed.; old F
       84. SD *Servant*] Ed.; *Messenger* F

	85.	SP SERVANT] Ed.; *Nicke.* F
3.2	29.	thy] F2; *omit* F
	30.	old] Ed.; *omit* F
	33.	hear] Q; heard F
	54.	swayed] Ed.; Waid F
	129.	SD *Exit.* F
	130.	to] Ed.; *omit* F
	132.	I] F2; *omit* F
	202.	SP GREMIO] F2; *Gra.* F
4.1	24.	SP CURTIS] Q; *Gru.* F
	45.	their] F3; the F
	110.	SP GRUMIO] F3; *Gre.* F
	180.	SD *Enter Curtis*] *Enter Curtis a Seruant.* F
4.2	4.	SP HORTENSIO] F2; *Luc.* F
	6.	SP LUCENTIO] F2; *Hor.* F
	8.	SP LUCENTIO] F2; *Hor.* F
	13.	none] Ed.; me F
	31.	her] F3; them F
	74.	Take] F2; *Par.* Take F
	74.	in] Ed.; me F
	74	SD *and hereafter. Merchant*] Ed.; *Pedant* F (*Ped.* in SP's)
4.3		Ed.; *Actus Quartus, Scena Prima.* F
	67.	SP HABERDASHER] Ed.; *Fel.* F
	86.	a] Q; *omit* F
	93.	a] Q; *omit* F
	187.	account'st] Ed.; accountedst F
4.4	0.	SD *booted, and*] F *at line 19* SD *repeats the Pedant-Merchant's entrance:* "Enter . . . Pedant booted and bare headed."
	1.	Sir] Ed.; Sirs F
	5.	Where] Ed.; *Tra.* Where F
	19.	SD *See note to 4.4.0 SD.*
	67.	SD *Exit.* F
	69.	SD *Enter Peter.* F

73. SD *Enter Lucentio.*] Ed.; *Enter Lucentio and Biondello.* F
92. except] F2; expect F

4.5
21. is] Q; in F
42. where] F2; whether F
45. Allots] Q; A lots F
83. be] F2; *omit* F

5.1
4. SD *Exit.* F
6. master's] Ed.; Mistris F
14. SD *He knocks.*] Ed.; *Knock.* F
54. master's] F2; Mistris F

5.2
Ed.; *Actus Quintus* F
0. SD *Enter Baptista, Vincentio, Gremio, the Pedant, Lucentio, and Bianca. Tranio, Biondello Grumio, and Widdow: The Seruingmen with Tranio bringing in a Banquet.* F
2. done] Ed.; come F
47. bitter] Ed.; better F
67. for] F2; sir F
142. a] Ed.; fiue F
147. you're] F3; your F

A
MIDSUMMER
NIGHT'S DREAM

Shakespeare's
A Midsummer Night's Dream

In *A Midsummer Night's Dream*, Shakespeare confronts us with mysterious images of romantic desire. There are Theseus and Hippolyta, about to be married; both are strange and wonderful figures from classical mythology. Theseus is a great warrior, a kinsman of Hercules; she is an Amazon, a warrior-woman, defeated in battle by Theseus. His longing for the wedding day opens the play, and the play closes with their exit to their marriage bed.

Within Theseus's world of Athens, two young men and two young women sort themselves out into marriageable couples, but only after one triangle, with Hermia at the apex and Helena excluded, is temporarily replaced by another, this time with Helena at the apex and Hermia excluded. At each point the fickle young men think they are behaving rationally and responsibly as infatuation (sometimes caused by a magic flower, sometimes not) leads them into fierce claims and counterclaims, and the audience is shown the power of desire to take over one's vision and one's actions. By presenting the young lovers as almost interchangeable, Shakespeare displays and probes the mystery of how lovers find differences—compelling, life-shaping differences—where there seem to be only likenesses.

In the woods outside of Athens, where the lovers suffer their strange love experiences, we find yet other images of desire, these involving the king and queen of Fairyland and an Athenian weaver transformed into an ass-headed monster. King Oberon and Queen Titania are engaged in a near-epic battle over custody of an orphan boy; the king uses magic to make the queen fall in love with the monster. The monster—a simple weaver named Bottom who came into the woods with his companions to rehearse a play for Theseus and Hippolyta's wedding—is himself the victim of magic. He has been turned into a monster by Oberon's helper, a hobgoblin or "puck" named Robin Goodfellow. The love-experience of Titania and Bottom plays out the familiar "beauty and the beast" story, and, like the stories of the young lovers, it makes us wonder at the power of infatuation to transform the image of the beloved in the lover's eyes.

Finally, there is the tragic love story of "Pyramus and Thisbe," ineptly written and staged by Bottom and his workingmen companions. In this story romantic love leads to a double suicide—provoking only mirth in the onstage audience but reminding us once again of the extraordinary power of desire.

Characters in the Play

HERMIA
LYSANDER
HELENA
DEMETRIUS
} *four lovers*

THESEUS, duke of Athens
HIPPOLYTA, queen of the Amazons
EGEUS, father to Hermia
PHILOSTRATE, master of the revels to Theseus

NICK BOTTOM, weaver
PETER QUINCE, carpenter
FRANCIS FLUTE, bellows-mender
TOM SNOUT, tinker
SNUG, joiner
ROBIN STARVELING, tailor

OBERON, king of the Fairies
TITANIA, queen of the Fairies
ROBIN GOODFELLOW, a "puck," or hobgoblin, in Oberon's service
A FAIRY, in the service of Titania
PEASEBLOSSOM
COBWEB
MOTE
MUSTARDSEED
} *fairies attending upon Titania*

Lords and Attendants on Theseus and Hippolyta
Other Fairies in the trains of Titania and Oberon

161

⌜ACT 1⌝

⌜Scene 1⌝

Enter Theseus, Hippolyta, ⌜and Philostrate,⌝ with others.

THESEUS
Now, fair Hippolyta, our nuptial hour
Draws on apace. Four happy days bring in
Another moon. But, O, methinks how slow
This old moon ⌜wanes!⌝ She lingers my desires
Like to a stepdame or a dowager   5
Long withering out a young man's revenue.

HIPPOLYTA
Four days will quickly steep themselves in night;
Four nights will quickly dream away the time;
And then the moon, like to a silver bow
⌜New⌝-bent in heaven, shall behold the night   10
Of our solemnities.

THESEUS   Go, Philostrate,
Stir up the Athenian youth to merriments.
Awake the pert and nimble spirit of mirth.
Turn melancholy forth to funerals;   15
The pale companion is not for our pomp.
                              ⌜*Philostrate exits.*⌝
Hippolyta, I wooed thee with my sword
And won thy love doing thee injuries,
But I will wed thee in another key,
With pomp, with triumph, and with reveling.   20

163

*Enter Egeus and his daughter Hermia, and Lysander
and Demetrius.*

EGEUS
　Happy be Theseus, our renownèd duke!
THESEUS
　Thanks, good Egeus. What's the news with thee?
EGEUS
　Full of vexation come I, with complaint
　Against my child, my daughter Hermia.—
　Stand forth, Demetrius.—My noble lord,　　　　　25
　This man hath my consent to marry her.—
　Stand forth, Lysander.—And, my gracious duke,
　This man hath bewitched the bosom of my child.—
　Thou, thou, Lysander, thou hast given her rhymes
　And interchanged love tokens with my child.　　30
　Thou hast by moonlight at her window sung
　With feigning voice verses of feigning love
　And stol'n the impression of her fantasy
　With bracelets of thy hair, rings, gauds, conceits,
　Knacks, trifles, nosegays, sweetmeats—messengers　35
　Of strong prevailment in unhardened youth.
　With cunning hast thou filched my daughter's heart,
　Turned her obedience (which is due to me)
　To stubborn harshness.—And, my gracious duke,
　Be it so she will not here before your Grace　　40
　Consent to marry with Demetrius,
　I beg the ancient privilege of Athens:
　As she is mine, I may dispose of her,
　Which shall be either to this gentleman
　Or to her death, according to our law　　　　　45
　Immediately provided in that case.
THESEUS
　What say you, Hermia? Be advised, fair maid.
　To you, your father should be as a god,
　One that composed your beauties, yea, and one

To whom you are but as a form in wax   50
By him imprinted, and within his power
To leave the figure or disfigure it.
Demetrius is a worthy gentleman.

HERMIA
So is Lysander.

THESEUS   In himself he is,   55
But in this kind, wanting your father's voice,
The other must be held the worthier.

HERMIA
I would my father looked but with my eyes.

THESEUS
Rather your eyes must with his judgment look.

HERMIA
I do entreat your Grace to pardon me.   60
I know not by what power I am made bold,
Nor how it may concern my modesty
In such a presence here to plead my thoughts;
But I beseech your Grace that I may know
The worst that may befall me in this case   65
If I refuse to wed Demetrius.

THESEUS
Either to die the death, or to abjure
Forever the society of men.
Therefore, fair Hermia, question your desires,
Know of your youth, examine well your blood,   70
Whether (if you yield not to your father's choice)
You can endure the livery of a nun,
For aye to be in shady cloister mewed,
To live a barren sister all your life,
Chanting faint hymns to the cold fruitless moon.   75
Thrice-blessèd they that master so their blood
To undergo such maiden pilgrimage,
But earthlier happy is the rose distilled
Than that which, withering on the virgin thorn,
Grows, lives, and dies in single blessedness.   80

HERMIA
So will I grow, so live, so die, my lord,
Ere I will yield my virgin patent up
Unto his lordship whose unwishèd yoke
My soul consents not to give sovereignty.

THESEUS
Take time to pause, and by the next new moon   85
(The sealing day betwixt my love and me
For everlasting bond of fellowship),
Upon that day either prepare to die
For disobedience to your father's will,
Or else to wed Demetrius, as he would,   90
Or on Diana's altar to protest
For aye austerity and single life.

DEMETRIUS
Relent, sweet Hermia, and, Lysander, yield
Thy crazèd title to my certain right.

LYSANDER
You have her father's love, Demetrius.   95
Let me have Hermia's. Do you marry him.

EGEUS
Scornful Lysander, true, he hath my love;
And what is mine my love shall render him.
And she is mine, and all my right of her
I do estate unto Demetrius.   100

LYSANDER, ⌜to Theseus⌝
I am, my lord, as well derived as he,
As well possessed. My love is more than his;
My fortunes every way as fairly ranked
(If not with vantage) as Demetrius';
And (which is more than all these boasts can be) 105
I am beloved of beauteous Hermia.
Why should not I then prosecute my right?
Demetrius, I'll avouch it to his head,
Made love to Nedar's daughter, Helena,
And won her soul; and she, sweet lady, dotes,   110

Devoutly dotes, dotes in idolatry,
Upon this spotted and inconstant man.

THESEUS
I must confess that I have heard so much,
And with Demetrius thought to have spoke thereof;
But, being overfull of self-affairs, 115
My mind did lose it.—But, Demetrius, come,
And come, Egeus; you shall go with me.
I have some private schooling for you both.—
For you, fair Hermia, look you arm yourself
To fit your fancies to your father's will, 120
Or else the law of Athens yields you up
(Which by no means we may extenuate)
To death or to a vow of single life.—
Come, my Hippolyta. What cheer, my love?—
Demetrius and Egeus, go along. 125
I must employ you in some business
Against our nuptial, and confer with you
Of something nearly that concerns yourselves.

EGEUS
With duty and desire we follow you.
⌜*All but Hermia and Lysander*⌝ *exit.*

LYSANDER
How now, my love? Why is your cheek so palc? 130
How chance the roses there do fade so fast?

HERMIA
Belike for want of rain, which I could well
Beteem them from the tempest of my eyes.

LYSANDER
Ay me! For aught that I could ever read,
Could ever hear by tale or history, 135
The course of true love never did run smooth.
But either it was different in blood—

HERMIA
O cross! Too high to be enthralled to ⌜low.⌝

LYSANDER
Or else misgraffèd in respect of years—

HERMIA
  O spite! Too old to be engaged to young.   140
LYSANDER
  Or else it stood upon the choice of friends—
HERMIA
  O hell, to choose love by another's eyes!
LYSANDER
  Or, if there were a sympathy in choice,
  War, death, or sickness did lay siege to it,
  Making it momentany as a sound,   145
  Swift as a shadow, short as any dream,
  Brief as the lightning in the collied night,
  That, in a spleen, unfolds both heaven and earth,
  And, ere a man hath power to say "Behold!"
  The jaws of darkness do devour it up.   150
  So quick bright things come to confusion.
HERMIA
  If then true lovers have been ever crossed,
  It stands as an edict in destiny.
  Then let us teach our trial patience
  Because it is a customary cross,   155
  As due to love as thoughts and dreams and sighs,
  Wishes and tears, poor fancy's followers.
LYSANDER
  A good persuasion. Therefore, hear me, Hermia:
  I have a widow aunt, a dowager
  Of great revenue, and she hath no child.   160
  From Athens is her house remote seven leagues,
  And she respects me as her only son.
  There, gentle Hermia, may I marry thee;
  And to that place the sharp Athenian law
  Cannot pursue us. If thou lovest me, then   165
  Steal forth thy father's house tomorrow night,
  And in the wood a league without the town
  (Where I did meet thee once with Helena
  To do observance to a morn of May),
  There will I stay for thee.   170

HERMIA   My good Lysander,
  I swear to thee by Cupid's strongest bow,
  By his best arrow with the golden head,
  By the simplicity of Venus' doves,
  By that which knitteth souls and prospers loves,   175
  And by that fire which burned the Carthage queen
  When the false Trojan under sail was seen,
  By all the vows that ever men have broke
  (In number more than ever women spoke),
  In that same place thou hast appointed me,   180
  Tomorrow truly will I meet with thee.

LYSANDER
  Keep promise, love. Look, here comes Helena.

                    Enter Helena.

HERMIA
  Godspeed, fair Helena. Whither away?

HELENA
  Call you me "fair"? That "fair" again unsay.
  Demetrius loves your fair. O happy fair!   185
  Your eyes are lodestars and your tongue's sweet air
  More tunable than lark to shepherd's ear
  When wheat is green, when hawthorn buds appear.
  Sickness is catching. O, were favor so!
  ⌜Yours would⌝ I catch, fair Hermia, ere I go.   190
  My ear should catch your voice, my eye your eye;
  My tongue should catch your tongue's sweet
    melody.
  Were the world mine, Demetrius being bated,
  The rest ⌜I'd⌝ give to be to you translated.   195
  O, teach me how you look and with what art
  You sway the motion of Demetrius' heart!

HERMIA
  I frown upon him, yet he loves me still.

HELENA
  O, that your frowns would teach my smiles such
    skill!   200

HERMIA
I give him curses, yet he gives me love.
HELENA
O, that my prayers could such affection move!
HERMIA
The more I hate, the more he follows me.
HELENA
The more I love, the more he hateth me.
HERMIA
His folly, Helena, is no fault of mine.   205
HELENA
None but your beauty. Would that fault were mine!
HERMIA
Take comfort: he no more shall see my face.
Lysander and myself will fly this place.
Before the time I did Lysander see
Seemed Athens as a paradise to me.   210
O, then, what graces in my love do dwell
That he hath turned a heaven unto a hell!
LYSANDER
Helen, to you our minds we will unfold.
Tomorrow night when Phoebe doth behold
Her silver visage in the wat'ry glass,   215
Decking with liquid pearl the bladed grass
(A time that lovers' flights doth still conceal),
Through Athens' gates have we devised to steal.
HERMIA
And in the wood where often you and I
Upon faint primrose beds were wont to lie,   220
Emptying our bosoms of their counsel ⌜sweet,⌝
There my Lysander and myself shall meet,
And thence from Athens turn away our eyes
To seek new friends and ⌜stranger companies.⌝
Farewell, sweet playfellow. Pray thou for us,   225
And good luck grant thee thy Demetrius.—

Keep word, Lysander. We must starve our sight
From lovers' food till morrow deep midnight.

LYSANDER
I will, my Hermia.   *Hermia exits.*
              Helena, adieu.   230
As you on him, Demetrius dote on you!
                                Lysander exits.

HELENA
How happy some o'er other some can be!
Through Athens I am thought as fair as she.
But what of that? Demetrius thinks not so.
He will not know what all but he do know.   235
And, as he errs, doting on Hermia's eyes,
So I, admiring of his qualities.
Things base and vile, holding no quantity,
Love can transpose to form and dignity.
Love looks not with the eyes but with the mind;   240
And therefore is winged Cupid painted blind.
Nor hath Love's mind of any judgment taste.
Wings, and no eyes, figure unheedy haste.
And therefore is Love said to be a child
Because in choice he is so oft beguiled.   245
As waggish boys in game themselves forswear,
So the boy Love is perjured everywhere.
For, ere Demetrius looked on Hermia's eyne,
He hailed down oaths that he was only mine;
And when this hail some heat from Hermia felt,   250
So he dissolved, and show'rs of oaths did melt.
I will go tell him of fair Hermia's flight.
Then to the wood will he tomorrow night
Pursue her. And, for this intelligence
If I have thanks, it is a dear expense.   255
But herein mean I to enrich my pain,
To have his sight thither and back again.
                                She exits.

⌜Scene 2⌝

Enter Quince the carpenter, and Snug the joiner, and
Bottom the weaver, and Flute the bellows-mender, and
Snout the tinker, and Starveling the tailor.

QUINCE Is all our company here?

BOTTOM You were best to call them generally, man by man, according to the scrip.

QUINCE Here is the scroll of every man's name which is thought fit, through all Athens, to play in our 5 interlude before the Duke and the Duchess on his wedding day at night.

BOTTOM First, good Peter Quince, say what the play treats on, then read the names of the actors, and so grow to a point. 10

QUINCE Marry, our play is "The most lamentable comedy and most cruel death of Pyramus and Thisbe."

BOTTOM A very good piece of work, I assure you, and a merry. Now, good Peter Quince, call forth your 15 actors by the scroll. Masters, spread yourselves.

QUINCE Answer as I call you. Nick Bottom, the weaver.

BOTTOM Ready. Name what part I am for, and proceed.

QUINCE You, Nick Bottom, are set down for Pyramus. 20

BOTTOM What is Pyramus—a lover or a tyrant?

QUINCE A lover that kills himself most gallant for love.

BOTTOM That will ask some tears in the true performing of it. If I do it, let the audience look to their eyes. I will move storms; I will condole in some 25 measure. To the rest.—Yet my chief humor is for a tyrant. I could play Ercles rarely, or a part to tear a cat in, to make all split:

> *The raging rocks*
> *And shivering shocks* 30
> *Shall break the locks*

> Of prison gates.
> And Phibbus' car
> Shall shine from far
> And make and mar   35
> The foolish Fates.

This was lofty. Now name the rest of the players.
This is Ercles' vein, a tyrant's vein. A lover is more
condoling.

QUINCE Francis Flute, the bellows-mender.   40

FLUTE Here, Peter Quince.

QUINCE Flute, you must take Thisbe on you.

FLUTE What is Thisbe—a wand'ring knight?

QUINCE It is the lady that Pyramus must love.

FLUTE Nay, faith, let not me play a woman. I have a   45
beard coming.

QUINCE That's all one. You shall play it in a mask, and
you may speak as small as you will.

BOTTOM An I may hide my face, let me play Thisbe too.
I'll speak in a monstrous little voice: "Thisne,   50
Thisne!"—"Ah Pyramus, my lover dear! Thy Thisbe
dear and lady dear!"

QUINCE No, no, you must play Pyramus—and, Flute,
you Thisbe.

BOTTOM Well, proceed.   55

QUINCE Robin Starveling, the tailor.

STARVELING Here, Peter Quince.

QUINCE Robin Starveling, you must play Thisbe's
mother.—Tom Snout, the tinker.

SNOUT Here, Peter Quince.   60

QUINCE You, Pyramus' father.—Myself, Thisbe's
father.—Snug the joiner, you the lion's part.—
And I hope here is a play fitted.

SNUG Have you the lion's part written? Pray you, if it
be, give it me, for I am slow of study.   65

QUINCE You may do it extempore, for it is nothing but
roaring.

BOTTOM   Let me play the lion too. I will roar that I will
    do any man's heart good to hear me. I will roar that
    I will make the Duke say "Let him roar again. Let   70
    him roar again!"

QUINCE   An you should do it too terribly, you would
    fright the Duchess and the ladies that they would
    shriek, and that were enough to hang us all.

ALL   That would hang us, every mother's son.   75

BOTTOM   I grant you, friends, if you should fright the
    ladies out of their wits, they would have no more
    discretion but to hang us. But I will aggravate my
    voice so that I will roar you as gently as any sucking
    dove. I will roar you an 'twere any nightingale.   80

QUINCE   You can play no part but Pyramus, for Pyra-
    mus is a sweet-faced man, a proper man as one
    shall see in a summer's day, a most lovely gentle-
    manlike man. Therefore you must needs play Pyr-
    amus.   85

BOTTOM   Well, I will undertake it. What beard were I
    best to play it in?

QUINCE   Why, what you will.

BOTTOM   I will discharge it in either your straw-color
    beard, your orange-tawny beard, your purple-   90
    in-grain beard, or your French-crown-color beard,
    your perfit yellow.

QUINCE   Some of your French crowns have no hair at
    all, and then you will play barefaced. But, masters,
    here are your parts, ⌜*giving out the parts,*⌝ and I am   95
    to entreat you, request you, and desire you, to con
    them by tomorrow night and meet me in the palace
    wood, a mile without the town, by moonlight. There
    will we rehearse, for if we meet in the city, we shall
    be dogged with company and our devices known. In   100
    the meantime I will draw a bill of properties such as
    our play wants. I pray you fail me not.

BOTTOM   We will meet, and there we may rehearse

most obscenely and courageously. Take pains. Be
perfit. Adieu.   105
QUINCE At the Duke's Oak we meet.
BOTTOM Enough. Hold, or cut bowstrings.

They exit.

⌜ACT 2⌝

⌜Scene 1⌝

*Enter a Fairy at one door and Robin Goodfellow at
another.*

ROBIN
  How now, spirit? Whither wander you?
FAIRY
            Over hill, over dale,
              Thorough bush, thorough brier,
            Over park, over pale,
              Thorough flood, thorough fire;   5
            I do wander everywhere,
            Swifter than the moon's sphere.
            And I serve the Fairy Queen,
            To dew her orbs upon the green.
            The cowslips tall her pensioners be;   10
            In their gold coats spots you see;
            Those be rubies, fairy favors;
            In those freckles live their savors.
      I must go seek some dewdrops here
      And hang a pearl in every cowslip's ear.   15
      Farewell, thou lob of spirits. I'll be gone.
      Our queen and all her elves come here anon.
ROBIN
  The King doth keep his revels here tonight.
  Take heed the Queen come not within his sight,

For Oberon is passing fell and wrath   20
Because that she, as her attendant, hath
A lovely boy stolen from an Indian king;
She never had so sweet a changeling.
And jealous Oberon would have the child
Knight of his train, to trace the forests wild.   25
But she perforce withholds the lovèd boy,
Crowns him with flowers, and makes him all her
     joy.
And now they never meet in grove or green,
By fountain clear, or spangled starlight sheen,   30
But they do square, that all their elves for fear
Creep into acorn cups and hide them there.

FAIRY
Either I mistake your shape and making quite,
Or else you are that shrewd and knavish sprite
Called Robin Goodfellow. Are not you he   35
That frights the maidens of the villagery,
Skim milk, and sometimes labor in the quern
And bootless make the breathless huswife churn,
And sometime make the drink to bear no barm,
Mislead night wanderers, laughing at their harm?   40
Those that "Hobgoblin" call you, and "sweet Puck,"
You do their work, and they shall have good luck.
Are not you he?

ROBIN   Thou speakest aright.
I am that merry wanderer of the night.   45
I jest to Oberon and make him smile
When I a fat and bean-fed horse beguile,
Neighing in likeness of a filly foal.
And sometime lurk I in a gossip's bowl
In very likeness of a roasted crab,   50
And, when she drinks, against her lips I bob
And on her withered dewlap pour the ale.
The wisest aunt, telling the saddest tale,
Sometime for three-foot stool mistaketh me;

Then slip I from her bum, down topples she,   55
And "Tailor!" cries, and falls into a cough,
And then the whole choir hold their hips and loffe
And waxen in their mirth and neeze and swear
A merrier hour was never wasted there.
But room, fairy. Here comes Oberon.   60

FAIRY
    And here my mistress. Would that he were gone!

Enter ⌐Oberon⌐ the King of Fairies at one door, with his
train, and ⌐Titania⌐ the Queen at another, with hers.

OBERON
    Ill met by moonlight, proud Titania.

TITANIA
    What, jealous Oberon? ⌐Fairies,⌐ skip hence.
    I have forsworn his bed and company.

OBERON
    Tarry, rash wanton. Am not I thy lord?   65

TITANIA
    Then I must be thy lady. But I know
    When thou hast stolen away from Fairyland
    And in the shape of Corin sat all day
    Playing on pipes of corn and versing love
    To amorous Phillida. Why art thou here,   70
    Come from the farthest steep of India,
    But that, forsooth, the bouncing Amazon,
    Your buskined mistress and your warrior love,
    To Theseus must be wedded, and you come
    To give their bed joy and prosperity?   75

OBERON
    How canst thou thus for shame, Titania,
    Glance at my credit with Hippolyta,
    Knowing I know thy love to Theseus?
    Didst not thou lead him through the glimmering
        night   80
    From ⌐Perigouna,⌐ whom he ravishèd,

And make him with fair ⌜Aegles⌝ break his faith,
With Ariadne and Antiopa?

TITANIA
These are the forgeries of jealousy;
And never, since the middle summer's spring,   85
Met we on hill, in dale, forest, or mead,
By pavèd fountain or by rushy brook,
Or in the beachèd margent of the sea,
To dance our ringlets to the whistling wind,
But with thy brawls thou hast disturbed our sport.   90
Therefore the winds, piping to us in vain,
As in revenge have sucked up from the sea
Contagious fogs, which, falling in the land,
Hath every pelting river made so proud
That they have overborne their continents.   95
The ox hath therefore stretched his yoke in vain,
The plowman lost his sweat, and the green corn
Hath rotted ere his youth attained a beard.
The fold stands empty in the drownèd field,
And crows are fatted with the murrain flock.   100
The nine-men's-morris is filled up with mud,
And the quaint mazes in the wanton green,
For lack of tread, are undistinguishable.
The human mortals want their winter here.
No night is now with hymn or carol blessed.   105
Therefore the moon, the governess of floods,
Pale in her anger, washes all the air,
That rheumatic diseases do abound.
And thorough this distemperature we see
The seasons alter: hoary-headed frosts   110
Fall in the fresh lap of the crimson rose,
And on old Hiems' ⌜thin⌝ and icy crown
An odorous chaplet of sweet summer buds
Is, as in mockery, set. The spring, the summer,
The childing autumn, angry winter, change   115
Their wonted liveries, and the mazèd world

By their increase now knows not which is which.
And this same progeny of evils comes
From our debate, from our dissension;
We are their parents and original.   120

OBERON
Do you amend it, then. It lies in you.
Why should Titania cross her Oberon?
I do but beg a little changeling boy
To be my henchman.

TITANIA   Set your heart at rest: 125
The Fairyland buys not the child of me.
His mother was a vot'ress of my order,
And in the spicèd Indian air by night
Full often hath she gossiped by my side
And sat with me on Neptune's yellow sands,   130
Marking th' embarkèd traders on the flood,
When we have laughed to see the sails conceive
And grow big-bellied with the wanton wind;
Which she, with pretty and with swimming gait,
Following (her womb then rich with my young   135
    squire),
Would imitate and sail upon the land
To fetch me trifles and return again,
As from a voyage, rich with merchandise.
But she, being mortal, of that boy did die,   140
And for her sake do I rear up her boy,
And for her sake I will not part with him.

OBERON
How long within this wood intend you stay?

TITANIA
Perchance till after Theseus' wedding day.
If you will patiently dance in our round   145
And see our moonlight revels, go with us.
If not, shun me, and I will spare your haunts.

OBERON
Give me that boy and I will go with thee.

TITANIA
  Not for thy fairy kingdom. Fairies, away.
  We shall chide downright if I longer stay.   150
        ⌜*Titania and her fairies*⌝ *exit.*

OBERON
  Well, go thy way. Thou shalt not from this grove
  Till I torment thee for this injury.—
  My gentle Puck, come hither. Thou rememb'rest
  Since once I sat upon a promontory
  And heard a mermaid on a dolphin's back   155
  Uttering such dulcet and harmonious breath
  That the rude sea grew civil at her song
  And certain stars shot madly from their spheres
  To hear the sea-maid's music.

ROBIN   I remember.   160

OBERON
  That very time I saw (but thou couldst not),
  Flying between the cold moon and the earth,
  Cupid all armed. A certain aim he took
  At a fair vestal thronèd by ⌜the⌝ west,
  And loosed his love-shaft smartly from his bow   165
  As it should pierce a hundred thousand hearts.
  But I might see young Cupid's fiery shaft
  Quenched in the chaste beams of the wat'ry moon,
  And the imperial vot'ress passèd on
  In maiden meditation, fancy-free.   170
  Yet marked I where the bolt of Cupid fell.
  It fell upon a little western flower,
  Before, milk-white, now purple with love's wound,
  And maidens call it "love-in-idleness."
  Fetch me that flower; the herb I showed thee once.   175
  The juice of it on sleeping eyelids laid
  Will make or man or woman madly dote
  Upon the next live creature that it sees.
  Fetch me this herb, and be thou here again
  Ere the leviathan can swim a league.   180

ROBIN
    I'll put a girdle round about the earth
    In forty minutes.   ⌜*He exits.*⌝
OBERON   Having once this juice,
    I'll watch Titania when she is asleep
    And drop the liquor of it in her eyes.   185
    The next thing then she, waking, looks upon
    (Be it on lion, bear, or wolf, or bull,
    On meddling monkey, or on busy ape)
    She shall pursue it with the soul of love.
    And ere I take this charm from off her sight   190
    (As I can take it with another herb),
    I'll make her render up her page to me.
    But who comes here? I am invisible,
    And I will overhear their conference.

        Enter Demetrius, Helena following him.

DEMETRIUS
    I love thee not; therefore pursue me not.   195
    Where is Lysander and fair Hermia?
    The one I'll stay; the other stayeth me.
    Thou told'st me they were stol'n unto this wood,
    And here am I, and wood within this wood
    Because I cannot meet my Hermia.   200
    Hence, get thee gone, and follow me no more.
HELENA
    You draw me, you hard-hearted adamant!
    But yet you draw not iron, for my heart
    Is true as steel. Leave you your power to draw,
    And I shall have no power to follow you.   205
DEMETRIUS
    Do I entice you? Do I speak you fair?
    Or rather do I not in plainest truth
    Tell you I do not, ⌜nor⌝ I cannot love you?
HELENA
    And even for that do I love you the more.

I am your spaniel, and, Demetrius,   210
The more you beat me I will fawn on you.
Use me but as your spaniel: spurn me, strike me,
Neglect me, lose me; only give me leave
(Unworthy as I am) to follow you.
What worser place can I beg in your love   215
(And yet a place of high respect with me)
Than to be usèd as you use your dog?

DEMETRIUS
Tempt not too much the hatred of my spirit,
For I am sick when I do look on thee.

HELENA
And I am sick when I look not on you.   220

DEMETRIUS
You do impeach your modesty too much
To leave the city and commit yourself
Into the hands of one that loves you not,
To trust the opportunity of night
And the ill counsel of a desert place   225
With the rich worth of your virginity.

HELENA
Your virtue is my privilege. For that
It is not night when I do see your face,
Therefore I think I am not in the night.
Nor doth this wood lack worlds of company,   230
For you, in my respect, are all the world.
Then, how can it be said I am alone
When all the world is here to look on me?

DEMETRIUS
I'll run from thee and hide me in the brakes
And leave thee to the mercy of wild beasts.   235

HELENA
The wildest hath not such a heart as you.
Run when you will. The story shall be changed:
Apollo flies and Daphne holds the chase;
The dove pursues the griffin; the mild hind

Makes speed to catch the tiger. Bootless speed   240
When cowardice pursues and valor flies!

DEMETRIUS
I will not stay thy questions. Let me go,
Or if thou follow me, do not believe
But I shall do thee mischief in the wood.

HELENA
Ay, in the temple, in the town, the field,   245
You do me mischief. Fie, Demetrius!
Your wrongs do set a scandal on my sex.
We cannot fight for love as men may do.
We should be wooed and were not made to woo.
                              ⌜*Demetrius exits.*⌝
I'll follow thee and make a heaven of hell   250
To die upon the hand I love so well.   ⌜*Helena exits.*⌝

OBERON
Fare thee well, nymph. Ere he do leave this grove,
Thou shalt fly him, and he shall seek thy love.

                    Enter ⌜*Robin.*⌝

Hast thou the flower there? Welcome, wanderer.

ROBIN
Ay, there it is.   255

OBERON   I pray thee give it me.
                    ⌜*Robin gives him the flower.*⌝
I know a bank where the wild thyme blows,
Where oxlips and the nodding violet grows,
Quite overcanopied with luscious woodbine,
With sweet muskroses, and with eglantine.   260
There sleeps Titania sometime of the night,
Lulled in these flowers with dances and delight.
And there the snake throws her enameled skin,
Weed wide enough to wrap a fairy in.
And with the juice of this I'll streak her eyes   265
And make her full of hateful fantasies.
Take thou some of it, and seek through this grove.

⌜*He gives Robin part of the flower.*⌝
A sweet Athenian lady is in love
With a disdainful youth. Anoint his eyes,
But do it when the next thing he espies   270
May be the lady. Thou shalt know the man
By the Athenian garments he hath on.
Effect it with some care, that he may prove
More fond on her than she upon her love.
And look thou meet me ere the first cock crow.   275

ROBIN
Fear not, my lord. Your servant shall do so.
                                        They exit.

⌜*Scene 2*⌝
Enter Titania, Queen of Fairies, with her train.

TITANIA
Come, now a roundel and a fairy song;
Then, for the third part of a minute, hence—
Some to kill cankers in the muskrose buds,
Some war with reremice for their leathern wings
To make my small elves coats, and some keep back   5
The clamorous owl that nightly hoots and wonders
At our quaint spirits. Sing me now asleep.
Then to your offices and let me rest.   ⌜*She lies down.*⌝

        Fairies sing.

⌜FIRST FAIRY⌝
        You spotted snakes with double tongue,
            Thorny hedgehogs, be not seen.   10
        Newts and blindworms, do no wrong,
            Come not near our Fairy Queen.
⌜CHORUS⌝
            Philomel, with melody
            Sing in our sweet lullaby.

Lulla, lulla, lullaby, lulla, lulla, lullaby.   15
　Never harm
　Nor spell nor charm
Come our lovely lady nigh.
So good night, with lullaby.

FIRST FAIRY
Weaving spiders, come not here.   20
　Hence, you long-legged spinners, hence.
Beetles black, approach not near.
　Worm nor snail, do no offence.

⌜CHORUS⌝
Philomel, with melody
Sing in our sweet lullaby.   25
Lulla, lulla, lullaby, lulla, lulla, lullaby.
　Never harm
　Nor spell nor charm
Come our lovely lady nigh.
So good night, with lullaby.   30
　　　　　　　　　　⌜*Titania sleeps.*⌝

SECOND FAIRY
Hence, away! Now all is well.
One aloof stand sentinel.　　　⌜*Fairies exit.*⌝

Enter Oberon, ⌜*who anoints Titania's eyelids with the nectar.*⌝

OBERON
What thou seest when thou dost wake,
Do it for thy true love take.
Love and languish for his sake.   35
Be it ounce, or cat, or bear,
Pard, or boar with bristled hair,
In thy eye that shall appear
When thou wak'st, it is thy dear.
Wake when some vile thing is near. ⌜*He exits.*⌝   40

Enter Lysander and Hermia.

LYSANDER
  Fair love, you faint with wand'ring in the wood.
    And, to speak troth, I have forgot our way.
  We'll rest us, Hermia, if you think it good,
    And tarry for the comfort of the day.

HERMIA
  ⌐Be¬ it so, Lysander. Find you out a bed,   45
  For I upon this bank will rest my head.

LYSANDER
  One turf shall serve as pillow for us both;
  One heart, one bed, two bosoms, and one troth.

HERMIA
  Nay, good Lysander. For my sake, my dear,
  Lie further off yet. Do not lie so near.   50

LYSANDER
  O, take the sense, sweet, of my innocence!
  Love takes the meaning in love's conference.
  I mean that my heart unto yours ⌐is¬ knit,
  So that but one heart we can make of it;
  Two bosoms interchainèd with an oath—   55
  So then two bosoms and a single troth.
  Then by your side no bed-room me deny,
  For lying so, Hermia, I do not lie.

HERMIA
  Lysander riddles very prettily.
  Now much beshrew my manners and my pride   60
  If Hermia meant to say Lysander lied.
  But, gentle friend, for love and courtesy,
  Lie further off in human modesty.
  Such separation, as may well be said,
  Becomes a virtuous bachelor and a maid.   65
  So far be distant; and good night, sweet friend.
  Thy love ne'er alter till thy sweet life end!

LYSANDER
  "Amen, amen" to that fair prayer, say I,
  And then end life when I end loyalty!
  Here is my bed. Sleep give thee all his rest!   70

HERMIA

With half that wish the wisher's eyes be pressed!
⌜*They sleep.*⌝

Enter ⌜*Robin.*⌝

ROBIN

Through the forest have I gone,
But Athenian found I none
On whose eyes I might approve
This flower's force in stirring love.   75
⌜*He sees Lysander.*⌝
Night and silence! Who is here?
Weeds of Athens he doth wear.
This is he my master said
Despisèd the Athenian maid.
And here the maiden, sleeping sound   80
On the dank and dirty ground.
Pretty soul, she durst not lie
Near this lack-love, this kill-courtesy.—
Churl, upon thy eyes I throw
All the power this charm doth owe.   85
⌜*He anoints Lysander's eyelids
with the nectar.*⌝
When thou wak'st, let love forbid
Sleep his seat on thy eyelid.
So, awake when I am gone,
For I must now to Oberon.   *He exits.*

Enter Demetrius and Helena, running.

HELENA

Stay, though thou kill me, sweet Demetrius.   90
DEMETRIUS

I charge thee, hence, and do not haunt me thus.
HELENA

O, wilt thou darkling leave me? Do not so.

DEMETRIUS
  Stay, on thy peril. I alone will go.　⌜*Demetrius exits.*⌝
HELENA
  O, I am out of breath in this fond chase.
  The more my prayer, the lesser is my grace.　　　　95
  Happy is Hermia, wheresoe'er she lies,
  For she hath blessèd and attractive eyes.
  How came her eyes so bright? Not with salt tears.
  If so, my eyes are oftener washed than hers.
  No, no, I am as ugly as a bear,　　　　　　　　100
  For beasts that meet me run away for fear.
  Therefore no marvel though Demetrius
  Do as a monster fly my presence thus.
  What wicked and dissembling glass of mine
  Made me compare with Hermia's sphery eyne?　　105
  But who is here? Lysander, on the ground!
  Dead or asleep? I see no blood, no wound.—
  Lysander, if you live, good sir, awake.
LYSANDER, ⌜*waking up*⌝
  And run through fire I will for thy sweet sake.
  Transparent Helena! Nature shows art,　　　　　110
  That through thy bosom makes me see thy heart.
  Where is Demetrius? O, how fit a word
  Is that vile name to perish on my sword!
HELENA
  Do not say so. Lysander, say not so.
  What though he love your Hermia? Lord, what　115
    though?
  Yet Hermia still loves you. Then be content.
LYSANDER
  Content with Hermia? No, I do repent
  The tedious minutes I with her have spent.
  Not Hermia, but Helena I love.　　　　　　　120
  Who will not change a raven for a dove?
  The will of man is by his reason swayed,
  And reason says you are the worthier maid.

Things growing are not ripe until their season;
So I, being young, till now ripe not to reason.   125
And touching now the point of human skill,
Reason becomes the marshal to my will
And leads me to your eyes, where I o'erlook
Love's stories written in love's richest book.

HELENA
Wherefore was I to this keen mockery born?   130
When at your hands did I deserve this scorn?
Is 't not enough, is 't not enough, young man,
That I did never, no, nor never can
Deserve a sweet look from Demetrius' eye,
But you must flout my insufficiency?   135
Good troth, you do me wrong, good sooth, you do,
In such disdainful manner me to woo.
But fare you well. Perforce I must confess
I thought you lord of more true gentleness.
O, that a lady of one man refused   140
Should of another therefore be abused!   *She exits.*

LYSANDER
She sees not Hermia.—Hermia, sleep thou there,
And never mayst thou come Lysander near.
For, as a surfeit of the sweetest things
The deepest loathing to the stomach brings,   145
Or as the heresies that men do leave
Are hated most of those they did deceive,
So thou, my surfeit and my heresy,
Of all be hated, but the most of me!
And, all my powers, address your love and might   150
To honor Helen and to be her knight.   *He exits.*

HERMIA, ⌈*waking up*⌉
Help me, Lysander, help me! Do thy best
To pluck this crawling serpent from my breast.
Ay me, for pity! What a dream was here!
Lysander, look how I do quake with fear.   155
Methought a serpent ate my heart away,

And you sat smiling at his cruel prey.
Lysander! What, removed? Lysander, lord!
What, out of hearing? Gone? No sound, no word?
Alack, where are you? Speak, an if you hear.   160
Speak, of all loves! I swoon almost with fear.—
No? Then I well perceive you are not nigh.
Either death or you I'll find immediately.

She exits.

⌜ACT 3⌝

⌜Scene 1⌝

⌜*With Titania still asleep onstage,*⌝ *enter the Clowns,*
⌜*Bottom, Quince, Snout, Starveling, Snug, and Flute.*⌝

BOTTOM   Are we all met?

QUINCE   Pat, pat. And here's a marvels convenient
place for our rehearsal. This green plot shall be
our stage, this hawthorn brake our tiring-house,
and we will do it in action as we will do it before   5
the Duke.

BOTTOM   Peter Quince?

QUINCE   What sayest thou, bully Bottom?

BOTTOM   There are things in this comedy of Pyramus
and Thisbe that will never please. First, Pyramus   10
must draw a sword to kill himself, which the ladies
cannot abide. How answer you that?

SNOUT   By 'r lakin, a parlous fear.

STARVELING   I believe we must leave the killing out,
when all is done.   15

BOTTOM   Not a whit! I have a device to make all well.
Write me a prologue, and let the prologue seem to
say we will do no harm with our swords, and that
Pyramus is not killed indeed. And, for the more
better assurance, tell them that I, Pyramus, am not   20
Pyramus, but Bottom the weaver. This will put them
out of fear.

192

QUINCE Well, we will have such a prologue, and it shall
be written in eight and six.

BOTTOM No, make it two more. Let it be written in 25
eight and eight.

SNOUT Will not the ladies be afeard of the lion?

STARVELING I fear it, I promise you.

BOTTOM Masters, you ought to consider with yourself,
to bring in (God shield us!) a lion among ladies is a 30
most dreadful thing. For there is not a more fearful
wildfowl than your lion living, and we ought to look
to 't.

SNOUT Therefore another prologue must tell he is not
a lion. 35

BOTTOM Nay, you must name his name, and half his
face must be seen through the lion's neck, and he
himself must speak through, saying thus, or to the
same defect: "Ladies," or "Fair ladies, I would
wish you," or "I would request you," or "I would 40
entreat you not to fear, not to tremble! My life for
yours. If you think I come hither as a lion, it were
pity of my life. No, I am no such thing. I am a man as
other men are." And there indeed let him name his
name and tell them plainly he is Snug the joiner. 45

QUINCE Well, it shall be so. But there is two hard
things: that is, to bring the moonlight into a chamber, for you know Pyramus and Thisbe meet by
moonlight.

SNOUT Doth the moon shine that night we play our 50
play?

BOTTOM A calendar, a calendar! Look in the almanac.
Find out moonshine, find out moonshine.
⌜*Quince takes out a book.*⌝

QUINCE Yes, it doth shine that night.

⌜BOTTOM⌝ Why, then, may you leave a casement of the 55
great chamber window, where we play, open, and
the moon may shine in at the casement.

QUINCE Ay, or else one must come in with a bush of
thorns and a lantern and say he comes to disfigure
or to present the person of Moonshine. Then there   60
is another thing: we must have a wall in the great
chamber, for Pyramus and Thisbe, says the story,
did talk through the chink of a wall.

SNOUT You can never bring in a wall. What say you,
Bottom?   65

BOTTOM Some man or other must present Wall. And
let him have some plaster, or some loam, or some
roughcast about him to signify wall, or let him
hold his fingers thus, and through that cranny shall
Pyramus and Thisbe whisper.   70

QUINCE If that may be, then all is well. Come, sit down,
every mother's son, and rehearse your parts. Pyramus, you begin. When you have spoken your
speech, enter into that brake, and so everyone
according to his cue.   75

Enter Robin ⌜*invisible to those onstage.*⌝

ROBIN, ⌜*aside*⌝
What hempen homespuns have we swagg'ring here
So near the cradle of the Fairy Queen?
What, a play toward? I'll be an auditor—
An actor too perhaps, if I see cause.

QUINCE Speak, Pyramus.—Thisbe, stand forth.   80

BOTTOM, *as Pyramus*
     Thisbe, the flowers of odious savors sweet—

QUINCE Odors, ⌜*odors!*⌝

BOTTOM, *as Pyramus*
                    . . . *odors savors sweet.*
     So hath thy breath, my dearest Thisbe dear.—
     But hark, a voice! Stay thou but here awhile,   85
     And by and by I will to thee appear.   He exits.

⌜ROBIN, *aside*⌝
A stranger Pyramus than e'er played here. ⌜*He exits.*⌝

FLUTE   Must I speak now?

QUINCE   Ay, marry, must you, for you must understand
he goes but to see a noise that he heard and is to   90
come again.

FLUTE, *as Thisbe*
    Most radiant Pyramus, most lily-white of hue,
    Of color like the red rose on triumphant brier,
    Most brisky juvenal and eke most lovely Jew,
    As true as truest horse, that yet would never tire.   95
    I'll meet thee, Pyramus, at Ninny's tomb.

QUINCE   "Ninus' tomb," man! Why, you must not
speak that yet. That you answer to Pyramus. You
speak all your part at once, cues and all.—Pyramus, enter. Your cue is past. It is "never tire."   100

FLUTE   O!
  ⌜*As Thisbe.*⌝ *As true as truest horse, that yet would never*
  tire.

    ⌜*Enter Robin, and Bottom as Pyramus with the*
               ass-head.⌝

BOTTOM, *as Pyramus*
    If I were fair, ⌜*fair*⌝ *Thisbe, I were only thine.*

QUINCE   O monstrous! O strange! We are haunted. Pray,   105
masters, fly, masters! Help!
    ⌜*Quince, Flute, Snout, Snug, and Starveling exit.*⌝

ROBIN
  I'll follow you. I'll lead you about a round,
    Through bog, through bush, through brake,
        through brier.
  Sometime a horse I'll be, sometime a hound,   110
    A hog, a headless bear, sometime a fire,
  And neigh, and bark, and grunt, and roar, and burn,
    Like horse, hound, hog, bear, fire, at every turn.
                        He exits.

BOTTOM   Why do they run away? This is a knavery of
them to make me afeard.   115

Enter Snout.

SNOUT   O Bottom, thou art changed! What do I see on
thee?

BOTTOM   What do you see? You see an ass-head of your
own, do you?   ⌐*Snout exits.*⌐

Enter Quince.

QUINCE   Bless thee, Bottom, bless thee! Thou art trans-   120
lated!   *He exits.*

BOTTOM   I see their knavery. This is to make an ass of
me, to fright me, if they could. But I will not stir
from this place, do what they can. I will walk up
and down here, and I will sing, that they shall hear   125
I am not afraid.

⌐*He sings.*⌐ *The ouzel cock, so black of hue,*
         With orange-tawny bill,
      The throstle with his note so true,
         The wren with little quill—   130

TITANIA, ⌐*waking up*⌐
What angel wakes me from my flow'ry bed?

BOTTOM ⌐*sings*⌐
      The finch, the sparrow, and the lark,
         The plainsong cuckoo gray,
      Whose note full many a man doth mark
         And dares not answer "nay"—   135
for, indeed, who would set his wit to so foolish a
bird? Who would give a bird the lie though he cry
"cuckoo" never so?

TITANIA
I pray thee, gentle mortal, sing again.
Mine ear is much enamored of thy note,   140
So is mine eye enthrallèd to thy shape,
And thy fair virtue's force perforce doth move me
On the first view to say, to swear, I love thee.

BOTTOM   Methinks, mistress, you should have little

reason for that. And yet, to say the truth, reason 145
and love keep little company together nowadays.
The more the pity that some honest neighbors will
not make them friends. Nay, I can gleek upon
occasion.

TITANIA
Thou art as wise as thou art beautiful.   150

BOTTOM   Not so neither; but if I had wit enough to get
out of this wood, I have enough to serve mine own
turn.

TITANIA
Out of this wood do not desire to go.
Thou shalt remain here whether thou wilt or no.   155
I am a spirit of no common rate.
The summer still doth tend upon my state,
And I do love thee. Therefore go with me.
I'll give thee fairies to attend on thee,
And they shall fetch thee jewels from the deep   160
And sing while thou on pressèd flowers dost sleep.
And I will purge thy mortal grossness so
That thou shalt like an airy spirit go.—
Peaseblossom, Cobweb, Mote, and Mustardseed!

*Enter four Fairies: ⌈Peaseblossom, Cobweb,
Mote, and Mustardseed.⌉*

⌈PEASEBLOSSOM⌉ Ready.   165
⌈COBWEB⌉ And I.
⌈MOTE⌉ And I.
⌈MUSTARDSEED⌉ And I.
⌈ALL⌉ Where shall we go?

TITANIA
Be kind and courteous to this gentleman.   170
Hop in his walks and gambol in his eyes;
Feed him with apricocks and dewberries,
With purple grapes, green figs, and mulberries;
The honey-bags steal from the humble-bees,

And for night-tapers crop their waxen thighs 175
And light them at the fiery glowworms' eyes
To have my love to bed and to arise;
And pluck the wings from painted butterflies
To fan the moonbeams from his sleeping eyes.
Nod to him, elves, and do him courtesies. 180

⌜PEASEBLOSSOM⌝ Hail, mortal!

⌜COBWEB⌝ Hail!

⌜MOTE⌝ Hail!

⌜MUSTARDSEED⌝ Hail!

BOTTOM I cry your Worships mercy, heartily.—I be- 185
seech your Worship's name.

COBWEB Cobweb.

BOTTOM I shall desire you of more acquaintance, good
Master Cobweb. If I cut my finger, I shall make
bold with you.—Your name, honest gentleman? 190

PEASEBLOSSOM Peaseblossom.

BOTTOM I pray you, commend me to Mistress Squash,
your mother, and to Master Peascod, your father.
Good Master Peaseblossom, I shall desire you of
more acquaintance, too.—Your name, I beseech 195
you, sir?

MUSTARDSEED Mustardseed.

BOTTOM Good Master Mustardseed, I know your patience well. That same cowardly, giantlike ox-beef
hath devoured many a gentleman of your house. I 200
promise you, your kindred hath made my eyes
water ere now. I desire you ⌜of⌝ more acquaintance, good Master Mustardseed.

TITANIA
Come, wait upon him. Lead him to my bower.
The moon, methinks, looks with a wat'ry eye, 205
And when she weeps, weeps every little flower,
Lamenting some enforcèd chastity.
Tie up my lover's tongue. Bring him silently.

⌜*They*⌝ *exit.*

⌐Scene 2⌐
Enter ⌐*Oberon,* ⌐ *King of Fairies.*

OBERON

I wonder if Titania be awaked;
Then what it was that next came in her eye,
Which she must dote on in extremity.

⌐*Enter Robin Goodfellow.*⌐

Here comes my messenger. How now, mad spirit?
What night-rule now about this haunted grove?   5

ROBIN

My mistress with a monster is in love.
Near to her close and consecrated bower,
While she was in her dull and sleeping hour,
A crew of patches, rude mechanicals,
That work for bread upon Athenian stalls,   10
Were met together to rehearse a play
Intended for great Theseus' nuptial day.
The shallowest thick-skin of that barren sort,
Who Pyramus presented in their sport,
Forsook his scene and entered in a brake.   15
When I did him at this advantage take,
An ass's noll I fixèd on his head.
Anon his Thisbe must be answerèd,
And forth my ⌐mimic⌐ comes. When they him spy,
As wild geese that the creeping fowler eye,   20
Or russet-pated choughs, many in sort,
Rising and cawing at the gun's report,
Sever themselves and madly sweep the sky,
So at his sight away his fellows fly,
And, at our stamp, here o'er and o'er one falls.   25
He "Murder" cries and help from Athens calls.
Their sense thus weak, lost with their fears thus
      strong,
Made senseless things begin to do them wrong;

For briers and thorns at their apparel snatch,   30
Some sleeves, some hats, from yielders all things
    catch.
I led them on in this distracted fear
And left sweet Pyramus translated there.
When in that moment, so it came to pass,   35
Titania waked and straightway loved an ass.

OBERON
This falls out better than I could devise.
But hast thou yet latched the Athenian's eyes
With the love juice, as I did bid thee do?

ROBIN
I took him sleeping—that is finished, too—   40
And the Athenian woman by his side,
That, when he waked, of force she must be eyed.

Enter Demetrius and Hermia.

OBERON
Stand close. This is the same Athenian.

ROBIN
This is the woman, but not this the man.
                                    ⌐*They step aside.*⌐

DEMETRIUS
O, why rebuke you him that loves you so?   45
Lay breath so bitter on your bitter foe!

HERMIA
Now I but chide, but I should use thee worse,
For thou, I fear, hast given me cause to curse.
If thou hast slain Lysander in his sleep,
Being o'er shoes in blood, plunge in the deep   50
And kill me too.
The sun was not so true unto the day
As he to me. Would he have stolen away
From sleeping Hermia? I'll believe as soon
This whole earth may be bored, and that the moon   55
May through the center creep and so displease

Her brother's noontide with th' Antipodes.
It cannot be but thou hast murdered him.
So should a murderer look, so dead, so grim.

DEMETRIUS
So should the murdered look, and so should I,   60
Pierced through the heart with your stern cruelty.
Yet you, the murderer, look as bright, as clear,
As yonder Venus in her glimmering sphere.

HERMIA
What's this to my Lysander? Where is he?
Ah, good Demetrius, wilt thou give him me?   65

DEMETRIUS
I had rather give his carcass to my hounds.

HERMIA
Out, dog! Out, cur! Thou driv'st me past the bounds
Of maiden's patience. Hast thou slain him, then?
Henceforth be never numbered among men.
O, once tell true! Tell true, even for my sake!   70
Durst thou have looked upon him, being awake?
And hast thou killed him sleeping? O brave touch!
Could not a worm, an adder, do so much?
An adder did it, for with doubler tongue
Than thine, thou serpent, never adder stung.   75

DEMETRIUS
You spend your passion on a misprised mood.
I am not guilty of Lysander's blood,
Nor is he dead, for aught that I can tell.

HERMIA
I pray thee, tell me then that he is well.

DEMETRIUS
An if I could, what should I get therefor?   80

HERMIA
A privilege never to see me more.
And from thy hated presence part I ⌜so.⌝
See me no more, whether he be dead or no.

                                        She exits.

DEMETRIUS
  There is no following her in this fierce vein.
  Here, therefore, for a while I will remain.   85
  So sorrow's heaviness doth heavier grow
  For debt that bankrout ⌜sleep⌝ doth sorrow owe,
  Which now in some slight measure it will pay,
  If for his tender here I make some stay.
               ⌜*He*⌝ *lies down* ⌜*and falls asleep.*⌝
OBERON, ⌜*to Robin*⌝
  What hast thou done? Thou hast mistaken quite   90
  And laid the love juice on some true-love's sight.
  Of thy misprision must perforce ensue
  Some true-love turned, and not a false turned true.
ROBIN
  Then fate o'errules, that, one man holding troth,
  A million fail, confounding oath on oath.   95
OBERON
  About the wood go swifter than the wind,
  And Helena of Athens look thou find.
  All fancy-sick she is and pale of cheer
  With sighs of love that costs the fresh blood dear.
  By some illusion see thou bring her here.   100
  I'll charm his eyes against she do appear.
ROBIN I go, I go, look how I go,
  Swifter than arrow from the Tartar's bow.   ⌜*He exits.*⌝
OBERON, ⌜*applying the nectar to Demetrius' eyes*⌝
      Flower of this purple dye,
      Hit with Cupid's archery,   105
      Sink in apple of his eye.
      When his love he doth espy,
      Let her shine as gloriously
      As the Venus of the sky.
      When thou wak'st, if she be by,   110
      Beg of her for remedy.

          Enter ⌜*Robin.*⌝

ROBIN

>   Captain of our fairy band,
>   Helena is here at hand,
>   And the youth, mistook by me,
>   Pleading for a lover's fee.   115
>   Shall we their fond pageant see?
>   Lord, what fools these mortals be!

OBERON

>   Stand aside. The noise they make
>   Will cause Demetrius to awake.

ROBIN

>   Then will two at once woo one.   120
>   That must needs be sport alone.
>   And those things do best please me
>   That befall prepost'rously.
>   ⌈*They step aside.*⌉

>   *Enter Lysander and Helena.*

LYSANDER
  Why should you think that I should woo in scorn?
    Scorn and derision never come in tears.   125
  Look when I vow, I weep; and vows so born,
    In their nativity all truth appears.
  How can these things in me seem scorn to you,
  Bearing the badge of faith to prove them true?

HELENA
  You do advance your cunning more and more.   130
    When truth kills truth, O devilish holy fray!
  These vows are Hermia's. Will you give her o'er?
    Weigh oath with oath, and you will nothing
      weigh.
  Your vows to her and me, put in two scales,   135
  Will even weigh, and both as light as tales.

LYSANDER
  I had no judgment when to her I swore.

HELENA
  Nor none, in my mind, now you give her o'er.

LYSANDER
  Demetrius loves her, and he loves not you.
DEMETRIUS, ⌜*waking up*⌝
  O Helen, goddess, nymph, perfect, divine!   140
  To what, my love, shall I compare thine eyne?
  Crystal is muddy. O, how ripe in show
  Thy lips, those kissing cherries, tempting grow!
  That pure congealèd white, high Taurus' snow,
  Fanned with the eastern wind, turns to a crow   145
  When thou hold'st up thy hand. O, let me kiss
  This princess of pure white, this seal of bliss!
HELENA
  O spite! O hell! I see you all are bent
  To set against me for your merriment.
  If you were civil and knew courtesy,   150
  You would not do me thus much injury.
  Can you not hate me, as I know you do,
  But you must join in souls to mock me too?
  If you were men, as men you are in show,
  You would not use a gentle lady so,   155
  To vow and swear and superpraise my parts,
  When, I am sure, you hate me with your hearts.
  You both are rivals and love Hermia,
  And now both rivals to mock Helena.
  A trim exploit, a manly enterprise,   160
  To conjure tears up in a poor maid's eyes
  With your derision! None of noble sort
  Would so offend a virgin and extort
  A poor soul's patience, all to make you sport.
LYSANDER
  You are unkind, Demetrius. Be not so,   165
  For you love Hermia; this you know I know.
  And here with all goodwill, with all my heart,
  In Hermia's love I yield you up my part.
  And yours of Helena to me bequeath,
  Whom I do love and will do till my death.   170

HELENA
Never did mockers waste more idle breath.
DEMETRIUS
Lysander, keep thy Hermia. I will none.
If e'er I loved her, all that love is gone.
My heart to her but as guest-wise sojourned,
And now to Helen is it home returned,   175
There to remain.
LYSANDER   Helen, it is not so.
DEMETRIUS
Disparage not the faith thou dost not know,
Lest to thy peril thou aby it dear.
Look where thy love comes. Yonder is thy dear.   180

Enter Hermia.

HERMIA, ⌈*to Lysander*⌉
Dark night, that from the eye his function takes,
The ear more quick of apprehension makes;
Wherein it doth impair the seeing sense,
It pays the hearing double recompense.
Thou art not by mine eye, Lysander, found;   185
Mine ear, I thank it, brought me to thy sound.
But why unkindly didst thou leave me so?
LYSANDER
Why should he stay whom love doth press to go?
HERMIA
What love could press Lysander from my side?
LYSANDER
Lysander's love, that would not let him bide,   190
Fair Helena, who more engilds the night
Than all yon fiery oes and eyes of light.
Why seek'st thou me? Could not this make thee
    know
The hate I bear thee made me leave thee so?   195
HERMIA
You speak not as you think. It cannot be.

HELENA
Lo, she is one of this confederacy!
Now I perceive they have conjoined all three
To fashion this false sport in spite of me.—
Injurious Hermia, most ungrateful maid,   200
Have you conspired, have you with these contrived,
To bait me with this foul derision?
Is all the counsel that we two have shared,
The sisters' vows, the hours that we have spent
When we have chid the hasty-footed time   205
For parting us—O, is all forgot?
All schooldays' friendship, childhood innocence?
We, Hermia, like two artificial gods,
Have with our needles created both one flower,
Both on one sampler, sitting on one cushion,   210
Both warbling of one song, both in one key,
As if our hands, our sides, voices, and minds
Had been incorporate. So we grew together
Like to a double cherry, seeming parted,
But yet an union in partition,   215
Two lovely berries molded on one stem;
So with two seeming bodies but one heart,
Two of the first, ⌜like⌝ coats in heraldry,
Due but to one, and crownèd with one crest.
And will you rent our ancient love asunder,   220
To join with men in scorning your poor friend?
It is not friendly; 'tis not maidenly.
Our sex, as well as I, may chide you for it,
Though I alone do feel the injury.
HERMIA
I am amazèd at your words.   225
I scorn you not. It seems that you scorn me.
HELENA
Have you not set Lysander, as in scorn,
To follow me and praise my eyes and face,
And made your other love, Demetrius,

Who even but now did spurn me with his foot,   230
To call me goddess, nymph, divine and rare,
Precious, celestial? Wherefore speaks he this
To her he hates? And wherefore doth Lysander
Deny your love (so rich within his soul)
And tender me, forsooth, affection,   235
But by your setting on, by your consent?
What though I be not so in grace as you,
So hung upon with love, so fortunate,
But miserable most, to love unloved?
This you should pity rather than despise.   240

HERMIA
I understand not what you mean by this.

HELENA
Ay, do. Persever, counterfeit sad looks,
Make mouths upon me when I turn my back,
Wink each at other, hold the sweet jest up.
This sport, well carried, shall be chronicled.   245
If you have any pity, grace, or manners,
You would not make me such an argument.
But fare you well. 'Tis partly my own fault,
Which death or absence soon shall remedy.

LYSANDER
Stay, gentle Helena. Hear my excuse,   250
My love, my life, my soul, fair Helena.

HELENA
O excellent!

HERMIA, ⌈*to Lysander*⌉
Sweet, do not scorn her so.

DEMETRIUS, ⌈*to Lysander*⌉
If she cannot entreat, I can compel.

LYSANDER
Thou canst compel no more than she entreat.   255
Thy threats have no more strength than her weak
   ⌈prayers.⌉—
Helen, I love thee. By my life, I do.

I swear by that which I will lose for thee,
To prove him false that says I love thee not.   260

DEMETRIUS
I say I love thee more than he can do.

LYSANDER
If thou say so, withdraw and prove it too.

DEMETRIUS
Quick, come.

HERMIA   Lysander, whereto tends all this?
                        ⌐*She takes hold of Lysander.*¬

LYSANDER
Away, you Ethiop!   265

DEMETRIUS, ⌐*to Hermia*¬
                        No, no. He'll
Seem to break loose. ⌐*To Lysander.*¬ Take on as you
    would follow,
But yet come not. You are a tame man, go!

LYSANDER, ⌐*to Hermia*¬
Hang off, thou cat, thou burr! Vile thing, let loose,   270
Or I will shake thee from me like a serpent.

HERMIA
Why are you grown so rude? What change is this,
Sweet love?

LYSANDER   Thy love? Out, tawny Tartar, out!
Out, loathèd med'cine! O, hated potion, hence!   275

HERMIA
Do you not jest?

HELENA   Yes, sooth, and so do you.

LYSANDER
Demetrius, I will keep my word with thee.

DEMETRIUS
I would I had your bond. For I perceive
A weak bond holds you. I'll not trust your word.   280

LYSANDER
What? Should I hurt her, strike her, kill her dead?
Although I hate her, I'll not harm her so.

HERMIA

What, can you do me greater harm than hate?
Hate me? Wherefore? O me, what news, my love?
Am not I Hermia? Are not you Lysander?　　285
I am as fair now as I was erewhile.
Since night you loved me; yet since night you left
　　me.
Why, then, you left me—O, the gods forbid!—
In earnest, shall I say?　　290

LYSANDER　　　　　　　　Ay, by my life,
And never did desire to see thee more.
Therefore be out of hope, of question, of doubt.
Be certain, nothing truer, 'tis no jest
That I do hate thee and love Helena.　　295

　　　　　　　　　　⌐*Hermia turns him loose.*⌐

HERMIA

O me! ⌐*To Helena.*⌐ You juggler, you cankerblossom,
You thief of love! What, have you come by night
And stol'n my love's heart from him?

HELENA　　　　　　　　　Fine, i' faith.
Have you no modesty, no maiden shame,　　300
No touch of bashfulness? What, will you tear
Impatient answers from my gentle tongue?
Fie, fie, you counterfeit, you puppet, you!

HERMIA

"Puppet"? Why so? Ay, that way goes the game.
Now I perceive that she hath made compare　　305
Between our statures; she hath urged her height,
And with her personage, her tall personage,
Her height, forsooth, she hath prevailed with him.
And are you grown so high in his esteem
Because I am so dwarfish and so low?　　310
How low am I, thou painted maypole? Speak!
How low am I? I am not yet so low
But that my nails can reach unto thine eyes.

HELENA
   I pray you, though you mock me, ⌈gentlemen,⌉
   Let her not hurt me. I was never curst;   315
   I have no gift at all in shrewishness.
   I am a right maid for my cowardice.
   Let her not strike me. You perhaps may think,
   Because she is something lower than myself,
   That I can match her.   320
HERMIA   "Lower"? Hark, again!
HELENA
   Good Hermia, do not be so bitter with me.
   I evermore did love you, Hermia,
   Did ever keep your counsels, never wronged you—
   Save that, in love unto Demetrius,   325
   I told him of your stealth unto this wood.
   He followed you; for love, I followed him.
   But he hath chid me hence and threatened me
   To strike me, spurn me, nay, to kill me too.
   And now, so you will let me quiet go,   330
   To Athens will I bear my folly back
   And follow you no further. Let me go.
   You see how simple and how fond I am.
HERMIA
   Why, get you gone. Who is 't that hinders you?
HELENA
   A foolish heart that I leave here behind.   335
HERMIA
   What, with Lysander?
HELENA   With Demetrius.
LYSANDER
   Be not afraid. She shall not harm thee, Helena.
DEMETRIUS
   No, sir, she shall not, though you take her part.
HELENA
   O, when she is angry, she is keen and shrewd.   340
   She was a vixen when she went to school,
   And though she be but little, she is fierce.

HERMIA
  "Little" again? Nothing ⌜but⌝ "low" and "little"?
  Why will you suffer her to flout me thus?
  Let me come to her.   345
LYSANDER   Get you gone, you dwarf,
  You minimus of hind'ring knotgrass made,
  You bead, you acorn—
DEMETRIUS   You are too officious
  In her behalf that scorns your services.   350
  Let her alone. Speak not of Helena.
  Take not her part. For if thou dost intend
  Never so little show of love to her,
  Thou shalt aby it.
LYSANDER   Now she holds me not.   355
  Now follow, if thou dar'st, to try whose right,
  Of thine or mine, is most in Helena.
DEMETRIUS
  "Follow"? Nay, I'll go with thee, cheek by jowl.
                      ⌜*Demetrius and Lysander exit.*⌝
HERMIA
  You, mistress, all this coil is long of you.
                            ⌜*Helena retreats.*⌝
  Nay, go not back.   360
HELENA   I will not trust you, I,
  Nor longer stay in your curst company.
  Your hands than mine are quicker for a fray.
  My legs are longer though, to run away.   ⌜*She exits.*⌝
HERMIA
  I am amazed and know not what to say.   ⌜*She exits.*⌝ 365
OBERON, ⌜*to Robin*⌝
  This is thy negligence. Still thou mistak'st,
  Or else committ'st thy knaveries willfully.
ROBIN
  Believe me, king of shadows, I mistook.
  Did not you tell me I should know the man
  By the Athenian garments he had on?   370

And so far blameless proves my enterprise
That I have 'nointed an Athenian's eyes;
And so far am I glad it so did sort,
As this their jangling I esteem a sport.

OBERON

Thou seest these lovers seek a place to fight.   375
Hie, therefore, Robin, overcast the night;
The starry welkin cover thou anon
With drooping fog as black as Acheron,
And lead these testy rivals so astray
As one come not within another's way.   380
Like to Lysander sometime frame thy tongue;
Then stir Demetrius up with bitter wrong.
And sometime rail thou like Demetrius.
And from each other look thou lead them thus,
Till o'er their brows death-counterfeiting sleep   385
With leaden legs and batty wings doth creep.
Then crush this herb into Lysander's eye,
                      ⌈*He gives the flower to Robin.*⌉
Whose liquor hath this virtuous property,
To take from thence all error with his might
And make his eyeballs roll with wonted sight.   390
When they next wake, all this derision
Shall seem a dream and fruitless vision.
And back to Athens shall the lovers wend,
With league whose date till death shall never end.
Whiles I in this affair do thee employ,   395
I'll to my queen and beg her Indian boy;
And then I will her charmèd eye release
From monster's view, and all things shall be peace.

ROBIN

My fairy lord, this must be done with haste,
For night's swift dragons cut the clouds full fast,   400
And yonder shines Aurora's harbinger,
At whose approach, ghosts wand'ring here and
    there

Troop home to churchyards. Damnèd spirits all,
That in crossways and floods have burial,   405
Already to their wormy beds are gone.
For fear lest day should look their shames upon,
They willfully themselves exile from light
And must for aye consort with black-browed night.

OBERON
But we are spirits of another sort.   410
I with the Morning's love have oft made sport
And, like a forester, the groves may tread
Even till the eastern gate, all fiery red,
Opening on Neptune with fair blessèd beams,
Turns into yellow gold his salt-green streams.   415
But notwithstanding, haste! Make no delay.
We may effect this business yet ere day.   ⌜*He exits.*⌝

ROBIN
            Up and down, up and down,
            I will lead them up and down.
            I am feared in field and town.   420
            Goblin, lead them up and down.
Here comes one.

                    Enter Lysander.

LYSANDER
Where art thou, proud Demetrius? Speak thou now.
ROBIN, ⌜*in Demetrius' voice*⌝
Here, villain, drawn and ready. Where art thou?
LYSANDER   I will be with thee straight.   425
ROBIN, ⌜*in Demetrius' voice*⌝   Follow me, then, to
plainer ground.   ⌜*Lysander exits.*⌝

                    Enter Demetrius.

DEMETRIUS   Lysander, speak again.
Thou runaway, thou coward, art thou fled?
Speak! In some bush? Where dost thou hide thy   430
    head?

ROBIN, ⌐*in Lysander's voice*⌐
  Thou coward, art thou bragging to the stars,
  Telling the bushes that thou look'st for wars,
  And wilt not come? Come, recreant! Come, thou
      child!   435
  I'll whip thee with a rod. He is defiled
  That draws a sword on thee.
DEMETRIUS   Yea, art thou there?
ROBIN, ⌐*in Lysander's voice*⌐
  Follow my voice. We'll try no manhood here.
                                      ⌐*They exit.*⌐

              ⌐*Enter Lysander.*⌐

LYSANDER
  He goes before me and still dares me on.   440
  When I come where he calls, then he is gone.
  The villain is much lighter-heeled than I.
  I followed fast, but faster he did fly,
  That fallen am I in dark uneven way,
  And here will rest me. Come, thou gentle day,   445
  For if but once thou show me thy gray light,
  I'll find Demetrius and revenge this spite.
                          ⌐*He lies down and sleeps.*⌐

          ⌐*Enter*⌐ *Robin and Demetrius.*

ROBIN, ⌐*in Lysander's voice*⌐
  Ho, ho, ho! Coward, why com'st thou not?
DEMETRIUS
  Abide me, if thou dar'st, for well I wot
  Thou runn'st before me, shifting every place,   450
  And dar'st not stand nor look me in the face.
  Where art thou now?
ROBIN, ⌐*in Lysander's voice*⌐
                      Come hither. I am here.
DEMETRIUS
  Nay, then, thou mock'st me. Thou shalt buy this
      dear   455

If ever I thy face by daylight see.
Now go thy way. Faintness constraineth me
To measure out my length on this cold bed.
By day's approach look to be visited.
⌐*He lies down and sleeps.* ⌐

Enter Helena.

HELENA
O weary night, O long and tedious night,   460
 Abate thy hours! Shine, comforts, from the east,
That I may back to Athens by daylight
 From these that my poor company detest.
And sleep, that sometimes shuts up sorrow's eye,
Steal me awhile from mine own company.   465
                    ⌐*She lies down and*⌐ *sleeps.*

ROBIN
            Yet but three? Come one more.
            Two of both kinds makes up four.
            Here she comes, curst and sad.
            Cupid is a knavish lad
            Thus to make poor females mad.   470

            ⌐*Enter Hermia.*⌐

HERMIA
Never so weary, never so in woe,
 Bedabbled with the dew and torn with briers,
I can no further crawl, no further go.
 My legs can keep no pace with my desires.
Here will I rest me till the break of day.   475
Heavens shield Lysander if they mean a fray!
                    ⌐*She lies down and sleeps.* ⌐
ROBIN
            On the ground
            Sleep sound.
            I'll apply
            ⌐To⌐ your eye,   480
            Gentle lover, remedy.

⌜*Robin applies the nectar
to Lysander's eyes.*⌝

When thou wak'st,
Thou tak'st
True delight
In the sight   485
Of thy former lady's eye.
And the country proverb known,
That every man should take his own,
In your waking shall be shown.
        Jack shall have Jill;   490
        Naught shall go ill;
The man shall have his mare again, and all shall be
    well.

⌜*He exits.*⌝

⌐ACT 4⌐

⌐Scene 1⌐

⌐With the four lovers still asleep onstage,⌐ enter
⌐Titania,⌐ Queen of Fairies, and ⌐Bottom⌐ and Fairies,
and ⌐Oberon,⌐ the King, behind them ⌐unseen by those
onstage.⌐

TITANIA
Come, sit thee down upon this flow'ry bed,
  While I thy amiable cheeks do coy,
And stick muskroses in thy sleek smooth head,
  And kiss thy fair large ears, my gentle joy.

BOTTOM Where's Peaseblossom?   5

PEASEBLOSSOM Ready.

BOTTOM Scratch my head, Peaseblossom. Where's
  Monsieur Cobweb?

COBWEB Ready.

BOTTOM Monsieur Cobweb, good monsieur, get you   10
  your weapons in your hand and kill me a red-hipped
  humble-bee on the top of a thistle, and, good
  monsieur, bring me the honey-bag. Do not fret
  yourself too much in the action, monsieur, and,
  good monsieur, have a care the honey-bag break   15
  not; I would be loath to have you overflown with a
  honey-bag, signior. ⌐*Cobweb exits.*⌐ Where's Monsieur Mustardseed?

MUSTARDSEED Ready.

217

BOTTOM   Give me your neaf, Monsieur Mustardseed.   20
    Pray you, leave your courtesy, good monsieur.
MUSTARDSEED   What's your will?
BOTTOM   Nothing, good monsieur, but to help Cava-
    lery Cobweb to scratch. I must to the barber's,
    monsieur, for methinks I am marvels hairy about   25
    the face. And I am such a tender ass, if my hair do
    but tickle me, I must scratch.
TITANIA
    What, wilt thou hear some music, my sweet love?
BOTTOM   I have a reasonable good ear in music. Let's
    have the tongs and the bones.   30
TITANIA
    Or say, sweet love, what thou desirest to eat.
BOTTOM   Truly, a peck of provender. I could munch
    your good dry oats. Methinks I have a great desire
    to a bottle of hay. Good hay, sweet hay, hath no
    fellow.   35
TITANIA
    I have a venturous fairy that shall seek
    The squirrel's hoard and fetch thee new nuts.
BOTTOM   I had rather have a handful or two of dried
    peas. But, I pray you, let none of your people stir
    me; I have an exposition of sleep come upon me.   40
TITANIA
    Sleep thou, and I will wind thee in my arms.—
    Fairies, begone, and be all ways away.
                                    ⌜*Fairies exit.*⌝
    So doth the woodbine the sweet honeysuckle
    Gently entwist; the female ivy so
    Enrings the barky fingers of the elm.   45
    O, how I love thee! How I dote on thee!
                          ⌜*Bottom and Titania sleep.*⌝

                Enter Robin Goodfellow.

OBERON
    Welcome, good Robin. Seest thou this sweet sight?

Her dotage now I do begin to pity.
For, meeting her of late behind the wood,
Seeking sweet favors for this hateful fool,   50
I did upbraid her and fall out with her.
For she his hairy temples then had rounded
With coronet of fresh and fragrant flowers;
And that same dew, which sometime on the buds
Was wont to swell like round and orient pearls,   55
Stood now within the pretty flouriets' eyes,
Like tears that did their own disgrace bewail.
When I had at my pleasure taunted her,
And she in mild terms begged my patience,
I then did ask of her her changeling child,   60
Which straight she gave me, and her fairy sent
To bear him to my bower in Fairyland.
And now I have the boy, I will undo
This hateful imperfection of her eyes.
And, gentle Puck, take this transformèd scalp   65
From off the head of this Athenian swain,
That he, awaking when the other do,
May all to Athens back again repair
And think no more of this night's accidents
But as the fierce vexation of a dream.   70
But first I will release the Fairy Queen.
                    ⌈*He applies the nectar to her eyes.*⌉
          Be as thou wast wont to be.
          See as thou wast wont to see.
          Dian's bud o'er Cupid's flower
          Hath such force and blessèd power.   75
     Now, my Titania, wake you, my sweet queen.
TITANIA, ⌈*waking*⌉
     My Oberon, what visions have I seen!
     Methought I was enamored of an ass.
OBERON
     There lies your love.
TITANIA   How came these things to pass?   80
     O, how mine eyes do loathe his visage now!

OBERON
    Silence awhile.—Robin, take off this head.—
    Titania, music call; and strike more dead
    Than common sleep of all these ⌈five⌉ the sense.
TITANIA
    Music, ho, music such as charmeth sleep!   85
ROBIN, ⌈*removing the ass-head from Bottom*⌉
    Now, when thou wak'st, with thine own fool's eyes
        peep.
OBERON
    Sound music.   ⌈*Music.*⌉
                Come, my queen, take hands with me,
    And rock the ground whereon these sleepers be.   90
                        ⌈*Titania and Oberon dance.*⌉
    Now thou and I are new in amity,
    And will tomorrow midnight solemnly
    Dance in Duke Theseus' house triumphantly,
    And bless it to all fair prosperity.
    There shall the pairs of faithful lovers be   95
    Wedded, with Theseus, all in jollity.
ROBIN
            Fairy king, attend and mark.
            I do hear the morning lark.
OBERON
            Then, my queen, in silence sad
            Trip we after night's shade.   100
            We the globe can compass soon,
            Swifter than the wand'ring moon.
TITANIA
            Come, my lord, and in our flight
            Tell me how it came this night
            That I sleeping here was found   105
            With these mortals on the ground.
                    ⌈*Oberon, Robin, and Titania*⌉ *exit.*

    Wind horn. Enter Theseus and all his train,
            ⌈*Hippolyta, Egeus.*⌉

THESEUS
  Go, one of you, find out the Forester.
  For now our observation is performed,
  And, since we have the vaward of the day,
  My love shall hear the music of my hounds.   110
  Uncouple in the western valley; let them go.
  Dispatch, I say, and find the Forester.
                                    ⌜*A Servant exits.*⌝
  We will, fair queen, up to the mountain's top
  And mark the musical confusion
  Of hounds and echo in conjunction.   115

HIPPOLYTA
  I was with Hercules and Cadmus once,
  When in a wood of Crete they bayed the bear
  With hounds of Sparta. Never did I hear
  Such gallant chiding, for, besides the groves,
  The skies, the fountains, every region near   120
  ⌜Seemed⌝ all one mutual cry. I never heard
  So musical a discord, such sweet thunder.

THESEUS
  My hounds are bred out of the Spartan kind,
  So flewed, so sanded; and their heads are hung
  With ears that sweep away the morning dew;   125
  Crook-kneed, and dewlapped like Thessalian bulls;
  Slow in pursuit, but matched in mouth like bells,
  Each under each. A cry more tunable
  Was never holloed to, nor cheered with horn,
  In Crete, in Sparta, nor in Thessaly.   130
  Judge when you hear.—But soft! What nymphs are
     these?

EGEUS
  My lord, this ⌜is⌝ my daughter here asleep,
  And this Lysander; this Demetrius is,
  This Helena, old Nedar's Helena.   135
  I wonder of their being here together.

THESEUS
No doubt they rose up early to observe
The rite of May, and hearing our intent,
Came here in grace of our solemnity.
But speak, Egeus. Is not this the day   140
That Hermia should give answer of her choice?
EGEUS   It is, my lord.
THESEUS
Go, bid the huntsmen wake them with their horns.
                              ⌜*A Servant exits.*⌝
              Shout within. Wind horns. They all start up.
THESEUS
Good morrow, friends. Saint Valentine is past.
Begin these woodbirds but to couple now?   145
      ⌜*Demetrius, Helena, Hermia, and Lysander kneel.*⌝
LYSANDER
Pardon, my lord.
THESEUS   I pray you all, stand up.
                                        ⌜*They rise.*⌝
I know you two are rival enemies.
How comes this gentle concord in the world,
That hatred is so far from jealousy   150
To sleep by hate and fear no enmity?
LYSANDER
My lord, I shall reply amazèdly,
Half sleep, half waking. But as yet, I swear,
I cannot truly say how I came here.
But, as I think—for truly would I speak,   155
And now I do bethink me, so it is:
I came with Hermia hither. Our intent
Was to be gone from Athens, where we might,
Without the peril of the Athenian law—
EGEUS
Enough, enough!—My lord, you have enough.   160
I beg the law, the law, upon his head.
They would have stol'n away.—They would,
  Demetrius,

Thereby to have defeated you and me:
You of your wife and me of my consent,   165
Of my consent that she should be your wife.

DEMETRIUS
My lord, fair Helen told me of their stealth,
Of this their purpose hither to this wood,
And I in fury hither followed them,
Fair Helena in fancy following me.   170
But, my good lord, I wot not by what power
(But by some power it is) my love to Hermia,
Melted as the snow, seems to me now
As the remembrance of an idle gaud
Which in my childhood I did dote upon,   175
And all the faith, the virtue of my heart,
The object and the pleasure of mine eye,
Is only Helena. To her, my lord,
Was I betrothed ere I ⌜saw⌝ Hermia.
But like a sickness did I loathe this food.   180
But, as in health, come to my natural taste,
Now I do wish it, love it, long for it,
And will forevermore be true to it.

THESEUS
Fair lovers, you are fortunately met.
Of this discourse we more will hear anon.—   185
Egeus, I will overbear your will,
For in the temple by and by, with us,
These couples shall eternally be knit.—
And, for the morning now is something worn,
Our purposed hunting shall be set aside.   190
Away with us to Athens. Three and three,
We'll hold a feast in great solemnity.
Come, Hippolyta.

                    ⌜*Theseus and his train,*
              including Hippolyta and Egeus, exit.⌝

DEMETRIUS
These things seem small and undistinguishable,
Like far-off mountains turnèd into clouds.   195

HERMIA
　Methinks I see these things with parted eye,
　When everything seems double.
HELENA   So methinks.
　And I have found Demetrius like a jewel,
　Mine own and not mine own.   200
DEMETRIUS   Are you sure
　That we are awake? It seems to me
　That yet we sleep, we dream. Do not you think
　The Duke was here and bid us follow him?
HERMIA
　Yea, and my father.   205
HELENA   And Hippolyta.
LYSANDER
　And he did bid us follow to the temple.
DEMETRIUS
　Why, then, we are awake. Let's follow him,
　And by the way let ⌜us⌝ recount our dreams.
                                              ⌜*Lovers exit.*⌝
BOTTOM, ⌜*waking up*⌝ When my cue comes, call me,   210
　and I will answer. My next is "Most fair Pyramus."
　Hey-ho! Peter Quince! Flute the bellows-mender!
　Snout the tinker! Starveling! God's my life! Stolen
　hence and left me asleep! I have had a most rare
　vision. I have had a dream past the wit of man to say   215
　what dream it was. Man is but an ass if he go about
　⌜to⌝ expound this dream. Methought I was—there
　is no man can tell what. Methought I was and
　methought I had—but man is but ⌜a patched⌝ fool if
　he will offer to say what methought I had. The eye of   220
　man hath not heard, the ear of man hath not seen,
　man's hand is not able to taste, his tongue to
　conceive, nor his heart to report what my dream
　was. I will get Peter Quince to write a ballad of this
　dream. It shall be called "Bottom's Dream" be-   225
　cause it hath no bottom; and I will sing it in the

latter end of a play, before the Duke. Peradventure,
to make it the more gracious, I shall sing it at her
death.

⌐*He exits.*⌐

⌐Scene 2⌐
Enter Quince, Flute, ⌐Snout, and Starveling.⌐

QUINCE Have you sent to Bottom's house? Is he come
home yet?

⌐STARVELING⌐ He cannot be heard of. Out of doubt he
is transported.

FLUTE If he come not, then the play is marred. It goes   5
not forward, doth it?

QUINCE It is not possible. You have not a man in all
Athens able to discharge Pyramus but he.

FLUTE No, he hath simply the best wit of any handi-
craftman in Athens.   10

QUINCE Yea, and the best person too, and he is a very
paramour for a sweet voice.

FLUTE You must say "paragon." A "paramour" is (God
bless us) a thing of naught.

Enter Snug the joiner.

SNUG Masters, the Duke is coming from the temple,   15
and there is two or three lords and ladies more
married. If our sport had gone forward, we had all
been made men.

FLUTE O, sweet bully Bottom! Thus hath he lost six
pence a day during his life. He could not have   20
'scaped six pence a day. An the Duke had not given
him six pence a day for playing Pyramus, I'll be
hanged. He would have deserved it. Six pence a day
in Pyramus, or nothing!

Enter Bottom.

BOTTOM Where are these lads? Where are these   25
  hearts?
QUINCE Bottom! O most courageous day! O most happy hour!
BOTTOM Masters, I am to discourse wonders. But ask
  me not what; for, if I tell you, I am not true   30
  Athenian. I will tell you everything right as it fell
  out.
QUINCE Let us hear, sweet Bottom.
BOTTOM Not a word of me. All that I will tell you is that
  the Duke hath dined. Get your apparel together,   35
  good strings to your beards, new ribbons to your
  pumps. Meet presently at the palace. Every man
  look o'er his part. For the short and the long is, our
  play is preferred. In any case, let Thisbe have clean
  linen, and let not him that plays the lion pare his   40
  nails, for they shall hang out for the lion's claws.
  And, most dear actors, eat no onions nor garlic, for
  we are to utter sweet breath, and I do not doubt but
  to hear them say it is a sweet comedy. No more
  words. Away! Go, away!   45
                                ⌜*They exit.*⌝

⌜ACT 5⌝

⌜Scene 1⌝

Enter Theseus, Hippolyta, and Philostrate, ⌜Lords, and Attendants.⌝

HIPPOLYTA
'Tis strange, my Theseus, that these lovers speak of.
THESEUS
More strange than true. I never may believe
These antique fables, nor these fairy toys.
Lovers and madmen have such seething brains,
Such shaping fantasies, that apprehend   5
More than cool reason ever comprehends.
The lunatic, the lover, and the poet
Are of imagination all compact.
One sees more devils than vast hell can hold:
That is the madman. The lover, all as frantic,   10
Sees Helen's beauty in a brow of Egypt.
The poet's eye, in a fine frenzy rolling,
Doth glance from heaven to earth, from earth to
    heaven,
And as imagination bodies forth   15
The forms of things unknown, the poet's pen
Turns them to shapes and gives to airy nothing
A local habitation and a name.
Such tricks hath strong imagination
That, if it would but apprehend some joy,   20

It comprehends some bringer of that joy.
Or in the night, imagining some fear,
How easy is a bush supposed a bear!

HIPPOLYTA
But all the story of the night told over,
And all their minds transfigured so together,   25
More witnesseth than fancy's images
And grows to something of great constancy,
But, howsoever, strange and admirable.

Enter Lovers: Lysander, Demetrius, Hermia, and Helena.

THESEUS
Here come the lovers full of joy and mirth.—
Joy, gentle friends! Joy and fresh days of love   30
Accompany your hearts!

LYSANDER   More than to us
Wait in your royal walks, your board, your bed!

THESEUS
Come now, what masques, what dances shall we
  have   35
To wear away this long age of three hours
Between ⌜our⌝ after-supper and bedtime?
Where is our usual manager of mirth?
What revels are in hand? Is there no play
To ease the anguish of a torturing hour?   40
Call Philostrate.

PHILOSTRATE, ⌜*coming forward*⌝
                    Here, mighty Theseus.

THESEUS
Say what abridgment have you for this evening,
What masque, what music? How shall we beguile
The lazy time if not with some delight?   45

PHILOSTRATE, ⌜*giving Theseus a paper*⌝
There is a brief how many sports are ripe.
Make choice of which your Highness will see first.

THESEUS
  "The battle with the Centaurs, to be sung
  By an Athenian eunuch to the harp."
  We'll none of that. That have I told my love   50
  In glory of my kinsman Hercules.
  "The riot of the tipsy Bacchanals,
  Tearing the Thracian singer in their rage."
  That is an old device, and it was played
  When I from Thebes came last a conqueror.   55
  "The thrice-three Muses mourning for the death
  Of learning, late deceased in beggary."
  That is some satire, keen and critical,
  Not sorting with a nuptial ceremony.
  "A tedious brief scene of young Pyramus   60
  And his love Thisbe, very tragical mirth."
  "Merry" and "tragical"? "Tedious" and "brief"?
  That is hot ice and wondrous strange snow!
  How shall we find the concord of this discord?
PHILOSTRATE
  A play there is, my lord, some ten words long   65
  (Which is as brief as I have known a play),
  But by ten words, my lord, it is too long,
  Which makes it tedious; for in all the play,
  There is not one word apt, one player fitted.
  And tragical, my noble lord, it is.   70
  For Pyramus therein doth kill himself,
  Which, when I saw rehearsed, I must confess,
  Made mine eyes water; but more merry tears
  The passion of loud laughter never shed.
THESEUS
  What are they that do play it?   75
PHILOSTRATE
  Hard-handed men that work in Athens here,
  Which never labored in their minds till now,
  And now have toiled their unbreathed memories
  With this same play, against your nuptial.

THESEUS
  And we will hear it.   80
PHILOSTRATE   No, my noble lord,
  It is not for you. I have heard it over,
  And it is nothing, nothing in the world,
  Unless you can find sport in their intents,
  Extremely stretched and conned with cruel pain   85
  To do you service.
THESEUS   I will hear that play,
  For never anything can be amiss
  When simpleness and duty tender it.
  Go, bring them in—and take your places, ladies.   90
                           ⌜*Philostrate exits.*⌝

HIPPOLYTA
  I love not to see wretchedness o'ercharged,
  And duty in his service perishing.
THESEUS
  Why, gentle sweet, you shall see no such thing.
HIPPOLYTA
  He says they can do nothing in this kind.
THESEUS
  The kinder we, to give them thanks for nothing.   95
  Our sport shall be to take what they mistake;
  And what poor duty cannot do, noble respect
  Takes it in might, not merit.
  Where I have come, great clerks have purposèd
  To greet me with premeditated welcomes,   100
  Where I have seen them shiver and look pale,
  Make periods in the midst of sentences,
  Throttle their practiced accent in their fears,
  And in conclusion dumbly have broke off,
  Not paying me a welcome. Trust me, sweet,   105
  Out of this silence yet I picked a welcome,
  And in the modesty of fearful duty,
  I read as much as from the rattling tongue
  Of saucy and audacious eloquence.

Love, therefore, and tongue-tied simplicity   110
In least speak most, to my capacity.

⌈*Enter Philostrate.*⌉

PHILOSTRATE
So please your Grace, the Prologue is addressed.
THESEUS   Let him approach.

Enter the Prologue.

PROLOGUE
If we offend, it is with our goodwill.
    That you should think we come not to offend,   115
But with goodwill. To show our simple skill,
    That is the true beginning of our end.
Consider, then, we come but in despite.
    We do not come, as minding to content you,
Our true intent is. All for your delight   120
    We are not here. That you should here repent
        you,
The actors are at hand, and, by their show,
You shall know all that you are like to know.
                            ⌈*Prologue exits.*⌉
THESEUS   This fellow doth not stand upon points.   125
LYSANDER   He hath rid his prologue like a rough colt;
    he knows not the stop. A good moral, my lord: it is
    not enough to speak, but to speak true.
HIPPOLYTA   Indeed he hath played on this prologue like
    a child on a recorder—a sound, but not in govern-   130
    ment.
THESEUS   His speech was like a tangled chain—noth-
    ing impaired, but all disordered. Who is next?

Enter Pyramus ⌈*(Bottom),*⌉ *and Thisbe* ⌈*(Flute),*⌉ *and
Wall* ⌈*(Snout),*⌉ *and Moonshine* ⌈*(Starveling),*⌉ *and Lion
        ⌈(Snug),*⌉⌈*and Prologue (Quince).*⌉

QUINCE, *as Prologue*
Gentles, perchance you wonder at this show.

But wonder on, till truth make all things plain.   135
This man is Pyramus, if you would know.
  This beauteous lady Thisbe is certain.
This man with lime and roughcast doth present
  "Wall," that vile wall which did these lovers
      sunder;   140
And through Wall's chink, poor souls, they are
      content
  To whisper, at the which let no man wonder.
This man, with lantern, dog, and bush of thorn,
  Presenteth "Moonshine," for, if you will know,   145
By moonshine did these lovers think no scorn
  To meet at Ninus' tomb, there, there to woo.
This grisly beast (which "Lion" hight by name)
  The trusty Thisbe coming first by night
Did ⌜scare⌝ away, or rather did affright;   150
  And, as she fled, her mantle she did fall,
  Which Lion vile with bloody mouth did stain.
Anon comes Pyramus, sweet youth and tall,
  And finds his trusty Thisbe's mantle slain.
Whereat, with blade, with bloody blameful blade,   155
  He bravely broached his boiling bloody breast.
And Thisbe, tarrying in mulberry shade,
  His dagger drew, and died. For all the rest,
Let Lion, Moonshine, Wall, and lovers twain
At large discourse, while here they do remain.   160
THESEUS I wonder if the lion be to speak.
DEMETRIUS No wonder, my lord. One lion may when
    many asses do.
          Lion, Thisbe, Moonshine, ⌜*and Prologue*⌝ *exit.*
SNOUT, *as Wall*
In this same interlude it doth befall
That I, one ⌜Snout⌝ by name, present a wall;   165
And such a wall as I would have you think
That had in it a crannied hole or chink,
Through which the lovers, Pyramus and Thisbe,

Did whisper often, very secretly.
This loam, this roughcast, and this stone doth show   170
That I am that same wall. The truth is so.
And this the cranny is, right and sinister,
Through which the fearful lovers are to whisper.

THESEUS   Would you desire lime and hair to speak
better?   175

DEMETRIUS   It is the wittiest partition that ever I heard
discourse, my lord.

THESEUS   Pyramus draws near the wall. Silence.

BOTTOM, *as Pyramus*
O grim-looked night! O night with hue so black!
O night, which ever art when day is not!   180
O night! O night! Alack, alack, alack!
I fear my Thisbe's promise is forgot.
And thou, O wall, O sweet, O lovely wall,
That stand'st between her father's ground and
mine,   185
Thou wall, O wall, O sweet and lovely wall,
Show me thy chink to blink through with mine
eyne.
Thanks, courteous wall. Jove shield thee well for
this.   190
But what see I? No Thisbe do I see.
O wicked wall, through whom I see no bliss,
Cursed be thy stones for thus deceiving me!

THESEUS   The wall, methinks, being sensible, should
curse again.   195

BOTTOM   No, in truth, sir, he should not. "Deceiving
me" is Thisbe's cue. She is to enter now, and I am
to spy her through the wall. You shall see it will fall
pat as I told you. Yonder she comes.

Enter Thisbe ⌈(Flute).⌉

FLUTE, *as Thisbe*
O wall, full often hast thou heard my moans   200

For parting my fair Pyramus and me.
My cherry lips have often kissed thy stones,
   Thy stones with lime and hair knit ⌈up in thee.⌉
BOTTOM, *as Pyramus*
I see a voice! Now will I to the chink
   To spy an I can hear my Thisbe's face.   205
Thisbe?
FLUTE, *as Thisbe*
            My love! Thou art my love, I think.
BOTTOM, *as Pyramus*
   Think what thou wilt, I am thy lover's grace,
   And, like Limander, am I trusty still.
FLUTE, *as Thisbe*
   And I like Helen, till the Fates me kill.   210
BOTTOM, *as Pyramus*
   Not Shafalus to Procrus was so true.
FLUTE, *as Thisbe*
   As Shafalus to Procrus, I to you.
BOTTOM, *as Pyramus*
   O kiss me through the hole of this vile wall.
FLUTE, *as Thisbe*
   I kiss the wall's hole, not your lips at all.
BOTTOM, *as Pyramus*
   Wilt thou at Ninny's tomb meet me straightway?   215
FLUTE, *as Thisbe*
   'Tide life, 'tide death, I come without delay.
                              ⌈*Bottom and Flute exit.*⌉
SNOUT, *as Wall*
   Thus have I, Wall, my part dischargèd so,
   And, being done, thus Wall away doth go.   ⌈*He exits.*⌉
THESEUS Now is the ⌈wall down⌉ between the two
   neighbors.   220
DEMETRIUS No remedy, my lord, when walls are so
   willful to hear without warning.
HIPPOLYTA This is the silliest stuff that ever I heard.
THESEUS The best in this kind are but shadows, and

the worst are no worse, if imagination amend 225
them.
HIPPOLYTA It must be your imagination, then, and not
theirs.
THESEUS If we imagine no worse of them than they of
themselves, they may pass for excellent men. Here 230
come two noble beasts in, a man and a lion.

Enter Lion ⌈(Snug)⌉ and Moonshine ⌈(Starveling).⌉

SNUG, *as Lion*
You ladies, you whose gentle hearts do fear
    The smallest monstrous mouse that creeps on
        floor,
May now perchance both quake and tremble here, 235
    When lion rough in wildest rage doth roar.
Then know that I, as Snug the joiner, am
A lion fell, nor else no lion's dam;
For if I should as lion come in strife
Into this place, 'twere pity on my life. 240
THESEUS A very gentle beast, and of a good con-
science.
DEMETRIUS The very best at a beast, my lord, that e'er I
saw.
LYSANDER This lion is a very fox for his valor. 245
THESEUS True, and a goose for his discretion.
DEMETRIUS Not so, my lord, for his valor cannot carry
his discretion, and the fox carries the goose.
THESEUS His discretion, I am sure, cannot carry his
valor, for the goose carries not the fox. It is well. 250
Leave it to his discretion, and let us listen to the
Moon.
STARVELING, *as Moonshine*
This lanthorn doth the hornèd moon present.
DEMETRIUS He should have worn the horns on his
head. 255
THESEUS He is no crescent, and his horns are invisible
within the circumference.

STARVELING, *as Moonshine*
    This lanthorn doth the hornèd moon present.
    Myself the man i' th' moon do seem to be.
THESEUS   This is the greatest error of all the rest; the   260
    man should be put into the lanthorn. How is it else
    "the man i' th' moon"?
DEMETRIUS   He dares not come there for the candle,
    for you see, it is already in snuff.
HIPPOLYTA   I am aweary of this moon. Would he would   265
    change.
THESEUS   It appears by his small light of discretion that
    he is in the wane; but yet, in courtesy, in all reason,
    we must stay the time.
LYSANDER   Proceed, Moon.   270
STARVELING, *as Moonshine*   All that I have to say is to tell
    you that the lanthorn is the moon, I the man i' th'
    moon, this thornbush my thornbush, and this dog
    my dog.
DEMETRIUS   Why, all these should be in the lanthorn,   275
    for all these are in the moon. But silence. Here
    comes Thisbe.

            Enter Thisbe ⌈(Flute).⌉

FLUTE, *as Thisbe*
    This is old Ninny's tomb. Where is my love?
SNUG, *as Lion*   O!
                    ⌈*The Lion roars. Thisbe runs off,*
                        dropping her mantle.⌉
DEMETRIUS   Well roared, Lion.   280
THESEUS   Well run, Thisbe.
HIPPOLYTA   Well shone, Moon. Truly, the Moon shines
    with a good grace.
                    ⌈*Lion worries the mantle.*⌉
THESEUS   Well moused, Lion.

            Enter Pyramus ⌈(Bottom).⌉

DEMETRIUS   And then came Pyramus.   285

⌜*Lion exits.*⌝

LYSANDER   And so the lion vanished.

BOTTOM, *as Pyramus*

Sweet Moon, I thank thee for thy sunny beams.
   I thank thee, Moon, for shining now so bright,
For by thy gracious, golden, glittering ⌜gleams,⌝
   I trust to take of truest Thisbe sight.—   290
      But stay! O spite!
      But mark, poor knight,
   What dreadful dole is here!
      Eyes, do you see!
      How can it be!   295
   O dainty duck! O dear!
      Thy mantle good—
   What, stained with blood?
   Approach, ye Furies fell!
      O Fates, come, come,   300
      Cut thread and thrum,
   Quail, crush, conclude, and quell!

THESEUS   This passion, and the death of a dear friend,
   would go near to make a man look sad.

HIPPOLYTA   Beshrew my heart but I pity the man.   305

BOTTOM, *as Pyramus*

O, wherefore, Nature, didst thou lions frame,
Since lion vile hath here deflowered my dear,
Which is—no, no—which was the fairest dame
That lived, that loved, that liked, that looked with
   cheer?   310
      Come, tears, confound!
      Out, sword, and wound
   The pap of Pyramus;
      Ay, that left pap,
      Where heart doth hop.   ⌜*Pyramus stabs himself.*⌝ 315
   Thus die I, thus, thus, thus.
      Now am I dead;

    Now am I fled;
My soul is in the sky.
    Tongue, lose thy light!   320
    Moon, take thy flight!   ⌈*Moonshine exits.*⌉
Now die, die, die, die, die.   ⌈*Pyramus falls.*⌉

DEMETRIUS No die, but an ace, for him, for he is but
    one.

LYSANDER Less than an ace, man, for he is dead, he is 325
    nothing.

THESEUS With the help of a surgeon he might yet
    recover and yet prove an ass.

HIPPOLYTA How chance Moonshine is gone before
    Thisbe comes back and finds her lover?   330

THESEUS She will find him by starlight.

⌈*Enter Thisbe (Flute).*⌉

Here she comes, and her passion ends the play.

HIPPOLYTA Methinks she should not use a long one for
    such a Pyramus. I hope she will be brief.

DEMETRIUS A mote will turn the balance, which Pyra- 335
    mus, which Thisbe, is the better: he for a man, God
    warrant us; she for a woman, God bless us.

LYSANDER She hath spied him already with those
    sweet eyes.

DEMETRIUS And thus she means, *videlicet*—   340

FLUTE, *as Thisbe*
    Asleep, my love?
    What, dead, my dove?
O Pyramus, arise!
    Speak, speak. Quite dumb?
    Dead? Dead? A tomb   345
Must cover thy sweet eyes.
    These lily lips,
    This cherry nose,
These yellow cowslip cheeks
    Are gone, are gone!   350

       Lovers, make moan;
      His eyes were green as leeks.
       O Sisters Three,
       Come, come to me
      With hands as pale as milk.   355
       Lay them in gore,
       Since you have shore
      With shears his thread of silk.
       Tongue, not a word!
       Come, trusty sword,   360
      Come, blade, my breast imbrue!
          ⌈*Thisbe stabs herself.*⌉

      And farewell, friends.
      Thus Thisbe ends.
     Adieu, adieu, adieu.   ⌈*Thisbe falls.*⌉

THESEUS Moonshine and Lion are left to bury the 365
    dead.

DEMETRIUS Ay, and Wall too.
             ⌈*Bottom and Flute arise.*⌉

⌈BOTTOM⌉ No, I assure you, the wall is down that
    parted their fathers. Will it please you to see the
    Epilogue or to hear a Bergomask dance between 370
    two of our company?

THESEUS No epilogue, I pray you. For your play needs
    no excuse. Never excuse. For when the players are
    all dead, there need none to be blamed. Marry, if
    he that writ it had played Pyramus and hanged 375
    himself in Thisbe's garter, it would have been a fine
    tragedy; and so it is, truly, and very notably dis-
    charged. But, come, your Bergomask. Let your
    epilogue alone.
           ⌈*Dance, and the players exit.*⌉

The iron tongue of midnight hath told twelve.   380
Lovers, to bed! 'Tis almost fairy time.
I fear we shall outsleep the coming morn
As much as we this night have overwatched.

This palpable-gross play hath well beguiled
The heavy gait of night. Sweet friends, to bed.   385
A fortnight hold we this solemnity
In nightly revels and new jollity.   *They exit.*

        Enter ⌜Robin Goodfellow.⌝

ROBIN
    Now the hungry ⌜lion⌝ roars,
      And the wolf ⌜behowls⌝ the moon,
    Whilst the heavy plowman snores,   390
      All with weary task fordone.
    Now the wasted brands do glow,
      Whilst the screech-owl, screeching loud,
    Puts the wretch that lies in woe
      In remembrance of a shroud.   395
    Now it is the time of night
      That the graves, all gaping wide,
    Every one lets forth his sprite
      In the church-way paths to glide.
    And we fairies, that do run   400
      By the triple Hecate's team
    From the presence of the sun,
      Following darkness like a dream,
    Now are frolic. Not a mouse
    Shall disturb this hallowed house.   405
    I am sent with broom before,
    To sweep the dust behind the door.

Enter ⌜Oberon and Titania,⌝ King and Queen of Fairies,
        with all their train.

OBERON
    Through the house give glimmering light,
      By the dead and drowsy fire.
    Every elf and fairy sprite,   410
      Hop as light as bird from brier,
    And this ditty after me,
    Sing and dance it trippingly.

TITANIA

    First rehearse your song by rote,
    To each word a warbling note.   415
    Hand in hand, with fairy grace,
    Will we sing and bless this place.
       ⌜*Oberon leads the Fairies in song and dance.*⌝

OBERON

    Now, until the break of day,
    Through this house each fairy stray.
    To the best bride-bed will we,   420
    Which by us shall blessèd be,
    And the issue there create
    Ever shall be fortunate.
    So shall all the couples three
    Ever true in loving be,   425
    And the blots of Nature's hand
    Shall not in their issue stand.
    Never mole, harelip, nor scar,
    Nor mark prodigious, such as are
    Despisèd in nativity,   430
    Shall upon their children be.
    With this field-dew consecrate
    Every fairy take his gait,
    And each several chamber bless,
    Through this palace, with sweet peace.   435
    And the owner of it blest,
    Ever shall in safety rest.
    Trip away. Make no stay.
    Meet me all by break of day.
              ⌜*All but Robin*⌝ *exit.*

ROBIN

    If we shadows have offended,   440
    Think but this and all is mended:
    That you have but slumbered here
    While these visions did appear.
    And this weak and idle theme,

No more yielding but a dream,   445
Gentles, do not reprehend.
If you pardon, we will mend.
And, as I am an honest Puck,
If we have unearnèd luck
Now to 'scape the serpent's tongue,   450
We will make amends ere long.
Else the Puck a liar call.
So good night unto you all.
Give me your hands, if we be friends,
And Robin shall restore amends.   455

⌜*He exits.*⌝

Explanatory Notes

1.1 Theseus, duke of Athens, is planning the festivities for his upcoming wedding to the newly captured Amazon, Hippolyta. Egeus arrives with his daughter Hermia and her two suitors, Lysander (the man she wants to marry) and Demetrius (the man her father wants her to marry). Egeus demands that Theseus enforce Athenian law upon Hermia and execute her if she refuses to marry Demetrius. Theseus threatens Hermia with either lifelong chastity or death if she continues to disobey her father. Lysander and Hermia make plans to flee Athens. They reveal their plan to Helena, Hermia's friend, who is in love with Demetrius. To win Demetrius's favor, Helena decides to tell him about Lysander and Hermia's planned elopement.

1. **our nuptial hour:** the time for our wedding

4. **lingers:** delays, prolongs

5–6. **Like ... revenue:** i.e., in the same way that a stepmother or a widow with rights in her dead husband's property (1) makes a young heir wait to inherit it, or (2) wastes it, or (3) has a claim on the young man's income until she dies

7. **steep themselves:** i.e., be absorbed (literally, soak themselves)

11. **solemnities:** festive ceremonies

14. **pert:** lively

16. **pale companion:** i.e., melancholy (**Companion** is a term of contempt, meaning "fellow.")

17–18. **I wooed ... injuries:** In stories about Theseus, he overcomes Hippolyta in battle with the Amazons and then marries her.

20. **triumph:** public festivity

243

32. **feigning voice:** a voice singing softly; **feigning love:** pretended love

33. **the impression of her fantasy:** i.e., her imagination, on which you have impressed your image

34. **gauds:** (1) playthings; (2) showy things; **conceits:** fancy trinkets

35. **Knacks:** knickknacks

36. **prevailment:** influence

40. **Be it so:** i.e., if

44. **this gentleman:** Demetrius

46. **Immediately:** directly, i.e., with nothing intervening between sentence and actual punishment

47. **Be advised:** i.e., think carefully

52. **leave:** i.e., leave undisturbed; or, perhaps, abandon

56. **in this kind:** in this case; **wanting . . . voice:** lacking your father's support

62. **concern my modesty:** affect my reputation for proper maidenly behavior

67. **die the death:** be put to death

69. **question:** examine carefully

70. **Know of:** learn from; **blood:** passions, feelings

72. **livery of a nun:** a nun's distinctive clothing (The term *nun* was used by writers in Shakespeare's day to refer not only to Christian nuns but also to pagan virgins dedicated to a life of chaste service to Diana or Vesta.)

73. **For aye:** forever; **mewed:** caged (A mew was a cage for hawks.)

75. **Chanting . . . moon:** Diana was both the moon goddess and the goddess of chastity.

76–77. **Thrice-blessèd . . . pilgrimage:** i.e., those who master their passions and live as chaste maidens separated from the world are **thrice-blessèd**

78–80. **But earthlier . . . blessedness:** i.e., those who marry have more happiness on this earth than those who live and die in **single blessedness** (The image is of the married woman as a **rose distilled** [plucked and its fragrance distilled into perfume] as opposed to the rose that remains unplucked.)

82. **my virgin patent:** my entitlement to my virginity; my freedom to live as a virgin

83. **Unto his lordship:** i.e., to the mastery of a man

90. **he would:** i.e., your father wishes

91. **protest:** vow

92. **austerity:** i.e., a life of self-denial

94. **crazèd title:** flawed claim

96. **Do you:** i.e., you

100. **estate unto:** give to

101. **derived:** born, descended

102. **well possessed:** i.e., wealthy

103. **fairly:** attractively

104. **with vantage:** i.e., even more (than his)

108. **avouch . . . head:** declare it to his face

109. **Made love to:** courted

112. **spotted:** i.e., morally stained, wicked

115. **self-affairs:** personal business

118. **schooling:** reproof, admonition

119. **arm:** prepare

122. **by no means we may extenuate:** i.e., I (speaking in my formal capacity) can in no way lessen or change

124. **What cheer . . . ?:** i.e., how are you? (literally, what is your mood or disposition?)

127. **Against:** in preparation for

128. **nearly that concerns yourselves:** i.e., that concerns you closely

131. **How chance . . . ?:** i.e., how does it happen that . . . ?

132. **Belike:** probably; **want:** lack

133. **Beteem:** grant, give

134. **For aught:** according to anything

137. **different in blood:** unequal in hereditary rank

138. **cross:** bar, barrier, obstruction

139. **misgraffèd . . . years:** mismatched in age

141. **stood upon:** depended on

143. **if . . . choice:** i.e., if the lovers were suitably matched

145. **momentany:** lasting but a moment; instantaneous

147. **collied:** coal-black

148. **That:** the lightning; **in a spleen:** i.e., suddenly, in an impulsive action (The spleen was regarded as the seat of angry impulsiveness.); **unfolds:** reveals

149. **ere:** before

151. **quick:** (1) living, intense; (2) quickly; **confusion:** ruin, defeat

152. **ever crossed:** always frustrated or thwarted

157. **fancy's:** love's

158. **A good persuasion:** i.e., a good attitude for us to take

160. **revenue:** accented here on the second syllable

162. **respects me as:** i.e., regards me as much as if I were

166. **forth:** i.e., forth from

167. **without:** outside of

169. **To do . . . May:** i.e., to celebrate May Day (perhaps by collecting branches and flowers)

173. **arrow with the golden head:** Cupid, the mythological god of love, was said to use arrows with golden heads to cause love, and arrows with leaden heads to repel love.

174. **simplicity:** innocence; **Venus' doves:** Doves were sacred to Venus (goddess of love and mother of Cupid) and were sometimes pictured as drawing her chariot.

176–77. **that fire . . . was seen:** Dido, queen of Carthage, both burned with love for Aeneas and burned herself on a pyre after Aeneas, **the false Trojan**, abandoned her by sailing off to found Rome.

183. **Godspeed:** a conventional greeting

185. **your fair:** your fairness, beauty; **happy:** fortunate

186. **lodestars:** stars (like the polestar) that sailors used to guide them

187. **tunable:** melodious

189. **catching:** contagious; **favor:** looks

190. **catch:** get as if by infection

194–95. **Demetrius . . . translated:** i.e., I'd give all the world, except for Demetrius, in order to be transformed into you. **bated:** excepted, omitted **translated:** transformed

206. **Would:** i.e., I wish

211. **what graces . . . dwell:** i.e., how much attractiveness lies in Lysander

214. **Phoebe:** i.e., the moon (Phoebe is another name for Diana, goddess of the moon.)

215. **wat'ry glass:** i.e., pond or lake, which acts as a glass or mirror

217. **still:** always

220. **faint:** pale; **wont:** accustomed

224. **stranger companies:** i.e., the company of strangers

228. **lovers' food:** i.e., the sight of each other

232. **o'er other some:** i.e., in comparison to certain others

238. **holding no quantity:** i.e., out of all proportion

240–47. **Love . . . everywhere:** Helena uses the ways in which Cupid is often pictured (as a blind boy with wings) to describe the qualities of love—its blindness, lack of judgment, folly, and inconstancy.

242. **of any judgment taste:** i.e., any taste of judgment

243. **figure:** represent; **unheedy:** heedless, reckless

245. **beguiled:** cheated

246. **game:** sport; **forswear:** swear falsely, perjure

247. **is perjured:** i.e., perjures himself

248. **eyne:** eyes

249. **hailed down:** showered, poured down like hail

254. **intelligence:** news

255. **If . . . expense:** Helena may be saying that she is purchasing Demetrius's thanks at great cost; or, she may mean that her efforts will be dear to her if they bring her Demetrius's thanks. **dear:** (1) high priced; (2) loved, precious

1.2 Six Athenian tradesmen decide to put on a play, called "Pyramus and Thisbe," for Theseus and Hippolyta's wedding. Pyramus will be played by Bottom the weaver and Thisbe by Francis Flute the bellows-mender. The men are given their parts to study, and they agree to meet for a rehearsal in the woods outside Athens.

0 SD. **joiner:** carpenter, cabinetmaker

2. **You were best:** i.e., you had better; **generally:** Bottom's mistake for "individually"

3. **scrip:** a piece of paper with writing on it

4. **which:** i.e., who

6. **interlude:** an entertainment that comes between other events (here, a play to fill the time between the wedding and bedtime)

10. **grow to a point:** As in many of Bottom's lines, one gets a sense of what he means even though he uses language oddly. Here, he seems to mean "come to a conclusion."

11. **Marry:** i.e., indeed (originally an oath on the name of the Virgin Mary)

12–13. **Pyramus and Thisbe:** The story of Pyramus and Thisbe—a story very much like that of Romeo and Juliet—is told in Ovid's *Metamorphoses*, book 4.

23. **ask:** require

25. **condole:** grieve, lament (Bottom probably means that he will act the part of the grieving lover.)

26. **humor:** inclination, preference

27. **Ercles:** Hercules (This may be an allusion to a lost play about the Greek hero; or, the role of Hercules may have been famous as an extravagant, ranting part.)

27–28. **tear a cat:** i.e., rant and rave

33. **Phibbus' car:** the chariot of the sun god, Phoebus Apollo

38. **Ercles' vein:** the style of Hercules (See note on line 27, above.)

42. **take . . . on you:** i.e., play the part of

43. **wand'ring knight:** knight-errant (i.e., a hero's role in medieval romance)

47. **That's all one:** i.e., no matter; **mask:** perhaps alluding to the masks that women frequently wore when out of doors to protect their skin from the sun

48. **small:** shrill, high-pitched

49. **An:** i.e., if

50. **monstrous little:** extremely small

74. **were:** i.e., would be

78. **discretion:** judgment (Bottom seems to mean that they would have no choice but to hang them.); **aggravate:** Bottom's mistake for "moderate" or "mitigate" (i.e., soften, tone down)

79. **roar you:** i.e., roar for you

79–80. **sucking dove:** Bottom's confusion of "sucking [i.e., unweaned] lamb" and "sitting [i.e., hatching] dove"

80. **an 'twere:** as if it were

82. **a proper:** i.e., as handsome a

84. **must needs:** i.e., must

88. **will:** i.e., wish

89. **discharge:** perform; **your:** i.e., a (a colloquialism)

90. **orange-tawny:** tan

90–91. **purple-in-grain:** crimson fast-dyed

91. **French-crown:** gold (the color of the French coin called a "crown" in English)

92. **perfit:** perfect (Since "perfect" became the preferred spelling around 1590, it is possible that the old form was deliberately chosen for Bottom—as again at line 105.)

93–94. **French . . . all:** an allusion to the baldness caused by syphilis (the "French disease")

96. **con:** learn

98. **without:** outside of

100. **devices:** plans; or, the plot of our play (The word *device* was sometimes used to denote a play or masque—as it is in Act 5 of this play.)

101. **bill of properties:** list of stage props

104. **obscenely:** Bottom perhaps means "seemly."

105. **perfit:** i.e., word-perfect

107. **Hold, or cut bowstrings:** This sounds like a proverb, or like an archery term, but seems to be Bottom's invention. (Perhaps it means "Keep your word or be disgraced.")

2.1 Oberon and Titania, king and queen of the fairies, quarrel over possession of a young Indian boy. Oberon orders Robin Goodfellow, a hobgoblin or "puck," to obtain a special flower that makes people fall in love with the next creature they see. Oberon wants to make Titania fall in love with a beast and use her infatuation to get the Indian boy from her. Demetrius enters pursued by Helena, whom he tries to drive off. When Robin returns, Oberon, who sympathizes with Helena's love, orders him to find the Athenian man (i.e., Demetrius) and apply some of the flower's magic nectar to his eyes.

0 SD. **Robin Goodfellow:** a "puck," or mischievous spirit, whose activities are described in lines 33–59 (Since Nicholas Rowe's 1709 edition of the play, the character has been known as "Puck.") Robin appears in stories, plays, and books on witchcraft, sometimes as simply mischievous, sometimes as an evil goblin.

3. **Thorough:** i.e., through

4. **pale:** fenced-in area

7. **moon's sphere:** In Ptolemaic astronomy, the moon (like the planets, the stars, and the sun) was carried around the earth in a crystalline sphere.

9. **orbs:** circles (A circle of darker, more luxuriant, grass in a meadow was called a "fairy ring" and was thought to be the dancing ground of fairies.)

10. **pensioners:** Because of their height and their brightly colored flowers (gold with ruby-red spots), **cowslips** are compared to the gaudily dressed body-guards (**pensioners**) that served Queen Elizabeth.

16. **lob:** oaf, lout

17. **anon:** soon

18. **revels:** At the court of Queen Elizabeth, **revels** were presented at special seasons, and included plays, masques, and sports. Here, the king of fairyland's **revels** might also include dancing.

20. **passing:** i.e., surpassingly, extremely; **fell and wrath:** i.e., fiercely angry

25. **trace:** travel through

26. **perforce:** forcibly

29. **they:** i.e., the king and queen of fairies

30. **fountain:** spring

31. **square:** quarrel; **that:** i.e., so that

34. **shrewd:** mischievous, malicious; **sprite:** spirit

35. **Robin Goodfellow:** See the note on 2.1.0 SD.

36. **villagery:** villages

37. **Skim milk:** i.e., steal the cream from the milk; **labor in the quern:** i.e., work at the quern (a small mill for grinding corn), to frustrate the grinding

38. **bootless . . . churn:** i.e., make her churning produce no butter   **bootless:** uselessly, fruitlessly   **huswife:** pronounced "hussif"

39. **barm:** yeasty "head" on beer.

47. **beguile:** deceive, trick

49. **gossip's bowl:** the cup from which the gossiping or tattling woman is drinking

50. **crab:** crab apple (Roasted crab apples and spices were added to hot ale to make a winter drink.)

52. **dewlap:** the fold of skin hanging from the neck of certain animals (here applied to the neck of the old woman)

53. **aunt:** perhaps, old woman or gossip; **telling ... tale:** "Winter's tales" and "old wives' tales," told to while away long evenings, could be merry or sad.

56. **"Tailor":** Since "tail" could mean "buttocks," it has been suggested that the old woman's cry might be translated as "O my bum!" (It remains uncertain just what the expression means.)

57. **choir:** company

57–58. **loffe ... waxen ... neeze:** These archaic forms of "laugh," "wax" (i.e., increase), and "sneeze" seem to reproduce the country setting Robin is describing.

60. **room:** i.e., make room, stand aside

64. **forsworn:** renounced, formally rejected

65. **rash wanton:** foolish rebel; **lord:** husband (and therefore having the right to control his wife)

66. **lady:** wife (and therefore having the right to expect her husband to be faithful)

68. **in ... Corin:** disguised as a lovesick shepherd

69. **of corn:** i.e., made from wheat straws

70. **Phillida:** traditional shepherdess of love poetry

71. **steep:** slope, cliff

72. **forsooth:** in truth, certainly; **Amazon:** In stories about Theseus, Hippolyta was one of the Amazon warriors (a tribe of women fighters) who attacked Athens. After four months of fighting, peace was reached through Hippolyta's efforts.

73. **buskined:** wearing buskins, or boots

74. **must be:** i.e., is to be

75. **their bed:** i.e., their marriage and offspring

77. **Glance at:** allude to; **credit:** reputation

81–83. **Perigouna ... Aegles ... Ariadne ... Antiopa:** In stories about Theseus, these are lovers whom Theseus deserted. Oberon lays the blame for these desertions on Titania. **break ... faith:** i.e., go back on his word, break his promise

84. **forgeries:** fictions, fictitious inventions

85. **middle summer's spring:** i.e., the beginning of midsummer

86. **mead:** meadow

87. **pavèd:** pebbled

88. **margent:** margin

89. **ringlets:** circle dances

91. **piping:** i.e., whistling, making music

94. **pelting:** paltry, insignificant

95. **continents:** i.e., banks (which contain them)

97–98. **green corn . . . beard:** As grain (called, in England, corn) ripens, its head develops bristle-like extensions; it is then called "bearded."

99. **fold:** i.e., sheepfold, or pen

100. **murrain flock:** i.e., sheep dead from murrain, an infectious disease

101. **nine-men's-morris:** an outdoor space carved, or cut in turf, for a game of the same name

102. **quaint:** elaborate; **mazes:** intricate interconnecting paths that lead confusingly to (and away from) a center; **wanton green:** luxuriant grass

103. **tread:** perhaps, human footsteps which, when tracing the maze, would keep its path clear; **undistinguishable:** not perceptible

104. **want:** lack

106. **Therefore:** i.e., because of Oberon's disturbance of the fairy dances (as in line 91)

108. **That:** i.e., so that; **rheumatic:** i.e., like colds or flu, with discharges of rheum or mucus (accent on first syllable)

109. **thorough:** i.e., through, as a consequence of; **distemperature:** (1) bad temper; (2) bad weather

112. **Hiems':** i.e., winter's

113. **odorous:** fragrant

115. **childing:** fruitful (producing "children"); **change:** exchange

116. **wonted liveries:** usual outfits

116–17. **the mazèd world ... which:** i.e., the bewildered world can no longer distinguish one season from another according to the produce (**increase**) normally brought forth in each   **mazèd:** bewildered

118–19. **this same ... debate:** these evils are the descendants of our quarrel   **debate:** quarrel

120. **original:** origin

122. **cross:** oppose, resist

124. **henchman:** page, squire

127. **vot'ress ... order:** woman vowed to serve me

129. **Full:** i.e., very

130. **Neptune:** the god of the sea

131. **Marking:** noticing, watching; **embarkèd ... flood:** i.e., merchant ships sailing on the ocean

133. **wanton:** (1) lewd; (2) playful

145. **round:** circle dance

147. **spare your haunts:** avoid the places you frequent

150. **chide:** fight, brawl; **downright:** i.e., outright

151. **from:** i.e., go from

152. **injury:** wrong, insult

154. **Since:** i.e., when

158. **stars ... spheres:** See note on 2.1.7, above.

164. **vestal:** i.e., virgin (This passage is often explained as referring to Queen Elizabeth I.)

165. **smartly:** briskly

166. **As:** i.e., as if

167. **might:** i.e., could

168. **wat'ry moon:** Because the moon controls the tides, it is often associated with water.

169. **imperial:** commanding, majestic; perhaps also (as a reference to Queen Elizabeth) pertaining to rulership of an empire (In the 1596 edition of Spenser's *Faerie Queene*, for example, Spenser refers to "The Most ... Magnificent Empresse ... Elizabeth ... Queene of England, France and Ireland and of Virginia...."); **vot'ress:** a woman under a vow (The word **vestal** suggests it is a vow of chastity.)

171. **bolt:** arrow
174. **love-in-idleness:** a name for the pansy or hearts-ease
175. **herb:** plant
177. **or . . . or:** either . . . or
180. **leviathan:** a monstrous sea creature mentioned in the Bible; **league:** approximately three miles
183. **juice:** nectar from the flower
192. **page:** boy attending on a knight
197. **stay:** halt, stop; **stayeth:** arrests, holds
199. **and wood:** and mad, insane
202. **adamant:** i.e., magnet
203. **draw:** attract
204. **Leave you:** i.e., give up
206. **speak you fair:** i.e., speak to you civilly
208. **nor:** i.e., and
221. **impeach:** call into question, discredit; **modesty:** i.e., properly chaste female behavior
222. **To leave:** i.e., in leaving
225. **ill:** evil; **desert:** uninhabited
227. **virtue:** (1) excellence; (2) moral goodness; **privilege:** i.e., protection; **For that:** i.e., because
231. **For:** because; **in my respect:** i.e., from my perspective
234. **brakes:** thickets
238–40. **Apollo . . . tiger:** Helena gives three examples of stories that are **changed** so that the weak pursue the strong: the chaste nymph Daphne chases the god Apollo (in mythology, Daphne fled from Apollo and escaped him by being transformed into a laurel tree); the dove attacks the mythical beast called the griffin; the female deer chases the tiger. **griffin:** an animal with the head of an eagle on the body of a lion
240. **Bootless:** useless, fruitless
242. **stay:** i.e., stay for
243–44. **do . . . But:** i.e., you may be sure that

244, 246. do . . . mischief: harm
247. my sex: i.e., all females
251. upon: by
253. fly: flee from
257. blows: bursts into flower
258. oxlips: flowers somewhat larger than cowslips
259. woodbine: honeysuckle
260. eglantine: sweetbrier
261. sometime of: sometimes during
263. throws: casts; **her:** i.e., its
264. Weed: garment
265. this: i.e., of the magic flower
273. that: i.e., so that
274. fond on: desperately in love with

2.2 Oberon anoints Titania's eyes as she sleeps. A weary Lysander and Hermia enter and fall asleep nearby. Robin, thinking he has found "the Athenian man," anoints the eyes of the sleeping Lysander and exits. Demetrius and Helena arrive, and he leaves her behind. Lysander awakes, sees Helena, and immediately falls in love with her. She mistakes his courtship for mockery and tries to elude him. After they exit, the abandoned Hermia awakes from a nightmare and goes in search of her beloved Lysander.

1. roundel: perhaps, a round dance; or, a song (a "roundelay")
3. cankers: canker worms, grubs
4. reremice: bats
7. quaint: dainty, brisk
8. offices: duties, responsibilities
9. double: forked
11. Newts and blindworms: species of salamanders and reptiles thought, in Shakespeare's day, to be poisonous
13. Philomel: the nightingale (named for Philomela, who, in Roman mythology, was transformed into a

nightingale after she was raped by her brother-in-law and her tongue cut out)

36. **ounce:** lynx; **cat:** i.e., lion or tiger

37. **Pard:** leopard

38. **that:** i.e., that which

42. **troth:** truth, truly

48. **troth:** faithful vow

51. **take . . . innocence:** perhaps, understand the innocent meaning—i.e., of what I just said (In lines 53–58, Lysander explains what he meant in line 48.)

52. **Love . . . conference:** i.e., when lovers talk, it is love that hears and understands

60. **beshrew:** literally, curse (but the harshness of the word was lost through repeated use)

63. **human:** humane, civil, courteous

70. **Here:** Lysander would be some distance from where Hermia is lying.

74. **approve:** demonstrate, confirm; or, test

77. **Weeds:** garments

85. **owe:** i.e., own, possess

86–87. **let love . . . eyelid:** i.e., let love so torment you that you cannot close your eyes in sleep **forbid . . . seat:** i.e., banish from its place

91. **charge:** command

92. **darkling:** in the dark

94. **fond:** (1) foolish; (2) infatuated

95. **grace:** favor or reward for prayer

103. **as:** i.e., as if I were

104. **glass:** mirror

105. **compare with:** i.e., rival, vie with; **sphery eyne:** perhaps, eyes belonging to the celestial spheres, like stars

110. **Transparent:** (1) radiant; (2) capable of being seen through; **Nature shows art:** In making Helena's body "transparent," so that Lysander can "see her heart," Nature acts like a magician. **art:** magic, power

121. **change:** i.e., exchange

122–29. **The will . . . book:** In this speech, Lysander attributes his sudden love for Helena to his having suddenly become mature and rational.   **will:** desire

124. **Things growing:** i.e., growing things

125. **ripe not:** i.e., did not ripen

126. **point:** i.e., the highest point; **skill:** judgment, discrimination

127. **marshal:** an officer who leads guests to their proper places

128. **o'erlook:** survey

130. **Wherefore:** why

136. **Good troth, good sooth:** i.e., in truth (mild oaths)

138. **Perforce:** of necessity

147. **of those they did deceive:** i.e., by the men who had mistakenly believed in the heresies

149. **Of:** i.e., by

157. **prey:** i.e., attack

160. **an if:** i.e., if

3.1   The tradesmen meet in the woods to rehearse. Robin Goodfellow happens upon them and transforms Bottom's head into that of an ass. Abandoned by his terrified friends, Bottom sings. His singing awakens Titania, who, under the influence of the flower's magic, falls in love with him. She takes him away to sleep in her bower.

0 SD. **Clowns:** i.e., actors who play comic roles

2. **Pat:** i.e., at exactly the right time; **marvels:** i.e., marvelously

3. **plot:** piece of ground

4. **brake:** thicket; **tiring-house:** i.e., attiring house, dressing room

8. **bully:** worthy, admirable

13. **By 'r lakin:** an oath "by our Lady"; **parlous:** perilous, terrible

15. **when all is done:** i.e., after all

24. **eight and six:** alternating eight- and six-syllable lines (the standard ballad meter)

39. **defect:** Bottom's error for "effect"

42–43. **it were pity of my life:** i.e., I would be risking my life

58–59. **bush of thorns:** In legend, there is in the moon a man who carries a bundle of sticks and a lantern and who is often accompanied by his dog.

59. **disfigure:** Quince's mistake for "figure" (i.e., represent)

67–68. **plaster ... loam ... roughcast:** Each of these is used for plastering walls. **Plaster** is a mixture of lime, sand, and hair; **loam** is a mixture of clay, sand, and straw (it was also used for making bricks); **roughcast** is a mixture of lime and gravel.

69. **thus:** The actor playing Bottom usually, at this point, makes a "V" with his first two fingers.

76. **hempen homespuns:** i.e., country bumpkins, wearing homespun clothes woven from hemp

77. **cradle:** i.e., the bower where Titania is sleeping

78. **toward:** about to take place

89. **marry:** i.e., indeed

92–95. **Most ... tire:** These lines include several words that simply fill out the six-beat doggerel lines (**brisky** [rather than "brisk"], **juvenal** [rather than "youth"], **eke** [i.e., also]) and words that seem desperate attempts to rhyme (**Jew** to rhyme with **hue, tire** to rhyme with **brier**). Part of the comedy in the "Pyramus and Thisbe" scenes turns on the very bad "poetry" of the script. **triumphant:** splendid **brier:** wild rose bush

97. **Ninus' tomb:** In Ovid's *Metamorphoses*, the lovers meet at the tomb of Ninus, legendary founder of the city of Nineveh.

99. **part:** Actors were provided with "parts" that contained cues of two or three words, as well as their own speeches. (Flute seems not to have read "cues and all," but

rather to have read two of Thisbe's speeches as if they were one.)

103 SD. **with the ass-head:** i.e., wearing the "ass head" (a stage prop)

104. **were only:** i.e., would be only

107. **round:** roundabout way; circle dance

111. **fire:** i.e., will-o'-the-wisp

120–21. **translated:** transformed

127. **ouzel:** blackbird

129. **throstle:** thrush

130. **little quill:** i.e., small note (literally, a small musical pipe)

133. **plainsong cuckoo gray:** i.e., gray cuckoo, whose repetitive call is as simple as the early church music called **plainsong**

134. **Whose . . . mark:** i.e., whose song many men hear and pay attention to (Because the cuckoo does not build nests but leaves its eggs for other birds to hatch and feed, its song of "cuckoo" is linked to "cuckold," a man whose wife is unfaithful and thus who might bear children fathered by other men. Its call was considered a mocking cry directed at married men.)

136. **who . . . foolish:** Proverbial: "Do not set your wit against a fool's." **set his wit:** use his intelligence to answer

137. **give . . . the lie:** accuse . . . of lying

138. **never so:** countless times (i.e., over and over)

140. **note:** song

142. **virtue's:** excellence's; **perforce:** i.e., whether I want to or not, willy-nilly; **move me:** persuade me; stir my emotions

146. **keep little company together:** i.e., are not good friends

148. **gleek:** make a joke

156. **common:** ordinary; **rate:** value

157. **still:** always; **doth tend upon:** serves, attends; **state:** greatness, position of power

160. **deep:** ocean

162–63. **I will purge . . . go:** i.e., I will transform you into a spirit **purge:** make pure or clean **mortal:** i.e., subject to death (It has been suggested that the medical meaning of **purge** [i.e., to cleanse the body through bleedings or laxatives] should be considered here.)

164 SD. **Peaseblossom . . . Mustardseed:** Each of these names indicates something very tiny or otherwise hard to see. **Peaseblossom:** the flower of the pea plant **Mote:** speck (Since the words *mote* and *moth* were pronounced the same way, and since the character's name is spelled "moth" in the early printings of this play, the character's name might mean, instead, a small flying insect. "Mote" is an almost-silent character, not described in the dialogue as the other fairies are. Thus editors have difficulty determining whether his/its name should, in modern spelling, be "Mote" or "Moth.") **Mustardseed:** It is from tiny mustardseeds that mustard is made.

171. **gambol:** skip, leap about; **in his eyes:** in his sight

172. **apricocks:** apricots; **dewberries:** blackberries

174. **humble-bees:** bumblebees

177. **have:** i.e., attend

185. **cry . . . mercy:** i.e., beg . . . pardon

189–90. **Cobweb . . . you:** Cobwebs were used to stop bleeding.

190. **honest:** honorable

192. **Squash:** an unripened pea-pod

193. **Peascod:** a ripe pea-pod

198–99. **your patience:** perhaps, referring to mustard's patience in being so often devoured; perhaps, "your Patience," as in "your Honor"

199. **ox-beef:** Mustard is often served as a condiment with beef. (Bottom is here sympathizing with Mustardseed for having lost kinsmen who have been eaten as mustard.)

207. **enforcèd chastity:** (1) chastity enforced, compelled; (2) chastity forced and destroyed, raped

3.2 Robin Goodfellow reports to Oberon about Titania and Bottom. When Demetrius enters wooing Hermia, Oberon discovers that Robin has anointed the eyes of the wrong Athenian. Oberon then orders Robin to fetch Helena while he anoints the eyes of the sleeping Demetrius. Helena enters pursued by Lysander vowing his love. Demetrius awakes, falls in love with Helena, and also begins to woo her. Helena believes both men are mocking her. When Hermia arrives and learns that Lysander has abandoned her for Helena, she threatens Helena, who thinks that Hermia is part of the conspiracy. Lysander and Demetrius prepare to duel to prove their right to Helena. At Oberon's command, Robin impersonates each of the two men in turn in order to lead the other astray until both, exhausted, fall asleep. Helena and Hermia also fall asleep. Robin applies nectar to Lysander's eyes to undo the spell that has drawn him to Helena.

3. **in extremity:** to the highest degree

5. **night-rule:** perhaps, disorder (night being associated with the irrational); **haunted:** much visited

7. **close:** hidden, secluded

8. **dull:** i.e., unconscious (because asleep)

9. **patches:** simpletons; **rude:** humble; uncivilized; **mechanicals:** workers

10. **work for bread:** i.e., earn their livings; **stalls:** booths, sheds (where cobblers, butchers, etc., worked and sold their wares)

13. **barren:** dull

14. **sport:** drama, theatrical activity

15. **scene:** stage

17. **noll:** head

18. **Anon:** soon

19. **mimic:** i.e., comic actor

20. **fowler:** one who hunts wild birds

21. **russet-pated . . . sort:** a large flock of brownish-headed jackdaws

23. **Sever themselves:** i.e., split up

25. **at our stamp:** Robin, as described in stories and ballads, has a powerful stamp. However, since his use of "our" is puzzling, it has been suggested that "at our stamp" is a misprint for "at a stump."

31–32. **from ... catch:** perhaps, everything snatches at cowards

34. **translated:** transformed

37. **falls out:** happens

38. **latched:** snared, caught

42. **That:** i.e., so that; **of force:** of necessity (i.e., inevitably)

43. **Stand close:** an order to step aside into hiding

50. **o'er shoes:** i.e., up to your ankles

55–57. **This whole earth ... Antipodes:** i.e., that the solid globe could be so pierced that the moon could travel through it, bringing night to the Antipodes when it should there be noon **bored:** pierced through, drilled **Her brother's:** i.e., the sun's **Antipodes:** the region on the opposite side of the globe

59. **dead:** (1) deadly; (2) dull; (3) deathly pale

64. **What's this to:** i.e., what does this have to do with

71. **being awake:** i.e., if Lysander were awake

73. **worm:** serpent

75. **never adder stung:** i.e., never did adder sting

76. **misprised:** mistaken; **mood:** perhaps, anger, or grief; perhaps, state of mind

80. **An if:** i.e., if; **therefor:** for it, in exchange

86–89. **So sorrow's ... stay:** Demetrius, explaining that he will now lie down and sleep, plays with two meanings of the word *heavy* (sad; sleepy). He says that sorrow grows heavier when sleep, like a bankrupt, cannot pay its debts; he lies down to wait for sleep to make him an offer (a **tender**) and pay part of its debt.

92. **Of thy misprision:** from your mistake; **perforce:** necessarily

93. **turned:** altered, changed

94–95. **Then fate . . . oath:** Robin attributes his mistake to fate, claiming that for every man who is faithful a million are fickle. **holding troth:** keeping his plighted oath **confounding:** breaking

96. **About the wood go:** i.e., go through the forest

97. **look thou:** i.e., make sure you

98. **fancy-sick:** lovesick; **cheer:** face

99. **costs . . . dear:** Sighs were thought to deplete the blood. **dear:** dearly

101. **against:** i.e., to prepare for the time

103. **Tartar's bow:** an Oriental bow, more powerful than English bows

106. **apple:** i.e., the pupil

107. **his love:** i.e., Helena

109. **Venus:** the planet Venus, known as the evening star (also named at line 63)

115. **fee:** reward

116. **fond pageant:** foolish spectacle or scene

121. **needs:** necessarily, inevitably; **sport alone:** an unrivaled entertainment

126. **Look when:** whenever, all the while

129. **badge of faith:** i.e., his tears

130. **advance:** display, exhibit

131. **When truth . . . fray:** Helena argues that Lysander is using the **truth** of his present vows to kill the **truth** of his vows to Hermia, thus creating a battle that is both **devilish** (in that he is breaking his oath) and **holy** (in that it is a battle between truths).

132. **give her o'er:** abandon her

133–34. **Weigh . . . weigh:** Balance your oaths to her against your oaths to me, and (1) you will weigh "nothing," because the scales will be evenly balanced; or, (2) since they are both empty, you will be weighing nothing.

141. **eyne:** eyes

142. **Crystal is muddy:** i.e., in comparison to her eyes

144. **Taurus:** a mountain range in Asia

147. **princess of pure white:** i.e., her hand; **seal:** i.e., guarantee, pledge

149. **set against:** attack

153. **join in souls:** perhaps, unite

156. **parts:** personal qualities

160. **trim:** fine (said sarcastically)

163–64. **extort . . . patience:** i.e., wring from a poor soul her patience, as if through torture   **extort:** wring out

164. **make you sport:** i.e., entertain yourselves

172. **I will none:** i.e., I want none of her

174. **to her but as guest-wise sojourned:** i.e., journeyed to (or stayed with) her only as a visitor   **but:** only **sojourned:** traveled; stayed

179. **aby it dear:** pay dearly for it

181. **his:** i.e., its

183. **Wherein:** i.e., in that respect (of affecting the senses) in which

188, 189. **press:** push, urge

192. **oes and eyes of light:** i.e., stars   **oes:** round spangles

199. **in spite of:** i.e., to spite

202. **bait:** harass, torment

205. **chid:** scolded

208. **artificial:** skillful

209. **needles:** pronounced "neeles"

211. **both in one key:** i.e., the two of us in perfect harmony

213. **incorporate:** united in one body

218–19. **Two . . . crest:** Helena here uses technical language of heraldry (**of the first, coats, crest**) to say again that she and Hermia, though in two bodies, once shared a single heart.

220. **rent:** rend, tear

223. **Our sex:** i.e., all females

225. **amazèd:** bewildered, dumbfounded (Many edi-

tions add the word "passionate" to this line, so that it reads "your passionate words," taking the word from the Folio text. For the relation of the Folio to the quarto texts, see page 280.)

230. **spurn:** kick

232, 233. **Wherefore:** why

235. **tender:** offer; **forsooth:** in truth (a very mild oath)

236. **setting on:** instigation

237. **in grace:** i.e., favored

242. **Persever:** persevere (accent on second syllable); **sad:** serious, grave

243. **Make mouths upon:** i.e., make faces at

245. **carried:** managed; **chronicled:** i.e., written up in chronicles or histories

247. **argument:** subject of contention

250. **excuse:** defense

254. **she:** i.e., Hermia; **entreat:** i.e., persuade you

259. **by that:** i.e., by my life

262. **withdraw ... prove it:** Lysander here challenges Demetrius to prove his love in a duel.

265. **Ethiop:** Like "tawny Tartar" at line 274, this seems a reference to the dark color of Hermia's hair or complexion. (An **Ethiop** was a dark-skinned African.)

266–68. **No ... follow:** These lines are difficult as printed in the quarto. Many editors substitute the Folio's "sir" for "he'll," thus solving the problem of the shift from "he" to "you." **Take on as:** i.e., act as if

274. **Tartar:** i.e., Gypsy

277. **sooth:** truly (a very mild oath)

278. **my word with thee:** i.e., my challenge to you

279–80. **bond ... bond:** a quibble on **bond** as a binding legal agreement and **bond** as a fetter or chain (Hermia is the **weak bond** holding Lysander.)

284. **what news:** i.e., what does this mean?

286. **erewhile:** a little while ago

296. **juggler:** trickster, deceiver; **cankerblossom:** i.e., cankerworm, a worm that destroys flower buds

306. **urged:** i.e., put forward as a recommendation

315, 316. **curst, shrewishness:** These words (like **shrewd** at 3.2.340) were used to describe women who were considered quarrelsome, talkative, or sharp-tongued.

317. **a right maid:** i.e., a girl indeed, a real sissy

319. **something:** i.e., somewhat

328. **chid me hence:** i.e., tried to drive me away through scolding

330. **so:** i.e., if

333. **fond:** foolish; or, doting

339. **she:** i.e., Hermia; **her:** i.e., Helena's

340. **keen:** cruel, fierce; **shrewd:** i.e., shrewish

344. **suffer:** allow

345. **come to her:** i.e., get at her

347. **minimus:** i.e., tiniest of creatures; **knotgrass:** a weed that was thought to stunt growth

354. **aby:** pay for

356–57. **whose right . . . is most in:** i.e., who has the most right to

359. **coil:** turmoil; **is long of:** i.e., is because of

365. **amazed:** astounded (as if lost in a maze)

366. **Still thou:** i.e., you always, you continue to

368. **shadows:** illusions, spirits; also, darkness

373. **it so did sort:** i.e., that it happened this way

374. **As:** since

376. **Hie:** hurry

377. **welkin:** sky; **anon:** immediately

378. **Acheron:** i.e., hell (literally, one of the four rivers of the classical underworld, Hades)

380. **As one come:** i.e., so that one comes

384. **from:** i.e., away from

386. **batty:** batlike

387. **herb:** plant, flower

388. **liquor:** juice; **virtuous property:** potent power

389. **his might:** i.e., its strength
390. **wonted sight:** i.e., usual (normal) vision
392. **fruitless:** idle, empty
394. **With league . . . end:** i.e., united in a compact that will last until death   **date:** duration, term
397. **charmèd:** bewitched
400. **night's swift dragons:** Night is here presented as driving across the sky in a chariot drawn by dragons.
401. **Aurora's harbinger:** i.e., Venus, the morning star, announcing the approach of dawn (**Aurora**)
405. **in crossways . . . burial:** i.e., those not buried in sacred ground   **crossways:** i.e., crossroads, where the bodies of suicides were buried
409. **for aye:** i.e., forever
411–15. **I . . . streams:** i.e., I do not have to flee the daylight (as do the ghosts of the damned)   **the Morning's love:** perhaps, Aurora herself   **the eastern gate:** i.e., where the sun rises   **Neptune:** i.e., the ocean
421. **Goblin:** i.e., hobgoblin (another name for Robin Goodfellow)
424. **drawn:** i.e., with my sword out
425. **straight:** straightway, immediately
427. **plainer:** flatter, more level
434. **recreant:** coward
436. **rod:** a stick used to whip a child; **defiled:** i.e., because Demetrius is such a coward, it would be shameful to fight him like a man
439. **try no manhood:** i.e., have no test of our courage
440. **still:** continually
444. **That:** i.e., so that; **in:** i.e., into a
449. **Abide me:** i.e., wait for me; **wot:** know
454–55. **buy this dear:** i.e., pay dearly for this
458. **this cold bed:** i.e., the ground
459. **By day's approach:** i.e., as soon as day breaks
461. **Abate:** cut short
468. **curst:** angry
476. **mean:** i.e., intend to have

4.1 Titania and her attendants pamper Bottom, who falls asleep with her. Oberon, watching them, tells Robin that Titania has given him the Indian boy and thus they can now remove the spells from Titania and Bottom. Reunited, Titania and Oberon use music to charm Bottom and the four lovers into a deep sleep, and then exit.

Theseus and Hippolyta, accompanied by Egeus and others, have come to the woods to celebrate May Day. They discover the four lovers asleep and wake them. Lysander now loves Hermia again, and Demetrius loves Helena. When Lysander reveals how he and Hermia fled Athens, Egeus begs Theseus to punish him. But when Demetrius announces that he now loves Helena, Theseus overrides Egeus and decrees that Lysander will marry Hermia and Demetrius Helena when Theseus himself weds Hippolyta. As the lovers depart for Athens, Bottom awakes and attempts to recall his night's experience, which seems to him now a dream.

  2. **amiable:** charming, lovable; **coy:** caress
 16. **overflown with:** submerged in
 20. **neaf:** fist
 21. **leave your courtesy:** i.e., perhaps, stop bowing
23–24. **Cavalery:** i.e., Cavalier
 24. **Cobweb:** Cobweb has been sent off already, and so this reference is considered an error by many editors. Some suggest "Peaseblossom" should be substituted for "Cobweb," but it is impossible to know how exactly to correct the "error."
 25. **marvels:** i.e., marvelously
 30. **the tongs and the bones:** instruments used in burlesque or rustic music (**Tongs** were played by hitting pieces of metal, like a modern triangle. **Bones** were pieces of bone clicked together.)
 32. **provender:** hay, food for cattle
 34. **bottle:** bundle

35. **fellow:** equal
40. **exposition of:** Bottom's error for "disposition to"
42. **all ways:** i.e., in every direction
48. **dotage:** infatuation
54. **sometime:** formerly
55. **orient:** bright, lustrous
56. **flouriets:** i.e., little flowers
61. **straight:** straightway, immediately
67. **other:** i.e., others
68. **May:** i.e., they may; **repair:** go, travel
69. **accidents:** incidents, events
72. **wast wont to:** i.e., used to
74–75. **Dian's bud . . . power:** Oberon earlier explains (at 2.1.191 and 3.2.387–92) that he has in his possession a second flower that can undo the effect of the flower he calls "love-in-idleness." Here, as he applies the juice to Titania's eyes, he links the curative flower to Diana (**Dian's bud**), the goddess of chastity, and love-in-idleness to Cupid, god of love.
81. **visage:** appearance, face
84. **these five:** i.e., Bottom and the four lovers
92. **solemnly:** ceremoniously
93. **triumphantly:** festively
97. **attend and mark:** i.e., pay attention, notice
99. **sad:** serious
106 SD. **Wind horn:** i.e., one or more hunting horns are blown
107. **Forester:** the official in charge of the forest land and responsible for the wild animals of the forest
108. **our observation:** i.e., our observance of May Day rites
109. **since . . . day:** i.e., since it is still early   **vaward:** vanguard
110. **music of my hounds:** The cry of a pack of hounds in pursuit of hunted animals was compared to orchestral or vocal music, and its sound was much prized.

At line 127, Theseus suggests that his hounds' music is more important to him than their speed.

111. **Uncouple:** i.e., unleash the hounds

114–15. **mark . . . conjunction:** i.e., listen to the sound created by the coming together of the cry of the hounds and its echo from the mountains

116. **Hercules:** a hero in Greek and Roman mythology; **Cadmus:** legendary founder of the city of Thebes

117. **bayed:** i.e., brought to bay

118. **hounds of Sparta:** Spartan hounds, celebrated for their hunting abilities

119. **chiding:** i.e., barking

124. **So:** i.e., like those of Sparta; **flewed:** with large folds of flesh about the mouth; **sanded:** i.e., sandy-colored

126. **dewlapped:** i.e., with folds of skin under their necks

127–28. **matched . . . each:** i.e., their cry was like a set of bells, each voice chiming in tune with the others **Each under each:** i.e., like notes on a scale

128. **cry:** pack; **tunable:** i.e., tuneful

131. **soft:** i.e., stop a minute

136. **of:** i.e., at

137–38. **observe / The rite of May:** i.e., celebrate May Day

139. **grace:** honor; **solemnity:** observance (i.e., of May Day rites)

144. **Saint Valentine:** i.e., Valentine's Day (when birds proverbially chose their mates)

150. **jealousy:** suspicion, mistrust

152. **amazèdly:** i.e., in a state of bewilderment (as if lost in a maze)

155. **truly . . . speak:** i.e., I wish to speak the truth

159. **Without:** outside of, beyond

168. **hither:** i.e., to come here

169. **hither:** here

170. **in fancy:** i.e., drawn by her love
171. **wot:** know
174. **idle gaud:** worthless trinket
176. **virtue:** power
180. **like a sickness:** i.e., like one who is sick
186. **overbear:** i.e., overrule
189. **for:** i.e., because; **something:** i.e., somewhat
192. **in great solemnity:** i.e., with great ceremony
196. **parted:** divided (i.e., out of focus)
199–200. **like a jewel . . . own:** i.e., as if I had found a jewel whom someone else might claim
211. **My next:** i.e., my next line
212. **Hey-ho!:** This may signal either a call or a big yawn.
213. **God's:** i.e., perhaps, may God save
216. **go about:** i.e., try
219. **patched:** i.e., dressed in motley, such as a professional fool would wear
220–24. **The eye . . . dream was:** This seems to be Bottom's confused memory of 1 Corinthians 2.9, where St. Paul writes: "The eye hath not seen, and the ear hath not heard, neither have entered into the heart of man, the things which God hath prepared for them that love him" (as translated in the Bishops' Bible [1568]).
225–26. **because it hath no bottom:** St. Paul's letter to the Corinthians continues (1 Corinthians 2.10): ". . . the spirit searcheth all things, yea the deep things of God," words that again may be confusingly echoed in Bottom's reflection on the bottomlessness of his vision.
227–29. **a play . . . her death:** It has been suggested that the vagueness here about "a play" and "her death" are signs that Bottom is still half asleep.

4.2 The tradesmen regret, for their own sakes and for Bottom's, the loss of their opportunity to perform the play, since Bottom is irreplaceable. Bottom arrives and announces that their play has been chosen by Theseus for performance that night.

   3. **Out of doubt:** i.e., surely
   4. **transported:** i.e., transformed; carried away
   5–6. **It goes . . . doth it?:** i.e., it won't go on, will it?
   8. **discharge:** i.e., play, perform
   11. **person:** personage, appearance
   14. **thing of naught:** an evil thing
   17–18. **we . . . men:** i.e., our fortunes would have been made
   19–20. **six pence . . . life:** Such a daily pension would have been very grand.
   21. **An:** if
   26. **hearts:** hearties, good fellows
   31–32. **right . . . fell out:** just . . . happened
   34. **of me:** i.e., from me
   36. **strings to your beards:** i.e., strings to tie on your false beards
   36–37. **ribbons to your pumps:** i.e., ribbons to decorate your fancy shoes
   37. **presently:** right away
   39. **preferred:** recommended

5.1 Theseus dismisses as imaginary the lovers' account of their night's experience, and then chooses "Pyramus and Thisbe" for the night's entertainment. The play is so ridiculous and the performance so bad that the courtly audience finds pleasure in mocking them. When the play is over and the newly married couples have retired to bed, the fairies enter, led by Titania and Oberon, to bless the three marriages. Robin Goodfellow asks the audience to think of the play as if it were a dream.

   1. **that:** i.e., that which, what
   2. **may:** i.e., can

3. **antique fables:** (1) old stories; (2) fantastic tales;
fairy toys: i.e., foolish tales (**toys**) about fairies

5. **shaping fantasies:** i.e., creative imaginations; **apprehend:** conceive, imagine

6. **comprehends:** grasps, understands

8. **of imagination all compact:** i.e., made up entirely of imagination

10. **all as frantic:** i.e., just as insane

11. **Helen's beauty:** i.e., the beauty of the legendary Helen of Troy; **a brow of Egypt:** i.e., a Gypsy-like face (another allusion to the supposed unattractiveness of women with darker coloring)

21. **comprehends:** includes (as a part of its conception of the joy); **some bringer of:** i.e., someone or something that brings

25. **all . . . together:** i.e., their minds all suffering the same transformation

26. **More witnesseth than fancy's images:** i.e., attests to more than imaginary delusions

27. **constancy:** consistency, unchangingness

28. **howsoever:** i.e., in any case; **admirable:** i.e., worthy of wonder

32. **More:** i.e., more joy

33. **Wait:** i.e., await you; **board:** table

34. **masques:** like **revels** (line 39), a name for courtly entertainment

37. **after-supper:** a light meal or dessert served after the main supper

43. **abridgment:** i.e., pastime (to abridge or shorten the evening)

46. **brief:** i.e., list, short account; **sports:** diversions;
ripe: ready, prepared

48. **battle with the Centaurs:** a famous incident in the life of Hercules

50. **We'll none:** i.e., we'll have none

51. **my kinsman:** Plutarch's "Life of Theseus" says that Hercules was Theseus's cousin.

52–53. **The riot . . . rage:** This would be the story of Orpheus (**the Thracian singer**), who was torn to pieces by women who worshiped Bacchus.

54. **device:** show, entertainment

56–57. **The thrice . . . beggary:** presumably a satirical play about the neglect of scholarship and learning **thrice-three Muses:** The nine muses presided over literature, arts, and sciences.

58. **critical:** judgmental

59. **sorting with:** i.e., suitable for, appropriate to

74. **passion of loud laughter:** i.e., intense or vehement laughter

78. **toiled:** fatigued, worn out; **unbreathed:** i.e., unexercised

79. **against:** i.e., in time for

85. **conned:** memorized

89. **simpleness:** sincerity; lack of sophistication

91. **wretchedness:** i.e., poor wretches; **o'ercharged:** overburdened

92. **his:** i.e., its

96. **take:** accept

97. **noble respect:** i.e., a generous regard or consideration

98. **Takes . . . merit:** i.e., perhaps, considers the effort, not the effect

99. **come:** i.e., journeyed; **clerks:** scholars

100. **premeditated:** previously designed

102. **periods:** i.e., stops

103. **their practiced accent:** i.e., the emphasis they had rehearsed

104. **dumbly:** silently

107. **fearful:** frightened

111. **to my capacity:** perhaps, in my opinion

112. **addressed:** ready

114–24. **If . . . know:** The comic effect of this prologue depends on its being delivered with the major pauses in the wrong places, in just the way that Theseus had earlier described.

117. **end:** aim, purpose

119. **minding:** i.e., intending

125. **stand upon points:** (1) is not a stickler for detail; (2) pays no attention to punctuation

126. **rid:** i.e., ridden; **rough:** i.e., untrained

127. **stop:** (1) signal to stop; (2) punctuation mark

130. **recorder:** a flutelike musical instrument

130–31. **in government:** i.e., controlled

132–33. **nothing:** not at all

148. **hight:** is called

151. **fall:** i.e., drop

153. **tall:** brave

156. **broached:** i.e., stabbed (with a comic allusion to broaching [i.e., tapping] a keg of beer or wine)

160. **At large:** i.e., at length

172. **sinister:** left (Here, in performance, "Wall" usually makes a "cranny" by holding his fingers in the shape of a V.)

174. **lime and hair:** the materials that make up roughcast

176. **wittiest:** most intelligent

188. **eyne:** i.e., eyes

189. **Thanks:** in response to Wall's gesture of showing the cranny; **Jove shield thee:** i.e., God reward you

194. **being sensible:** i.e., having senses

195. **curse again:** i.e., return the curse

198–99. **fall pat:** i.e., happen exactly

205. **an:** if

209. **Limander:** no doubt "Leander," a famous lover

210. **Helen:** perhaps, Helen of Troy (One would think that the name here should have been Hero, Leander's love.)

211. **Shafalus, Procrus:** no doubt Cephalus and Procris, famous tragic lovers

215. **Ninny's tomb:** i.e., Ninus's tomb (See note to 3.1.97.)

216. **'Tide . . . death:** i.e., come life or death   **'Tide:** betide

217. **dischargèd:** performed

222. **to:** i.e., as to

224. **in this kind:** i.e., plays and/or players; **shadows:** illusions, fictions

238. **A lion . . . dam:** perhaps, am neither a lion nor a lioness   **fell:** fierce   **dam:** mother

254-55. **horns . . . head:** a reference to the cuckold

256. **no crescent:** i.e., not a crescent (waxing, growing) moon

263. **for the candle:** i.e., for fear of the candle

264. **in snuff:** i.e., (1) in need of having its wick trimmed; (2) angry

269. **stay:** wait for

284. **moused:** torn or shaken (as a cat with a mouse)

293. **dole:** sorrow

299. **Furies:** the Erinys, mythological beings who punished those who offended against natural and moral laws; **fell:** fierce

300. **Fates:** In Greek mythology, the three Fates wove one's life and brought about one's death by cutting life's thread.

301. **thread and thrum:** i.e., the whole thread of my life   **thrum:** the tufted end of the warp

302. **Quail:** overcome; **quell:** kill

303. **passion:** i.e., staging of strong emotion

305. **Beshrew:** i.e., curse

306. **wherefore:** why

307. **deflowered:** a malapropism, or verbal confusion, perhaps for "devoured"

309-10. **with cheer:** i.e., with her face; also, perhaps, cheerfully

311. **confound:** destroy

313. **pap:** breast (usually used to refer to the nipple or breast of a woman or the teat of an animal)

323. **die:** one of a pair of dice; **ace:** a one-spot on a die

328. **ass:** perhaps a pun on the earlier **ace**

329. **How chance Moonshine is:** i.e., why has Moonshine

340. **means:** (1) moans, laments; (2) lodges a formal complaint; **videlicet:** to wit, as follows

344. **dumb:** silent

353. **Sisters Three:** i.e., the Fates

357. **shore:** i.e., shorn, cut (phrased to rhyme with **gore**)

358. **thread of silk:** i.e., the thread of his life (phrased to rhyme with **milk**)

361. **imbrue:** drench with blood

369–70. **see . . . hear:** Once again, Bottom confuses the senses of seeing and hearing.

370. **Bergomask dance:** a rustic dance

377–78. **discharged:** performed

380. **iron tongue of midnight:** i.e., the midnight bell (with its iron clapper); **told:** counted out

381. **fairy time:** i.e., the time between midnight and dawn

382. **outsleep:** i.e., sleep past, oversleep

383. **overwatched:** i.e., stayed up so late

384. **palpable-gross:** i.e., obviously dull

385. **heavy gait:** slow pace

386. **solemnity:** festive celebration

390. **heavy:** sleepy

391. **fordone:** exhausted

392. **wasted brands:** burned-up logs

394–95. **Puts . . . In remembrance of:** causes . . . to think of

398. **his:** i.e., its

401. **triple Hecate:** The goddess Hecate had three

forms (Luna, the moon, in the sky; Diana on earth; and Proserpina in the underworld).

404. **frolic:** frolicsome, merry

420. **will we:** i.e., Titania and I will go

422. **there create:** i.e., created there

426. **the blots of Nature's hand:** i.e., deformities

427. **in their issue stand:** appear in their offspring

429. **prodigious:** ominous; abnormal

432. **field-dew consecrate:** i.e., consecrated dew

434. **several:** separate, individual

440. **shadows:** illusions; actors

444. **idle:** trivial

445. **No . . . dream:** i.e., producing no more than a dream

447. **mend:** improve

450. **serpent's tongue:** i.e., hisses (from the audience)

454. **Give me your hands:** i.e., applaud

Textual Notes

The reading of the present text appears to the left of the square bracket. The earliest sources of readings not in **Q1,** the quarto of 1600, are indicated as follows: **Q2** is the quarto of 1619; **Qq** is "Q1 and Q2"; **F** is the Shakespeare First Folio of 1623, in which *A Midsummer Night's Dream* is a slightly edited reprint of Q2. **Ed.** is an earlier editor of Shakespeare, from the editor of the Second Folio of 1632 to the present. **SD** means stage direction; **SP** means speech heading.

1.1   4. wanes] Q2, F; waues Q1

               10. New] Ed.; Now Qq, F

               20. SD *Lysander and*] F; Lysander *and* Helena, *and* Qq

     25, 27. Stand forth, Demetrius . . . Stand forth, Lysander] Ed.; *set as stage directions in* Qq, F

             138. low] Ed.; loue Qq, F

             190. Yours would] Ed.; Your words Qq, F

             195. I'd] Ed.; ile Qq, F

             221. sweet] Ed.; sweld Qq, F

             224. stranger companies] Ed.; strange companions Qq, F

2.1   63. Fairies] Ed.; Fairy Qq, F

             81. Perigouna] Ed.; *Perigenia* Qq, F

             82. Aegles] Ed.; Eagles Qq, F

	112.	thin] Ed.; chinne Qq, F
	164.	the] F; *omit* Q
	208.	not, nor] F; not, not Qq
	253.	SD *Robin*] Ed.; Pucke Qq, F
2.2	9.	SP FIRST FAIRY] Ed.; *omit* Qq, F
	13, 24.	SP CHORUS] Ed.; *omit* Qq, F
	45.	Be] Q2, F; Bet Q1
	53.	is] Q2, F; it Q1
	71.	SD *Robin*] Ed.; Pucke Qq, F
3.1	55.	SP BOTTOM] Q2, F; *Cet.* Q1
	81, 83, 104.	SP BOTTOM, *as Pyramus*] Ed.; *Pyra.* Qq, F
	82.	odors] F; odorous Qq
	87.	SP ROBIN] F (*Puck*); *Quin.* Qq
	88.	SP FLUTE] Ed.; *Thys.* Qq, F
	92.	SP FLUTE, *as Thisbe*] Ed.; *Thys.* Qq, F
	101.	SP FLUTE] Ed.; *Thys.* Qq, F
	103.	SD *after line 113 in* F "Enter Piramus with the Asse head"; *omit* Q1
	104.	fair Thisbe] Ed.; *Thysby* Qq, F
	106.	SD *Quince . . . exit.*] *omit* Qq; *The Clownes all Exit.* F
	164.	SD *Enter foure Fairyes.* Qq; *Enter Peaseblossome, Cobweb, Moth, Mustardseede, and foure Fairies.* F
	165.	SP PEASEBLOSSOM] Ed.; *Fairies.* Qq, F
	166.	SP COBWEB] Ed.; *omit* Qq, F
	167.	SP MOTE] Ed.; *omit* Qq, F
	168.	SP MUSTARDSEED] Ed.; *omit* Qq, F
	169.	SP ALL] Ed.; *omit* Qq, F
	181.	SP PEASEBLOSSOM] Ed.; *1. Fai.* Qq, F
	182.	SP COBWEB] Ed.; *omit* Qq, F
	183.	SP MOTE] Ed.; *2. Fai.* Qq, F
	184.	SP MUSTARDSEED] Ed.; *3. Fai.* Qq, F
	202.	of] Ed.; *omit* Qq, F
3.2	0.	SD *Enter . . . Fairies.*] F (*adding "solus"*); Qq (*adding "and Robin goodfellow."*)

3. SD *Enter ... Goodfellow.*] F (*Enter Pucke.*); *omit* Qq

19. mimic] F; Minnick Q1; Minnock Q2

82. so] Ed.; *omit* Qq, F

87. sleep] Ed.; slippe Qq, F

111. SD *Robin*] Puck Qq, F

140. *waking up*] F (*Awa.*) *after line 139; omit* Qq

218. first, like] Ed.; first life Qq, F

257. prayers] Ed.; praise Qq, F

314. gentlemen] Q2, F; gentleman Q1

343. but] Q2, F; hut Q1

365. SD *She exits.*] *Exeunt.* Qq; *omit* F

480. To] Ed.; *omit* Qq, F

4.1

0. SD *Bottom*] Ed.; *Clowne* Qq, F. *At the end of Act 3 F reads "They sleepe all the Act."*

84. sleep ... these five] Ed.; sleepe: ... these, fine Qq, F

106. SD *Oberon ... Egeus.*] *Exeunt. Enter Theseus and all his traine. Winde horne.* Qq; *Exeunt. Winde Hornes. Enter Theseus, Egeus, Hippolita and all his traine.* F

121. Seemed] Ed.; Seeme Qq, F

133. is] Q2, F; *omit* Q1

143. SD *Shout ... up.*] *Shoute within: they all start vp. Winde hornes.* Qq; *Hornes and they wake. Shout within, they all start vp.* F

179. saw] Ed.; see Qq, F

193. SD *Theseus ... exit.*] *Exit Duke and Lords.* F

209. let us] Q2, F; lets Q1

210. SD *waking up*] F (*"Bottome wakes."* after line 209)

217. to] Q2, F; *omit* Q1

	219.	a patched] F; patcht a Qq
4.2	0.	SD *Enter ... Starveling.*] *Enter* Quince, Flute, Thisby *and the rabble.* Qq; *Enter Quince, Flute, Thisbie, Snout, and Starueling.* F
	3.	SP STARVELING] F; *Flut.* Qq
5.1	0.	SD *Enter ... Philostrate.*] Q1; *Enter Theseus, Hippolita, Egeus and his Lords.* F
	37.	our] F; Or Qq
	133.	SD *Prologue (Quince)*] F *at 113 SD has* "Prologue. Quince."
	150.	scare] Ed.; scarre Qq, F
	165.	Snout] F; *Flute* Qq
	203.	up in thee] F; now againe Qq
	218.	SD *He exits.*] *Exit Clow.* F
	219.	wall down] Ed.; morall downe F; Moon vsed Qq
	279.	SD *The ... off*] F; *omit* Q1
	289.	gleams] Ed.; beames Qq, F
	368.	SP BOTTOM] F; *Lyon* Qq
	387.	SD *Robin Goodfellow*] Ed.; Pucke Qq, F
	388.	lion] Ed.; Lyons Qq, F
	389.	behowls] Ed.; beholds Qq, F
	436–37.	*lines transposed in* Qq, F
	439.	SD *All ... exit.*] Ed.; *Exeunt.* Qq; *omit* F

TWELFTH NIGHT,
OR,
WHAT
YOU WILL

Shakespeare's
Twelfth Night, or, What You Will

In *Twelfth Night*, Shakespeare plays with the intersections of love and power. The Countess Olivia is presented to us at the play's beginning as an independent and powerful woman. The sudden deaths of her father and her brother have left her in charge of her own household and have thereby given her power over such male relatives as Sir Toby Belch. Her status as a wealthy, aristocratic single woman makes her the focus of male attention, and she is especially attractive to Duke (or Count) Orsino, who, as the play begins, is already pursuing her. There also circle about her two other would-be suitors: the pretentious and socially ambitious steward, Malvolio, a man whose ambitions make him vulnerable to manipulation by members of Olivia's household; and the weak and foolish Sir Andrew Aguecheek, who is altogether ignored by Olivia but whose delusions of possible marriage to her make him an easy victim of the flattering and swindling Sir Toby.

Onto this scene arrive the well-born twins Viola and Sebastian, and the love of power gives way to the power of love. The twins have been shipwrecked; each thinks the other is drowned; both are destitute. Without protection, Viola chooses to disguise herself as a page, call herself Cesario, and enter into the service of Orsino. In her role as the young Cesario, such is her beauty and her command of language that she immediately wins Orsino's complete trust; he enlists her as his envoy to his beloved Olivia—only to have Olivia fall desperately in love with the beautiful young messenger. Sebastian, too, although without either power or wealth, is similarly irresistible. Antonio, for example, not only saves him from death in the sea but also risks his own life to remain in Sebastian's company.

As is usual in comedy, the play complicates these tangled relationships before it finally and wonderfully untangles them. The title of the play suggests that there is a certain urgency to the need for this disentangling. "Twelfth Night" is the twelfth night after Christmas, the last night of what used to be the extended period of celebration of the Christmas season. Thus it marks the boundary between the time for games and disguisings and the business of the workaday world. The second part of the title, "What You Will," suggests that this play gives us a world that we would all choose (or "will") to enjoy, if we but could.

Characters in the Play

VIOLA, a lady of Messaline shipwrecked on the coast of
   Illyria (later disguised as CESARIO)

OLIVIA, an Illyrian countess
MARIA, her waiting-gentlewoman
SIR TOBY BELCH, Olivia's kinsman
SIR ANDREW AGUECHEEK, Sir Toby's companion
MALVOLIO, steward in Olivia's household
FOOL, Olivia's jester, named Feste
FABIAN, a gentleman in Olivia's household

ORSINO, duke (or count) of Illyria
VALENTINE ⎱ gentlemen serving Orsino
CURIO ⎰

SEBASTIAN, Viola's brother
ANTONIO, friend to Sebastian

CAPTAIN
PRIEST
TWO officers

Lords, Sailors, Musicians, and other Attendants

ACT 1

Scene 1

Enter Orsino, Duke of Illyria, Curio, and other Lords,
⌈*with Musicians playing.*⌉

ORSINO
  If music be the food of love, play on.
  Give me excess of it, that, surfeiting,
  The appetite may sicken and so die.
  That strain again! It had a dying fall.
  O, it came o'er my ear like the sweet sound   5
  That breathes upon a bank of violets,
  Stealing and giving odor. Enough; no more.
  'Tis not so sweet now as it was before.
  O spirit of love, how quick and fresh art thou,
  That, notwithstanding thy capacity   10
  Receiveth as the sea, naught enters there,
  Of what validity and pitch soe'er,
  But falls into abatement and low price
  Even in a minute. So full of shapes is fancy
  That it alone is high fantastical.   15

CURIO
  Will you go hunt, my lord?

ORSINO   What, Curio?

CURIO   The hart.

ORSINO
  Why, so I do, the noblest that I have.
  O, when mine eyes did see Olivia first,   20

291

Methought she purged the air of pestilence.
That instant was I turned into a hart,
And my desires, like fell and cruel hounds,
E'er since pursue me.

Enter Valentine.

How now, what news from her? 25

VALENTINE
So please my lord, I might not be admitted,
But from her handmaid do return this answer:
The element itself, till seven years' heat,
Shall not behold her face at ample view,
But like a cloistress she will veilèd walk, 30
And water once a day her chamber round
With eye-offending brine—all this to season
A brother's dead love, which she would keep fresh
And lasting in her sad remembrance.

ORSINO
O, she that hath a heart of that fine frame 35
To pay this debt of love but to a brother,
How will she love when the rich golden shaft
Hath killed the flock of all affections else
That live in her; when liver, brain, and heart,
These sovereign thrones, are all supplied, and filled 40
Her sweet perfections with one self king!
Away before me to sweet beds of flowers!
Love thoughts lie rich when canopied with bowers.

They exit.

Scene 2
Enter Viola, a Captain, and Sailors.

VIOLA   What country, friends, is this?
CAPTAIN   This is Illyria, lady.
VIOLA
And what should I do in Illyria?

My brother he is in Elysium.
Perchance he is not drowned.—What think you,   5
  sailors?

CAPTAIN
It is perchance that you yourself were saved.

VIOLA
O, my poor brother! And so perchance may he be.

CAPTAIN
True, madam. And to comfort you with chance,
Assure yourself, after our ship did split,   10
When you and those poor number saved with you
Hung on our driving boat, I saw your brother,
Most provident in peril, bind himself
(Courage and hope both teaching him the practice)
To a strong mast that lived upon the sea,   15
Where, like ⌈Arion⌉ on the dolphin's back,
I saw him hold acquaintance with the waves
So long as I could see.

VIOLA, ⌈*giving him money*⌉   For saying so, there's gold.
Mine own escape unfoldeth to my hope,   20
Whereto thy speech serves for authority,
The like of him. Know'st thou this country?

CAPTAIN
Ay, madam, well, for I was bred and born
Not three hours' travel from this very place.

VIOLA   Who governs here?   25

CAPTAIN
A noble duke, in nature as in name.

VIOLA   What is his name?

CAPTAIN   Orsino.

VIOLA
Orsino. I have heard my father name him.
He was a bachelor then.   30

CAPTAIN
And so is now, or was so very late;
For but a month ago I went from hence,

And then 'twas fresh in murmur (as, you know,
What great ones do the less will prattle of)
That he did seek the love of fair Olivia.   35

VIOLA   What's she?

CAPTAIN
A virtuous maid, the daughter of a count
That died some twelvemonth since, then leaving her
In the protection of his son, her brother,
Who shortly also died, for whose dear love,   40
They say, she hath abjured the sight
And company of men.

VIOLA   O, that I served that lady,
And might not be delivered to the world
Till I had made mine own occasion mellow,   45
What my estate is.

CAPTAIN   That were hard to compass
Because she will admit no kind of suit,
No, not the Duke's.

VIOLA
There is a fair behavior in thee, captain,   50
And though that nature with a beauteous wall
Doth oft close in pollution, yet of thee
I will believe thou hast a mind that suits
With this thy fair and outward character.
I prithee—and I'll pay thee bounteously—   55
Conceal me what I am, and be my aid
For such disguise as haply shall become
The form of my intent. I'll serve this duke.
Thou shalt present me as an eunuch to him.
It may be worth thy pains, for I can sing   60
And speak to him in many sorts of music
That will allow me very worth his service.
What else may hap, to time I will commit.
Only shape thou thy silence to my wit.

CAPTAIN
Be you his eunuch, and your mute I'll be.   65

When my tongue blabs, then let mine eyes not see.
VIOLA   I thank thee. Lead me on.

They exit.

Scene 3
Enter Sir Toby and Maria.

TOBY   What a plague means my niece to take the death
of her brother thus? I am sure care's an enemy to
life.
MARIA   By my troth, Sir Toby, you must come in earlier
o' nights. Your cousin, my lady, takes great excep-   5
tions to your ill hours.
TOBY   Why, let her except before excepted!
MARIA   Ay, but you must confine yourself within the
modest limits of order.
TOBY   Confine? I'll confine myself no finer than I am.   10
These clothes are good enough to drink in, and so
be these boots too. An they be not, let them hang
themselves in their own straps!
MARIA   That quaffing and drinking will undo you. I
heard my lady talk of it yesterday, and of a foolish   15
knight that you brought in one night here to be her
wooer.
TOBY   Who, Sir Andrew Aguecheek?
MARIA   Ay, he.
TOBY   He's as tall a man as any 's in Illyria.   20
MARIA   What's that to th' purpose?
TOBY   Why, he has three thousand ducats a year!
MARIA   Ay, but he'll have but a year in all these ducats.
He's a very fool and a prodigal.
TOBY   Fie, that you'll say so! He plays o' th' viol-de-   25
gamboys, and speaks three or four languages word
for word without book, and hath all the good gifts of
nature.

MARIA He hath indeed, almost natural, for, besides
that he's a fool, he's a great quarreler, and, but that   30
he hath the gift of a coward to allay the gust he hath
in quarreling, 'tis thought among the prudent he
would quickly have the gift of a grave.

TOBY By this hand, they are scoundrels and substractors that say so of him. Who are they?   35

MARIA They that add, moreover, he's drunk nightly in
your company.

TOBY With drinking healths to my niece. I'll drink to
her as long as there is a passage in my throat and
drink in Illyria. He's a coward and a coistrel that   40
will not drink to my niece till his brains turn o' th'
toe like a parish top. What, wench! *Castiliano vulgo*,
for here comes Sir Andrew Agueface.

Enter Sir Andrew.

ANDREW Sir Toby Belch! How now, Sir Toby Belch?

TOBY Sweet Sir Andrew!   45

ANDREW, ⌜*to Maria*⌝ Bless you, fair shrew.

MARIA And you too, sir.

TOBY Accost, Sir Andrew, accost!

ANDREW What's that?

TOBY My niece's chambermaid.   50

⌜ANDREW⌝ Good Mistress Accost, I desire better acquaintance.

MARIA My name is Mary, sir.

ANDREW Good Mistress Mary Accost—

TOBY You mistake, knight. "Accost" is front her, board   55
her, woo her, assail her.

ANDREW By my troth, I would not undertake her in
this company. Is that the meaning of "accost"?

MARIA Fare you well, gentlemen.   ⌜*She begins to exit.*⌝

TOBY An thou let part so, Sir Andrew, would thou   60
mightst never draw sword again.

ANDREW An you part so, mistress, I would I might

never draw sword again. Fair lady, do you think you
have fools in hand?

MARIA　Sir, I have not you by th' hand.　　　　　　65

ANDREW　Marry, but you shall have, and here's my
hand.　　　　　　　　　　　　⌐*He offers his hand.*⌐

MARIA, ⌐*taking his hand*⌐ Now, sir, thought is free. I
pray you, bring your hand to th' butt'ry bar and let
it drink.　　　　　　　　　　　　　　　　　70

ANDREW　Wherefore, sweetheart? What's your metaphor?

MARIA　It's dry, sir.

ANDREW　Why, I think so. I am not such an ass but I
can keep my hand dry. But what's your jest?　　　75

MARIA　A dry jest, sir.

ANDREW　Are you full of them?

MARIA　Ay, sir, I have them at my fingers' ends. Marry,
now I let go your hand, I am barren.　　*Maria exits.*

TOBY　O knight, thou lack'st a cup of canary! When did　80
I see thee so put down?

ANDREW　Never in your life, I think, unless you see
canary put me down. Methinks sometimes I have
no more wit than a Christian or an ordinary man
has. But I am a great eater of beef, and I believe that　85
does harm to my wit.

TOBY　No question.

ANDREW　An I thought that, I'd forswear it. I'll ride
home tomorrow, Sir Toby.

TOBY　*Pourquoi*, my dear knight?　　　　　　90

ANDREW　What is *"pourquoi"*? Do, or not do? I would I
had bestowed that time in the tongues that I have in
fencing, dancing, and bearbaiting. O, had I but
followed the arts!

TOBY　Then hadst thou had an excellent head of hair.　95

ANDREW　Why, would that have mended my hair?

TOBY　Past question, for thou seest it will not ⌐curl by⌐
nature.

ANDREW But it becomes ⌜me⌝ well enough, does 't not?

TOBY Excellent! It hangs like flax on a distaff, and I 100
hope to see a huswife take thee between her legs
and spin it off.

ANDREW Faith, I'll home tomorrow, Sir Toby. Your
niece will not be seen, or if she be, it's four to one
she'll none of me. The Count himself here hard by 105
woos her.

TOBY She'll none o' th' Count. She'll not match above
her degree, neither in estate, years, nor wit. I have
heard her swear 't. Tut, there's life in 't, man.

ANDREW I'll stay a month longer. I am a fellow o' th' 110
strangest mind i' th' world. I delight in masques
and revels sometimes altogether.

TOBY Art thou good at these kickshawses, knight?

ANDREW As any man in Illyria, whatsoever he be,
under the degree of my betters, and yet I will not 115
compare with an old man.

TOBY What is thy excellence in a galliard, knight?

ANDREW Faith, I can cut a caper.

TOBY And I can cut the mutton to 't.

ANDREW And I think I have the back-trick simply as 120
strong as any man in Illyria.

TOBY Wherefore are these things hid? Wherefore have
these gifts a curtain before 'em? Are they like to
take dust, like Mistress Mall's picture? Why dost
thou not go to church in a galliard and come home 125
in a coranto? My very walk should be a jig. I would
not so much as make water but in a sink-a-pace.
What dost thou mean? Is it a world to hide virtues
in? I did think, by the excellent constitution of thy
leg, it was formed under the star of a galliard. 130

ANDREW Ay, 'tis strong, and it does indifferent well in a
⌜dun-colored⌝ stock. Shall we ⌜set⌝ about some
revels?

TOBY What shall we do else? Were we not born under
    Taurus?   135

ANDREW Taurus? ⌜That's⌝ sides and heart.

TOBY No, sir, it is legs and thighs. Let me see thee
    caper. ⌜*Sir Andrew dances.*⌝ Ha, higher! Ha, ha,
    excellent!

                                                   They exit.

Scene 4

Enter Valentine, and Viola in man's attire ⌜as Cesario.⌝

VALENTINE If the Duke continue these favors towards
    you, Cesario, you are like to be much advanced. He
    hath known you but three days, and already you
    are no stranger.

VIOLA You either fear his humor or my negligence, that   5
    you call in question the continuance of his love. Is
    he inconstant, sir, in his favors?

VALENTINE No, believe me.

VIOLA I thank you.

       Enter ⌜Orsino,⌝ Curio, and Attendants.

    Here comes the Count.   10

ORSINO Who saw Cesario, ho?

VIOLA On your attendance, my lord, here.

ORSINO, ⌜*to Curio and Attendants*⌝
    Stand you awhile aloof.—Cesario,
    Thou know'st no less but all. I have unclasped
    To thee the book even of my secret soul.   15
    Therefore, good youth, address thy gait unto her.
    Be not denied access. Stand at her doors
    And tell them, there thy fixèd foot shall grow
    Till thou have audience.

VIOLA   Sure, my noble lord,   20
    If she be so abandoned to her sorrow
    As it is spoke, she never will admit me.

ORSINO
　Be clamorous and leap all civil bounds
　Rather than make unprofited return.

VIOLA
　Say I do speak with her, my lord, what then?　25

ORSINO
　O, then unfold the passion of my love.
　Surprise her with discourse of my dear faith.
　It shall become thee well to act my woes.
　She will attend it better in thy youth
　Than in a nuncio's of more grave aspect.　30

VIOLA
　I think not so, my lord.

ORSINO　　　　　　　　Dear lad, believe it;
　For they shall yet belie thy happy years
　That say thou art a man. Diana's lip
　Is not more smooth and rubious, thy small pipe　35
　Is as the maiden's organ, shrill and sound,
　And all is semblative a woman's part.
　I know thy constellation is right apt
　For this affair.—Some four or five attend him,
　All, if you will, for I myself am best　40
　When least in company.—Prosper well in this
　And thou shalt live as freely as thy lord,
　To call his fortunes thine.

VIOLA　　　　　　　　I'll do my best
　To woo your lady. ⌜*Aside.*⌝ Yet a barful strife!　45
　Whoe'er I woo, myself would be his wife.

　　　　　　　　　　　　　　　　　They exit.

Scene 5
Enter Maria and ⌜*Feste, the Fool.*⌝

MARIA　Nay, either tell me where thou hast been, or I
　　will not open my lips so wide as a bristle may enter

in way of thy excuse. My lady will hang thee for thy
absence.

FOOL   Let her hang me. He that is well hanged in this   5
world needs to fear no colors.

MARIA   Make that good.

FOOL   He shall see none to fear.

MARIA   A good Lenten answer. I can tell thee where
that saying was born, of "I fear no colors."   10

FOOL   Where, good Mistress Mary?

MARIA   In the wars; and that may you be bold to say in
your foolery.

FOOL   Well, God give them wisdom that have it, and
those that are Fools, let them use their talents.   15

MARIA   Yet you will be hanged for being so long absent.
Or to be turned away, is not that as good as a
hanging to you?

FOOL   Many a good hanging prevents a bad marriage,
and, for turning away, let summer bear it out.   20

MARIA   You are resolute, then?

FOOL   Not so, neither, but I am resolved on two points.

MARIA   That if one break, the other will hold, or, if both
break, your gaskins fall.

FOOL   Apt, in good faith, very apt. Well, go thy way. If Sir   25
Toby would leave drinking, thou wert as witty a
piece of Eve's flesh as any in Illyria.

MARIA   Peace, you rogue. No more o' that. Here comes
my lady. Make your excuse wisely, you were best.

⌐*She exits.*¬

Enter Lady Olivia with Malvolio ⌐*and Attendants.*¬

FOOL ⌐*aside*¬   Wit, an 't be thy will, put me into good   30
fooling! Those wits that think they have thee do very
oft prove fools, and I that am sure I lack thee may
pass for a wise man. For what says Quinapalus?
"Better a witty Fool than a foolish wit."—God bless
thee, lady!   35

OLIVIA Take the Fool away.

FOOL Do you not hear, fellows? Take away the Lady.

OLIVIA Go to, you're a dry Fool. I'll no more of you. Besides, you grow dishonest.

FOOL Two faults, madonna, that drink and good coun- 40
sel will amend. For give the dry Fool drink, then is
the Fool not dry. Bid the dishonest man mend
himself; if he mend, he is no longer dishonest; if he
cannot, let the botcher mend him. Anything that's
mended is but patched; virtue that transgresses is 45
but patched with sin, and sin that amends is but
patched with virtue. If that this simple syllogism
will serve, so; if it will not, what remedy? As there is
no true cuckold but calamity, so beauty's a flower.
The Lady bade take away the Fool. Therefore, I say 50
again, take her away.

OLIVIA Sir, I bade them take away you.

FOOL Misprision in the highest degree! Lady, *cucullus
non facit monachum.* That's as much to say as, I
wear not motley in my brain. Good madonna, give 55
me leave to prove you a fool.

OLIVIA Can you do it?

FOOL Dexteriously, good madonna.

OLIVIA Make your proof.

FOOL I must catechize you for it, madonna. Good my 60
mouse of virtue, answer me.

OLIVIA Well, sir, for want of other idleness, I'll bide
your proof.

FOOL Good madonna, why mourn'st thou?

OLIVIA Good Fool, for my brother's death. 65

FOOL I think his soul is in hell, madonna.

OLIVIA I know his soul is in heaven, Fool.

FOOL The more fool, madonna, to mourn for your
brother's soul, being in heaven. Take away the fool,
gentlemen. 70

OLIVIA What think you of this Fool, Malvolio? Doth he
not mend?

MALVOLIO Yes, and shall do till the pangs of death
　　shake him. Infirmity, that decays the wise, doth
　　ever make the better Fool.　　　　　　　　　　　75
FOOL God send you, sir, a speedy infirmity, for the
　　better increasing your folly! Sir Toby will be sworn
　　that I am no fox, but he will not pass his word for
　　twopence that you are no fool.
OLIVIA How say you to that, Malvolio?　　　　　　80
MALVOLIO I marvel your Ladyship takes delight in
　　such a barren rascal. I saw him put down the other
　　day with an ordinary fool that has no more brain
　　than a stone. Look you now, he's out of his guard
　　already. Unless you laugh and minister occasion to　85
　　him, he is gagged. I protest I take these wise men
　　that crow so at these set kind of Fools no better than
　　the Fools' zanies.
OLIVIA O, you are sick of self-love, Malvolio, and taste
　　with a distempered appetite. To be generous, guilt-　90
　　less, and of free disposition is to take those things
　　for bird-bolts that you deem cannon bullets. There
　　is no slander in an allowed Fool, though he do
　　nothing but rail; nor no railing in a known discreet
　　man, though he do nothing but reprove.　　　　　95
FOOL Now Mercury endue thee with leasing, for thou
　　speak'st well of Fools!

Enter Maria.

MARIA Madam, there is at the gate a young gentleman
　　much desires to speak with you.
OLIVIA From the Count Orsino, is it?　　　　　　100
MARIA I know not, madam. 'Tis a fair young man, and
　　well attended.
OLIVIA Who of my people hold him in delay?
MARIA Sir Toby, madam, your kinsman.
OLIVIA Fetch him off, I pray you. He speaks nothing　105
　　but madman. Fie on him! ⌈*Maria exits.*⌉ Go you,
　　Malvolio. If it be a suit from the Count, I am sick,

or not at home; what you will, to dismiss it. (*Malvolio exits.*) Now you see, sir, how your fooling grows old, and people dislike it. 110

FOOL Thou hast spoke for us, madonna, as if thy eldest son should be a Fool, whose skull Jove cram with brains, for—here he comes—one of thy kin has a most weak *pia mater.*

Enter Sir Toby.

OLIVIA By mine honor, half drunk!—What is he at the 115 gate, cousin?

TOBY A gentleman.

OLIVIA A gentleman? What gentleman?

TOBY 'Tis a gentleman here—a plague o' these pickle herring!—How now, sot? 120

FOOL Good Sir Toby.

OLIVIA Cousin, cousin, how have you come so early by this lethargy?

TOBY Lechery? I defy lechery. There's one at the gate.

OLIVIA Ay, marry, what is he? 125

TOBY Let him be the devil an he will, I care not. Give me faith, say I. Well, it's all one. *He exits.*

OLIVIA What's a drunken man like, Fool?

FOOL Like a drowned man, a fool, and a madman. One draught above heat makes him a fool, the second 130 mads him, and a third drowns him.

OLIVIA Go thou and seek the crowner and let him sit o' my coz, for he's in the third degree of drink: he's drowned. Go look after him.

FOOL He is but mad yet, madonna, and the Fool shall 135 look to the madman. ⌜*He exits.*⌝

Enter Malvolio.

MALVOLIO Madam, yond young fellow swears he will speak with you. I told him you were sick; he takes

on him to understand so much, and therefore
comes to speak with you. I told him you were   140
asleep; he seems to have a foreknowledge of that
too, and therefore comes to speak with you. What is
to be said to him, lady? He's fortified against any
denial.

OLIVIA   Tell him he shall not speak with me.   145

MALVOLIO   Has been told so, and he says he'll stand at
your door like a sheriff's post and be the supporter
to a bench, but he'll speak with you.

OLIVIA   What kind o' man is he?

MALVOLIO   Why, of mankind.   150

OLIVIA   What manner of man?

MALVOLIO   Of very ill manner. He'll speak with you,
will you or no.

OLIVIA   Of what personage and years is he?

MALVOLIO   Not yet old enough for a man, nor young   155
enough for a boy—as a squash is before 'tis a
peascod, or a codling when 'tis almost an apple. 'Tis
with him in standing water, between boy and man.
He is very well-favored, and he speaks very shrewishly. One would think his mother's milk were   160
scarce out of him.

OLIVIA
Let him approach. Call in my gentlewoman.

MALVOLIO   Gentlewoman, my lady calls.   *He exits.*

Enter Maria.

OLIVIA
Give me my veil. Come, throw it o'er my face.
                                    ⌜*Olivia veils.*⌝
We'll once more hear Orsino's embassy.   165

Enter ⌜Viola.⌝

VIOLA   The honorable lady of the house, which is she?

OLIVIA   Speak to me. I shall answer for her. Your will?

VIOLA   Most radiant, exquisite, and unmatchable
beauty—I pray you, tell me if this be the lady of the
house, for I never saw her. I would be loath to cast   170
away my speech, for, besides that it is excellently
well penned, I have taken great pains to con it. Good
beauties, let me sustain no scorn. I am very comptible, even to the least sinister usage.

OLIVIA   Whence came you, sir?   175

VIOLA   I can say little more than I have studied, and
that question's out of my part. Good gentle one,
give me modest assurance if you be the lady of the
house, that I may proceed in my speech.

OLIVIA   Are you a comedian?   180

VIOLA   No, my profound heart. And yet, by the very
fangs of malice, I swear I am not that I play. Are
you the lady of the house?

OLIVIA   If I do not usurp myself, I am.

VIOLA   Most certain, if you are she, you do usurp   185
yourself, for what is yours to bestow is not yours to
reserve. But this is from my commission. I will on
with my speech in your praise and then show you
the heart of my message.

OLIVIA   Come to what is important in 't. I forgive you   190
the praise.

VIOLA   Alas, I took great pains to study it, and 'tis
poetical.

OLIVIA   It is the more like to be feigned. I pray you,
keep it in. I heard you were saucy at my gates, and   195
allowed your approach rather to wonder at you than
to hear you. If you be not mad, begone; if you have
reason, be brief. 'Tis not that time of moon with me
to make one in so skipping a dialogue.

MARIA   Will you hoist sail, sir? Here lies your way.   200

VIOLA   No, good swabber, I am to hull here a little

longer.—Some mollification for your giant, sweet
lady.

⌈OLIVIA⌉ Tell me your mind.

⌈VIOLA⌉ I am a messenger.   205

OLIVIA Sure you have some hideous matter to deliver
when the courtesy of it is so fearful. Speak your
office.

VIOLA It alone concerns your ear. I bring no overture
of war, no taxation of homage. I hold the olive in 210
my hand. My words are as full of peace as matter.

OLIVIA Yet you began rudely. What are you? What
would you?

VIOLA The rudeness that hath appeared in me have I
learned from my entertainment. What I am and 215
what I would are as secret as maidenhead: to your
ears, divinity; to any other's, profanation.

OLIVIA Give us the place alone. We will hear this
divinity. ⌈*Maria and Attendants exit.*⌉ Now, sir, what
is your text?   220

VIOLA Most sweet lady—

OLIVIA A comfortable doctrine, and much may be said
of it. Where lies your text?

VIOLA In Orsino's bosom.

OLIVIA In his bosom? In what chapter of his bosom? 225

VIOLA To answer by the method, in the first of his heart.

OLIVIA O, I have read it; it is heresy. Have you no more
to say?

VIOLA Good madam, let me see your face.

OLIVIA Have you any commission from your lord to 230
negotiate with my face? You are now out of your
text. But we will draw the curtain and show you the
picture. ⌈*She removes her veil.*⌉ Look you, sir, such a
one I was this present. Is 't not well done?

VIOLA Excellently done, if God did all.   235

OLIVIA 'Tis in grain, sir; 'twill endure wind and
weather.

VIOLA

'Tis beauty truly blent, whose red and white
Nature's own sweet and cunning hand laid on.
Lady, you are the cruel'st she alive   240
If you will lead these graces to the grave
And leave the world no copy.

OLIVIA   O, sir, I will not be so hard-hearted! I will give
out divers schedules of my beauty. It shall be
inventoried and every particle and utensil labeled 245
to my will: as, *item,* two lips indifferent red; *item,*
two gray eyes, with lids to them; *item,* one neck, one
chin, and so forth. Were you sent hither to praise
me?

VIOLA

I see you what you are. You are too proud.   250
But, if you were the devil, you are fair.
My lord and master loves you. O, such love
Could be but recompensed though you were
  crowned
The nonpareil of beauty.   255

OLIVIA   How does he love me?

VIOLA   With adorations, fertile tears,
With groans that thunder love, with sighs of fire.

OLIVIA

Your lord does know my mind. I cannot love him.
Yet I suppose him virtuous, know him noble,   260
Of great estate, of fresh and stainless youth;
In voices well divulged, free, learned, and valiant,
And in dimension and the shape of nature
A gracious person. But yet I cannot love him.
He might have took his answer long ago.   265

VIOLA

If I did love you in my master's flame,
With such a suff'ring, such a deadly life,
In your denial I would find no sense.
I would not understand it.

OLIVIA   Why, what would you?   270
VIOLA
  Make me a willow cabin at your gate
  And call upon my soul within the house,
  Write loyal cantons of contemnèd love
  And sing them loud even in the dead of night,
  Hallow your name to the reverberate hills   275
  And make the babbling gossip of the air
  Cry out "Olivia!" O, you should not rest
  Between the elements of air and earth
  But you should pity me.
OLIVIA   You might do much.   280
  What is your parentage?
VIOLA
  Above my fortunes, yet my state is well.
  I am a gentleman.
OLIVIA   Get you to your lord.
  I cannot love him. Let him send no more—   285
  Unless perchance you come to me again
  To tell me how he takes it. Fare you well.
  I thank you for your pains. Spend this for me.
                              ⌜*She offers money.*⌝
VIOLA
  I am no fee'd post, lady. Keep your purse.
  My master, not myself, lacks recompense.   290
  Love make his heart of flint that you shall love,
  And let your fervor, like my master's, be
  Placed in contempt. Farewell, fair cruelty.   *She exits.*
OLIVIA "What is your parentage?"
  "Above my fortunes, yet my state is well.   295
  I am a gentleman." I'll be sworn thou art.
  Thy tongue, thy face, thy limbs, actions, and spirit
  Do give thee fivefold blazon. Not too fast! Soft,
      soft!
  Unless the master were the man. How now?   300
  Even so quickly may one catch the plague?

Methinks I feel this youth's perfections
With an invisible and subtle stealth
To creep in at mine eyes. Well, let it be.—
What ho, Malvolio!   305

Enter Malvolio.

MALVOLIO   Here, madam, at your service.
OLIVIA
Run after that same peevish messenger,
The County's man. He left this ring behind him,
Would I or not. Tell him I'll none of it.
⌜*She hands him a ring.*⌝
Desire him not to flatter with his lord,   310
Nor hold him up with hopes. I am not for him.
If that the youth will come this way tomorrow,
I'll give him reasons for 't. Hie thee, Malvolio.
MALVOLIO   Madam, I will.   *He exits.*
OLIVIA
I do I know not what, and fear to find   315
Mine eye too great a flatterer for my mind.
Fate, show thy force. Ourselves we do not owe.
What is decreed must be, and be this so.
⌜*She exits.*⌝

ACT 2

Scene 1
Enter Antonio and Sebastian.

ANTONIO   Will you stay no longer? Nor will you not that
I go with you?

SEBASTIAN   By your patience, no. My stars shine darkly
over me. The malignancy of my fate might perhaps
distemper yours. Therefore I shall crave of you your   5
leave that I may bear my evils alone. It were a bad
recompense for your love to lay any of them on you.

ANTONIO   Let me yet know of you whither you are
bound.

SEBASTIAN   No, sooth, sir. My determinate voyage is   10
mere extravagancy. But I perceive in you so excellent a touch of modesty that you will not extort
from me what I am willing to keep in. Therefore it
charges me in manners the rather to express myself. You must know of me, then, Antonio, my name   15
is Sebastian, which I called Roderigo. My father was
that Sebastian of Messaline whom I know you have
heard of. He left behind him myself and a sister,
both born in an hour. If the heavens had been
pleased, would we had so ended! But you, sir,   20
altered that, for some hour before you took me
from the breach of the sea was my sister drowned.

ANTONIO   Alas the day!

311

SEBASTIAN   A lady, sir, though it was said she much
resembled me, was yet of many accounted beauti-   25
ful. But though I could not with such estimable
wonder overfar believe that, yet thus far I will boldly
publish her: she bore a mind that envy could not but
call fair. She is drowned already, sir, with salt water,
though I seem to drown her remembrance again   30
with more.

ANTONIO   Pardon me, sir, your bad entertainment.

SEBASTIAN   O good Antonio, forgive me your trouble.

ANTONIO   If you will not murder me for my love, let me
be your servant.   35

SEBASTIAN   If you will not undo what you have done—
that is, kill him whom you have recovered—desire
it not. Fare you well at once. My bosom is full of
kindness, and I am yet so near the manners of my
mother that, upon the least occasion more, mine   40
eyes will tell tales of me. I am bound to the Count
Orsino's court. Farewell.   *He exits.*

ANTONIO
The gentleness of all the gods go with thee!
I have many enemies in Orsino's court,
Else would I very shortly see thee there.   45
But come what may, I do adore thee so
That danger shall seem sport, and I will go.
                                        He exits.

Scene 2
Enter Viola and Malvolio, at several doors.

MALVOLIO   Were not you even now with the Countess
Olivia?

VIOLA   Even now, sir. On a moderate pace I have since
arrived but hither.

MALVOLIO   She returns this ring to you, sir. You might   5

have saved me my pains to have taken it away
yourself. She adds, moreover, that you should put
your lord into a desperate assurance she will none
of him. And one thing more, that you be never so
hardy to come again in his affairs, unless it be to   10
report your lord's taking of this. Receive it so.

VIOLA   She took the ring of me. I'll none of it.

MALVOLIO   Come, sir, you peevishly threw it to her, and
her will is it should be so returned. ⌜*He throws
down the ring.*⌝ If it be worth stooping for, there it   15
lies, in your eye; if not, be it his that finds it.

                                                   He exits.

VIOLA

I left no ring with her. What means this lady?
                     ⌜*She picks up the ring.*⌝
Fortune forbid my outside have not charmed her!
She made good view of me, indeed so much
That methought her eyes had lost her tongue,   20
For she did speak in starts distractedly.
She loves me, sure! The cunning of her passion
Invites me in this churlish messenger.
None of my lord's ring? Why, he sent her none!
I am the man. If it be so, as 'tis,   25
Poor lady, she were better love a dream.
Disguise, I see thou art a wickedness
Wherein the pregnant enemy does much.
How easy is it for the proper false
In women's waxen hearts to set their forms!   30
Alas, ⌜our⌝ frailty is the cause, not we,
For such as we are made ⌜of,⌝ such we be.
How will this fadge? My master loves her dearly,
And I, poor monster, fond as much on him,
And she, mistaken, seems to dote on me.   35
What will become of this? As I am man,
My state is desperate for my master's love.
As I am woman (now, alas the day!),

What thriftless sighs shall poor Olivia breathe!
O Time, thou must untangle this, not I.   40
It is too hard a knot for me t' untie.

⌈*She exits.*⌉

Scene 3
Enter Sir Toby and Sir Andrew.

TOBY   Approach, Sir Andrew. Not to be abed after
   midnight is to be up betimes, and *"diluculo sur-*
   gere," thou know'st—
ANDREW   Nay, by my troth, I know not. But I know to
   be up late is to be up late.   5
TOBY   A false conclusion. I hate it as an unfilled can. To
   be up after midnight and to go to bed then, is early,
   so that to go to bed after midnight is to go to bed
   betimes. Does not our lives consist of the four
   elements?   10
ANDREW   Faith, so they say, but I think it rather con-
   sists of eating and drinking.
TOBY   Thou'rt a scholar. Let us therefore eat and
   drink. Marian, I say, a stoup of wine!

Enter ⌈Feste, the Fool.⌉

ANDREW   Here comes the Fool, i' faith.   15
FOOL   How now, my hearts? Did you never see the
   picture of "We Three"?
TOBY   Welcome, ass! Now let's have a catch.
ANDREW   By my troth, the Fool has an excellent breast.
   I had rather than forty shillings I had such a leg,   20
   and so sweet a breath to sing, as the Fool has.—In
   sooth, thou wast in very gracious fooling last night
   when thou spok'st of Pigrogromitus, of the Vapians
   passing the equinoctial of Queubus. 'Twas very
   good, i' faith. I sent thee sixpence for thy leman.   25
   Hadst it?

FOOL   I did impeticos thy gratillity, for Malvolio's nose
      is no whipstock, my lady has a white hand, and the
      Myrmidons are no bottle-ale houses.

ANDREW   Excellent! Why, this is the best fooling when   30
      all is done. Now, a song.

TOBY, ⌜*giving money to the Fool*⌝ Come on, there is
      sixpence for you. Let's have a song.

ANDREW, ⌜*giving money to the Fool*⌝ There's a testril of
      me, too. If one knight give a—   35

FOOL   Would you have a love song or a song of good
      life?

TOBY   A love song, a love song.

ANDREW   Ay, ay, I care not for good life.

FOOL *sings*

> O mistress mine, where are you roaming?   40
> O, stay and hear! Your truelove's coming,
>   That can sing both high and low.
> Trip no further, pretty sweeting.
> Journeys end in lovers meeting,
>   Every wise man's son doth know.   45

ANDREW   Excellent good, i' faith.

TOBY   Good, good.

FOOL ⌜*sings*⌝

> What is love? 'Tis not hereafter.
> Present mirth hath present laughter.
>   What's to come is still unsure.   50
> In delay there lies no plenty,
> Then come kiss me, sweet and twenty.
>   Youth's a stuff will not endure.

ANDREW   A mellifluous voice, as I am true knight.

TOBY   A contagious breath.   55

ANDREW   Very sweet and contagious, i' faith.

TOBY   To hear by the nose, it is dulcet in contagion.
      But shall we make the welkin dance indeed? Shall
      we rouse the night owl in a catch that will draw
      three souls out of one weaver? Shall we do that?   60

ANDREW An you love me, let's do 't. I am dog at a
catch.

FOOL By 'r Lady, sir, and some dogs will catch well.

ANDREW Most certain. Let our catch be "Thou
Knave."   65

FOOL "Hold thy peace, thou knave," knight? I shall be
constrained in 't to call thee "knave," knight.

ANDREW 'Tis not the first time I have constrained one
to call me "knave." Begin, Fool. It begins "Hold
thy peace."   70

FOOL I shall never begin if I hold my peace.

ANDREW Good, i' faith. Come, begin.   *Catch sung.*

Enter Maria.

MARIA What a caterwauling do you keep here! If my
lady have not called up her steward Malvolio and
bid him turn you out of doors, never trust me.   75

TOBY My lady's a Cataian, we are politicians, Malvolio's
a Peg-a-Ramsey, and ⌜*Sings.*⌝ *Three merry men be
we.* Am not I consanguineous? Am I not of her
blood? Tillyvally! "Lady"! ⌜*Sings.*⌝ *There dwelt a man
in Babylon, lady, lady.*   80

FOOL Beshrew me, the knight's in admirable fooling.

ANDREW Ay, he does well enough if he be disposed,
and so do I, too. He does it with a better grace, but
I do it more natural.

TOBY ⌜*sings*⌝ *O' the twelfth day of December—*   85

MARIA For the love o' God, peace!

Enter Malvolio.

MALVOLIO My masters, are you mad? Or what are you?
Have you no wit, manners, nor honesty but to
gabble like tinkers at this time of night? Do you
make an ale-house of my lady's house, that you   90
squeak out your coziers' catches without any mitigation or remorse of voice? Is there no respect of
place, persons, nor time in you?

TOBY   We did keep time, sir, in our catches. Sneck up!

MALVOLIO   Sir Toby, I must be round with you. My lady   95
bade me tell you that, though she harbors you as her
kinsman, she's nothing allied to your disorders. If
you can separate yourself and your misdemeanors,
you are welcome to the house; if not, an it would
please you to take leave of her, she is very willing to   100
bid you farewell.

TOBY ⌐*sings*⌐
Farewell, dear heart, since I must needs be gone.

MARIA   Nay, good Sir Toby.

FOOL ⌐*sings*⌐
    His eyes do show his days are almost done.

MALVOLIO   Is 't even so?   105

TOBY ⌐*sings*⌐
        But I will never die.

FOOL ⌐*sings*⌐
        Sir Toby, there you lie.

MALVOLIO   This is much credit to you.

TOBY ⌐*sings*⌐
        Shall I bid him go?

FOOL ⌐*sings*⌐
        What an if you do?   110

TOBY ⌐*sings*⌐
        Shall I bid him go, and spare not?

FOOL ⌐*sings*⌐
        O no, no, no, no, you dare not.

TOBY   Out o' tune, sir? You lie. Art any more than a
steward? Dost thou think, because thou art virtu-
ous, there shall be no more cakes and ale?   115

FOOL   Yes, by Saint Anne, and ginger shall be hot i' th'
mouth, too.

TOBY   Thou'rt i' th' right.—Go, sir, rub your chain
with crumbs.—A stoup of wine, Maria!

MALVOLIO   Mistress Mary, if you prized my lady's favor   120
at anything more than contempt, you would not give

means for this uncivil rule. She shall know of it, by
this hand.   *He exits.*

MARIA Go shake your ears!

ANDREW 'Twere as good a deed as to drink when a   125
man's a-hungry, to challenge him the field and
then to break promise with him and make a fool of
him.

TOBY Do 't, knight. I'll write thee a challenge. Or I'll
deliver thy indignation to him by word of mouth.   130

MARIA Sweet Sir Toby, be patient for tonight. Since the
youth of the Count's was today with my lady, she is
much out of quiet. For Monsieur Malvolio, let me
alone with him. If I do not gull him into ⌜a nayword⌝
and make him a common recreation, do not think I   135
have wit enough to lie straight in my bed. I know I
can do it.

TOBY Possess us, possess us, tell us something of him.

MARIA Marry, sir, sometimes he is a kind of puritan.

ANDREW O, if I thought that, I'd beat him like a dog!   140

TOBY What, for being a puritan? Thy exquisite reason,
dear knight?

ANDREW I have no exquisite reason for 't, but I have
reason good enough.

MARIA The devil a puritan that he is, or anything   145
constantly but a time-pleaser; an affectioned ass
that cons state without book and utters it by great
swaths; the best persuaded of himself, so crammed,
as he thinks, with excellencies, that it is his grounds
of faith that all that look on him love him. And on   150
that vice in him will my revenge find notable cause
to work.

TOBY What wilt thou do?

MARIA I will drop in his way some obscure epistles of
love, wherein by the color of his beard, the shape of   155
his leg, the manner of his gait, the expressure of his
eye, forehead, and complexion, he shall find himself

most feelingly personated. I can write very like my
lady your niece; on a forgotten matter, we can
hardly make distinction of our hands.   160

TOBY Excellent! I smell a device.

ANDREW I have 't in my nose, too.

TOBY He shall think, by the letters that thou wilt drop,
that they come from my niece, and that she's in
love with him.   165

MARIA My purpose is indeed a horse of that color.

ANDREW And your horse now would make him an ass.

MARIA Ass, I doubt not.

ANDREW O, 'twill be admirable!

MARIA Sport royal, I warrant you. I know my physic   170
will work with him. I will plant you two, and let the
Fool make a third, where he shall find the letter.
Observe his construction of it. For this night, to bed,
and dream on the event. Farewell.

TOBY Good night, Penthesilea.   *She exits.*   175

ANDREW Before me, she's a good wench.

TOBY She's a beagle true bred, and one that adores
me. What o' that?

ANDREW I was adored once, too.

TOBY Let's to bed, knight. Thou hadst need send for   180
more money.

ANDREW If I cannot recover your niece, I am a foul way
out.

TOBY Send for money, knight. If thou hast her not i'
th' end, call me "Cut."   185

ANDREW If I do not, never trust me, take it how you
will.

TOBY Come, come, I'll go burn some sack. 'Tis too
late to go to bed now. Come, knight; come, knight.
                                        They exit.

Scene 4
Enter ⌜Orsino,⌝ Viola, Curio, and others.

ORSINO
Give me some music. ⌜*Music plays.*⌝ Now, good
morrow, friends.—
Now, good Cesario, but that piece of song,
That old and antique song we heard last night.
Methought it did relieve my passion much, 5
More than light airs and recollected terms
Of these most brisk and giddy-pacèd times.
Come, but one verse.
CURIO He is not here, so please your Lordship, that
should sing it. 10
ORSINO Who was it?
CURIO Feste the jester, my lord, a Fool that the Lady
Olivia's father took much delight in. He is about
the house.
ORSINO
Seek him out ⌜*Curio exits,*⌝ and play the tune the 15
while.   *Music plays.*
⌜*To Viola.*⌝ Come hither, boy. If ever thou shalt love,
In the sweet pangs of it remember me,
For such as I am, all true lovers are,
Unstaid and skittish in all motions else 20
Save in the constant image of the creature
That is beloved. How dost thou like this tune?
VIOLA
It gives a very echo to the seat
Where love is throned.
ORSINO   Thou dost speak masterly. 25
My life upon 't, young though thou art, thine eye
Hath stayed upon some favor that it loves.
Hath it not, boy?
VIOLA   A little, by your favor.

ORSINO
  What kind of woman is 't?   30
VIOLA   Of your complexion.
ORSINO
  She is not worth thee, then. What years, i' faith?
VIOLA About your years, my lord.
ORSINO
  Too old, by heaven. Let still the woman take
  An elder than herself. So wears she to him;   35
  So sways she level in her husband's heart.
  For, boy, however we do praise ourselves,
  Our fancies are more giddy and unfirm,
  More longing, wavering, sooner lost and worn,
  Than women's are.   40
VIOLA   I think it well, my lord.
ORSINO
  Then let thy love be younger than thyself,
  Or thy affection cannot hold the bent.
  For women are as roses, whose fair flower,
  Being once displayed, doth fall that very hour.   45
VIOLA
  And so they are. Alas, that they are so,
  To die even when they to perfection grow!

        Enter Curio and ⌜Feste, the Fool.⌝

ORSINO
  O, fellow, come, the song we had last night.—
  Mark it, Cesario. It is old and plain;
  The spinsters and the knitters in the sun   50
  And the free maids that weave their thread with
    bones
  Do use to chant it. It is silly sooth,
  And dallies with the innocence of love
  Like the old age.   55
FOOL Are you ready, sir?
ORSINO Ay, prithee, sing.   *Music.*

The Song.

⌜FOOL⌝

    Come away, come away, death,
      And in sad cypress let me be laid.
    ⌜*Fly*⌝ *away,* ⌜*fly*⌝ *away, breath,*   60
      I am slain by a fair cruel maid.
    My shroud of white, stuck all with yew,
      O, prepare it!
    My part of death, no one so true
      Did share it.   65

    Not a flower, not a flower sweet
      On my black coffin let there be strown;
    Not a friend, not a friend greet
      My poor corpse, where my bones shall be thrown.
    A thousand thousand sighs to save,   70
      Lay me, O, where
    Sad true lover never find my grave,
      To weep there.

ORSINO, ⌜*giving money*⌝ There's for thy pains.

FOOL No pains, sir. I take pleasure in singing, sir.   75

ORSINO I'll pay thy pleasure, then.

FOOL Truly, sir, and pleasure will be paid, one time or another.

ORSINO Give me now leave to leave thee.

FOOL Now the melancholy god protect thee, and the   80
    tailor make thy doublet of changeable taffeta, for thy
    mind is a very opal. I would have men of such
    constancy put to sea, that their business might be
    everything and their intent everywhere, for that's it
    that always makes a good voyage of nothing. Fare-   85
    well.   *He exits.*

ORSINO

    Let all the rest give place.

                ⌜*All but Orsino and Viola exit.*⌝
                Once more, Cesario,

Get thee to yond same sovereign cruelty.
Tell her my love, more noble than the world,   90
Prizes not quantity of dirty lands.
The parts that fortune hath bestowed upon her,
Tell her, I hold as giddily as fortune.
But 'tis that miracle and queen of gems
That nature pranks her in attracts my soul.   95

VIOLA   But if she cannot love you, sir—

ORSINO
⌈I⌉ cannot be so answered.

VIOLA   Sooth, but you must.
Say that some lady, as perhaps there is,
Hath for your love as great a pang of heart   100
As you have for Olivia. You cannot love her;
You tell her so. Must she not then be answered?

ORSINO   There is no woman's sides
Can bide the beating of so strong a passion
As love doth give my heart; no woman's heart   105
So big, to hold so much; they lack retention.
Alas, their love may be called appetite,
No motion of the liver, but the palate,
That suffer surfeit, cloyment, and revolt;
But mine is all as hungry as the sea,   110
And can digest as much. Make no compare
Between that love a woman can bear me
And that I owe Olivia.

VIOLA   Ay, but I know—

ORSINO   What dost thou know?   115

VIOLA
Too well what love women to men may owe.
In faith, they are as true of heart as we.
My father had a daughter loved a man
As it might be, perhaps, were I a woman,
I should your Lordship.   120

ORSINO   And what's her history?

VIOLA
A blank, my lord. She never told her love,
But let concealment, like a worm i' th' bud,
Feed on her damask cheek. She pined in thought,
And with a green and yellow melancholy   125
She sat like Patience on a monument,
Smiling at grief. Was not this love indeed?
We men may say more, swear more, but indeed
Our shows are more than will; for still we prove
Much in our vows but little in our love.   130

ORSINO
But died thy sister of her love, my boy?

VIOLA
I am all the daughters of my father's house,
And all the brothers, too—and yet I know not.
Sir, shall I to this lady?

ORSINO   Ay, that's the theme.   135
To her in haste. Give her this jewel. Say
My love can give no place, bide no denay.
            ⌜*He hands her a jewel and*⌝ *they exit.*

Scene 5
Enter Sir Toby, Sir Andrew, and Fabian.

TOBY   Come thy ways, Signior Fabian.

FABIAN   Nay, I'll come. If I lose a scruple of this sport,
let me be boiled to death with melancholy.

TOBY   Wouldst thou not be glad to have the niggardly
rascally sheep-biter come by some notable shame?   5

FABIAN   I would exult, man. You know he brought me
out o' favor with my lady about a bearbaiting here.

TOBY   To anger him, we'll have the bear again, and we
will fool him black and blue, shall we not, Sir
Andrew?   10

ANDREW   An we do not, it is pity of our lives.

Enter Maria.

TOBY   Here comes the little villain.—How now, my
metal of India?

MARIA   Get you all three into the boxtree. Malvolio's
coming down this walk. He has been yonder i' the   15
sun practicing behavior to his own shadow this half
hour. Observe him, for the love of mockery, for I
know this letter will make a contemplative idiot of
him. Close, in the name of jesting! ⌜*They hide.*⌝ Lie
thou there ⌜*putting down the letter,*⌝ for here comes   20
the trout that must be caught with tickling.

                                        She exits.

Enter Malvolio.

MALVOLIO   'Tis but fortune, all is fortune. Maria once
told me she did affect me, and I have heard herself
come thus near, that should she fancy, it should be
one of my complexion. Besides, she uses me with a   25
more exalted respect than anyone else that follows
her. What should I think on 't?

TOBY, ⌜*aside*⌝   Here's an overweening rogue.

FABIAN, ⌜*aside*⌝   O, peace! Contemplation makes a rare
turkeycock of him. How he jets under his advanced   30
plumes!

ANDREW, ⌜*aside*⌝   'Slight, I could so beat the rogue!

TOBY, ⌜*aside*⌝   Peace, I say.

MALVOLIO   To be Count Malvolio.

TOBY, ⌜*aside*⌝   Ah, rogue!   35

ANDREW, ⌜*aside*⌝   Pistol him, pistol him!

TOBY, ⌜*aside*⌝   Peace, peace!

MALVOLIO   There is example for 't. The lady of the
Strachy married the yeoman of the wardrobe.

ANDREW, ⌜*aside*⌝   Fie on him, Jezebel!   40

FABIAN, ⌜*aside*⌝   O, peace, now he's deeply in. Look how
imagination blows him.

MALVOLIO Having been three months married to her, sitting in my state—

TOBY, ⌐*aside*¬ O, for a stone-bow, to hit him in the eye! 45

MALVOLIO Calling my officers about me, in my branched velvet gown, having come from a daybed, where I have left Olivia sleeping—

TOBY, ⌐*aside*¬ Fire and brimstone!

FABIAN, ⌐*aside*¬ O, peace, peace! 50

MALVOLIO And then to have the humor of state; and after a demure travel of regard, telling them I know my place, as I would they should do theirs, to ask for my kinsman Toby—

TOBY, ⌐*aside*¬ Bolts and shackles! 55

FABIAN, ⌐*aside*¬ O, peace, peace, peace! Now, now.

MALVOLIO Seven of my people, with an obedient start, make out for him. I frown the while, and perchance wind up my watch, or play with my—some rich jewel. Toby approaches; curtsies there to me— 60

TOBY, ⌐*aside*¬ Shall this fellow live?

FABIAN, ⌐*aside*¬ Though our silence be drawn from us with cars, yet peace.

MALVOLIO I extend my hand to him thus, quenching my familiar smile with an austere regard of control— 65

TOBY, ⌐*aside*¬ And does not Toby take you a blow o' the lips then?

MALVOLIO Saying "Cousin Toby, my fortunes, having cast me on your niece, give me this prerogative of speech—" 70

TOBY, ⌐*aside*¬ What, what?

MALVOLIO "You must amend your drunkenness."

TOBY, ⌐*aside*¬ Out, scab!

FABIAN, ⌐*aside*¬ Nay, patience, or we break the sinews of our plot. 75

MALVOLIO "Besides, you waste the treasure of your time with a foolish knight—"

ANDREW, ⌜*aside*⌝ That's me, I warrant you.

MALVOLIO "One Sir Andrew." 80

ANDREW, ⌜*aside*⌝ I knew 'twas I, for many do call me fool.

MALVOLIO, ⌜*seeing the letter*⌝ What employment have we here?

FABIAN, ⌜*aside*⌝ Now is the woodcock near the gin. 85

TOBY, ⌜*aside*⌝ O, peace, and the spirit of humors intimate reading aloud to him.

MALVOLIO, ⌜*taking up the letter*⌝ By my life, this is my lady's hand! These be her very *c*'s, her *u*'s, and her *t*'s, and thus makes she her great *P*'s. It is in 90 contempt of question her hand.

ANDREW, ⌜*aside*⌝ Her *c*'s, her *u*'s, and her *t*'s. Why that?

MALVOLIO ⌜*reads*⌝ *To the unknown beloved, this, and my good wishes*—Her very phrases! By your leave, wax. Soft. And the impressure her Lucrece, with which 95 she uses to seal—'tis my lady! ⌜*He opens the letter.*⌝ To whom should this be?

FABIAN, ⌜*aside*⌝ This wins him, liver and all.

MALVOLIO ⌜*reads*⌝

> *Jove knows I love,*
> > *But who?* 100
> *Lips, do not move;*
> *No man must know.*

"No man must know." What follows? The numbers altered. "No man must know." If this should be thee, Malvolio! 105

TOBY, ⌜*aside*⌝ Marry, hang thee, brock!

MALVOLIO ⌜*reads*⌝

> *I may command where I adore,*
> > *But silence, like a Lucrece knife,*
> *With bloodless stroke my heart doth gore;*
> *M.O.A.I. doth sway my life.* 110

FABIAN, ⌜*aside*⌝ A fustian riddle!

TOBY, ⌜*aside*⌝ Excellent wench, say I.

MALVOLIO "M.O.A.I. doth sway my life." Nay, but first
let me see, let me see, let me see.

FABIAN, ⌈*aside*⌉ What dish o' poison has she dressed   115
him!

TOBY, ⌈*aside*⌉ And with what wing the ⌈staniel⌉ checks
at it!

MALVOLIO "I may command where I adore." Why, she
may command me; I serve her, she is my lady. Why,   120
this is evident to any formal capacity. There is no
obstruction in this. And the end—what should that
alphabetical position portend? If I could make that
resemble something in me! Softly! "M.O.A.I."—

TOBY, ⌈*aside*⌉ O, ay, make up that.—He is now at a cold   125
scent.

FABIAN, ⌈*aside*⌉ Sowter will cry upon 't for all this,
though it be as rank as a fox.

MALVOLIO "M"—Malvolio. "M"—why, that begins
my name!   130

FABIAN, ⌈*aside*⌉ Did not I say he would work it out? The
cur is excellent at faults.

MALVOLIO "M." But then there is no consonancy in
the sequel that suffers under probation. "A" should
follow, but "O" does.   135

FABIAN, ⌈*aside*⌉ And "O" shall end, I hope.

TOBY, ⌈*aside*⌉ Ay, or I'll cudgel him and make him cry
"O."

MALVOLIO And then "I" comes behind.

FABIAN, ⌈*aside*⌉ Ay, an you had any eye behind you, you   140
might see more detraction at your heels than fortunes before you.

MALVOLIO "M.O.A.I." This simulation is not as the
former, and yet to crush this a little, it would bow
to me, for every one of these letters are in my name.   145
Soft, here follows prose.

⌈*He reads.*⌉ *If this fall into thy hand, revolve. In my*
stars I am above thee, but be not afraid of greatness.

Some are ⌈*born*⌉ *great, some* ⌈*achieve*⌉ *greatness, and
some have greatness thrust upon 'em. Thy fates open* 150
*their hands. Let thy blood and spirit embrace them.
And, to inure thyself to what thou art like to be, cast
thy humble slough and appear fresh. Be opposite with
a kinsman, surly with servants. Let thy tongue tang
arguments of state. Put thyself into the trick of singu-* 155
*larity. She thus advises thee that sighs for thee.
Remember who commended thy yellow stockings and
wished to see thee ever cross-gartered. I say, remember. Go to, thou art made, if thou desir'st to be so. If
not, let me see thee a steward still, the fellow of* 160
*servants, and not worthy to touch Fortune's fingers.
Farewell. She that would alter services with thee.*
                                The Fortunate-Unhappy.
Daylight and champian discovers not more! This is
open. I will be proud, I will read politic authors, I 165
will baffle Sir Toby, I will wash off gross acquaintance, I will be point-devise the very man. I do not
now fool myself, to let imagination jade me; for
every reason excites to this, that my lady loves me.
She did commend my yellow stockings of late, she 170
did praise my leg being cross-gartered, and in this
she manifests herself to my love and, with a kind of
injunction, drives me to these habits of her liking. I
thank my stars, I am happy. I will be strange, stout,
in yellow stockings, and cross-gartered, even with 175
the swiftness of putting on. Jove and my stars be
praised! Here is yet a postscript.
⌈*He reads.*⌉ *Thou canst not choose but know who I
am. If thou entertain'st my love, let it appear in thy
smiling; thy smiles become thee well. Therefore in my* 180
presence still smile, dear my sweet, I prithee.
Jove, I thank thee! I will smile. I will do everything
that thou wilt have me.   *He exits.*

FABIAN I will not give my part of this sport for a
pension of thousands to be paid from the Sophy. 185
TOBY I could marry this wench for this device.
ANDREW So could I, too.
TOBY And ask no other dowry with her but such
another jest.
ANDREW Nor I neither. 190

Enter Maria.

FABIAN Here comes my noble gull-catcher.
TOBY Wilt thou set thy foot o' my neck?
ANDREW Or o' mine either?
TOBY Shall I play my freedom at tray-trip and become
thy bondslave? 195
ANDREW I' faith, or I either?
TOBY Why, thou hast put him in such a dream that
when the image of it leaves him he must run mad.
MARIA Nay, but say true, does it work upon him?
TOBY Like aqua vitae with a midwife. 200
MARIA If you will then see the fruits of the sport,
mark his first approach before my lady. He will
come to her in yellow stockings, and 'tis a color
she abhors, and cross-gartered, a fashion she de-
tests; and he will smile upon her, which will now 205
be so unsuitable to her disposition, being ad-
dicted to a melancholy as she is, that it cannot
but turn him into a notable contempt. If you will
see it, follow me.
TOBY To the gates of Tartar, thou most excellent dev- 210
il of wit!
ANDREW I'll make one, too.
They exit.

ACT 3

Scene 1

Enter Viola and ⌐Feste, the Fool, playing a tabor.⌐

VIOLA   Save thee, friend, and thy music. Dost thou live
    by thy tabor?

FOOL   No, sir, I live by the church.

VIOLA   Art thou a churchman?

FOOL   No such matter, sir. I do live by the church, for I   5
    do live at my house, and my house doth stand by the
    church.

VIOLA   So thou mayst say the ⌐king⌐ lies by a beggar if a
    beggar dwell near him, or the church stands by thy
    tabor if thy tabor stand by the church.   10

FOOL   You have said, sir. To see this age! A sentence is
    but a chev'ril glove to a good wit. How quickly the
    wrong side may be turned outward!

VIOLA   Nay, that's certain. They that dally nicely with
    words may quickly make them wanton.   15

FOOL   I would therefore my sister had had no name,
    sir.

VIOLA   Why, man?

FOOL   Why, sir, her name's a word, and to dally with
    that word might make my sister wanton. But,   20
    indeed, words are very rascals since bonds dis-
    graced them.

VIOLA   Thy reason, man?

FOOL   Troth, sir, I can yield you none without words,
and words are grown so false I am loath to prove   25
reason with them.

VIOLA   I warrant thou art a merry fellow and car'st for
nothing.

FOOL   Not so, sir. I do care for something. But in my
conscience, sir, I do not care for you. If that be to   30
care for nothing, sir, I would it would make you
invisible.

VIOLA   Art not thou the Lady Olivia's Fool?

FOOL   No, indeed, sir. The Lady Olivia has no folly. She
will keep no Fool, sir, till she be married, and Fools   35
are as like husbands as pilchers are to herrings: the
husband's the bigger. I am indeed not her Fool but
her corrupter of words.

VIOLA   I saw thee late at the Count Orsino's.

FOOL   Foolery, sir, does walk about the orb like the   40
sun; it shines everywhere. I would be sorry, sir, but
the Fool should be as oft with your master as with
my mistress. I think I saw your Wisdom there.

VIOLA   Nay, an thou pass upon me, I'll no more with
thee. Hold, there's expenses for thee. ⌜*Giving a*   45
coin.⌝

FOOL   Now Jove, in his next commodity of hair, send
thee a beard!

VIOLA   By my troth I'll tell thee, I am almost sick for
one, ⌜*aside*⌝ though I would not have it grow on my
chin.—Is thy lady within?   50

FOOL   Would not a pair of these have bred, sir?

VIOLA   Yes, being kept together and put to use.

FOOL   I would play Lord Pandarus of Phrygia, sir, to
bring a Cressida to this Troilus.

VIOLA   I understand you, sir. 'Tis well begged. ⌜*Giving*   55
another coin.⌝

FOOL   The matter I hope is not great, sir, begging but a
beggar: Cressida was a beggar. My lady is within, sir.

I will conster to them whence you come. Who you
are and what you would are out of my welkin—I
might say "element," but the word is overworn.   60
                                                    He exits.

VIOLA
This fellow is wise enough to play the Fool,
And to do that well craves a kind of wit.
He must observe their mood on whom he jests,
The quality of persons, and the time,
And, like the haggard, check at every feather   65
That comes before his eye. This is a practice
As full of labor as a wise man's art:
For folly that he wisely shows is fit;
But ⌜wise men,⌝ folly-fall'n, quite taint their wit.

          Enter Sir Toby and Andrew.

TOBY   Save you, gentleman.   70
VIOLA   And you, sir.
ANDREW   *Dieu vous garde, monsieur.*
VIOLA   *Et vous aussi. Votre serviteur!*
ANDREW   I hope, sir, you are, and I am yours.
TOBY   Will you encounter the house? My niece is   75
   desirous you should enter, if your trade be to her.
VIOLA   I am bound to your niece, sir; I mean, she is the
   list of my voyage.
TOBY   Taste your legs, sir; put them to motion.
VIOLA   My legs do better understand me, sir, than I   80
   understand what you mean by bidding me taste my
   legs.
TOBY   I mean, to go, sir, to enter.
VIOLA   I will answer you with gait and entrance—but
   we are prevented.   85

     Enter Olivia, and ⌜Maria, her⌝ Gentlewoman.

Most excellent accomplished lady, the heavens rain
odors on you!

ANDREW, ⌜*aside*⌝ That youth's a rare courtier. "Rain
  odors," well.

VIOLA My matter hath no voice, lady, but to your own 90
  most pregnant and vouchsafed ear.

ANDREW, ⌜*aside*⌝ "Odors," "pregnant," and "vouchsafed." I'll get 'em all three all ready.

OLIVIA Let the garden door be shut, and leave me to
  my hearing. ⌜*Sir Toby, Sir Andrew, and Maria exit.*⌝ 95
  Give me your hand, sir.

VIOLA
  My duty, madam, and most humble service.

OLIVIA What is your name?

VIOLA
  Cesario is your servant's name, fair princess.

OLIVIA
  My servant, sir? 'Twas never merry world 100
  Since lowly feigning was called compliment.
  You're servant to the Count Orsino, youth.

VIOLA
  And he is yours, and his must needs be yours.
  Your servant's servant is your servant, madam.

OLIVIA
  For him, I think not on him. For his thoughts, 105
  Would they were blanks rather than filled with me.

VIOLA
  Madam, I come to whet your gentle thoughts
  On his behalf.

OLIVIA   O, by your leave, I pray you.
  I bade you never speak again of him. 110
  But would you undertake another suit,
  I had rather hear you to solicit that
  Than music from the spheres.

VIOLA   Dear lady—

OLIVIA
  Give me leave, beseech you. I did send, 115
  After the last enchantment you did here,

A ring in chase of you. So did I abuse
Myself, my servant, and, I fear me, you.
Under your hard construction must I sit,
To force that on you in a shameful cunning   120
Which you knew none of yours. What might you
     think?
Have you not set mine honor at the stake,
And baited it with all th' unmuzzled thoughts
That tyrannous heart can think? To one of your   125
     receiving
Enough is shown. A cypress, not a bosom,
Hides my heart. So, let me hear you speak.

VIOLA
  I pity you.
OLIVIA   That's a degree to love.   130
VIOLA
  No, not a grize, for 'tis a vulgar proof
  That very oft we pity enemies.
OLIVIA
  Why then methinks 'tis time to smile again.
  O world, how apt the poor are to be proud!
  If one should be a prey, how much the better   135
  To fall before the lion than the wolf.   *Clock strikes.*
  The clock upbraids me with the waste of time.
  Be not afraid, good youth, I will not have you.
  And yet when wit and youth is come to harvest,
  Your wife is like to reap a proper man.   140
  There lies your way, due west.
VIOLA   Then westward ho!
  Grace and good disposition attend your Ladyship.
  You'll nothing, madam, to my lord by me?
OLIVIA
  Stay. I prithee, tell me what thou think'st of me.   145
VIOLA
  That you do think you are not what you are.

OLIVIA
  If I think so, I think the same of you.
VIOLA
  Then think you right. I am not what I am.
OLIVIA
  I would you were as I would have you be.
VIOLA
  Would it be better, madam, than I am?   150
  I wish it might, for now I am your fool.
OLIVIA, ⌜*aside*⌝
  O, what a deal of scorn looks beautiful
  In the contempt and anger of his lip!
  A murd'rous guilt shows not itself more soon
  Than love that would seem hid. Love's night is   155
      noon.—
  Cesario, by the roses of the spring,
  By maidhood, honor, truth, and everything,
  I love thee so, that, maugre all thy pride,
  Nor wit nor reason can my passion hide.   160
  Do not extort thy reasons from this clause,
  For that I woo, thou therefore hast no cause;
  But rather reason thus with reason fetter:
  Love sought is good, but given unsought is better.
VIOLA
  By innocence I swear, and by my youth,   165
  I have one heart, one bosom, and one truth,
  And that no woman has, nor never none
  Shall mistress be of it, save I alone.
  And so adieu, good madam. Nevermore
  Will I my master's tears to you deplore.   170
OLIVIA
  Yet come again, for thou perhaps mayst move
  That heart, which now abhors, to like his love.
              They exit ⌜*in different directions.*⌝

Scene 2
Enter Sir Toby, Sir Andrew, and Fabian.

ANDREW   No, faith, I'll not stay a jot longer.

TOBY   Thy reason, dear venom, give thy reason.

FABIAN   You must needs yield your reason, Sir Andrew.

ANDREW   Marry, I saw your niece do more favors to the
Count's servingman than ever she bestowed upon   5
me. I saw 't i' th' orchard.

TOBY   Did she see ⌜thee⌝ the while, old boy? Tell me
that.

ANDREW   As plain as I see you now.

FABIAN   This was a great argument of love in her toward   10
you.

ANDREW   'Slight, will you make an ass o' me?

FABIAN   I will prove it legitimate, sir, upon the oaths of
judgment and reason.

TOBY   And they have been grand-jurymen since before   15
Noah was a sailor.

FABIAN   She did show favor to the youth in your sight
only to exasperate you, to awake your dormouse
valor, to put fire in your heart and brimstone in
your liver. You should then have accosted her, and   20
with some excellent jests, fire-new from the mint,
you should have banged the youth into dumbness.
This was looked for at your hand, and this was
balked. The double gilt of this opportunity you let
time wash off, and you are now sailed into the north   25
of my lady's opinion, where you will hang like an
icicle on a Dutchman's beard, unless you do redeem it by some laudable attempt either of valor or
policy.

ANDREW   An 't be any way, it must be with valor, for   30
policy I hate. I had as lief be a Brownist as a
politician.

TOBY   Why, then, build me thy fortunes upon the basis

of valor. Challenge me the Count's youth to fight
with him. Hurt him in eleven places. My niece shall   35
take note of it, and assure thyself, there is no
love-broker in the world can more prevail in man's
commendation with woman than report of valor.

FABIAN There is no way but this, Sir Andrew.

ANDREW Will either of you bear me a challenge to him?   40

TOBY Go, write it in a martial hand. Be curst and
brief. It is no matter how witty, so it be eloquent
and full of invention. Taunt him with the license of
ink. If thou "thou"-est him some thrice, it shall not
be amiss, and as many lies as will lie in thy sheet of   45
paper, although the sheet were big enough for the
bed of Ware in England, set 'em down. Go, about it.
Let there be gall enough in thy ink, though thou
write with a goose-pen, no matter. About it.

ANDREW Where shall I find you?   50

TOBY We'll call thee at the cubiculo. Go.

Sir Andrew exits.

FABIAN This is a dear manikin to you, Sir Toby.

TOBY I have been dear to him, lad, some two thousand
strong, or so.

FABIAN We shall have a rare letter from him. But you'll   55
not deliver 't?

TOBY Never trust me, then. And by all means stir on
the youth to an answer. I think oxen and wainropes
cannot hale them together. For Andrew, if he were
opened and you find so much blood in his liver as   60
will clog the foot of a flea, I'll eat the rest of th'
anatomy.

FABIAN And his opposite, the youth, bears in his visage
no great presage of cruelty.

Enter Maria.

TOBY Look where the youngest wren of mine comes.   65

MARIA If you desire the spleen, and will laugh your-

selves into stitches, follow me. Yond gull Malvolio is
turned heathen, a very renegado; for there is no
Christian that means to be saved by believing rightly
can ever believe such impossible passages of gross-   70
ness. He's in yellow stockings.

TOBY   And cross-gartered?

MARIA   Most villainously, like a pedant that keeps a
school i' th' church. I have dogged him like his
murderer. He does obey every point of the letter   75
that I dropped to betray him. He does smile his face
into more lines than is in the new map with the
augmentation of the Indies. You have not seen such
a thing as 'tis. I can hardly forbear hurling things at
him. I know my lady will strike him. If she do, he'll   80
smile and take 't for a great favor.

TOBY   Come, bring us, bring us where he is.

                                        They all exit.

Scene 3
Enter Sebastian and Antonio.

SEBASTIAN
   I would not by my will have troubled you,
   But, since you make your pleasure of your pains,
   I will no further chide you.

ANTONIO
   I could not stay behind you. My desire,
   More sharp than filèd steel, did spur me forth;   5
   And not all love to see you, though so much
   As might have drawn one to a longer voyage,
   But jealousy what might befall your travel,
   Being skill-less in these parts, which to a stranger,
   Unguided and unfriended, often prove   10
   Rough and unhospitable. My willing love,
   The rather by these arguments of fear,
   Set forth in your pursuit.

SEBASTIAN   My kind Antonio,
I can no other answer make but thanks,   15
And thanks, and ever ⌜thanks; and⌝ oft good turns
Are shuffled off with such uncurrent pay.
But were my worth, as is my conscience, firm,
You should find better dealing. What's to do?
Shall we go see the relics of this town?   20

ANTONIO
Tomorrow, sir. Best first go see your lodging.

SEBASTIAN
I am not weary, and 'tis long to night.
I pray you, let us satisfy our eyes
With the memorials and the things of fame
That do renown this city.   25

ANTONIO   Would you'd pardon me.
I do not without danger walk these streets.
Once in a sea fight 'gainst the Count his galleys
I did some service, of such note indeed
That were I ta'en here it would scarce be answered.   30

SEBASTIAN
Belike you slew great number of his people?

ANTONIO
Th' offense is not of such a bloody nature,
Albeit the quality of the time and quarrel
Might well have given us bloody argument.
It might have since been answered in repaying   35
What we took from them, which, for traffic's sake,
Most of our city did. Only myself stood out,
For which, if I be lapsèd in this place,
I shall pay dear.

SEBASTIAN   Do not then walk too open.   40

ANTONIO
It doth not fit me. Hold, sir, here's my purse.
                         ⌜*Giving him money.*⌝
In the south suburbs, at the Elephant,
Is best to lodge. I will bespeak our diet

Whiles you beguile the time and feed your
    knowledge   45
With viewing of the town. There shall you have me.

SEBASTIAN   Why I your purse?

ANTONIO
Haply your eye shall light upon some toy
You have desire to purchase, and your store,
I think, is not for idle markets, sir.   50

SEBASTIAN
I'll be your purse-bearer and leave you
For an hour.

ANTONIO   To th' Elephant.

SEBASTIAN   I do remember.
They exit ⌜in different directions.⌝

Scene 4
Enter Olivia and Maria.

OLIVIA, ⌜*aside*⌝
I have sent after him. He says he'll come.
How shall I feast him? What bestow of him?
For youth is bought more oft than begged or
    borrowed.
I speak too loud.—   5
Where's Malvolio? He is sad and civil
And suits well for a servant with my fortunes.
Where is Malvolio?

MARIA   He's coming, madam, but in very strange manner. He is sure possessed, madam.   10

OLIVIA   Why, what's the matter? Does he rave?

MARIA   No, madam, he does nothing but smile. Your
Ladyship were best to have some guard about you if
he come, for sure the man is tainted in 's wits.

OLIVIA
Go call him hither. ⌜*Maria exits.*⌝ I am as mad as he,   15
If sad and merry madness equal be.

Enter ⌈Maria with⌉ Malvolio.

How now, Malvolio?

MALVOLIO   Sweet lady, ho, ho!

OLIVIA   Smil'st thou? I sent for thee upon a sad
occasion.   20

MALVOLIO   Sad, lady? I could be sad. This does make
some obstruction in the blood, this cross-garter-
ing, but what of that? If it please the eye of one, it is
with me as the very true sonnet is: "Please one, and
please all."   25

⌈OLIVIA⌉   Why, how dost thou, man? What is the matter
with thee?

MALVOLIO   Not black in my mind, though yellow in my
legs. It did come to his hands, and commands shall
be executed. I think we do know the sweet Roman   30
hand.

OLIVIA   Wilt thou go to bed, Malvolio?

MALVOLIO   To bed? "Ay, sweetheart, and I'll come to
thee."

OLIVIA   God comfort thee! Why dost thou smile so, and   35
kiss thy hand so oft?

MARIA   How do you, Malvolio?

MALVOLIO   At your request? Yes, nightingales answer
daws!

MARIA   Why appear you with this ridiculous boldness   40
before my lady?

MALVOLIO   "Be not afraid of greatness." 'Twas well
writ.

OLIVIA   What mean'st thou by that, Malvolio?

MALVOLIO   "Some are born great—"   45

OLIVIA   Ha?

MALVOLIO   "Some achieve greatness—"

OLIVIA   What sayst thou?

MALVOLIO   "And some have greatness thrust upon
them."   50

OLIVIA Heaven restore thee!

MALVOLIO "Remember who commended thy yellow
stockings—"

OLIVIA Thy yellow stockings?

MALVOLIO "And wished to see thee cross-gartered."   55

OLIVIA Cross-gartered?

MALVOLIO "Go to, thou art made, if thou desir'st to be
so—"

OLIVIA Am I made?

MALVOLIO "If not, let me see thee a servant still."   60

OLIVIA Why, this is very midsummer madness!

Enter Servant.

SERVANT Madam, the young gentleman of the Count
Orsino's is returned. I could hardly entreat him
back. He attends your Ladyship's pleasure.

OLIVIA I'll come to him. ⌜*Servant exits.*⌝ Good Maria, let   65
this fellow be looked to. Where's my Cousin Toby?
Let some of my people have a special care of him. I
would not have him miscarry for the half of my
dowry.
⌜*Olivia and Maria*⌝ *exit* ⌜*in different directions.*⌝

MALVOLIO O ho, do you come near me now? No worse   70
man than Sir Toby to look to me. This concurs
directly with the letter. She sends him on purpose
that I may appear stubborn to him, for she incites
me to that in the letter: "Cast thy humble slough,"
says she. "Be opposite with a kinsman, surly with   75
servants; let thy tongue ⌜tang⌝ with arguments of
state; put thyself into the trick of singularity," and
consequently sets down the manner how: as, a sad
face, a reverend carriage, a slow tongue, in the habit
of some Sir of note, and so forth. I have limed her,   80
but it is Jove's doing, and Jove make me thankful!
And when she went away now, "Let this fellow be
looked to." "Fellow!" Not "Malvolio," nor after my

degree, but "fellow." Why, everything adheres together, that no dram of a scruple, no scruple of a   85
scruple, no obstacle, no incredulous or unsafe
circumstance—what can be said? Nothing that can
be can come between me and the full prospect of
my hopes. Well, Jove, not I, is the doer of this, and
he is to be thanked.   90

Enter Toby, Fabian, and Maria.

TOBY   Which way is he, in the name of sanctity? If all
the devils of hell be drawn in little, and Legion
himself possessed him, yet I'll speak to him.

FABIAN   Here he is, here he is.—How is 't with you, sir?
How is 't with you, man?   95

MALVOLIO   Go off, I discard you. Let me enjoy my
private. Go off.

MARIA, ⌜*to Toby*⌝ Lo, how hollow the fiend speaks
within him! Did not I tell you? Sir Toby, my lady
prays you to have a care of him.   100

MALVOLIO   Aha, does she so?

TOBY, ⌜*to Fabian and Maria*⌝ Go to, go to! Peace, peace.
We must deal gently with him. Let me alone.—How
do you, Malvolio? How is 't with you? What, man,
defy the devil! Consider, he's an enemy to mankind.   105

MALVOLIO   Do you know what you say?

MARIA, ⌜*to Toby*⌝ La you, an you speak ill of the devil,
how he takes it at heart! Pray God he be not
bewitched!

FABIAN   Carry his water to th' wisewoman.   110

MARIA   Marry, and it shall be done tomorrow morning
if I live. My lady would not lose him for more than
I'll say.

MALVOLIO   How now, mistress?

MARIA   O Lord!   115

TOBY   Prithee, hold thy peace. This is not the way. Do
you not see you move him? Let me alone with
him.

FABIAN   No way but gentleness, gently, gently. The
   fiend is rough and will not be roughly used.   120
TOBY, ⌈to Malvolio⌉   Why, how now, my bawcock? How
   dost thou, chuck?
MALVOLIO   Sir!
TOBY   Ay, biddy, come with me.—What, man, 'tis not
   for gravity to play at cherry-pit with Satan. Hang   125
   him, foul collier!
MARIA   Get him to say his prayers, good Sir Toby; get
   him to pray.
MALVOLIO   My prayers, minx?
MARIA, ⌈to Toby⌉   No, I warrant you, he will not hear of   130
   godliness.
MALVOLIO   Go hang yourselves all! You are idle, shal-
   low things. I am not of your element. You shall
   know more hereafter.   *He exits.*
TOBY   Is 't possible?   135
FABIAN   If this were played upon a stage now, I could
   condemn it as an improbable fiction.
TOBY   His very genius hath taken the infection of the
   device, man.
MARIA   Nay, pursue him now, lest the device take air   140
   and taint.
FABIAN   Why, we shall make him mad indeed.
MARIA   The house will be the quieter.
TOBY   Come, we'll have him in a dark room and
   bound. My niece is already in the belief that he's   145
   mad. We may carry it thus, for our pleasure and his
   penance, till our very pastime, tired out of breath,
   prompt us to have mercy on him, at which time we
   will bring the device to the bar and crown thee for a
   finder of madmen. But see, but see!   150

Enter Sir Andrew.

FABIAN   More matter for a May morning.
ANDREW, ⌈presenting a paper⌉   Here's the challenge.
   Read it. I warrant there's vinegar and pepper in 't.

FABIAN Is 't so saucy?

ANDREW Ay, is 't. I warrant him. Do but read.   155

TOBY Give me. ⌜*He reads.*⌝ *Youth, whatsoever thou art,*
thou art but a scurvy fellow.

FABIAN Good, and valiant.

TOBY ⌜*reads*⌝ *Wonder not, nor admire not in thy mind,*
why I do call thee so, for I will show thee no reason   160
for 't.

FABIAN A good note, that keeps you from the blow of
the law.

TOBY ⌜*reads*⌝ *Thou com'st to the Lady Olivia, and in my*
sight she uses thee kindly. But thou liest in thy throat; 165
that is not the matter I challenge thee for.

FABIAN Very brief, and to exceeding good sense—less.

TOBY ⌜*reads*⌝ *I will waylay thee going home, where if it be*
thy chance to kill me—

FABIAN Good.   170

TOBY ⌜*reads*⌝ *Thou kill'st me like a rogue and a villain.*

FABIAN Still you keep o' th' windy side of the law.
Good.

TOBY ⌜*reads*⌝ *Fare thee well, and God have mercy upon*
one of our souls. He may have mercy upon mine, but 175
my hope is better, and so look to thyself. Thy friend, as
thou usest him, and thy sworn enemy,

Andrew Aguecheek.

If this letter move him not, his legs cannot. I'll
give 't him.   180

MARIA You may have very fit occasion for 't. He is now
in some commerce with my lady, and will by and
by depart.

TOBY Go, Sir Andrew. Scout me for him at the corner
of the orchard like a bum-baily. So soon as ever   185
thou seest him, draw, and as thou draw'st, swear
horrible, for it comes to pass oft that a terrible oath,
with a swaggering accent sharply twanged off, gives
manhood more approbation than ever proof itself
would have earned him. Away!   190

ANDREW   Nay, let me alone for swearing.   *He exits.*

TOBY   Now will not I deliver his letter, for the behavior
   of the young gentleman gives him out to be of good
   capacity and breeding; his employment between
   his lord and my niece confirms no less. Therefore,   195
   this letter, being so excellently ignorant, will breed
   no terror in the youth. He will find it comes from a
   clodpoll. But, sir, I will deliver his challenge by
   word of mouth, set upon Aguecheek a notable
   report of valor, and drive the gentleman (as I know   200
   his youth will aptly receive it) into a most hideous
   opinion of his rage, skill, fury, and impetuosity. This
   will so fright them both that they will kill one
   another by the look, like cockatrices.

                  Enter Olivia and Viola.

FABIAN   Here he comes with your niece. Give them   205
   way till he take leave, and presently after him.

TOBY   I will meditate the while upon some horrid
   message for a challenge.
                  ⌜*Toby, Fabian, and Maria exit.*⌝

OLIVIA
   I have said too much unto a heart of stone
   And laid mine honor too unchary on 't.   210
   There's something in me that reproves my fault,
   But such a headstrong potent fault it is
   That it but mocks reproof.

VIOLA
   With the same 'havior that your passion bears
   Goes on my master's griefs.   215

OLIVIA
   Here, wear this jewel for me. 'Tis my picture.
   Refuse it not. It hath no tongue to vex you.
   And I beseech you come again tomorrow.
   What shall you ask of me that I'll deny,
   That honor, saved, may upon asking give?   220

VIOLA
Nothing but this: your true love for my master.

OLIVIA
How with mine honor may I give him that
Which I have given to you?

VIOLA   I will acquit you.

OLIVIA
Well, come again tomorrow. Fare thee well.   225
A fiend like thee might bear my soul to hell.
                                    ⌜*She exits.*⌝

Enter Toby and Fabian.

TOBY Gentleman, God save thee.

VIOLA And you, sir.

TOBY That defense thou hast, betake thee to 't. Of what
nature the wrongs are thou hast done him, I know   230
not, but thy intercepter, full of despite, bloody as
the hunter, attends thee at the orchard end. Dismount thy tuck, be yare in thy preparation, for thy
assailant is quick, skillful, and deadly.

VIOLA You mistake, sir. I am sure no man hath any   235
quarrel to me. My remembrance is very free and
clear from any image of offense done to any man.

TOBY You'll find it otherwise, I assure you. Therefore,
if you hold your life at any price, betake you to your
guard, for your opposite hath in him what youth,   240
strength, skill, and wrath can furnish man withal.

VIOLA I pray you, sir, what is he?

TOBY He is knight dubbed with unhatched rapier and
on carpet consideration, but he is a devil in private
brawl. Souls and bodies hath he divorced three, and 245
his incensement at this moment is so implacable
that satisfaction can be none but by pangs of death
and sepulcher. "Hob, nob" is his word; "give 't or
take 't."

VIOLA I will return again into the house and desire   250

some conduct of the lady. I am no fighter. I have
heard of some kind of men that put quarrels pur-
posely on others to taste their valor. Belike this is a
man of that quirk.

TOBY   Sir, no. His indignation derives itself out of a very   255
competent injury. Therefore get you on and give
him his desire. Back you shall not to the house,
unless you undertake that with me which with as
much safety you might answer him. Therefore on,
or strip your sword stark naked, for meddle you   260
must, that's certain, or forswear to wear iron about
you.

VIOLA   This is as uncivil as strange. I beseech you, do
me this courteous office, as to know of the knight
what my offense to him is. It is something of my   265
negligence, nothing of my purpose.

TOBY   I will do so.—Signior Fabian, stay you by this
gentleman till my return.   *Toby exits.*

VIOLA   Pray you, sir, do you know of this matter?

FABIAN   I know the knight is incensed against you even   270
to a mortal arbitrament, but nothing of the circumstance more.

VIOLA   I beseech you, what manner of man is he?

FABIAN   Nothing of that wonderful promise, to read
him by his form, as you are like to find him in the   275
proof of his valor. He is indeed, sir, the most skillful,
bloody, and fatal opposite that you could possibly
have found in any part of Illyria. Will you walk
towards him? I will make your peace with him if I
can.   280

VIOLA   I shall be much bound to you for 't. I am one
that had rather go with Sir Priest than Sir Knight, I
care not who knows so much of my mettle.

They exit.

Enter Toby and Andrew.

TOBY Why, man, he's a very devil. I have not seen such
a firago. I had a pass with him, rapier, scabbard, 285
and all, and he gives me the stuck-in with such
a mortal motion that it is inevitable; and on the
answer, he pays you as surely as your feet hits the
ground they step on. They say he has been fencer
to the Sophy. 290

ANDREW Pox on 't ! I'll not meddle with him.

TOBY Ay, but he will not now be pacified. Fabian can
scarce hold him yonder.

ANDREW Plague on 't! An I thought he had been
valiant and so cunning in fence, I'd have seen him 295
damned ere I'd have challenged him. Let him let
the matter slip, and I'll give him my horse, gray
Capilet.

TOBY I'll make the motion. Stand here, make a good
show on 't. This shall end without the perdition of 300
souls. ⌜*Aside.*⌝ Marry, I'll ride your horse as well as I
ride you.

Enter Fabian and Viola.

⌜*Toby crosses to meet them.*⌝
⌜*Aside to Fabian.*⌝ I have his horse to take up the
quarrel. I have persuaded him the youth's a devil.

FABIAN, ⌜*aside to Toby*⌝ He is as horribly conceited of 305
him, and pants and looks pale as if a bear were at his
heels.

TOBY, ⌜*to Viola*⌝ There's no remedy, sir; he will fight
with you for 's oath sake. Marry, he hath better
bethought him of his quarrel, and he finds that now 310
scarce to be worth talking of. Therefore, draw for
the supportance of his vow. He protests he will not
hurt you.

VIOLA Pray God defend me! ⌜*Aside.*⌝ A little thing
would make me tell them how much I lack of a 315
man.

FABIAN   Give ground if you see him furious.
                              ⌜*Toby crosses to Andrew.*⌝
TOBY   Come, Sir Andrew, there's no remedy. The
   gentleman will, for his honor's sake, have one bout
   with you. He cannot by the *duello* avoid it. But he   320
   has promised me, as he is a gentleman and a soldier,
   he will not hurt you. Come on, to 't.
ANDREW, ⌜*drawing his sword*⌝ Pray God he keep his
   oath!
VIOLA, ⌜*drawing her sword*⌝
   I do assure you, 'tis against my will.   325

              Enter Antonio.

ANTONIO, ⌜*to Andrew*⌝
   Put up your sword. If this young gentleman
   Have done offense, I take the fault on me.
   If you offend him, I for him defy you.
TOBY   You, sir? Why, what are you?
ANTONIO, ⌜*drawing his sword*⌝
   One, sir, that for his love dares yet do more   330
   Than you have heard him brag to you he will.
TOBY, ⌜*drawing his sword*⌝
   Nay, if you be an undertaker, I am for you.

              Enter Officers.

FABIAN   O, good Sir Toby, hold! Here come the officers.
TOBY, ⌜*to Antonio*⌝ I'll be with you anon.
VIOLA, ⌜*to Andrew*⌝ Pray, sir, put your sword up, if   335
   you please.
ANDREW   Marry, will I, sir. And for that I promised
   you, I'll be as good as my word. He will bear you
   easily, and reins well.
FIRST OFFICER   This is the man. Do thy office.   340
SECOND OFFICER   Antonio, I arrest thee at the suit of
   Count Orsino.
ANTONIO   You do mistake me, sir.

FIRST OFFICER
　No, sir, no jot. I know your favor well,
　Though now you have no sea-cap on your head.—　345
　Take him away. He knows I know him well.
ANTONIO
　I must obey. ⌈*To Viola.*⌉ This comes with seeking
　　you.
　But there's no remedy. I shall answer it.
　What will you do, now my necessity　　　350
　Makes me to ask you for my purse? It grieves me
　Much more for what I cannot do for you
　Than what befalls myself. You stand amazed,
　But be of comfort.
SECOND OFFICER　　　Come, sir, away.　　　355
ANTONIO, ⌈*to Viola*⌉
　I must entreat of you some of that money.
VIOLA　What money, sir?
　For the fair kindness you have showed me here,
　And part being prompted by your present trouble,
　Out of my lean and low ability　　　360
　I'll lend you something. My having is not much.
　I'll make division of my present with you.
　Hold, there's half my coffer.　　⌈*Offering him money.*⌉
ANTONIO　Will you deny me now?
　Is 't possible that my deserts to you　　　365
　Can lack persuasion? Do not tempt my misery,
　Lest that it make me so unsound a man
　As to upbraid you with those kindnesses
　That I have done for you.
VIOLA　　　　　　　　I know of none,　　　370
　Nor know I you by voice or any feature.
　I hate ingratitude more in a man
　Than lying, vainness, babbling drunkenness,
　Or any taint of vice whose strong corruption
　Inhabits our frail blood—　　　375
ANTONIO　　　　　　　　O heavens themselves!

SECOND OFFICER Come, sir, I pray you go.

ANTONIO
Let me speak a little. This youth that you see here
I snatched one half out of the jaws of death,
Relieved him with such sanctity of love,   380
And to his image, which methought did promise
Most venerable worth, did I devotion.

FIRST OFFICER
What's that to us? The time goes by. Away!

ANTONIO
But O, how vile an idol proves this god!
Thou hast, Sebastian, done good feature shame.   385
In nature there's no blemish but the mind;
None can be called deformed but the unkind.
Virtue is beauty, but the beauteous evil
Are empty trunks o'erflourished by the devil.

FIRST OFFICER
The man grows mad. Away with him.—Come,   390
    come, sir.

ANTONIO Lead me on.

⌈*Antonio and Officers*⌉ *exit.*

VIOLA, ⌈*aside*⌉
Methinks his words do from such passion fly
That he believes himself; so do not I.
Prove true, imagination, O, prove true,   395
That I, dear brother, be now ta'en for you!

TOBY Come hither, knight; come hither, Fabian. We'll
    whisper o'er a couplet or two of most sage saws.
        ⌈*Toby, Fabian, and Andrew move aside.*⌉

VIOLA
He named Sebastian. I my brother know
Yet living in my glass. Even such and so   400
In favor was my brother, and he went
Still in this fashion, color, ornament,
For him I imitate. O, if it prove,
Tempests are kind, and salt waves fresh in love!
        ⌈*She exits.*⌉

TOBY   A very dishonest, paltry boy, and more a coward 405
    than a hare. His dishonesty appears in leaving his
    friend here in necessity and denying him; and for
    his cowardship, ask Fabian.

FABIAN   A coward, a most devout coward, religious
    in it.   410

ANDREW   'Slid, I'll after him again and beat him.

TOBY   Do, cuff him soundly, but never draw thy
    sword.

ANDREW   An I do not—

FABIAN   Come, let's see the event.   415

TOBY   I dare lay any money 'twill be nothing yet.

                                   ⌜*They*⌝ *exit.*

ACT 4

Scene 1
Enter Sebastian and ⌜*Feste, the Fool.*⌝

FOOL   Will you make me believe that I am not sent for
you?

SEBASTIAN   Go to, go to, thou art a foolish fellow. Let
me be clear of thee.

FOOL   Well held out, i' faith. No, I do not know you, nor   5
I am not sent to you by my lady to bid you come
speak with her, nor your name is not Master
Cesario, nor this is not my nose neither. Nothing
that is so is so.

SEBASTIAN   I prithee, vent thy folly somewhere else.   10
Thou know'st not me.

FOOL   Vent my folly? He has heard that word of some
great man and now applies it to a Fool. Vent my
folly? I am afraid this great lubber the world will
prove a cockney. I prithee now, ungird thy strange-   15
ness and tell me what I shall vent to my lady. Shall I
vent to her that thou art coming?

SEBASTIAN   I prithee, foolish Greek, depart from me.
There's money for thee. ⌜*Giving money.*⌝ If you
tarry longer, I shall give worse payment.   20

FOOL   By my troth, thou hast an open hand. These wise
men that give Fools money get themselves a good
report—after fourteen years' purchase.

Enter Andrew, Toby, and Fabian.

ANDREW, ⌜*to Sebastian*⌝   Now, sir, have I met you again?
    There's for you.   ⌜*He strikes Sebastian.*⌝   25
SEBASTIAN, ⌜*returning the blow*⌝   Why, there's for thee,
    and there, and there.—Are all the people mad?
TOBY   Hold, sir, or I'll throw your dagger o'er the
    house.
FOOL, ⌜*aside*⌝   This will I tell my lady straight. I would   30
    not be in some of your coats for twopence.
                                   ⌜*He exits.*⌝
TOBY, ⌜*seizing Sebastian*⌝   Come on, sir, hold!
ANDREW   Nay, let him alone. I'll go another way to
    work with him. I'll have an action of battery against
    him, if there be any law in Illyria. Though I struck   35
    him first, yet it's no matter for that.
SEBASTIAN, ⌜*to Toby*⌝   Let go thy hand!
TOBY   Come, sir, I will not let you go. Come, my young
    soldier, put up your iron. You are well fleshed.
    Come on.   40
SEBASTIAN
    I will be free from thee.
                  ⌜*He pulls free and draws his sword.*⌝
                        What wouldst thou now?
    If thou dar'st tempt me further, draw thy sword.
TOBY   What, what? Nay, then, I must have an ounce or
    two of this malapert blood from you.   45
                          ⌜*He draws his sword.*⌝

Enter Olivia.

OLIVIA
    Hold, Toby! On thy life I charge thee, hold!
TOBY   Madam.
OLIVIA
    Will it be ever thus? Ungracious wretch,
    Fit for the mountains and the barbarous caves,

Where manners ne'er were preached! Out of my   50
   sight!—
Be not offended, dear Cesario.—
Rudesby, begone!   ⌜*Toby, Andrew, and Fabian exit.*⌝
             I prithee, gentle friend,
Let thy fair wisdom, not thy passion, sway   55
In this uncivil and unjust extent
Against thy peace. Go with me to my house,
And hear thou there how many fruitless pranks
This ruffian hath botched up, that thou thereby
Mayst smile at this. Thou shalt not choose but go.   60
Do not deny. Beshrew his soul for me!
He started one poor heart of mine, in thee.

SEBASTIAN, ⌜*aside*⌝
What relish is in this? How runs the stream?
Or I am mad, or else this is a dream.
Let fancy still my sense in Lethe steep;   65
If it be thus to dream, still let me sleep!

OLIVIA
Nay, come, I prithee. Would thou'dst be ruled by
   me!

SEBASTIAN
Madam, I will.

OLIVIA   O, say so, and so be!   70
                              They exit.

Scene 2
Enter Maria and ⌜*Feste, the Fool.*⌝

MARIA Nay, I prithee, put on this gown and this beard;
   make him believe thou art Sir Topas the curate. Do
   it quickly. I'll call Sir Toby the whilst.   ⌜*She exits.*⌝
FOOL Well, I'll put it on, and I will dissemble myself in
   't, and I would I were the first that ever dissembled   5
   in such a gown. ⌜*He puts on gown and beard.*⌝ I am

not tall enough to become the function well, nor
lean enough to be thought a good student, but to be
said an honest man and a good housekeeper goes as
fairly as to say a careful man and a great scholar.   10
The competitors enter.

Enter Toby ⌐and Maria.⌐

TOBY   Jove bless thee, Master Parson.

FOOL   *Bonos dies*, Sir Toby; for, as the old hermit of
Prague, that never saw pen and ink, very wittily said
to a niece of King Gorboduc "That that is, is," so I,   15
being Master Parson, am Master Parson; for what is
"that" but "that" and "is" but "is"?

TOBY   To him, Sir Topas.

FOOL, ⌐*disguising his voice*⌐   What ho, I say! Peace in this
prison!   20

TOBY   The knave counterfeits well. A good knave.

Malvolio within.

MALVOLIO   Who calls there?

FOOL   Sir Topas the curate, who comes to visit Malvolio the lunatic.

MALVOLIO   Sir Topas, Sir Topas, good Sir Topas, go to   25
my lady—

FOOL   Out, hyperbolical fiend! How vexest thou this
man! Talkest thou nothing but of ladies?

TOBY, ⌐*aside*⌐   Well said, Master Parson.

MALVOLIO   Sir Topas, never was man thus wronged.   30
Good Sir Topas, do not think I am mad. They have
laid me here in hideous darkness—

FOOL   Fie, thou dishonest Satan! I call thee by the most
modest terms, for I am one of those gentle ones
that will use the devil himself with courtesy. Sayst   35
thou that house is dark?

MALVOLIO   As hell, Sir Topas.

FOOL Why, it hath bay windows transparent as barricadoes, and the ⌈clerestories⌉ toward the south-
north are as lustrous as ebony; and yet complainest 40
thou of obstruction?

MALVOLIO I am not mad, Sir Topas. I say to you this
house is dark.

FOOL Madman, thou errest. I say there is no darkness
but ignorance, in which thou art more puzzled than 45
the Egyptians in their fog.

MALVOLIO I say this house is as dark as ignorance,
though ignorance were as dark as hell. And I say
there was never man thus abused. I am no more
mad than you are. Make the trial of it in any 50
constant question.

FOOL What is the opinion of Pythagoras concerning
wildfowl?

MALVOLIO That the soul of our grandam might haply
inhabit a bird. 55

FOOL What thinkst thou of his opinion?

MALVOLIO I think nobly of the soul, and no way
approve his opinion.

FOOL Fare thee well. Remain thou still in darkness.
Thou shalt hold th' opinion of Pythagoras ere I will 60
allow of thy wits, and fear to kill a woodcock lest
thou dispossess the soul of thy grandam. Fare thee
well.

MALVOLIO Sir Topas, Sir Topas!

TOBY My most exquisite Sir Topas! 65

FOOL Nay, I am for all waters.

MARIA Thou mightst have done this without thy beard
and gown. He sees thee not.

TOBY To him in thine own voice, and bring me word
how thou find'st him. I would we were well rid 70
of this knavery. If he may be conveniently delivered, I would he were, for I am now so far in
offense with my niece that I cannot pursue with

any safety this sport the upshot. Come by and by
to my chamber.   75

⌜*Toby and Maria* ⌝ *exit.*

FOOL ⌜*sings, in his own voice* ⌝
Hey, Robin, jolly Robin,
Tell me how thy lady does.

MALVOLIO Fool!

FOOL ⌜*sings* ⌝
My lady is unkind, perdy.

MALVOLIO Fool!   80

FOOL ⌜*sings* ⌝
Alas, why is she so?

MALVOLIO Fool, I say!

FOOL ⌜*sings* ⌝
She loves another—
Who calls, ha?

MALVOLIO Good Fool, as ever thou wilt deserve well at   85
my hand, help me to a candle, and pen, ink, and
paper. As I am a gentleman, I will live to be thankful
to thee for 't.

FOOL Master Malvolio?

MALVOLIO Ay, good Fool.   90

FOOL Alas, sir, how fell you besides your five wits?

MALVOLIO Fool, there was never man so notoriously
abused. I am as well in my wits, Fool, as thou art.

FOOL But as well? Then you are mad indeed, if you be
no better in your wits than a Fool.   95

MALVOLIO They have here propertied me, keep me in
darkness, send ministers to me—asses!—and do
all they can to face me out of my wits.

FOOL Advise you what you say. The minister is here.
⌜*In the voice of Sir Topas.* ⌝ Malvolio, Malvolio, thy   100
wits the heavens restore. Endeavor thyself to sleep
and leave thy vain bibble-babble.

MALVOLIO Sir Topas!

FOOL, ⌜*as Sir Topas*⌝ Maintain no words with him, good
    fellow. ⌜*As Fool.*⌝ Who, I, sir? Not I, sir! God buy   105
    you, good Sir Topas. ⌜*As Sir Topas.*⌝ Marry, amen.
    ⌜*As Fool.*⌝ I will, sir, I will.

MALVOLIO   Fool! Fool! Fool, I say!

FOOL   Alas, sir, be patient. What say you, sir? I am
    shent for speaking to you.   110

MALVOLIO   Good Fool, help me to some light and some
    paper. I tell thee, I am as well in my wits as any
    man in Illyria.

FOOL   Welladay that you were, sir!

MALVOLIO   By this hand, I am. Good Fool, some ink,   115
    paper, and light; and convey what I will set down to
    my lady. It shall advantage thee more than ever the
    bearing of letter did.

FOOL   I will help you to 't. But tell me true, are you not
    mad indeed, or do you but counterfeit?   120

MALVOLIO   Believe me, I am not. I tell thee true.

FOOL   Nay, I'll ne'er believe a madman till I see his
    brains. I will fetch you light and paper and ink.

MALVOLIO   Fool, I'll requite it in the highest degree. I
    prithee, begone.   125

FOOL ⌜*sings*⌝
    I am gone, sir, and anon, sir,
        I'll be with you again,
    In a trice, like to the old Vice,
        Your need to sustain.
    Who with dagger of lath, in his rage and his wrath,   130
        Cries "aha!" to the devil;
    Like a mad lad, "Pare thy nails, dad!
        Adieu, goodman devil."

                                          He exits.

Scene 3
Enter Sebastian.

⌈SEBASTIAN⌉
  This is the air; that is the glorious sun.
  This pearl she gave me, I do feel 't and see 't.
  And though 'tis wonder that enwraps me thus,
  Yet 'tis not madness. Where's Antonio, then?
  I could not find him at the Elephant.   5
  Yet there he was; and there I found this credit,
  That he did range the town to seek me out.
  His counsel now might do me golden service.
  For though my soul disputes well with my sense
  That this may be some error, but no madness,   10
  Yet doth this accident and flood of fortune
  So far exceed all instance, all discourse,
  That I am ready to distrust mine eyes
  And wrangle with my reason that persuades me
  To any other trust but that I am mad—   15
  Or else the lady's mad. Yet if 'twere so,
  She could not sway her house, command her
      followers,
  Take and give back affairs and their dispatch
  With such a smooth, discreet, and stable bearing   20
  As I perceive she does. There's something in 't
  That is deceivable. But here the lady comes.

          Enter Olivia and ⌈a⌉ Priest.

OLIVIA, ⌈*to Sebastian*⌉
  Blame not this haste of mine. If you mean well,
  Now go with me and with this holy man
  Into the chantry by. There, before him   25
  And underneath that consecrated roof,
  Plight me the full assurance of your faith,
  That my most jealous and too doubtful soul
  May live at peace. He shall conceal it

Whiles you are willing it shall come to note,   30
What time we will our celebration keep
According to my birth. What do you say?
SEBASTIAN
I'll follow this good man and go with you
And, having sworn truth, ever will be true.
OLIVIA
Then lead the way, good father, and heavens so   35
    shine
That they may fairly note this act of mine.

They exit.

ACT 5

Scene 1
Enter ⌐Feste, the Fool⌐ and Fabian.

FABIAN   Now, as thou lov'st me, let me see his letter.

FOOL   Good Master Fabian, grant me another request.

FABIAN   Anything.

FOOL   Do not desire to see this letter.

FABIAN   This is to give a dog and in recompense desire   5
   my dog again.

Enter ⌐Orsino,⌐ Viola, Curio, and Lords.

ORSINO
  Belong you to the Lady Olivia, friends?

FOOL   Ay, sir, we are some of her trappings.

ORSINO
  I know thee well. How dost thou, my good fellow?

FOOL   Truly, sir, the better for my foes and the worse   10
   for my friends.

ORSINO
  Just the contrary: the better for thy friends.

FOOL   No, sir, the worse.

ORSINO   How can that be?

FOOL   Marry, sir, they praise me and make an ass of me.   15
   Now my foes tell me plainly I am an ass; so that by
   my foes, sir, I profit in the knowledge of myself, and
   by my friends I am abused. So that, conclusions to
   be as kisses, if your four negatives make your two

affirmatives, why then the worse for my friends and   20
the better for my foes.

ORSINO   Why, this is excellent.

FOOL   By my troth, sir, no—though it please you to be
one of my friends.

ORSINO, ⌜*giving a coin*⌝
Thou shalt not be the worse for me; there's gold.   25

FOOL   But that it would be double-dealing, sir, I would
you could make it another.

ORSINO   O, you give me ill counsel.

FOOL   Put your grace in your pocket, sir, for this once,
and let your flesh and blood obey it.   30

ORSINO   Well, I will be so much a sinner to be a
double-dealer: there's another.   ⌜*He gives a coin.*⌝

FOOL   *Primo, secundo, tertio* is a good play, and the old
saying is, the third pays for all. The triplex, sir, is a
good tripping measure, or the bells of Saint Bennet,   35
sir, may put you in mind—one, two, three.

ORSINO   You can fool no more money out of me at this
throw. If you will let your lady know I am here to
speak with her, and bring her along with you, it
may awake my bounty further.   40

FOOL   Marry, sir, lullaby to your bounty till I come
again. I go, sir, but I would not have you to think
that my desire of having is the sin of covetousness.
But, as you say, sir, let your bounty take a nap. I
will awake it anon.   *He exits.*   45

Enter Antonio and Officers.

VIOLA
Here comes the man, sir, that did rescue me.

ORSINO
That face of his I do remember well.
Yet when I saw it last, it was besmeared
As black as Vulcan in the smoke of war.
A baubling vessel was he captain of,   50

For shallow draught and bulk unprizable,
With which such scatheful grapple did he make
With the most noble bottom of our fleet
That very envy and the tongue of loss
Cried fame and honor on him.—What's the matter? 55

FIRST OFFICER
Orsino, this is that Antonio
That took the *Phoenix* and her fraught from Candy,
And this is he that did the *Tiger* board
When your young nephew Titus lost his leg.
Here in the streets, desperate of shame and state, 60
In private brabble did we apprehend him.

VIOLA
He did me kindness, sir, drew on my side,
But in conclusion put strange speech upon me.
I know not what 'twas but distraction.

ORSINO
Notable pirate, thou saltwater thief, 65
What foolish boldness brought thee to their mercies
Whom thou, in terms so bloody and so dear,
Hast made thine enemies?

ANTONIO   Orsino, noble sir,
Be pleased that I shake off these names you give 70
    me.
Antonio never yet was thief or pirate,
Though, I confess, on base and ground enough,
Orsino's enemy. A witchcraft drew me hither.
That most ingrateful boy there by your side 75
From the rude sea's enraged and foamy mouth
Did I redeem; a wrack past hope he was.
His life I gave him and did thereto add
My love, without retention or restraint,
All his in dedication. For his sake 80
Did I expose myself, pure for his love,
Into the danger of this adverse town;
Drew to defend him when he was beset;

Where, being apprehended, his false cunning
(Not meaning to partake with me in danger)   85
Taught him to face me out of his acquaintance
And grew a twenty years' removèd thing
While one would wink; denied me mine own purse,
Which I had recommended to his use
Not half an hour before.   90
VIOLA   How can this be?
ORSINO, ⌜*to Antonio*⌝   When came he to this town?
ANTONIO
Today, my lord; and for three months before,
No int'rim, not a minute's vacancy,
Both day and night did we keep company.   95

        Enter Olivia and Attendants.

ORSINO
Here comes the Countess. Now heaven walks on
    earth!—
But for thee, fellow: fellow, thy words are madness.
Three months this youth hath tended upon me—
But more of that anon. ⌜*To an Officer.*⌝ Take him   100
    aside.
OLIVIA
What would my lord, but that he may not have,
Wherein Olivia may seem serviceable?—
Cesario, you do not keep promise with me.
VIOLA   Madam?   105
ORSINO   Gracious Olivia—
OLIVIA
What do you say, Cesario?—Good my lord—
VIOLA
My lord would speak; my duty hushes me.
OLIVIA
If it be aught to the old tune, my lord,
It is as fat and fulsome to mine ear   110
As howling after music.

ORSINO
  Still so cruel?
OLIVIA   Still so constant, lord.
ORSINO
  What, to perverseness? You, uncivil lady,
  To whose ingrate and unauspicious altars   115
  My soul the faithful'st off'rings have breathed out
  That e'er devotion tendered—what shall I do?
OLIVIA
  Even what it please my lord that shall become him.
ORSINO
  Why should I not, had I the heart to do it,
  Like to th' Egyptian thief at point of death,   120
  Kill what I love?—a savage jealousy
  That sometimes savors nobly. But hear me this:
  Since you to nonregardance cast my faith,
  And that I partly know the instrument
  That screws me from my true place in your favor,   125
  Live you the marble-breasted tyrant still.
  But this your minion, whom I know you love,
  And whom, by heaven I swear, I tender dearly,
  Him will I tear out of that cruel eye
  Where he sits crownèd in his master's spite.—   130
  Come, boy, with me. My thoughts are ripe in
    mischief.
  I'll sacrifice the lamb that I do love
  To spite a raven's heart within a dove.
VIOLA
  And I, most jocund, apt, and willingly,   135
  To do you rest a thousand deaths would die.
OLIVIA
  Where goes Cesario?
VIOLA   After him I love
  More than I love these eyes, more than my life,
  More by all mores than e'er I shall love wife.   140
  If I do feign, you witnesses above,
  Punish my life for tainting of my love.

OLIVIA
  Ay me, detested! How am I beguiled!
VIOLA
  Who does beguile you? Who does do you wrong?
OLIVIA
  Hast thou forgot thyself? Is it so long?—   145
  Call forth the holy father.   ⌜*An Attendant exits.*⌝
ORSINO, ⌜*to Viola*⌝   Come, away!
OLIVIA
  Whither, my lord?—Cesario, husband, stay.
ORSINO
  Husband?
OLIVIA   Ay, husband. Can he that deny?   150
ORSINO
  Her husband, sirrah?
VIOLA   No, my lord, not I.
OLIVIA
  Alas, it is the baseness of thy fear
  That makes thee strangle thy propriety.
  Fear not, Cesario. Take thy fortunes up.   155
  Be that thou know'st thou art, and then thou art
  As great as that thou fear'st.

                    Enter Priest.

                              O, welcome, father.
  Father, I charge thee by thy reverence
  Here to unfold (though lately we intended   160
  To keep in darkness what occasion now
  Reveals before 'tis ripe) what thou dost know
  Hath newly passed between this youth and me.
PRIEST
  A contract of eternal bond of love,
  Confirmed by mutual joinder of your hands,   165
  Attested by the holy close of lips,
  Strengthened by interchangement of your rings,
  And all the ceremony of this compact

Sealed in my function, by my testimony;
Since when, my watch hath told me, toward my 170
  grave
I have traveled but two hours.

ORSINO ⌜*to Viola*⌝
O thou dissembling cub! What wilt thou be
When time hath sowed a grizzle on thy case?
Or will not else thy craft so quickly grow 175
That thine own trip shall be thine overthrow?
Farewell, and take her, but direct thy feet
Where thou and I henceforth may never meet.

VIOLA
My lord, I do protest—

OLIVIA   O, do not swear. 180
Hold little faith, though thou hast too much fear.

Enter Sir Andrew.

ANDREW For the love of God, a surgeon! Send one
  presently to Sir Toby.

OLIVIA What's the matter?

ANDREW Has broke my head across, and has given Sir 185
  Toby a bloody coxcomb too. For the love of God,
  your help! I had rather than forty pound I were at
  home.

OLIVIA Who has done this, Sir Andrew?

ANDREW The Count's gentleman, one Cesario. We took 190
  him for a coward, but he's the very devil incardinate.

ORSINO My gentleman Cesario?

ANDREW 'Od's lifelings, here he is!—You broke my
  head for nothing, and that that I did, I was set on to 195
  do 't by Sir Toby.

VIOLA
Why do you speak to me? I never hurt you.
You drew your sword upon me without cause,
But I bespake you fair and hurt you not.

ANDREW   If a bloody coxcomb be a hurt, you have hurt   200
me. I think you set nothing by a bloody coxcomb.

Enter Toby and ⌐Feste, the Fool.⌐

Here comes Sir Toby halting. You shall hear
more. But if he had not been in drink, he would
have tickled you othergates than he did.
ORSINO   How now, gentleman? How is 't with you?   205
TOBY   That's all one. Has hurt me, and there's th' end
on 't. ⌐*To Fool.*⌐ Sot, didst see Dick Surgeon, sot?
FOOL   O, he's drunk, Sir Toby, an hour agone; his eyes
were set at eight i' th' morning.
TOBY   Then he's a rogue and a passy-measures pavin. I   210
hate a drunken rogue.
OLIVIA   Away with him! Who hath made this havoc
with them?
ANDREW   I'll help you, Sir Toby, because we'll be
dressed together.   215
TOBY   Will you help?—an ass-head, and a coxcomb,
and a knave, a thin-faced knave, a gull?
OLIVIA
Get him to bed, and let his hurt be looked to.
⌐*Toby, Andrew, Fool, and Fabian exit.*⌐

Enter Sebastian.

SEBASTIAN
I am sorry, madam, I have hurt your kinsman,
But, had it been the brother of my blood,   220
I must have done no less with wit and safety.
You throw a strange regard upon me, and by that
I do perceive it hath offended you.
Pardon me, sweet one, even for the vows
We made each other but so late ago.   225
ORSINO
One face, one voice, one habit, and two persons!
A natural perspective, that is and is not!

SEBASTIAN
  Antonio, O, my dear Antonio!
  How have the hours racked and tortured me
  Since I have lost thee!   230
ANTONIO
  Sebastian are you?
SEBASTIAN   Fear'st thou that, Antonio?
ANTONIO
  How have you made division of yourself?
  An apple cleft in two is not more twin
  Than these two creatures. Which is Sebastian?   235
OLIVIA   Most wonderful!
SEBASTIAN, ⌜*looking at Viola*⌝
  Do I stand there? I never had a brother,
  Nor can there be that deity in my nature
  Of here and everywhere. I had a sister,
  Whom the blind waves and surges have devoured.   240
  Of charity, what kin are you to me?
  What countryman? What name? What parentage?
VIOLA
  Of Messaline. Sebastian was my father.
  Such a Sebastian was my brother, too.
  So went he suited to his watery tomb.   245
  If spirits can assume both form and suit,
  You come to fright us.
SEBASTIAN   A spirit I am indeed,
  But am in that dimension grossly clad
  Which from the womb I did participate.   250
  Were you a woman, as the rest goes even,
  I should my tears let fall upon your cheek
  And say "Thrice welcome, drownèd Viola."
VIOLA
  My father had a mole upon his brow.
SEBASTIAN   And so had mine.   255
VIOLA
  And died that day when Viola from her birth
  Had numbered thirteen years.

SEBASTIAN

  O, that record is lively in my soul!
  He finishèd indeed his mortal act
  That day that made my sister thirteen years.   260

VIOLA

  If nothing lets to make us happy both
  But this my masculine usurped attire,
  Do not embrace me till each circumstance
  Of place, time, fortune, do cohere and jump
  That I am Viola; which to confirm,   265
  I'll bring you to a captain in this town,
  Where lie my maiden weeds; by whose gentle help
  I was preserved to serve this noble count.
  All the occurrence of my fortune since
  Hath been between this lady and this lord.   270

SEBASTIAN, ⌜*to Olivia*⌝

  So comes it, lady, you have been mistook.
  But nature to her bias drew in that.
  You would have been contracted to a maid.
  Nor are you therein, by my life, deceived:
  You are betrothed both to a maid and man.   275

ORSINO, ⌜*to Olivia*⌝

  Be not amazed; right noble is his blood.
  If this be so, as yet the glass seems true,
  I shall have share in this most happy wrack.—
  Boy, thou hast said to me a thousand times
  Thou never shouldst love woman like to me.   280

VIOLA

  And all those sayings will I overswear,
  And all those swearings keep as true in soul
  As doth that orbèd continent the fire
  That severs day from night.

ORSINO   Give me thy hand,   285
  And let me see thee in thy woman's weeds.

VIOLA

  The Captain that did bring me first on shore

Hath my maid's garments. He, upon some action,
Is now in durance at Malvolio's suit,
A gentleman and follower of my lady's.   290

OLIVIA
He shall enlarge him.

Enter ⌜Feste, the Fool⌝ with a letter, and Fabian.

              Fetch Malvolio hither.
And yet, alas, now I remember me,
They say, poor gentleman, he's much distract.
A most extracting frenzy of mine own   295
From my remembrance clearly banished his.
⌜*To the Fool.*⌝ How does he, sirrah?

FOOL   Truly, madam, he holds Beelzebub at the stave's
end as well as a man in his case may do. Has here
writ a letter to you. I should have given 't you today   300
morning. But as a madman's epistles are no gos-
pels, so it skills not much when they are delivered.

OLIVIA   Open 't and read it.

FOOL   Look then to be well edified, when the Fool
delivers the madman. ⌜*He reads.*⌝ *By the Lord,*   305
madam—

OLIVIA   How now, art thou mad?

FOOL   No, madam, I do but read madness. An your
Ladyship will have it as it ought to be, you must
allow *vox.*   310

OLIVIA   Prithee, read i' thy right wits.

FOOL   So I do, madonna. But to read his right wits is to
read thus. Therefore, perpend, my princess, and
give ear.

OLIVIA, ⌜*giving letter to Fabian*⌝ Read it you, sirrah.   315

FABIAN (*reads*)   *By the Lord, madam, you wrong me, and*
the world shall know it. Though you have put me into
darkness and given your drunken cousin rule over
me, yet have I the benefit of my senses as well as your
Ladyship. I have your own letter that induced me to   320

the semblance I put on, with the which I doubt not but
to do myself much right or you much shame. Think of
me as you please. I leave my duty a little unthought of
and speak out of my injury.
The madly used Malvolio. 325

OLIVIA Did he write this?

FOOL Ay, madam.

ORSINO
  This savors not much of distraction.

OLIVIA
  See him delivered, Fabian. Bring him hither.
⌐*Fabian exits.*⌐

  ⌐*To Orsino.*⌐ My lord, so please you, these things   330
    further thought on,
  To think me as well a sister as a wife,
  One day shall crown th' alliance on 't, so please
    you,
  Here at my house, and at my proper cost.   335

ORSINO
  Madam, I am most apt t' embrace your offer.
  ⌐*To Viola.*⌐ Your master quits you; and for your
    service done him,
  So much against the mettle of your sex,
  So far beneath your soft and tender breeding,   340
  And since you called me "master" for so long,
  Here is my hand. You shall from this time be
  Your master's mistress.

OLIVIA, ⌐*to Viola*⌐   A sister! You are she.

Enter Malvolio ⌐*and Fabian.*⌐

ORSINO
  Is this the madman?   345

OLIVIA   Ay, my lord, this same.—
  How now, Malvolio?

MALVOLIO   Madam, you have done me
    wrong,
  Notorious wrong.   350

OLIVIA   Have I, Malvolio? No.

MALVOLIO, ⌜*handing her a paper*⌝

Lady, you have. Pray you peruse that letter.
You must not now deny it is your hand.
Write from it if you can, in hand or phrase,
Or say 'tis not your seal, not your invention.   355
You can say none of this. Well, grant it then,
And tell me, in the modesty of honor,
Why you have given me such clear lights of favor?
Bade me come smiling and cross-gartered to you,
To put on yellow stockings, and to frown   360
Upon Sir Toby and the lighter people?
And, acting this in an obedient hope,
Why have you suffered me to be imprisoned,
Kept in a dark house, visited by the priest,
And made the most notorious geck and gull   365
That e'er invention played on? Tell me why.

OLIVIA

Alas, Malvolio, this is not my writing,
Though I confess much like the character.
But out of question, 'tis Maria's hand.
And now I do bethink me, it was she   370
First told me thou wast mad; then cam'st in smiling,
And in such forms which here were presupposed
Upon thee in the letter. Prithee, be content.
This practice hath most shrewdly passed upon thee.
But when we know the grounds and authors of it,   375
Thou shalt be both the plaintiff and the judge
Of thine own cause.

FABIAN   Good madam, hear me speak,
And let no quarrel nor no brawl to come
Taint the condition of this present hour,   380
Which I have wondered at. In hope it shall not,
Most freely I confess, myself and Toby
Set this device against Malvolio here,
Upon some stubborn and uncourteous parts
We had conceived against him. Maria writ   385

The letter at Sir Toby's great importance,
In recompense whereof he hath married her.
How with a sportful malice it was followed
May rather pluck on laughter than revenge,
If that the injuries be justly weighed   390
That have on both sides passed.

OLIVIA, ⌜*to Malvolio*⌝
Alas, poor fool, how have they baffled thee!

FOOL   Why, "some are born great, some achieve greatness, and some have greatness thrown upon them."
   I was one, sir, in this interlude, one Sir Topas, sir,   395
   but that's all one. "By the Lord, Fool, I am not
   mad"—but, do you remember "Madam, why laugh
   you at such a barren rascal; an you smile not, he's
   gagged"? And thus the whirligig of time brings in
   his revenges.   400

MALVOLIO
I'll be revenged on the whole pack of you!   ⌜*He exits.*⌝

OLIVIA
He hath been most notoriously abused.

ORSINO
Pursue him and entreat him to a peace.   ⌜*Some exit.*⌝
He hath not told us of the Captain yet.
When that is known, and golden time convents,   405
A solemn combination shall be made
Of our dear souls.—Meantime, sweet sister,
We will not part from hence.—Cesario, come,
For so you shall be while you are a man.
But when in other habits you are seen,   410
Orsino's mistress, and his fancy's queen.
                              ⌜*All but the Fool*⌝ exit.

FOOL *sings*
   When that I was and a little tiny boy,
      With hey, ho, the wind and the rain,
   A foolish thing was but a toy,
      For the rain it raineth every day.   415

But when I came to man's estate,
    With hey, ho, the wind and the rain,
'Gainst knaves and thieves men shut their gate,
    For the rain it raineth every day.

But when I came, alas, to wive,   420
    With hey, ho, the wind and the rain,
By swaggering could I never thrive,
    For the rain it raineth every day.

But when I came unto my beds,
    With hey, ho, the wind and the rain,   425
With tosspots still had drunken heads,
    For the rain it raineth every day.

A great while ago the world begun,
    ⌜*With*⌝ *hey, ho, the wind and the rain,*
But that's all one, our play is done,   430
    And we'll strive to please you every day.
                                        ⌜*He exits.*⌝

Explanatory Notes

1.1   At his court, Orsino, sick with love for the Lady Olivia, learns from his messenger that she is grieving for her dead brother and refuses to be seen for seven years.

0 SD. **Illyria:** an ancient country in southern Europe, on the Adriatic Sea

2–3. **that . . . appetite:** i.e., so that my passion, glutted

4. **fall:** cadence (i.e., a sequence of chords ending the **strain** of music)

9–14. **O spirit . . . minute:** Love is described here as so hungry that it can devour everything and destroy the value of even the most precious things.   **quick and fresh:** keen and eager (to devour)   **validity:** worth   **pitch:** i.e., excellence (The pitch is the highest point in a falcon's flight.)

14–15. **fancy, high fantastical: Fancy** is both "love" and "imagination"; **high fantastical** carries the sense both of "highly imaginative, most able to create powerful images," and "extremely passionate." Orsino seems to be playing with the double meanings of these related words as he tries to describe the intensity of his lovesickness.

18. **hart:** stag (Orsino, in the following line, plays on the fact that *hart* sounds like *heart*.)

21. **Methought:** it seemed to me; **purged . . . pestilence:** i.e., purified the air of everything infectious

22–24. **That instant . . . pursue me:** Orsino compares himself to the mythological figure Acteon, who, having seen the goddess Diana bathing, was turned into a **hart** and destroyed by his own hounds.   **fell:** fierce, deadly

26. **So please my lord:** a polite phrase addressed to one's superior; **might not be:** i.e., was not

28. **element itself:** i.e., the very sky; **till seven years' heat:** i.e., until seven summers have passed

30. **cloistress:** a nun in a cloister

32. **eye-offending brine:** i.e., tears; **season:** preserve, keep fresh (**Brine** is salt water used for preserving food.)

33. **brother's ... love:** i.e., love for her dead brother

36. **but to a:** i.e., to a mere

37. **golden shaft:** In the mythology of romantic love, anyone struck by Cupid's arrow with the golden head falls desperately in love.

38. **affections else:** other feelings or desires

40. **thrones:** The **liver** was considered the seat of the passions, the **brain** the seat of reason, and the **heart** the seat of feeling.

40–41. **and ... perfections:** i.e., and her sweet perfections filled

41. **one self king:** a single monarch

1.2 On the Adriatic seacoast, Viola, who has been saved from a shipwreck in which her brother may have drowned, hears about Orsino and Olivia. She wishes to join Olivia's household, but is told that Olivia will admit no one into her presence. Viola decides to disguise herself as a boy so that she can join Orsino's male retinue.

4. **Elysium:** in Greek mythology, where the blessed go after death

5. **Perchance:** perhaps, possibly

7. **perchance:** i.e., by chance, through good luck

12. **driving:** i.e., drifting

15. **lived:** i.e., floated

16. **Arion ... back:** Arion, a Greek poet and musician, so charmed the dolphins with his music that one saved him from drowning

20–22. **Mine ... him:** i.e., my escape makes me hope

that my brother escaped too, and your speech encourages that hope

31. **late:** recently
34. **the less:** i.e., those of lower rank
38. **some twelvemonth since:** i.e., about a year ago
44. **delivered:** revealed
45. **mellow:** ripe
46. **estate:** social rank, position
47. **compass:** achieve, accomplish
48. **suit:** petition, formal request
51–52. **though ... pollution:** i.e., although natural beauty often hides inner corruption
53–54. **suits / With:** corresponds with, matches
54. **character:** i.e., personal appearance and behavior
56. **Conceal me:** i.e., conceal, keep secret
57. **become:** be suitable to
59. **eunuch:** a male soprano or castrato
62. **allow ... worth:** i.e., commend me as worthy to be in
64. **wit:** plan
65. **mute:** a person unable to speak

1.3 At the estate of Lady Olivia, Sir Toby Belch, Olivia's kinsman, has brought in Sir Andrew Aguecheek to be her suitor. Maria, Olivia's lady-in-waiting, says that Andrew is a fool, and Andrew himself doubts his ability to win Olivia, but Toby encourages him to woo her.

1, 5. **niece, cousin:** Both of these terms indicate close kinship; neither was as specific as it is today.
2. **care:** sorrow
4. **By my troth:** a mild oath
7. **except before excepted:** Toby's adaptation of the legal phrase *exceptis excipiendis* ("excepting those things which are to be excepted"), which he uses to dismiss Olivia's criticism

9. **modest:** moderate

10. **confine myself:** i.e., dress myself

12. **An:** if

14. **undo you:** ruin you; cause your downfall

20. **tall:** brave (Maria takes the word in its usual sense.)

22. **has . . . ducats:** i.e., has an income of three thousand gold coins

23. **have . . . ducats:** i.e., spend all his inheritance in a single year

24. **prodigal:** wastrel, spendthrift

25–26. **viol-de-gamboys:** i.e., viola da gamba, the predecessor of the modern cello

27. **without book:** i.e., from memory

29. **natural:** i.e., like a "natural" or idiot

30. **but that:** except for the fact that

31–32. **gust . . . in:** i.e., taste . . . for

34–35. **substractors:** i.e., detractors, slanderers

40. **coistrel:** lowborn contemptible fellow

42. **parish top:** a large public whipping-top; **Castiliano vulgo:** The meaning of this Spanish-sounding phrase (if it had one) is lost.

43. **Agueface:** This misnaming of Sir Andrew calls attention to the meaning of "Aguecheek," i.e., the pale, thin cheek (or face) of someone suffering from a fever or ague.

46. **shrew:** Andrew may be alluding to Maria's size (the shrew is among the smallest of mammals), or he may be using **shrew** (a word applied to a scolding or brawling woman) to mean simply "woman."

48. **Accost:** i.e., approach her, **woo her** (line 56) (In nautical terms, one ship accosts another by going alongside. The nautical language continues in **front**—i.e., confront— and **board** [line 55] and perhaps in **undertake** [line 57].)

60. **An . . . so:** i.e., if you let her leave so unceremoniously

64. **have fools in hand:** i.e., are dealing with fools

66. **Marry:** a mild oath, meaning "truly" or "indeed" (originally, an oath "by the Virgin Mary")

68. **thought is free:** a proverbial response to the question "Do you think I'm a fool?"

69. **butt'ry bar:** the ledge on top of the half door to the buttery, the storeroom for food and drink

71. **Wherefore:** i.e., why

73. **dry:** withered (indicating Andrew's lack of vigor, with a probable pun on **dry** as "thirsty")

76. **dry jest:** sarcastic or ironic joke

79. **barren:** i.e., no longer full of jests

80. **canary:** sweet wine

81. **put down:** snubbed, silenced

83. **put me down:** i.e., lay me out

84. **Christian:** often used, as here, to mean an ordinary human being

90. **Pourquoi:** French for "why"

92. **tongues:** i.e., foreign languages

93. **bearbaiting:** a blood sport in which dogs attack a bear chained to a stake

100. **distaff:** staff used in spinning thread from wool or flax

101. **huswife:** housewife (**Huswife,** pronounced "hussif," also had the sense of "hussy.")

103. **Faith:** a mild oath

105. **she'll ... me:** i.e., she does not want me; **Count:** i.e., Orsino, referred to as a duke in the first two scenes, but referred to hereafter in the dialogue as a count; **hard by:** nearby

108. **degree:** position; **estate:** fortune

111–12. **masques and revels:** entertainments, plays, dances

113. **kickshawses:** kickshaws, trifles (French: *quelques choses*)

117. **galliard:** a popular dance

118. **caper:** leap (A **caper** is also a condiment used in sauces. Toby plays on this sense when he mentions **mutton.**)

120. **back-trick:** probably, a backward leap or caper

123. **like:** i.e., likely

124. **take ... picture:** i.e., get dusty, and therefore need a curtain to protect them (It is unclear who "Mistress Mall" might be.)

126–27. **coranto, jig, sink-a-pace:** names for various dances

128. **virtues:** accomplishments

130. **star of a galliard:** a dancing star; or, a star propitious for dancing

132. **dun-colored stock:** i.e., brown stocking

135. **Taurus:** one of the twelve signs of the zodiac, which, at least according to Chaucer, governed the neck and the throat

1.4 At Orsino's court, Viola, disguised as a page and calling herself Cesario, has gained the trust of Orsino, who decides to send her to woo Olivia for him. Viola confides to the audience that she loves Orsino herself.

2. **Cesario:** the name chosen by Viola for her male disguise, which she will wear for the rest of the play; **be much advanced:** i.e., achieve advancement, promotion

5. **either ... negligence:** i.e., are concerned either that he is whimsical or that I cannot serve him well **fear:** distrust, suspect **humor:** disposition, whim

12. **On your attendance:** i.e., at your service

13. **aloof:** i.e., aside, apart

14. **no less but all:** i.e., everything

16. **address ... unto:** i.e., go to

18. **them:** i.e., Olivia's servants

19. **have audience:** i.e., are admitted to speak with her

23. **leap ... bounds:** i.e., go beyond the limits of courtesy

24. **unprofited:** i.e., unsuccessful

26. **unfold:** reveal, disclose

27. **Surprise:** overcome, capture (a military term)

28. **become thee well:** be appropriate for you

29. **attend:** pay attention to

30. **nuncio's:** messenger's; **more grave aspect:** i.e., older or more serious face

34. **Diana:** the virgin goddess, here the personification of youth and beauty

35. **rubious:** ruby red; **pipe:** i.e., voice

36. **organ:** i.e., voice (literally, vocal chords, larynx); **sound:** i.e., not cracked

37. **is semblative . . . part:** i.e., is like a woman (**Part** may be a theatrical term. In Shakespeare's theater, boys played women's parts.)

38. **thy constellation:** i.e., the stars that govern your success (or, that have shaped you)

39. **attend:** i.e., go along with

45. **barful strife:** i.e., an undertaking full of obstacles or "bars" (barriers)

1.5 Viola, in her disguise as Cesario, appears at Olivia's estate. Olivia allows Cesario to speak with her privately about Orsino's love. As Cesario presents Orsino's love-suit, Olivia falls in love with Cesario. She sends her steward, Malvolio, after Cesario with a ring.

0 SD. **Feste, the Fool:** In the Folio, this character, in stage directions and speech prefixes, is simply called "Clown" (an indication that the role was played by the troupe's comic actor). In dialogue, he is always called "Fool." He is at one point (in 2.4) referred to as "Feste, the jester," which leads some editors to name him "Feste" in speech prefixes and stage directions.

3. **in . . . excuse:** i.e., to defend you

6. **fear no colors:** proverbial for "fear nothing"

7. **Make ... good:** i.e., prove that; explain that

9. **Lenten:** i.e., weak, poor (good enough only for Lent, a time of fasting)

12. **In the wars:** Military flags were called **colors.**

13. **foolery:** Feste is a professional fool; i.e., he makes his living by entertaining his aristocratic patron and by amusing others in the household, who reward him for his **foolery.** Feste's foolery depends primarily on the way he uses words.

17. **turned away:** i.e., dismissed

20. **for:** i.e., as for; **let ... out:** i.e., may the warm weather of summer make it bearable

23. **if one break:** Maria plays on **points** (line 22) as meaning the laces that hold up a man's breeches.

24. **gaskins:** breeches or hose

27. **piece of Eve's flesh:** i.e., woman

29. **you were best:** We would say: "If you know what's good for you."

30. **Wit:** i.e., intelligence, brain; **an 't:** i.e., if it

31. **wits:** clever people

33. **Quinapalus:** a philosopher invented by Feste

34. **witty:** clever

38. **Go to:** an expression of impatience; **dry:** i.e., dull, not amusing

39. **dishonest:** dishonorable (i.e., unreliable)

40. **madonna:** my lady, madam (an Italian form of address)

42. **dry:** thirsty; **mend:** (1) reform; (2) repair

44. **botcher:** a tailor who repairs clothing

45. **is but:** is merely

49. **cuckold:** a man whose wife is unfaithful; **calamity:** i.e., one whom Fortune has deserted

50. **bade:** commanded (**Bade** is the past tense of "bid.")

53. **Misprision:** a mistake, an error

53–54. **cucullus ... monachum:** Proverbial: "A cowl does not make a monk."

55. **motley:** multicolored garments worn by professional fools

58. **Dexteriously:** i.e., dexterously, easily

60. **catechize:** question rigorously

60–61. **Good ... virtue:** i.e., my good, virtuous mouse (as if addressed to a young girl being catechized by the priest)

62. **want ... idleness:** lack of other pastime; **bide:** abide, listen to

72. **mend:** improve

78. **no fox:** i.e., not clever

78–79. **pass ... twopence:** i.e., bet tuppence

82–83. **put down ... with:** i.e., defeated (in a battle of wits) by

83. **ordinary fool:** perhaps, a simpleton; or, perhaps, a Fool without an aristocratic patron

84. **out of his guard:** defenseless, without an answer (a fencing metaphor)

85–86. **minister ... him:** give him opportunities

87. **crow:** cry out in pleasure; **set ... Fools:** i.e., professional fools   **set:** deliberate, intentional

88. **zanies:** (1) subordinate fools in comedies, whose function is to imitate the main comic character; (2) assistants, flatterers

90. **distempered:** diseased, disturbed; **generous:** high-minded

91. **free:** magnanimous

92. **bird-bolts:** blunt arrows

93. **allowed Fool:** i.e., a Fool who has been given permission always to speak freely

94–95. **known discreet man:** i.e., a man known to be judicious, wise

96. **Mercury ... leasing:** i.e., may Mercury, god of trickery, endow you with the gift of lying

106. **madman:** i.e., nonsense

107. **suit:** love-plea

112. **Jove:** king of the Roman gods

114. **pia mater:** i.e., brain

115. **What:** i.e., who

119–20. **a plague . . . herring:** perhaps Toby's explanation for his having belched or hiccoughed

120. **sot:** fool

126. **an he will:** if he wants to

127. **it's all one:** i.e., it doesn't matter

130. **draught:** i.e., cup of wine; **above heat:** Wine was thought to warm the liver.

132. **crowner:** i.e., coroner; **sit o':** i.e., hold an inquest on

147. **sheriff's post:** a large carved post

147–48. **the . . . bench:** i.e., a bench-support

153. **will . . . no:** i.e., whether you want to or not

154. **personage:** appearance

156. **squash:** unripe **peascod** (pea pod)

157. **codling:** unripe apple

158. **in standing . . . man:** i.e., halfway between boy and man, like a tide between ebb and flow

159–60. **shrewishly:** This word usually means "like a bad-tempered woman," but here it seems to mean merely "like a woman."

167. **Your will?:** i.e., what do you want?

172. **con:** memorize

173–74. **comptible . . . usage:** sensitive to even the smallest slight

178. **modest:** moderate

180. **comedian:** actor

182. **that I play:** i.e., that which I act

184. **usurp myself:** i.e., hold possession of myself wrongfully (Olivia's joking way of admitting that she is herself)

185–86. **usurp yourself:** i.e., wrongfully hold possession of yourself (in that you are refusing to marry and reproduce)

187. **reserve:** keep for yourself; **from:** i.e., not part of

190. **forgive you:** i.e., excuse you from reciting

194. **like:** i.e., likely

197. **be not mad:** This odd phrase may represent a scribal or printing error. Some editors omit the word **not;** others interpret "not" to mean "not entirely."

198. **'Tis . . . me:** i.e., I am not myself lunatic—under the influence of Luna, the moon

199. **make one:** i.e., take part

201. **swabber:** a sailor who swabs the decks; **hull:** remain, like a ship with furled sails

202. **giant:** perhaps a sarcastic reference to Maria's size

208. **office:** i.e., what you have been ordered to say

209. **alone . . . ear:** i.e., concerns no one but you

210. **taxation of:** i.e., demand that you pay; **olive:** olive branch, a symbol of peace and goodwill

212–13. **What would you?:** i.e., what do you want?

215. **my entertainment:** the way I was received

217. **divinity:** i.e., religious truth, theology; **profanation:** a violation of something sacred

220. **your text:** the scriptural passage on which you are to expound

222. **comfortable:** comforting

226. **by the method:** according to the division of the text in the table of contents

233–34. **such . . . present:** i.e., this is a portrait of me as I am at this moment

236. **in grain:** indelible (**Grain** was a "fast" or permanent dye.)

238. **blent:** blended

242. **leave . . . copy:** i.e., leave no children to carry on your beauty (Olivia responds as if **copy** here meant a written record.)

244. **divers schedules:** various lists

245. **utensil:** i.e., part of my body; **labeled:** described on paper and attached as a codicil

246. **item:** Latin for "likewise" (used to introduce each article in a formal inventory)

248. **praise:** perhaps, appraise

251. **if:** i.e., even if; **the devil:** perhaps a reference to Lucifer, the archangel who, through pride, led the revolt of the angels against God, and who, after his fall, was named Satan (Proverbial: "As proud as Lucifer.")

253. **but recompensed:** i.e., no more than returned on equal terms

255. **The nonpareil of beauty:** i.e., a beauty without equal

257. **fertile:** abundant

261. **estate:** fortune, status

262. **voices:** public opinion; **divulged:** spoken of; **free:** noble

263. **in dimension . . . nature:** i.e., in his physical shape

264. **A gracious:** an attractive

271. **willow cabin:** a small shelter made of willow (The **willow** is the symbol of grief for unrequited love.)

272. **call . . . house:** i.e., call out to Olivia, outside of whose **house** the **cabin** is built

273. **cantons:** i.e., cantos, ballads; **contemnèd:** disdained, viewed with contempt

275. **Hallow:** shout

276. **babbling . . . air:** i.e., Echo (the nymph who, in Greek mythology, pined away for love until only her voice was left to "babble")

279. **But . . . me:** i.e., unless you took pity on me

282. **fortunes:** (current) situation; **state:** social standing; or, condition in life

289. **fee'd post:** hired messenger

291. **Love:** i.e., may the god of love (Cupid); **make . . . flint:** i.e., turn . . . into flint; **that . . . love:** i.e., the man you will one day love

298. **give . . . blazon:** i.e., proclaim your high rank five times over (A **blazon** is a coat of arms.); **Soft:** an exclamation meaning "wait a minute"

300. **man:** i.e., servant

308. **County's man:** count's servant

309. **Would I:** i.e., whether I wanted it; **I'll . . . it:** i.e., I do not want it

310. **flatter with:** i.e., encourage

313. **Hie thee:** hurry

317. **owe:** own

2.1 A young gentleman named Sebastian, who has recently been saved from a shipwreck in which his sister has been lost, sets off for Orsino's court. Antonio, the sailor who saved him, follows him, even though Antonio risks his own life to do so.

1. **will you not:** i.e., do you not wish

3. **By your patience:** a polite phrase, "with your permission"

4. **malignancy:** evil influence (astrological term, carried also in the preceding phrase, "My stars shine darkly over me.")

5. **distemper:** disturb, damage

10. **sooth:** i.e., truly; **My . . . voyage:** the journey I've set for myself

11. **mere extravagancy:** no more than wandering

12. **modesty:** reserve, lack of presumption

13. **what . . . keep in:** i.e., what I wish to hide

13–14. **it . . . manners:** i.e., courtesy compels me

14. **the rather:** all the more

19. **in an:** i.e., within the same

22. **breach of the sea:** i.e., the breaking waves

26–27. **with . . . that:** i.e., **believe** too much in this admiring judgment of my sister's beauty

28. **publish:** proclaim

28–29. **that envy . . . fair:** i.e., that even the envious must call beautiful

32. **entertainment:** reception as my guest

34. **murder me for my love:** i.e., destroy me (1) in exchange for my love, or (2) because I care so much about you

37. **recovered:** rescued

39–40. **so near . . . mother:** i.e., so close to behaving like a woman

41. **will . . . me:** will weep, thus revealing my weakness

45. **Else:** otherwise

2.2 Malvolio finds the disguised Viola and "returns" the ring. Viola, alone, realizes that Olivia has fallen in love with Cesario and understands that Orsino, Olivia, and Viola/Cesario are now in a love triangle that she is helpless to resolve.

0 SD. **at several doors:** i.e., through separate stage entrances

4. **arrived . . . hither:** i.e., just reached this place

8. **a . . . assurance:** a certainty that offers him no hope

8–9. **will none of:** i.e., will not have

11. **this:** i.e., this message of rejection; **Receive it so:** i.e., take the ring with this understanding

12. **She . . . it:** This response seems to be a resourceful lie by Viola.

19. **made . . . me:** i.e., looked me over carefully

20. **had lost:** i.e., had made her lose

22. **cunning:** craftiness

23. **Invites:** encourages, tempts

24. **None of:** i.e., she will not have (a possible reference to lines 8–9)

25. **the man:** i.e., the one she loves

28. **the pregnant enemy:** i.e., the devil, who uses such deceits as **disguise** in his wicked practices **pregnant:** resourceful

29. **the proper false:** those who are unfaithful but handsome

30. **In . . . forms:** i.e., to imprint their images in women's impressionable hearts

31–32. **our . . . be:** Proverbial: "Women are the weaker vessels."

33. **fadge:** i.e., work out, fit together

34. **monster:** i.e., a man/woman; **fond . . . on:** just as infatuated with

37. **My . . . for:** i.e., it is impossible that I should win

39. **thriftless:** useless, fruitless

2.3 At Olivia's estate, Toby, Andrew, and the Fool hold a late night party. Maria comes in to quiet them, followed by Malvolio, who orders them to behave or be dismissed from the house. In retaliation, Maria plots to trap Malvolio with a forged letter that will persuade him that Olivia loves him.

2. **betimes:** early

2–3. **diluculo surgere:** the first two words of a familiar Latin sentence that means "To rise early is good for the health"

6. **as:** i.e., as much as I do; **can:** drinking cup

9–10. **the . . . elements:** air, earth, water, and fire

14. **stoup:** tankard (a large drinking vessel)

17. **"We Three":** a familiar picture of two fools, the title of which, "We Three," suggests that the viewer is the third fool

18. **catch:** music written for three voices, sung as a round

19. **breast:** i.e., breath, singing voice

22. **fooling:** See note on **foolery** at 1.5.13.

23–24. Pigrogromitus . . . Queubus: examples of the Fool's wordplay (here, apparent mockery of astrological language)

25. leman: mistress, lover

27. impeticos thy gratillity: more of the Fool's wordplay (**Gratillity** sounds like "gratuity," i.e., tip.)

27–29. for . . . houses: apparent nonsense to please Sir Andrew **whipstock:** whip handle **white:** then synonymous with "beautiful" **Myrmidons:** the followers of Achilles, the mightiest Greek warrior in Homer's *Iliad* **bottle-ale houses:** inferior taverns

34. testril: tester, sixpence; **of:** from

35. give a: In the Folio, there is no punctuation after these words, which come at the end of the line. It is possible that the next line of Andrew's speech was simply dropped.

36–37. song . . . life: a drinking song (Andrew, at line 39, appears to understand **good life** to mean a moral life.)

40. "O mistress mine": Tunes by this name were published in Shakespeare's time, but the words here are thought to be Shakespeare's.

44. in lovers meeting: i.e., when lovers meet

48. hereafter: at some future time

50. still: always

55. contagious: foul (but understood by Andrew to be a compliment)

57. To . . . nose: i.e., if we heard with our noses

58. welkin: heavens

59. catch: See note to 2.3.18.

60. weaver: Weavers were said to be fond of singing.

61. An: if; **dog:** i.e., expert

63. By 'r Lady: an oath, "By our Lady" (i.e., the Virgin Mary)

64–65. "Thou Knave": a catch in which the singers call each other, in turn, "thou knave" (**Knave** meant variously "servant, menial," "boy," and "villain.")

68. **one:** someone

69–70. **Hold thy peace:** i.e., be quiet, keep silent

76. **Cataian:** (1) Cathayan, someone from Cathay—i.e., China; (2) scoundrel; **politicians:** shrewd fellows

77. **Peg-a-Ramsey:** the name of a popular song

77–78. **Three . . . we:** a line from another popular song

78–79. **of her blood:** related to her (i.e., **consanguineous**)

79. **Tillyvally:** an expression of impatience; **"Lady":** Toby's mockery of Maria's reference to Olivia

79–80. **There . . . lady:** a line from a popular song

81. **Beshrew me:** i.e., curse me (a mild oath)

84. **natural:** i.e., naturally (with an unintended pun on "natural" meaning "like an idiot")

87. **My masters:** i.e., gentlemen

88. **wit:** sense; **honesty:** decency, decorum

89. **tinkers:** wandering menders of utensils, known for their drinking

91. **coziers:** cobblers

91–92. **mitigation or remorse:** These words suggest "softening," but neither seems appropriate as used here to refer to the **voice. Mitigation** is usually applied to a lessening of violence or disease; **remorse** is a theological term that applies to the conscience of a sinner. Malvolio's language often has odd quirks that contemporary audiences might have associated with his supposed puritanism. (See line 139.)

94. **Sneck up:** i.e., shut up

95. **round:** straightforward

102. **Farewell . . . gone:** the beginning of a song called "Corydon's Farewell to Phyllis," which continues through line 112.

107. **lie:** i.e., do not tell the truth (In "Corydon's Farewell," the words are "So long as I can spy.")

115. **cakes and ale:** associated with festivity

116. **Saint Anne:** mother of the Virgin Mary; **ginger:** used to spice ale

118–19. **rub . . . crumbs:** i.e., polish your steward's chain

122. **uncivil rule:** uncivilized conduct

125–28. **'Twere . . . him:** In confused language (e.g., he means "thirsty" when he says **a-hungry**), Andrew threatens to challenge Malvolio to a duel and then not show up.

133. **out of quiet:** disquieted, troubled

133–34. **let . . . him:** i.e., leave him to me

134. **gull . . . nayword:** i.e., through trickery turn him into a byword (a figure of scorn)

135. **recreation:** i.e., figure of fun

138. **Possess:** inform

139. **puritan:** originally, a term of abuse used against members of the Church of England who were strict moralists, intent on stamping out sin and doing away with frivolity (The word comes from the Latin *purus,* "pure.")

145. **The devil . . . is:** i.e., he is not a puritan

146. **constantly:** consistently; **time-pleaser:** flatterer, self-server; **affectioned:** affected

147. **cons . . . book:** i.e., memorizes high-sounding phrases

148. **best . . . of:** i.e., holding the highest opinion of

156. **expressure:** expression

158. **personated:** represented

159–60. **on . . . hands:** i.e., when we have forgotten who wrote something, we can barely distinguish her handwriting from mine

161. **device:** plan, scheme

170. **physic:** medicine

173. **construction:** interpretation

175. **Penthesilea:** queen of the Amazons (fierce warrior women)

176. **Before me:** a mild oath

182. **recover:** obtain

182–83. **a foul way out:** i.e., in financial trouble (literally, out in the dirt)

185. **Cut:** a horse (with a docked tail; or, gelded)
188. **burn some sack:** warm up some sherry

2.4 Orsino asks for a song to relieve his love-longing. In conversation about the capacities for love in men and in women, Viola expresses her love for Orsino through a story about "Cesario's sister." Orsino becomes curious about this sister's fate, but then turns back to his own longings and sends Cesario once again to visit Olivia.

1–2. **good morrow:** good morning
4. **antique:** old-fashioned (accent on first syllable)
5. **passion:** emotional suffering
6. **airs:** tunes, melodies; **recollected terms:** perhaps, unspontaneous or studied verse
20. **Unstaid and skittish:** fickle, inconstant; **in . . . else:** in all other emotions or desires
23. **It . . . echo:** i.e., it echoes exactly
23–24. **the seat . . . throned:** i.e., the lover's heart
27. **stayed . . . favor:** lingered over some face
29. **by your favor:** a courteous phrase, "if you please," with a punning reference to Orsino's "favor," or face
31. **complexion:** temperament; appearance
34. **still:** always
35. **wears . . . him:** i.e., shapes herself to fit him (like a garment to its owner)
36. **sways she level:** The image may be of a ruler holding sway, or of a balance scale.
38. **fancies:** loves
43. **hold the bent:** i.e., endure at its maximum tension, like a fully stretched bow
45. **Being . . . displayed:** i.e., having blossomed
49. **Mark:** pay attention to
50. **spinsters:** those who spin thread or yarn
51. **free:** carefree
51–52. **weave . . . bones:** use bone bobbins in making lace

53. **Do use to:** customarily; **silly sooth:** simple truth
54. **dallies:** plays
55. **the old age:** i.e., the good old days
59. **sad cypress:** i.e., a coffin of dark cypress wood
62. **yew:** i.e., sprigs of yew (The yew tree was often planted in churchyards and was a symbol of sadness.)
67. **strown:** strewn
74. **There's for:** i.e., there's payment for
77–78. **pleasure . . . another:** i.e., pleasure must eventually be paid for (proverbial)
79. **Give . . . thee:** a polite request for the Fool to leave
80. **the . . . god:** i.e., Saturn, god of melancholy
81. **doublet:** jacket; **changeable taffeta:** a thin silky fabric woven so that the color appears to change when viewed from different perspectives
82. **opal:** a stone of variable colors
82–83. **such constancy:** i.e., so little constancy
84. **intent:** i.e., intended destination
89. **sovereign cruelty:** (1) the cruel woman who rules my life; (2) the queen of cruelty (Orsino speaks the exaggerated language of love poetry.)
91. **quantity . . . lands:** i.e., her property
92. **parts . . . her:** i.e., her wealth and status
93. **hold as giddily as fortune:** Fortune is proverbially fickle.
94–95. **that miracle . . . in:** i.e., her own beauty, a gift of nature   **pranks:** dresses
102. **be answered:** i.e., take that as final
104. **bide:** endure
108. **No . . . palate:** i.e., not a strong emotion whose seat is in the liver, but a casual appetite
109. **suffer:** experience; **revolt:** revulsion
111–12. **Make . . . Between:** i.e., do not compare
113. **that:** i.e., that which
117. **In faith:** a mild oath
123. **worm i' th' bud:** i.e., a cankerworm inside a rosebud

124. **damask:** pink, rosy

129. **shows . . . will:** outer expressions are larger than actual desires; **still:** always

137. **give no place:** give way to no one; **bide no denay:** accept no denial

2.5 Maria lays her trap for Malvolio by placing her forged letter in his path. From their hiding place, Toby, Andrew, and Fabian observe Malvolio's delight in discovering the love letter. Malvolio promises to obey the letter: to smile, to put on yellow stockings cross-gartered, and to be haughty to Sir Toby. Delighted with their success, Maria and the others prepare to enjoy Malvolio's downfall.

1. **Come thy ways:** i.e., come along

2. **scruple:** i.e., tiny amount

5. **sheep-biter:** i.e., dog (Thomas Nashe, in his *An Almond for a Parrat*, 1590, uses the term to describe a hypocritical puritan.)

7. **bearbaiting:** See note to 1.3.93.

12. **villain:** here, a term of affection

13. **metal of India:** i.e., golden one (an allusion to the Americas, source of gold in Shakespeare's day)

14. **boxtree:** boxwood shrubbery

19. **Close:** i.e., stay hidden

21. **trout . . . tickling: Trout** can be lured from hiding places by stroking the gills. Here, Malvolio will be "stroked" with flattery.

23. **she did affect me:** i.e., Olivia loved me

24. **come . . . near:** i.e., say something close to this; **fancy:** fall in love

25. **complexion:** nature, appearance

26. **follows:** serves

29. **Contemplation:** anticipation, expectation

30–31. **jets . . . plumes:** struts (like a **turkeycock**) with his feathers spread

32. **'Slight:** By God's light (a strong oath)

36. **Pistol:** i.e., shoot

38–39. **The lady . . . wardrobe:** probably a topical allusion, now lost **yeoman:** servant, officer

40. **Jezebel:** a proud queen in the Bible

41. **deeply in:** i.e., mired in his fantasy

42. **blows:** swells

44. **state:** i.e., chair of state (as Count Malvolio)

45. **stone-bow:** a crossbow that propels stones

46. **officers:** underlings who manage the estate

47. **branched:** perhaps, embroidered with flowers

51. **have . . . state:** assume a haughty manner fitting my position

52. **a demure . . . regard:** perhaps, soberly surveying my officers

54. **Toby:** Malvolio drops Sir Toby's title, here and in the lines that follow.

62–63. **drawn . . . cars:** i.e., forced from us through torture **cars:** chariots

65–66. **regard of control:** look of mastery

67. **take . . . o':** i.e., give you a blow on

75–76. **break . . . plot:** i.e., cripple, destroy, our scheme

83. **employment:** i.e., business

85. **woodcock:** a proverbially stupid bird; **gin:** trap

86. **spirit of humors:** i.e., that which controls moods

86–87. **intimate . . . him:** i.e., suggest to him that he read aloud

89. **hand:** handwriting

89–90. **c's . . . u's . . . t's:** Some editors believe that Shakespeare's audience would have heard a bawdy joke in these lines. They argue that "cut" was a word for the pudendum. Evidence that the word had this meaning is, however, far from conclusive.

90–91. **in contempt of question:** i.e., without a doubt

94. **By your leave:** i.e., with your permission (Malvolio's apology to the wax seal before he breaks it)

95. **impressure:** image stamped on the wax; **Lucrece:** i.e., a picture of the chaste Lucretia, whose story Shakespeare had told in *The Rape of Lucrece*

96. **uses to seal:** is accustomed to sealing

103. **numbers:** meter

106. **brock:** a term of contempt (literally, badger)

108. **Lucrece knife:** Lucretia stabbed herself after being raped by Tarquin. (See note on line 95 above.)

110. **sway:** rule

111. **fustian:** pretentious, pompous

112. **Excellent wench:** i.e., Maria

115. **What dish:** i.e., what a dish; **dressed:** prepared for

117. **staniel:** an inferior kind of hawk

117–18. **checks at it:** turns to follow it

121. **formal capacity:** i.e., sane mind

122. **obstruction:** difficulty

125. **make up:** i.e., make sense out of

125–26. **He . . . scent:** i.e., he's like a hound who has lost the trail of his quarry (Language describing Malvolio as a dog following a scent continues in lines 127–28, where **Sowter** seems to be the dog's name and **cry upon 't** means "bark loudly," and in line 132, where **fault** is a technical term for a lost scent.)

128. **rank:** strong smelling

133–34. **no consonancy . . . sequel:** i.e., no harmony in the letters that follow (See note about Malvolio's language at 2.3.91–92.)

134. **suffers under probation:** i.e., stands up to testing

143–44. **This simulation . . . former:** i.e., this part of the letter does not resemble me as clearly as does the first part ("I may command where I adore")

147. **revolve:** consider

148. **stars:** i.e., destiny

150–51. **open their hands:** i.e., have become generous

152. **inure:** accustom; **like:** likely

152–53. **cast . . . slough:** discard your humble attitude (as a snake discards its old skin)

153. **opposite:** confrontational

154–55. **tang . . . state:** ring out with political opinions

155–56. **Put . . . singularity:** i.e., adopt idiosyncrasies

158. **cross-gartered:** wearing ribbons tied around the knees

159. **Go to:** an expression of protest (like "Come, come")

164. **champian:** open country; **discovers:** reveals

165. **open:** perfectly clear; **politic:** (1) political; (2) wise

166. **baffle:** publicly humiliate; **gross:** base

167. **point-devise . . . man:** i.e., precisely the man described in the letter

168. **jade:** dupe, delude

173. **these . . . liking:** i.e., wear the kind of clothes that she likes

174. **strange:** extraordinary, exceptional; **stout:** proud, arrogant

179. **thou entertain'st:** you accept

185. **Sophy:** shah of Persia

191. **gull-catcher:** A **gull** is a person easily cheated.

194. **play:** bet; **tray-trip:** a gambling game

200. **aqua vitae:** strong drink, usually brandy

208. **notable contempt:** i.e., well-known object of contempt

210. **Tartar:** i.e., Tartarus, hell

212. **make one, too:** i.e., join you

3.1 Viola (as Cesario), on her way to see Olivia, encounters first the Fool and then Sir Toby and Sir Andrew. Olivia, meeting Cesario, sends the others away and declares her love.

0 SD. **tabor:** small drum

1. **Save thee:** i.e., God save thee (a friendly greeting)

1–2. **Dost thou live by:** i.e., do you make your living by playing

4. **churchman:** clergyman

5. **No such matter:** i.e., not at all

11. **You have said:** i.e., you're right; **this age:** i.e., the age in which we live

12. **chev'ril:** kid leather, which stretches easily

14. **dally nicely:** play with precise meanings (**Dally** also means "flirt, play with amorously.")

15. **wanton:** changeable, ambiguous (also "immoral, unchaste")

21. **bonds:** i.e., the legal requirement that one's pledge (**word**) be backed by a written contract, or **bond**

27. **I warrant:** i.e., I'm sure

36. **pilchers:** pilchards, small fish related to the herring

39. **late:** lately, recently

40. **walk . . . orb:** move around the earth

41–42. **but . . . be:** i.e., unless the Fool were

43. **your Wisdom:** an ironic title (analogous to "your Honor")

44. **an thou . . . me:** i.e., if you attack me; **I'll no more:** i.e., I'll have no more to do

46. **in . . . commodity:** i.e., out of his next supply

51. **Would . . . bred:** The Fool, begging for money, suggests that money can breed, i.e., reproduce. Viola continues the wordplay in her response, where **put to use** means "invested to earn interest," but also has a sexual meaning.

53–54. **Lord . . . Troilus:** The allusion is to the story of Troilus and Cressida, lovers who were brought together by Pandarus. The story was told by Chaucer, and by Shakespeare in his *Troilus and Cressida*.

57. **Cressida . . . beggar:** In some versions of the story, Cressida becomes a beggar before her death.

58. **conster to them:** i.e., construe (explain) to those in the house

59. **out . . . welkin:** i.e., beyond my comprehension, out of my element (The wordplay here is on **welkin** as "sky," which, as "air," is an **element.**)

64. **quality:** rank; nature

65. **haggard:** wild hawk; **check at:** turn to follow

66. **practice:** profession
67. **art:** learning, skill
68. **fit:** i.e., fitting, appropriate
69. **wit:** intelligence (or reputation for it)
72. **Dieu ... monsieur:** God save you, sir.
73. **Et ... serviteur!:** And you as well, your servant!
75. **encounter:** i.e., approach (Toby uses affected language, and Viola answers him in kind.)
78. **list:** limit, boundary
80. **understand:** i.e., stand under, hold me up
84. **with ... entrance:** i.e., by going and entering
85. **we are prevented:** i.e., Olivia's appearance anticipates our entrance
90. **My ... but:** i.e., my message cannot be spoken except
91. **pregnant:** receptive; **vouchsafed:** willing, graciously attentive
101. **lowly feigning:** i.e., pretending to be humble; **was called:** i.e., began to be considered
105. **For:** as for; **on him:** i.e., about him
113. **music ... spheres:** In Ptolemaic astronomy, the stars move about the earth in crystalline spheres, giving out incredibly beautiful music that humans cannot hear.
115. **Give ... you:** i.e., permit me to speak, I beg you
117. **abuse:** deceive; wrong
119–21. **Under ... yours:** i.e., I must be judged harshly by you, since I used shameful cunning to force on you something you knew was not yours
123–25. **Have ... think:** The image here is of a bear-baiting. Olivia imagines her honor as a bear tied to the stake, attacked (**baited**) by the **unmuzzled** dogs that are Cesario's **thoughts.**
127. **cypress:** thin (almost transparent) cloth veil
130, 131. **degree, grize:** step
131. **a ... proof:** an ordinary experience
140. **proper:** handsome

142. **westward ho!:** the cry of Thames watermen headed from London to Westminster

144. **You'll nothing . . . ?:** i.e., you have no message . . . ?

148. **think you right:** i.e., you think correctly

155–56. **Love's . . . noon:** i.e., love cannot be hidden

159. **maugre . . . pride:** i.e., despite your scorn

160. **Nor . . . nor:** neither . . . nor

161. **extort thy reasons:** i.e., force out excuses; **clause:** premise

162. **For . . . cause:** i.e., because I am the wooer, you have no cause (to woo me)

163. **reason . . . fetter:** i.e., restrain such rationalizing by considering the following sentence

167. **nor never none:** nor anyone ever

3.2 Sir Andrew, convinced that Olivia will never love him, threatens to leave. Sir Toby persuades him that he can win her love if he challenges Cesario to a duel. Sir Andrew goes off to prepare a letter for Cesario. Maria enters to say that Malvolio has followed every point in the letter and is about to incur disaster when he appears before Olivia.

3. **must needs yield:** i.e., must give

6. **orchard:** garden

10. **argument:** token, evidence

13. **prove it legitimate:** i.e., make good my case; **oaths of:** i.e., testimony sworn under oath by

15. **they:** i.e., judgment and reason; **grand-jurymen:** those who decide whether there is sufficient evidence to bring a case to trial

18. **dormouse:** i.e., sleeping (The **dormouse** becomes torpid in cold weather.)

23. **at your hand:** i.e., from you

24. **balked:** passed up, neglected; **gilt:** gold plating (Fabian plays with the idea of a missed "golden **opportunity.**")

25–26. sailed . . . opinion: i.e., earned my lady's cold regard

29. policy: statesmanlike wisdom (Andrew, in his response, gives the word its meaning of "political cunning.")

31. as lief: i.e., just as soon; **Brownist:** a believer in the then-revolutionary ideas about religion preached by Robert Browne (c. 1550–1633)

33. build me: i.e., build

34. Challenge me: i.e., challenge

37. love-broker: go-between

41. curst: fierce, savage

42. so it be: i.e., as long as it is

43. invention: arguments; inventiveness

43–44. with . . . ink: i.e., with the freedom given to one who puts his challenge in writing

44. "thou"-est . . . thrice: i.e., address him three times as "thou" instead of "you" (The use of the familiar "thou" to a stranger would be an insult.)

47. bed of Ware: a famous ten-foot-wide bed (now in a museum in London)

48. gall: (1) oak galls, used in making ink; (2) bitterness

49. goose-pen: (1) a pen made with a goose quill; (2) a pen used by a goose (i.e., a fool)

51. cubiculo: bedchamber

52. dear manikin: i.e., valued little man (**Manikin** is a term of contempt.)

53. dear: expensive, costly

58. wainropes: i.e., wagon ropes

59. hale: haul, pull, drag

60. blood . . . liver: Cowards were supposed to have white or bloodless livers.

62. anatomy: i.e., the body being dissected

63. opposite: rival

66. desire the spleen: i.e., want to laugh

67. gull: dupe

68. a very renegado: i.e., no longer a Christian

69. **means:** intends
70. **passages:** acts
73. **villainously:** atrociously; **pedant:** i.e., teacher
77. **new map:** an allusion to a map published in 1599, among the first to use Mercator projection, and thus filled with prominent lines
78. **augmentation . . . Indies:** i.e., more complete mappings of the East Indies

3.3 Antonio, having followed Sebastian, explains the incident in his past that keeps him from safely venturing into the streets of Orsino's city. Giving his money to Sebastian, Antonio sets off to their inn while Sebastian goes off to see the sights.

1. **by my will:** i.e., willingly
5. **filèd:** ground to a sharp edge with a file
6. **not all love:** i.e., not only a desire
8. **jealousy:** fear of
9. **skill-less in:** i.e., without knowledge of
12. **The . . . fear:** i.e., spurred by these anxieties
16–17. **oft . . . pay:** i.e., good acts are often rewarded with mere words   **uncurrent:** not negotiable, worthless
18. **worth:** possessions, wealth; **conscience:** i.e., recognition of obligation (to you)
20. **relics:** i.e., antiquities, old buildings, etc.
25. **renown this city:** i.e., make this city famous
26. **Would . . . me:** i.e., please excuse me
28. **Count his:** Count's
29. **of such note:** i.e., so memorable
30. **it . . . answered:** i.e., I would hardly be able (1) to defend myself before the law, or (2) to endure the penalty exacted from me
31. **Belike:** perhaps
34. **bloody argument:** a reason worth shedding blood for

35. **answered:** recompensed
36. **for traffic's sake:** i.e., for the sake of trade
37. **stood out:** i.e., refused
38. **be lapsèd:** i.e., am caught
39. **dear:** dearly, at great cost
41. **It . . . me:** it is not fitting for me
43. **bespeak:** arrange for; **diet:** meals
44. **beguile:** while away
46. **There . . . me:** i.e., you will find me there (**at the Elephant**)
48. **Haply:** perhaps; **toy:** trifle
49. **store:** supply of money
50. **is . . . markets:** i.e., will not cover whimsical purchases

3.4 Malvolio, dressed ridiculously and smiling grotesquely, appears before an astonished Olivia. Thinking him insane, she puts him in the care of Sir Toby, who decides to treat him as a madman by having him bound and put in a dark room. Toby also decides to deliver Sir Andrew's challenge to Cesario in person in order to force the two of them into a duel. Terrified, they prepare to fight. At that moment, Antonio enters, thinks that Cesario is Sebastian, and comes to his defense. Antonio is immediately arrested by Orsino's officers. Since he is sure that Viola is Sebastian, Antonio is bitter about the apparent denial of their friendship. Viola is herself delighted by Antonio's angry words because, since he called her Sebastian, there is hope that her brother may in fact be alive.

2. **bestow of:** bestow on, give
6. **sad and civil:** serious-minded and polite
10. **possessed:** i.e., by the devil (This was one popular explanation of insanity.)
11. **rave:** speak incoherently
14. **in 's:** in his

16. **equal be:** i.e., are equal

19. **sad:** serious (Malvolio takes the word to mean "sorrowful.")

24. **sonnet:** song ("Please one, and please all" is the refrain of a ballad about the wishes of women.)

28. **black in my mind:** i.e., melancholy

30–31. **Roman hand:** Italian-style handwriting

33–34. **Ay . . . thee:** a line from a popular song

38–39. **nightingales answer daws:** i.e., fine birds don't respond to the call of crows

61. **very:** genuine, true; **midsummer madness:** insanity (The midsummer moon was thought to cause madness.)

63. **hardly:** i.e., only with great difficulty

68. **miscarry:** come to harm

78. **consequently:** i.e., subsequently, later

79–80. **in . . . note:** i.e., dressed like some noteworthy gentleman

80. **limed:** trapped, as with birdlime

81. **it is Jove's doing:** a possible allusion to Psalm 188.23, "This is the Lord's doing." (The names "God" and "Jove" are used almost interchangeably in this play.)

82. **fellow:** used dismissively by Olivia but heard by Malvolio as meaning "companion"

84. **degree:** i.e., my rank as her steward

84–85. **adheres together:** i.e., coheres, fits

85. **dram:** tiniest bit (literally, an apothecaries' weight of 60 grains); **scruple:** doubt (also, an apothecaries' weight of 20 grains)

86. **incredulous:** incredible; **unsafe:** unreliable, untrustworthy

92. **drawn in little:** (1) made into a miniature painting; (2) brought together into the small space (of Malvolio's body); **Legion:** the name of the "unclean spirit" possessing the demoniac in Mark 5.9, whose response to Jesus was "My name is Legion; for we are many."

97. **private:** i.e., privacy

107. **an:** if
108. **at heart:** i.e., to heart
110. **water:** urine (for medical diagnosis); **wisewoman:** a woman who used charms or herbs to treat diseases
111. **Marry:** a mild oath, meaning "truly" or "indeed"
117. **move:** excite
117–18. **Let . . . him:** i.e., don't interfere
120. **rough:** violent; **used:** treated
121. **bawcock:** fine bird (French: *beau coq*) This word, along with **chuck** and **biddy** (both of which mean "chicken"), seems to be addressed to "the fiend" supposedly possessing Malvolio.
125. **for gravity:** i.e., appropriate for a dignified person; **cherry-pit:** a children's game
126. **foul collier:** dirty coal-dealer (applicable to Satan, who is pictured as black)
132. **idle:** frivolous
138. **genius:** i.e., soul
139. **device:** plot
140–41. **take . . . taint:** be exposed to the air (i.e., become known) and thus be ruined
144–45. **in . . . bound:** a standard treatment for insanity at the time
146. **carry it thus:** proceed in this way
149. **bar:** perhaps, the bar of justice, the open court
151. **matter . . . morning:** perhaps, sport fit for a holiday
154. **saucy:** (1) flavored with seasoning; (2) insolent, rude
155. **warrant him:** perhaps, I can assure him (Cesario)
159. **admire:** marvel
162–63. **keeps . . . law:** i.e., protects you from arrest (for disturbing the peace, or for libel)
165. **thou liest in thy throat:** i.e., you are a complete liar
172. **o' th' windy side:** on the windward side, and therefore safe from attack
176. **look to:** i.e., look out for, take care of

179. **move him:** prompt him to action; or, arouse his feelings

182. **in some commerce:** in conversation about something

182–83. **by and by:** soon

184. **Scout me:** i.e., keep a lookout

185. **bum-baily:** a bailiff (sheriff's officer)

186. **draw:** i.e., draw your sword

189. **approbation:** reputation (for courage); **proof:** testing, trial

191. **let . . . swearing:** i.e., don't worry about my ability to swear

193. **gives him out:** shows him

194. **capacity:** intelligence; **breeding:** education; or, parentage; **his employment:** i.e., the service he performs

198. **clodpoll:** blockhead

199–200. **set . . . valor:** i.e., describe Aguecheek as notably courageous

204. **cockatrices:** mythical serpents (with the head, wings, and feet of a cock) whose looks could kill

205–206. **Give them way:** i.e., let them alone

206. **presently after him:** immediately go after him

207. **horrid:** terrifying

210. **laid:** wagered; **unchary:** impetuously; **on 't:** perhaps, on that stony heart (Many editors change "on 't" to "out," and interpret the phrase as meaning "expended my honor too lavishly.")

214. **With . . . 'havior:** i.e., in the same way

215. **Goes on:** i.e., go on, persist

216. **jewel:** i.e., jeweled miniature portrait

220. **saved:** i.e., uncompromised

229. **defense:** ability as a fencer; **betake thee:** commit yourself (Sir Toby speaks to Cesario in very contorted language throughout this scene.)

231. **thy intercepter:** i.e., the one who wants to cut you off; **despite:** anger, defiance

232. **hunter:** perhaps, huntsman; or, perhaps, hunting dog; **attends thee:** waits for you

232–33. **Dismount thy tuck:** draw your sword

233. **yare:** quick

236. **to:** i.e., with; **remembrance:** memory; **free:** innocent

239. **price:** value

239–40. **betake . . . guard:** put yourself in a defensive position

240. **opposite:** adversary

241. **withal:** i.e., with

243. **dubbed:** made a knight; **unhatched:** unhacked, not used (This charge, and the admission that Sir Andrew's knighthood was for **carpet consideration**—i.e., that he was knighted at court rather than on the battlefield—acknowledges that he is no soldier.)

246. **incensement:** anger

247. **satisfaction . . . by:** i.e., he can be satisfied only by

248–49. **"Hob, nob," "give 't or take 't":** Both phrases mean that the challenger wants to fight to the death. **word:** motto

251. **conduct:** escort; **of:** from

252–53. **put quarrels . . . on:** i.e., provoke quarrels with

253. **taste:** test; **Belike:** perhaps

255. **derives itself:** i.e., grows

256. **competent injury:** i.e., an insult sufficient to demand satisfaction

258. **that:** i.e., a duel

259. **answer:** fight with

260. **meddle:** fight

261–62. **forswear . . . you:** i.e., give up your right to wear a sword (admit your cowardice)

263. **uncivil:** rude

264. **office:** kindness, service; **as . . . of:** i.e., find out from

266. **negligence:** oversight; **purpose:** intention

271. **a . . . arbitrament:** i.e., a fight to the death
274. **read:** judge
275. **form:** appearance; **like:** likely
285. **firago:** virago; **pass:** bout
286. **stuck-in:** stoccata (a fencing thrust)
288. **answer:** return thrust
290. **Sophy:** shah of Persia
291. **Pox on 't:** a mild oath
295. **fence:** i.e., fencing
299. **motion:** offer
300. **on 't:** of it
303. **take up:** settle
305. **He:** Cesario; **is . . . conceited:** has as horrible an image
310. **his quarrel:** i.e., the insult to him
311–12. **for . . . vow:** so that he can keep his oath
320. **duello:** dueling code
332. **undertaker:** i.e., one who undertakes to fight
334. **anon:** soon
337. **for that:** as for that which (i.e., my horse)
344. **favor:** face
353. **amazed:** bewildered, perplexed
359. **part:** i.e., partly
361. **My having:** i.e., the money that I have
362. **present:** i.e., my present funds
365. **deserts:** good deeds, services
366. **lack persuasion:** i.e., fail to persuade (you to help me)
367. **unsound:** wicked
373. **vainness:** (1) vanity; (2) foolishness
375. **blood:** nature
379. **one half . . . death:** i.e., half-dead
385. **done . . . shame:** i.e., disgraced your good looks
386. **the mind:** i.e., what happens in one's mind or heart
389. **empty . . . devil:** i.e., elaborately decorated chests, made beautiful by the devil but with nothing inside

393. **passion:** intense feelings
398. **saws:** sayings
400. **glass:** mirror
401. **favor:** looks, features
402. **Still:** always
405. **dishonest:** dishonorable, shameful
409–10. **religious in:** i.e., devoted to
411. **'Slid:** an oath "by God's eyelid"
415. **event:** outcome

4.1 The Fool encounters Sebastian, whom he mistakes for Cesario. When Sir Andrew and Sir Toby attack Sebastian, the Fool fetches Olivia, who again declares her love—this time to a delighted Sebastian.

3. **Go to:** an expression of impatience
5. **held out:** kept up, maintained
5–9. **I . . . so:** These lines are said sarcastically.
10. **vent:** give expression to
14. **lubber:** oaf
15. **cockney:** sissy; **ungird:** remove
15–16. **strangeness:** distance (i.e., pretense that you and I are strangers)
18. **foolish Greek:** A "merry Greek" was a buffoon or jester.
28. **your dagger:** These words have suggested to some editors that Sebastian beats Andrew with the hilt of his dagger. If such is the case, Toby's command to Sebastian at line 39, "put up your iron," would mean "sheathe your dagger."
30. **straight:** straightway, immediately
34. **action of battery:** i.e., lawsuit accusing him of unlawfully beating me
39. **fleshed:** eager for battle; or, hardened to battle
45. **malapert:** impudent
53. **Rudesby:** ruffian
56. **extent:** assault

59. **botched up:** clumsily put together

61. **deny:** refuse; **Beshrew:** literally, curse (but the harshness of the word was lost through repeated use)

62. **started . . . thee:** i.e., made my heart (residing in you) leap with fear (There is a play on **heart** and "hart" and on **start** as "startle" and "rouse an animal from its hiding place.")

63. **What . . . this:** i.e., what does this mean (literally, how does this taste?)

64. **Or . . . or:** either . . . or

65. **Let . . . steep:** i.e., let me continue in this dream-like state **fancy:** imagination **sense:** senses, awareness of the waking world **Lethe:** the mythological river in the underworld that washes away one's memory of one's former life **steep:** immerse

67. **Would:** i.e., I wish

4.2 Under directions from Sir Toby, the Fool disguises himself as a parish priest and visits the imprisoned Malvolio. In his own person, the Fool agrees to fetch pen, paper, and a candle for the supposed madman.

2. **curate:** parish priest

3. **the whilst:** i.e., in the meantime

4. **dissemble:** disguise

5. **dissembled:** played the hypocrite

7. **the function:** i.e., of a priest

9. **housekeeper:** hospitable person

11. **The competitors:** i.e., my colleagues

13. **Bonos dies:** good day (in bad Latin)

13–14. **the . . . Prague:** The Fool once again invents an authority to quote in his foolery.

15. **Gorboduc:** a legendary king of Britain

18. **To him:** i.e., begin your attack on Malvolio

21 SD. **Malvolio within:** This Folio direction indicates that Malvolio speaks from offstage or from behind a door or curtain.

27. **Out . . . fiend:** addressed to the devil that supposedly possesses Malvolio **hyperbolical:** i.e., ranting (literally, using hyperbole or exaggeration)

33. **dishonest:** dishonorable; lying

34. **modest:** moderate

38–39. **barricadoes:** barricades, barriers

39. **clerestories:** high windows

45. **puzzled:** confused

46. **the . . . fog:** In stories about Moses, one of the plagues visited by God on the Egyptians was "a thick darkness in all the land of Egypt three days" (Exodus 10.22).

50–51. **any constant question:** perhaps, any consistent line of questioning

52. **Pythagoras:** This ancient Greek philosopher taught the transmigration of souls. Ovid's *Metamorphoses* (a book used frequently by Shakespeare) has a speech by Pythagoras urging humans not to kill animals because "Our souls survive . . . death; as they depart / Their local habitations in the flesh, / They enter new-found bodies that preserve them. / . . . the spirit takes its way / To different kinds of being as it chooses, / From beast to man, from man to beast" (Book 15, trans. Horace Gregory).

54. **haply:** perhaps

61. **allow . . . wits:** agree that you're sane; **and fear:** and (until) you shall fear

66. **I . . . waters:** perhaps, I can do anything

71–72. **delivered:** freed

74. **the upshot:** i.e., to its final conclusion

76. **Hey, Robin . . . :** a song the words for which are attributed to Thomas Wyatt

79. **perdy:** for sure (*par Dieu*, by God)

91. **fell you besides:** i.e., did you lose; **five wits:** five senses; or, according to Stephen Hawes in *The Pastime of Pleasure*, the five wits are common wit, imagination, fantasy, estimation, and memory

94. **But:** i.e., only, no more than

96. **propertied me:** treated me like a lifeless object
98. **face:** bully
99. **Advise you:** i.e., be careful
105–6. **God buy you:** i.e., God be with you, good-bye
110. **shent:** rebuked
114. **Welladay that:** i.e., alas, if only
117. **advantage:** benefit, profit
118. **letter:** i.e., a letter
128. **the old Vice:** a comic character in earlier drama, whose props (dagger of **lath,** or wood) and antics are described in the lines of the song
133. **goodman:** a title indicating a low social rank

4.3   While Sebastian is sure that neither he nor Olivia is insane, he is amazed by the wonder of his new situation. When Olivia asks him to enter into a formal betrothal with her, he readily agrees.

3. **wonder:** a state of mind caused by experiencing the wonderful or miraculous
6. **there he was:** i.e., he had been there; **credit:** report
7. **range:** roam, wander around
9. **my soul . . . sense:** i.e., my reason and my senses agree in arguing
12. **instance:** example; **discourse:** reasoning
15. **trust:** belief
17. **sway:** rule
19. **Take . . . dispatch:** i.e., "take affairs" (undertake business matters) and "give back their dispatch" (complete them promptly)
22. **deceivable:** deceptive
25. **chantry:** chapel; **by:** nearby
27. **Plight . . . faith:** i.e., assure me of your fidelity (through a betrothal)
28. **jealous:** anxious; **doubtful:** filled with doubts, insecure

29. **He:** i.e., the priest
30. **Whiles:** until; **come to note:** become known
31. **What time:** at which time; **our . . . keep:** i.e., celebrate our marriage
32. **birth:** social rank
37. **fairly note:** look favorably on; or, show that they approve

5.1 Orsino, at Olivia's estate, sends the Fool to bring Olivia to him. Antonio is brought in by officers and he tells the incredulous Orsino about Cesario's treacherous behavior. At Olivia's entrance, Orsino expresses his anger that Cesario has become Olivia's darling. Cesario's expressions of love for Orsino lead Olivia to send for the "holy father," who confirms Olivia's claim that she is formally betrothed to Cesario. Sir Andrew and Sir Toby enter with bloody heads, which they blame on Cesario. Sebastian's entry at this moment untangles a series of knots: Sebastian addresses Olivia with love, greets Antonio warmly, and recognizes Cesario as the image of himself. When Cesario admits to being Sebastian's sister Viola, Orsino asks Viola to become his wife. On the day that Sebastian marries Olivia, Viola will marry Orsino.

18. **abused:** deceived
18–20. **conclusions . . . affirmatives:** possibly an allusion to a sonnet by Sir Philip Sidney, in which the lady's twice saying "no" is taken as a "yes" because, in grammar, two negatives make an affirmative
26. **double-dealing:** (1) giving twice; (2) duplicity
29. **grace:** virtue (with a pun on the phrase—"your Grace"—with which the duke is normally addressed)
30. **obey it:** i.e., obey the Fool's **ill counsel** (line 28)
33. **Primo, secundo, tertio:** first, second, third (perhaps an allusion to a children's game, or **play**)
34. **triplex:** triple time in music (i.e., a three-beat rhythm)

35. **tripping:** quick and light
35. **Saint Bennet:** i.e., the church of St. Benedict
37. **fool:** beg through clever wordplay
38. **throw:** i.e., time (literally, throw of the dice)
43. **desire of having:** i.e., wish to possess
45. **anon:** very soon
49. **Vulcan:** Roman god of fire and blacksmith to the gods
50. **baubling:** tiny, insignificant
51. **For . . . unprizable:** i.e., worthless because of its **shallow draught** and its small **bulk**
52. **With which:** i.e., with which worthless vessel; **scatheful:** harmful
53. **bottom:** ship
54. **very:** even; **tongue of loss:** i.e., voices of those whom he defeated
55. **Cried:** called out
57. **fraught:** freight, that which the ship carries; **Candy:** Candia (capital of Crete)
60. **desperate of:** i.e., as if unconcerned with; **state:** i.e., his situation
61. **brabble:** brawl
62. **drew . . . side:** i.e., drew his sword to defend me
63. **put . . . me:** talked to me strangely
64. **distraction:** madness
67. **dear:** dire
73. **base and ground:** evidence
77. **wrack:** piece of wreckage
79. **retention:** holding back
80. **All . . . dedication:** i.e., dedicating all (my love) to him
81. **pure:** purely, simply
82. **adverse:** hostile
85. **Not meaning to:** i.e., choosing not to
86. **face . . . out of:** shamelessly exclude . . . from
88. **While . . . wink:** i.e., in the time it takes to blink one's eyes

89. **recommended:** consigned, given

94. **No int'rim:** without interruption

102. **What . . . that:** i.e., what does my lord wish, except for that

104. **keep promise with:** i.e., keep your promise to

110. **fat, fulsome:** disgusting

113. **constant:** steadfast, immovable

114. **uncivil:** cruel

115. **ingrate:** ungrateful; **unauspicious:** inauspicious, unfavorable

117. **tendered:** offered

120. **th' Egyptian thief:** an allusion to a novel by Heliodorus, in which the robber chief, threatened with death, tries to kill the woman he loves to prevent her being taken by another

122. **savors nobly:** i.e., smacks of nobility

123. **to nonregardance cast:** i.e., fail to take notice of

124. **that:** i.e., since

125. **screws:** twists

126. **Live you:** i.e., continue to live as

127. **minion:** darling

128. **tender:** regard, esteem

135. **jocund, apt:** jocundly, aptly (i.e., happily, readily)

136. **do you rest:** i.e., give you peace

141. **you witnesses above:** i.e., you heavenly powers

142. **tainting:** corrupting, injuring

143. **beguiled:** cheated, deceived

151. **sirrah:** a term of address that, here, emphasizes the speaker's authority

153. **baseness:** contemptibleness, ignobleness

154. **strangle thy propriety:** i.e., conceal what you are; or, perhaps, hide the fact that I belong to you

156. **that:** that which (i.e., my husband)

157. **that thou fear'st:** i.e., Orsino **that:** that which

160. **unfold:** disclose

163. **newly:** recently
165. **joinder:** joining
166. **close:** union
169. **Sealed . . . function:** ratified by me in my role as priest
173. **dissembling:** hypocritical
174. **a grizzle:** gray hair; **case:** skin
175. **craft:** craftiness
176. **trip:** wrestling move in which one trips one's opponent
181. **Hold little:** i.e., keep a bit of
183. **presently:** immediately
185. **Has . . . across:** i.e., he has cut my head
186. **coxcomb:** i.e., head
191–92. **incardinate:** a mistake for "incarnate"
194. **'Od's lifelings:** by God's little lives
199. **bespake . . . fair:** addressed . . . courteously
201. **set nothing by:** think nothing of
202. **halting:** limping
203. **in drink:** drunk
204. **othergates:** otherwise
206. **That's all one:** i.e., it doesn't matter
209. **set:** perhaps, closed; or, fixed; or, sunk out of sight
210. **passy-measures pavin:** perhaps a comment on the surgeon's slowness (A **pavin** is a stately dance, and the Italian word *passamezzo* means a slow tune.)
215. **dressed:** i.e., have our wounds dressed
216. **coxcomb:** fool; literally, the cap worn by a Fool
220. **the . . . blood:** i.e., my own brother
221. **with wit and safety:** i.e., with reasonable regard for my safety
222. **throw . . . me:** look at me strangely (or, perhaps, coldly)
225. **so late ago:** so recently
226. **habit:** outfit

227. **A . . . perspective:** i.e., an optical illusion created naturally, without mirrors or other optical devices (**perspectives**)

229. **racked:** The **rack** was an instrument of torture that tore the body apart.

232. **Fear'st thou:** i.e., are you in doubt about

238–39. **Nor . . . everywhere:** i.e., nor do I have the power to be omnipresent, like a god

241. **Of charity:** i.e., out of kindness (i.e., please tell me)

245. **suited:** dressed

246. **suit:** clothing

249–50. **am . . . participate:** i.e., am the same flesh-and-blood creature that I've been from my birth   **dimension:** bodily form   **grossly:** materially   **clad:** dressed   **participate:** possess

251. **as . . . even:** i.e., since everything else fits together

258. **record:** memory (accent on second syllable)

261. **lets:** hinders

262. **But . . . attire:** except for the male clothing I have appropriated

264. **cohere, jump:** agree

267. **maiden weeds:** woman's clothing; **gentle:** kind, courteous

271. **mistook:** mistaken

272. **nature . . . that:** i.e., nature caused your desire, mistakenly directed to Viola, to swerve to me (The **bias** is the curve that brings the ball to the desired point in the game of bowls.)

275. **maid and man:** i.e., a man who is a virgin

277. **the glass seems true:** i.e., the **perspective** glass seems to be representing the truth rather than a distortion

278. **wrack:** wreck, shipwreck; or, that which has washed up from the shipwreck

280. **like to me:** i.e., as much as you love me

281. **overswear:** i.e., swear over again

283. that orbèd continent: i.e., the sun (**A continent** is a container; the sun is pictured as containing **fire**.)

288. upon some action: as a result of legal action

289. in durance: imprisoned

291. He . . . him: i.e., Malvolio shall free the captain

293. remember me: i.e., remember

294. much distract: quite mad

295. extracting frenzy: a temporary insanity that drew everything from my mind (except thoughts of Cesario)

296. his: i.e., Malvolio's "frenzy"

298-99. he . . . end: i.e., he keeps the devil at a distance

300-301. today morning: i.e., this morning

302. skills not much: makes little difference

305. delivers: reads the words of

310. allow vox: permit me to use the appropriate "voice"

313. thus: i.e., like a madman; **perpend:** ponder, consider

321. the which: i.e., **your own letter** (line 320)

329. delivered: released

330-32. so . . . wife: i.e., if you are willing, once we've thought more about these things, to think as well of me as a sister-in-law as you were thinking of me as a wife

333. crown . . . on 't: i.e., celebrate the alliance that will make us kin (i.e., you can marry Viola at the same time I marry Sebastian)

335. at my proper cost: i.e., at my expense

336. apt: ready

337. quits: releases

339. mettle: nature

340. breeding: upbringing

353. hand: handwriting

354. from it: differently (from the way you wrote in the letter)

355. **invention:** composition

357. **in . . . honor:** i.e., with the moderation that should go with honor

358. **lights:** perhaps, signs

361. **lighter:** lesser

362. **acting this:** i.e., doing what you said

363. **suffered:** allowed

365. **geck, gull:** dupe

366. **invention:** i.e., plotting, scheming; **played on:** victimized

368. **the character:** my handwriting

371. **cam'st:** i.e., you came

372–73. **forms . . . were presupposed / Upon:** i.e., style . . . was prescribed for

374. **This . . . thee:** i.e., this plot has maliciously tricked you

375. **authors:** inventors

381. **wondered at:** See note to 4.3.3.

384–85. **Upon . . . him:** i.e., because of some rude and ill-mannered characteristics of his that made us dislike him

386. **importance:** importuning, urgent request

388. **it was followed:** i.e., the plot was carried out

389. **pluck on:** induce

392. **baffled thee:** put you to shame

395. **interlude:** comedy

399. **whirligig:** continual whirling

405. **convents:** perhaps, is convenient for all

409. **so you shall be:** i.e., that's what I'll call you

410. **habits:** clothes

411. **mistress:** (1) the woman he loves; (2) the person he obeys; **fancy's:** love's

414. **toy:** trifle

416. **came . . . estate:** i.e., grew up to be a man

426. **tosspots:** drunkards (The meaning of this stanza continues to be debated.)

430. **that's all one:** i.e., none of that matters

Textual Notes

The reading of the present text appears to the left of the square bracket. The earliest sources of readings not in **F**, the First Folio text, are indicated as follows: **F2** is the Second Folio of 1632; **F3** is the Third Folio of 1663–64; **F4** is the Fourth Folio of 1685. **Ed.** is an earlier editor of Shakespeare, beginning with Rowe in 1709. **SD** means stage direction; **SP** means speech prefix.

1.2	16.	Arion] Ed.; *Orion* F
1.3	1.	SP TOBY] F (*Sir To.*)
	51.	SP ANDREW] F2; *Ma.* F
	97.	curl by] Ed.; coole my F
	99.	me] F2; we F
	132.	dun-colored] Ed.; dam'd colour'd F
	132.	set] Ed.; sit F
	136.	That's] F3; That F
1.4	9.	SD *Orsino*] Ed.; *Duke* F
1.5	0.	SD *Feste, the Fool*] This ed.; *Clowne* F
	165.	SD *Viola*] F2; *Violenta* F
	204, 205.	SP OLIVIA, VIOLA] Ed.; *speech continues as Viola's in* F
	318.	SD *She exits.*] *Finis, Actus primus.* F
2.2	31.	our] F2; O F
	32.	made of,] Ed.; made, if F
2.3	2.	*diluculo*] Ed.; *Deliculo* F
	14.	SD *Feste, the Fool*] This ed.; *Clowne* F

	134.	a nayword] Ed.; an ayword F
2.4	0.	SD *Orsino*] Ed.; *Duke* F
	47.	SD *Feste, the Fool*] This ed.; *Clowne* F
	60.	*Fly . . . fly*] Ed.; *Fye . . . fie* F
	97.	I] Ed.; It F
2.5	117.	staniel] Ed.; stallion F
	149.	*born*] Ed.; become F
	149.	*achieve*] F2; atcheeues F
	212.	SD *They exit.*] *Exeunt. Finis Actus secnndus* [*sic*] F
3.1	0.	SD *Feste, the Fool*] This ed.; *Clowne* F
	8.	king] F2; Kings F
	69.	wise men, folly-fall'n] Ed.; wisemens folly falne F
3.2	7.	thee] F3; the F
3.3	16.	thanks, and ever thanks; and oft] Ed.; thankes; and euer oft F
3.4	26.	SP OLIVIA] F2; *Mal.* F
	179.	If] *To.* If F
	181.	You . . . fit . . . for 't] Yon . . . sit . . . fot't F
4.1	0.	SD *Feste, the Fool*] This ed.; *Clowne* F
4.2	0.	SD *Feste, the Fool*] This ed.; *Clowne* F
	6.	in] in in F
	39.	clerestories] Ed.; cleere stores F
4.3	1.	SP *omit* F
	37.	SD *They exit.*] *Exeunt. Finis Actus Quartus.* F
5.1	0.	SD *Feste, the Fool*] This ed.; *Clowne* F
	6.	SD *Orsino*] Ed.; *Duke* F
	201.	SD *Feste, the Fool*] This ed.; *Clowne* F
	291.	SD *Feste, the Fool*] This ed.; *Clowne* F
	428.	*begun*] Ed.; *begon* F
	429.	*With hey, ho, the wind and the rain*] F2 (*which adds "With"*); *hey ho, &c.* F
	431.	SD *He exits.*] FINIS. F